NEAL-SCHUMAN

DISCARD

W9-AGV-776

County Community College
901 South Haverhill Road
El Dorado, Kansas 67042-3280

Guide to

CELEBRATIONS AND HOLIDAYS AROUND THE WORLD

THE BEST BOOKS, MEDIA, AND MULTICULTURAL LEARNING ACTIVITIES

BY **KATHRYN I. MATTHEW** AND **JOY L. LOWE**

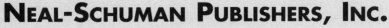

NEAL-SCHUMAN PUBLISHERS, INC.

New York   London

Published by Neal-Schuman Publishers, Inc.
100 William Street, Suite 2004
New York, NY 10038

The paper used in this publication meets the minimum requirements of American National Standard for Informational Sciences—Permanence of Paper for Printed Library Materials, ANSI Z39.48—1992 ♾

Copyright © 2004 by Kathryn I. Matthew and Joy L. Lowe

All rights reserved. Reproduction of this book, in whole or in part, without the written permission of the publisher is prohibited.

Printed and bound in the United States of America.

Library of Congress Cataloging-in-Publication Data

Matthew, Kathryn I.
    Neal-Schuman guide to celebrations & holidays around the world / Kathryn I. Matthew, Joy L. Lowe.
        p. cm.
    Includes bibliographical references and index.
    ISBN 1-55570-479-4 (alk. paper)
    1. Holidays–Bibliography. 2. Festivals–Bibliography. 3. Children's literature–Bibliography. 4. Children–Books and reading–United States–Bibliography. 5. Children's literature–Study and teaching (Elementary)–United States–Bibliography. I. Lowe, Joy L. II. Title.

Z5710.M38 2004   2003059940
394.26–dc21

394.26 MAT 2004

Matthew, Kathryn I.
Neal-Schuman guide to
celebrations and holidays

TABLE OF CONTENTS

List of Figures ix

Preface xi

Introduction xv

Part I: Quick Guides to Celebrations and Holidays

Section 1   Celebrations and Holidays at a Glance 3

Celebrations and Holidays for Each Month 4

Asian Celebrations and Holidays 22

Central American and Hispanic Celebrations and
Holidays 27

Jewish Celebrations and Holidays 30

Native American Celebrations 33

Special Celebrations .34

**Section 2   Key Titles for Integrating Celebrations and
Holidays into the Social Studies Curriculum** . . .37

Kindergarten and First Grade 37

Second Grade and Third Grade 49

Fourth Grade 62

Fifth Grade 67

Sixth Grade 77

Seventh Grade and Eighth Grade 81

Part II: Autumn

**Chapter 1   Autumn Celebrations and Holidays with
Moveable Dates** 93

Diwali (Festival of Lights) 93

Rosh Hashanah and Yom Kippur 95

Sukkot and Simchat Torah 99

Ramadan 101

Id-Ul-Fitr 104

Zhongqiu Jie (Mid-Autumn Moon Festival) 105

Chapter 2   September Holidays and Celebrations 109

Chongyang Jie (Double Nine Festival) 109

Labor Day 112

Grandparents' Day 117

Mexican Independence Day 122

Citizenship Day 123

Itse Selu (Green Corn Festival) 127

Chapter 3   October Holidays and Celebrations 131

Columbus Day 131

United Nations Day .134

Halloween 137

Chapter 4   November Holidays and Celebrations 145

All Saints' Day and All Souls' Day 145

Dia de los Muertos .147

National Sandwich Day 150

Guy Fawkes Day 152

Veterans' Day 153

Election Day 157

Thanksgiving Day 160

Part III: Winter

**Chapter 5   Winter Celebrations and Holidays with
              Moveable Dates 175**

Hanukkah 175

TET Nguyen-Dan (Vietnamese New Year) 182

Xin Nian and Deng Jie (Chinese Lunar New
Year and Lantern Festival) 184

Tu Bi-Shevat (Jewish Arbor Day) 189

Eid-Al-Adha 190

Chapter 6   December Holidays and Celebrations 193

St. Nicholas Day 194

Our Lady of Guadalupe Day 195

Santa Lucia Day 196

Las Posadas 198

Advent 199

Christmas—Religious 200

Christmas—Secular .203

Kwanzaa 212

Chapter 7   January Holidays and Celebrations 219

New Year's Day 219

Epiphany (Three Kings' Day) 222

Martin Luther King, Jr. Day 224

Chapter 8   February Holidays and Celebrations 231

Groundhog Day 231

Valentine's Day 235

Presidents' Day 242

Part IV: Spring

**Chapter 9   Spring Celebrations and Holidays with
Moveable Dates 251**

Carnival and Mardi Gras 251

Lent 255

Easter—Religious 256

Easter—Secular 258

Purim 266

Passover 267

Qing Ming (Clear Brightness Festival) 272

Holi (Festival of Color) 272

Chapter 10 March Holidays and Celebrations 275

Hina Matsuri (Doll Festival) 275

St. Patrick's Day 277

St. Joseph's Day 283

Chapter 11 April Holidays and Celebrations 285

April Fools' Day 285

International Children's Book Day 289

Hana Matsuri (Buddha's Birthday) 291

Earth Day 292

Arbor Day 299

Chapter 12 May Holidays and Celebrations 303

May Day 303

Cinco de Mayo 305

Tango-no-sekku (Boys' Day) 307

Kodomono-Hi (Children's Day) 309

Mother's Day 310

Memorial Day 315

Part V: Summer

**Chapter 13 Summer Celebrations and Holidays with
Moveable Dates 323**

Shavuot 323

Obon Festival 325

Duanwu Jie (Dragon Boat Festival) 327

Summer Excursions 328

Chapter 14 June Holidays and Celebrations 335

Father's Day 335

Flag Day 339

Juneteenth 343

Stonewall Rebellion 346

Chapter 15 July Holidays and Celebrations **349**

Fourth of July 349

Tanabata 355

Bastille Day 356

Mormon Pioneer Day 359

Chapter 16 August Holidays and Celebrations **363**

Hiroshima Day 363

Assumption Day 366

Women's Equality Day .368

Part VI: World Cultures, Unusual Events, and Special Days

Chapter 17 Celebrations and Holidays Collections **375**

Celebrations and Holidays around the World . . .375

American Celebrations and Holidays 382

Asian Celebrations and Holidays 387

Central American and Hispanic Celebrations
and Holidays 391

Jewish Celebrations and Holidays 393

Teacher Resources 396

Chapter 18 Special Celebrations **401**

Bar Mitzvahs and Bat Mitzvahs 402

Birthdays 403

Circuses, Fairs, Fiestas, and Jamborees 407

Graduations 409

Native American Celebrations 411

Quinceañeras 414

Snow Days 417

Tooth Fairy Visits 419

Weddings 423

Visiting Days 427

Indices

Author Index 429

Illustrator Index 435

Title Index 439

Subject Index 447

About the Authors **453**

LIST OF FIGURES

Figure 2-1. Personal Responses 116

Figure 2-2. Independence Day Traditions 123

Figure 3-1. Columbus Day 133

Figure 3-2. Halloween Candy 137

Figure 3-3. Comparison Chart 142

Figure 4-1. Character Analysis 156

Figure 4-2. Vocabulary Chart 159

Figure 4-3. Pilgrims 160

Figure 4-4. Feelings Chart 168

Figure 5-1. Comparing Definitions 182

Figure 5-2. Comparing Parades 188

Figure 6-1. Concept Map 197

Figure 6-2. Sequence of Events 210

Figure 6-3. Kwanzaa 216

Figure 7-1. Concept Map 221

Figure 8-1. Opinions 234

Figure 8-2. Valentines 235

Figure 8-3. Story Map 241

Figure 8-4. Abraham Lincoln 247

Figure 9-1. Comparison Chart 255

Figure 9-2. Easter Candy 258

Figure 9-3. Easter Symbol 265

Figure 10-1. St. Patrick's Day Parade 277

Figure 10-2. Problem Solution Diagram 281

Figure 10-3. Story Map 282

Figure 11-1. Flow Diagram 290

Figure 11-2. Circle Map Template 301

Figure 12-1. Mother's Day Card 313

Figure 12-2. Korean War Veteran 315

Figure 13-1. Cause and Effect Diagram 325

Figure 13-2. Venn Diagram 327

Figure 15-1. Independence Day Celebrations
around the World 354

Figure 17-1. New Year's Rituals 380

Figure 17-2. Christmas Symbols 381

Figure 18-1. Senses Chart 416

Figure 18-2. Snow Day 417

Figure 18-3. Tooth Fairy Note 419

Figure 18-4. Wedding 423

PREFACE

The *Neal-Schuman Guide to Celebrations and Holidays around the World* recommends resources and activities that librarians and teachers can use for understanding and teaching the special times of the year that children and their families celebrate in our multicultural society. The *Guide* grew from our direct experiences working in culturally diverse school systems. Students from different cultures sought to commemorate both the holidays specific to their own countries and religions and to understand the traditional American ones. We designed this handbook because locating background information and identifying appropriate books and media to share with students in the library and classroom on the celebrations of various countries was often difficult and time-consuming.

Our culturally diverse society gives us the opportunity to appreciate and participate in a wide variety of special occasions. Studying a wide variety of these observances helps children appreciate their own culture and become aware of the similarities and differences among other cultures (de Atiles, 2002). Children also discover that traditions associated with familiar festivities originated in other countries. Immigrants brought many of these traditions to America. Over the years these customs have been assimilated into our celebrations. For example, you can trace trick-or-treating and jack-o'-lanterns to Irish immigrants, and our New Year's fireworks and parades come from the ancient Chinese New Year celebration with its Dragon Parade and fireworks.

SPECIAL CONSIDERATIONS

We paid particular attention to the church and state separation issue, stressing the need to discuss the cultural perspective of a holiday, rather than a religious one, in nonreligious educational settings. For example, the *Neal-Schuman Guide to Celebrations and Holidays around the World* divides Christmas and Easter books and media into those with sacred and with secular themes.

Distinctive traditions and observances vary from family to family, from region to region, from country to country, and from religion to religion. For example, some families favor birthday cakes with "Happy Birthday" written across the top, while others serve the honoree's cake of choice. Reform Jews observe Sukkot for one week, while Orthodox Jews observe for nine days. Discovering these variations adds to the enjoyment and excitement.

Some holidays are known by both their traditional names and by translations of those names. For example, the translation for Qing Ming is the Clear Brightness Festival. There are different spellings for the holidays; Qing Ming is also spelled Qingming. We have chosen to use the most common spellings we found for the holidays and have included other spellings and translations in the descriptions of the holidays.

Sometimes, dates vary from year to year because they are based on different calendars, including the Gregorian, Jewish, Hindu, Chinese, and Islamic. Some calendars are lunar calendars and make adjustments to keep up with the solar cycle, while others do not (Moehn, 2000). These holidays are included in the chapters that focus on seasons, and we have provided ranges of dates based on the Gregorian calendar. Individual states set the dates for holidays that are not national holidays; the dates for Arbor Day celebrations vary from state to state, for example.

HOW TO USE THE GUIDE

Teachers and librarians need an easily accessible reference source. The *Neal-Schuman Guide to Celebrations and Holidays around the World* is organized with quick guides to the material, followed by a seasonal listing of holidays, and ending with special holidays.

The "Introduction" examines some concerns about teaching this subject, including the issue of religion in the classroom or library and the challenges of multicultural literature. We conclude with tips for selecting and using books and media.

Part I, "Quick Guides to Celebrations and Holidays," offers fast reference and resource locators to over eighty specific special occasions. The first chapter, "Celebrations and Holidays at a Glance," provides a chart showing the major American holidays, followed by a month-by-month breakdown, with our top book and media recommendations. There are five more charts providing the same essential information for other groups or types of celebrations.

Chapter 2, "Key Titles for Integrating Celebrations and Holidays into the Social Studies Curriculum," organizes a quick guide to many of the broad themes children are taught in school. Beginning in the early grades with an understanding of our own national patriotic holidays, through the upper elementary and middle school focus on United States history and world history, children learn how different countries and religions have shaped history. The themes range from families, citizenship, and patriotism, to ethnic identities and traditional American observations. Throughout the grade levels, students learn about the importance of being good citizens, how to take care of their environment, and about cultures of the world. The charts are divided into six grade levels: kindergarten and first grade, second and third grade, fourth grade, fifth grade, sixth grade, and seventh and eighth grade. Repeating the design of the other charts, each theme is matched to one or more holidays and our top book and media recommendations.

Parts II through V are the heart of the book, and present a year of celebrations season-by-season. Each season begins with a chapter featuring celebrations with moveable dates, followed by chapters providing a month-by-month breakdown. The information on these holidays features hundreds of resources and associated activities.

Each entry's bibliographic annotation begins with the author's name, the title of the book and, for many, the illustrator or photographer's name. Next, we provide the publisher, the year of publication, and the number of pages in the book. We follow with grade levels as guides for selecting appropriate books. A brief description of the book follows. Here is a sample:

> Livingston, Myra Cohn. *Festivals*. Illustrated by Leonard Everett Fisher. New York: Holiday House, 1996. 32p.
> Grades: P–4. This exciting, vibrant book explores a variety of multicultural festivals in lyrical poems and glowing illustrations. Poems about these multicultural festivals are included: Chinese New Year, Tet Nguyen-Dan, Mardi Gras, Purim, Cherry Blossom Festival, Now-Ruz, Arbor Day, Ramadan and Id-Ul-Fitr, Creek Indian Busk, Diwali, El Dia de Muertos, the Feast of St. Lucy, Las Posadas, and Kwanzaa. Bright, colorful illustrations by Leonard Everett Fisher enhance the text and capture the readers' attention. A glossary contains additional information about the holidays.

These annotations are followed by suggested learning activities.

Part VI, "World Cultures, Unusual Events, and Special Days," examines these unique holidays and resources.

Author, illustrator, title, and subject indices provide pinpoint access to wide-ranging material.

The *Neal-Schuman Guide to Celebrations and Holidays around the World* is designed to assist teachers and librarians in gathering and using high-quality materials to assure that children learn to appreciate and understand the diverse special events and festivities that are recognized in various countries, cultures, and religions around the world. Learning about multicultural celebrations and holidays is one way to ensure that children develop multicultural literacy. Multicultural literacy enables students to see that differences are not deficiencies (Diamond and Moore, 1995), enabling all children to draw from their own cultural heritage as the basis for learning to appreciate other cultures of the world.

REFERENCES

de Atiles, Julia Reguero. 2002. *Celebration Central*. (Accessed 3 February 2002.) Available: www.scholastic.com/atschool/celebtradit.htm.

Diamond, Barbara J., and Margaret A. Moore. 1995. *Multicultural Literacy: Mirroring the Reality of the Classroom*. White Plains, New York: Longman Publishers.

Moehn, Heather. 2000. *World Holidays: A Watts Guide for Children*. New York: Franklin Watts.

INTRODUCTION

There is a great deal of professional inquiry into one essential question: Why teach children about celebrations and holidays? There are many benefits, social and cultural as well as academic. Children who recognize themselves in books can make personal connections between the information and stories presented in the books and their own lives. Engaging their natural curiosity about other cultures and ethnic groups and learning about the special occasions and festivities of others expands their view of the world. Identifying the different cultures of the children, parents, faculty, and staff in libraries and schools ensures respect for everyone's customs and beliefs (Singer and Singer, 1997).

Exploring different cultures shows that you and your school or library accept and value diversity, showing children that diversity enriches society (Diamond and Moore, 1995). Understanding the diversity of people of all cultures demonstrates the similarities and differences between the most familiar and the most foreign (Steele, 1995). Distinguishing the diversity within cultural groups in values, lifestyles, and histories can lead to practical positive changes. For example, rather than using the general terms Hispanic Americans or Latinos, you can differentiate Mexican Americans, Puerto Ricans, or Brazilians (Diamond and Moore, 1995).

Interesting books and media stimulate children's critical thinking and deepen their cultural understanding. Children involved in compelling learning experiences grasp who they are and enhance their own self-esteem (Creaser and Dau, 1994). Actively learning about the customs they observe and the counterparts in other groups, rather than participating in rote activities and projects, affords children the information and opportunities to become insightful and grow in exciting directions (Dimidjian, 1989).

CONCERNS ABOUT CELEBRATIONS AND HOLIDAYS

Before embarking in this endeavor, be aware that there are no pat answers to the questions posed by studying this area. Should public schools and public libraries participate in activities and events centered on these special occasions? If you decide the answer is yes, should you focus on the ones favored by the media and merchants, or on the holidays of a variety of cultures? If families in the same cultures celebrate the same events differently, is it important to provide parents and children opportunities to share their own traditions and customs?

Practical advice prevails. As one way to gather valuable information, follow the children's lead as they talk about their family holidays (Musa and Prince-Clark, 2001). Talk to parents. Ask them about their preferences and practices. Parents need to express any concerns they may harbor. Find out if any celebrations require children missing school. Enlist parents' suggestions for ways to furnish alternatives if the class observes an occasion in which the individual student does not want to participate (Dimidjian, 1989). If you send notes home, determine if the parents understand the message. Often, families from other cultures may not understand the traditions associated with many American traditions. Communicating effectively with parents confirms that children from other cultures understand our celebrations (Schmidt, 1995).

Increasing cultural knowledge shapes a student's view of the world and their reaction to what they are learning (Diamond and Moore, 1995). Examine both familiar and unusual holidays through books and activities in the library and classroom. Establish the important shared cultural experiences (Musa and Prince-Clark, 2001). Children can appreciate the similarities and differences in different cultures. This practice enables children to see shared cultural experiences and understand that one is not better than another. Remember that when you study diversity it is important not to equate unlike experiences. For example, Hanukkah and Christmas both occur in December, but they honor very different events.

Be sensitive to the notion that although festivities are usually times to enjoy oneself and contemplate on the significance of the event to the group, individual reactions may vary. Rather than joyous revels, these may be unhappy times for children as they remember family members and friends who were at past celebrations but are no longer present due to death, divorce, or moving. An awareness of each student's reactions to the event can help you provide these children with the kind support and responsive guidance they may need.

RELIGION IN THE CLASSROOM OR LIBRARY

In a religious school or library, the teaching of sacred holidays is an everyday event. In public settings, where a wide variety of beliefs are present, teaching about a variety of religious holidays is acceptable, but celebrating them is not acceptable (Haynes, 1999). You need to distinguish between learning about religious occasions and celebrating religious events (Ribak-Rosenthal and Russell, 1994). Emphasize that learning about different religions does not mean that children have to accept the beliefs. This knowledge helps children understand and live more fully in a diverse society (Haynes, 1999).

It is also important to discern the needs of an individual student from the needs of the group. How does a particular student observe special occasions? Children with nonmajority religious beliefs may feel alienated, marginalized, and excluded during classroom celebrations that focus on majority religious beliefs (Ribak-Rosenthal and Russell, 1994). For example, if you want to explore Christmas, clarify if the families celebrate the religious rather than commercial aspects of Christmas, or if they do not celebrate Christmas because is not part of their culture (Creaser and Dau, 1994). Seemingly simple activities, like asking children to bring a present to school to exchange with other children, may cause problems for families who do not celebrate Christmas.

More guidelines for understanding this distinction can be found at www.teachingaboutreligion.org. The National Education Association Web site (available at www.nea.org/neatoday/0211/cover.html) contains sound ideas for discussing religion in the classroom.

MULTICULTURAL LITERATURE

Sharing multicultural literature offers a starting point for children as they explore, understand, and appreciate the diversity of our society (Diamond and Moore, 1995). Students learn about different cultures and develop common understandings. They see how they share similar experiences with others and identify with their own culture. For example, Dever and Barta (1997) suggest that when children learn about the ritual of giving thanks—a culturally diverse practice with common themes—they comprehend the similarities and differences between and even within cultures. This experience helps them learn to accept others.

Multicultural books make it easier for children to build on their prior knowledge and create connections between the texts and their own life experiences. Such books present positive information from a variety of perspectives. Additionally, Pang, Colvin, Tran, and Barba (1992) suggest that the best books feature strong characterization, authentic illustrations, strong plot, and historical accuracy.

SELECTING BOOKS

How do you approach the daunting task of selecting the best books from the large number available about the traditional American holidays and celebrations? Look for books written by the children's favorite authors, being sure to select a variety of fiction and informational books. Examine the books; note the style of writing, the typesetting, and the illustrations. Does the author present a biased or stereotypical view of the culture? Is the information accurate and relevant? What are the author's credentials for writing the book? Is the book one that students will be able to read on their own, or is it a book for reading aloud? Are the illustrations colorful and appealing? Do they accurately portray the culture? Will the book help students from different cultures understand the event? Aim for books that are interesting, well-written, and that children will want to read again and again.

Mindful of the above criteria, the authors selected books that fit these criteria and our own personal criteria. We selected books that appeal to children and ones that have universal appeal. The selections reflect our favorite books; books we read to our own children, grandchildren, and children in schools and libraries. We included books by our favorite authors and illustrators, books with good stories, books that have been around for many years, new books that we believe will become favorites, books that enticed us, and books with striking or colorful illustrations. We selected books that made us laugh out loud, books that made us cry, and books that we could not wait to share with each other—or with anyone else who would let us read the book out loud to them, no matter their age, no matter the season. We also selected books that we know are readily available and accessible to teachers and librarians.

IDEAS FOR USING THE BOOKS AND MEDIA

Before you introduce the books and media about a specific occasion to the children, talk to them about the holiday. Determine if they have sufficient prior knowledge. Do they understand the event? Does it contain meaning for them (Creaser and Dau, 1994)? Remember that children from other countries may need help understanding American holidays (Schmidt, 1995). First, try introducing the subject with a video that may be watched again to reinforce what the children learned. Place taped books in a listening center. This gives students the chance to listen to the books repeatedly, aiding in comprehending the information.

Read aloud to children and then offer the opportunity for them to share relevant experiences. Guide students as they learn to listen to others' comments and respond appropriately. This practice will model appropriate ways to discuss books (Taylor, 1998). Present meaning-oriented discussions. Students will stretch their thinking and enhance their ability to form and support their personal views (McKeown, 1998).

Extension activities need to relate to students and be significant. Do not stereotype or trivialize the cultures being explored in the classroom (Creaser and Dau, 1994). Be sure to take advantage of innovative and interactive Internet sites. They can often easily help students more fully understand and appreciate the celebration and holiday being explored.

REFERENCES

Creaser, Barbara, and Elizabeth Dau. 1994. *Who's in Charge of Celebrations? A Child-Centered Approach*. Watson, Australia: Australian Early Childhood Association, Inc.
Dever, Martha T., and James J. Barta. 1997. "Giving Thanks: Observing Thanksgiving, Kwanzaa, and Day of the Dead."

Social Studies and the Young Learner 10, no. 2 (November/December): 6–9.

Diamond, Barbara J., and Margaret A. Moore. 1995. *Multicultural Literacy: Mirroring the Reality of the Classroom*. White Plains, New York: Longman Publishers.

Dimidjian, Victoria Jean. 1989. "Holidays, Holy Days, and Wholly Dazed: Approaches to Special Days." *Young Children* 44, no. 6 (September): 70–75.

Haynes, Charles C. 1999. *A Teacher's Guide to Religion in the Public Schools*. Nashville, Tenn.: First Amendment Center.

McKeown, Margaret G. 1998. "Discussion of Text for Understanding." Pp. 365–370 in *Literature-Based Instruction: Reshaping the Curriculum*, ed. Taffy E. Raphael and Kathryn H. Au. Norwood, Mass.: Christopher-Gordon Publishers.

Musa, Diana, and Heather Prince-Clarke. *Should We Celebrate Holidays in School?* (Accessed January 2002.) Available: http://www.educationupdate.com/archives/2001/nov01/articles/child_bankst.html.

Pang, Valerie Ooka, Carolyn Colvin, MyLuong Tran, and Roberta H. Barba. 1992. "Beyond Chopsticks and Dragons: Selecting Asian-American Literature for Children." *The Reading Teacher* 46, no. 3 (November): 216–224.

Ribak-Rosenthal, Nina, and Todd T. Russell. 1994. "Dealing with Religious Differences in December: A School Counselor's Role." *Elementary School Guidance & Counseling* 28, no. 4 (April): 295–301.

Schmidt, Patricia R. 1995. *Tensions for Language Minority Children: Celebrations in a Kindergarten Classroom*. Paper presented at the Annual Meeting of the American Educational Research Association. ERIC Document, 38353.

Singer, Judith Y., and Alan Singer. 1997. " 'Festivals of Light': A Multicultural Celebration in Brooklyn." *Social Studies and the Young Learner* 10, no. 2 (November/December): 31–32.

Steele, Anitra T. 1995. "Raising the Issue." *Wilson Library Bulletin* 69 (January): 60–61.

Taylor, Barbara M. 1998. "Preserving What is Most Vital." Pp. 361–364 in *Literature-Based Instruction: Reshaping the Curriculum*, ed. Taffy E. Raphael and Kathryn H. Au. Norwood, Mass.: Christopher-Gordon Publishers.

DEDICATION

For Evelyn Hymel Ingraham and Robert Edward Ingraham—KIM

For Norma Cutrer Lambert and Robert Milton Lambert—JLL

PART I: QUICK GUIDES TO CELEBRATIONS AND HOLIDAYS

CELEBRATIONS AND HOLIDAYS AT A GLANCE   1

Celebrations and Holidays at a Glance

Fall	September	October	November	Winter	December	January	February	Spring
Diwali (Festival of Lights)	Chongyang Jie (Double Nine Festival)	Columbus Day	All Saints' Day and All Souls' Day	Hanukkah	St. Nicholas Day	New Year's Day	Groundhog Day	Carnival and Mardi Gras
Rosh Hashanah and Yom Kippur	Labor Day	United Nations Day	Dia de los Muertos	TET Nguyen-Dan (Vietnamese New Year)	Our Lady of Guadalupe Day	Epiphany (Three Kings' Day)	Valentine's Day	Lent
	Grandparents Day	Halloween	National Sandwich Day	Xin Nian and Deng Jie (Chinese Lunar New Year and Lantern Festival)	Santa Lucia Day	Martin Luther King, Jr. Day	Presidents' Day	Easter—Religious
Sukkot and Simchat Torah	Mexican Independence Day		Guy Fawkes Day		Las Posadas			Easter—Secular
Ramadan	Citizenship Day		Veterans Day		Advent			Purim
Id-Ul-Fitr	Itse Selu (Green Corn Festival)		Election Day	Tu Bi-Shevat (Jewish Arbor Day)	Christmas—Religious			Passover
Zhongqiu Jie (Mid-Autumn Moon Festival)			Thanksgiving Day	Eid-Al-Adha	Christmas—Secular			Qing Ming (Clear Brightness Festival)
					Kwanzaa			Holi (Festival of Color)

March	April	May	Summer	June	July	August	Holiday Collections	Special Occasions
Hina Masuri (Doll Festival)	April Fools' Day	May Day	Shavuot	Father's Day	Fourth of July	Hiroshima Day	Holidays Around the World	Bar Mitzvahs and Bat Mitzvahs
St. Patrick's Day	International Children's Book Day	Cinco de Mayo	Obon Festival	Flag Day	Tanabata	Assumption Day	American Holidays	Birthdays
St. Joseph's Day	Hana Matsuri (Buddha's Birthday)	Tango-no-sekku (Boys' Day)	Duanwu Jie (Dragon Boat Festival)	Juneteenth	Bastille Day	Women's Equality Day	Asian Holidays	Circuses, Fairs, Fiestas, & Jamborees
	Earth Day	Kodomono-Hi (Children's Day)	Summer Excursions	Stonewall Rebellion	Mormon Pioneer Day		Central America & Hispanic Holidays	Graduations
	Arbor Day	Mother's Day					Jewish Holidays	Native American
		Memorial Day					Teacher Resources	Quinceañeras
								Snow Days
								Tooth Fairy
								Weddings
								Visiting Days

CELEBRATIONS AND HOLIDAYS
FOR EACH MONTH

Below is a quick reference chart for teachers and librarians of some of the holidays and celebrations observed each month of the year. Following this chart is another chart containing books and media appropriate for prekindergarten through eighth grade for each of the holidays listed below. Information on the holidays, as well as annotations for a variety of books and media, can be found in individual book chapters.

September Chapter 2	Labor Day Grandparents Day
October Chapter 3	Columbus Day Halloween
November Chapter 4	Veterans Day Election Day Thanksgiving
December Chapter 6	Christmas Kwanzaa
January Chapter 7	New Year's Day Martin Luther King, Jr. Day
February Chapter 8	Groundhog Day Valentine's Day Presidents' Day
March Chapter 9, Chapter 10	Easter St. Patrick's Day
April Chapter 11	April Fools' Day Earth Day Arbor Day
May Chapter 12	Mother's Day Memorial Day
June Chapter 14	Father's Day Flag Day
July Chapter 15	Fourth of July
August Chapter 16	Women's Equality Day

SEPTEMBER

Labor Day First Monday	Bredeson, Carmen. *Labor Day*. New York: Children's Press, 2003. 32p. Grades: P–2.
	Hoyt-Goldsmith, Diane. *Migrant Worker: A Boy from the Rio Grande Valley*. Photographs by Lawrence Migdale. New York: Holiday House, 1996. 32p. Grades: 3–6.
	Gourley, Catherine. *Good Girl Work: Factories, Sweatshops, and How Women Changed Their Role in the American Workforce*. Brookfield, Conn.: The Millbrook Press, 1999. 96p. Grades: 4 and up.
	Labor Day: Celebrating the Work We Do. Video. Bala Cynwyd, Penn.: Schlessinger Video Productions-Library Video Company, 1999. 44 min. Grades: 6 and up.
Grandparents Day First Sunday after Labor Day	Rotner, Shelley, and Sheila Kelly. *Lots of Grandparents*. Photographs by Shelley Rotner. Brookfield, Conn.: The Millbrook Press, 2001. Unp. Grades: P–2.
	Carlson, Nancy L. *Hooray for Grandparents' Day*. New York: Viking, 2000. Unp. Grades: P–3.
	Plourde, Lynn. *Thank You, Grandpa*. Illustrated by Jason Cockroft. New York: Penguin Putnam, 2003. Unp. Grades: K–3.
	Koutsky, Jan Dale. *Pen Pals*. Honesdale, Penn.: Boyds Mills Press, 2002. Unp. Grades: K–5.

OCTOBER

Columbus Day Second Monday	Gardeski, Christina Mia. *Columbus Day*. New York: Children's Press, 2001. 32p. Grades: P–2.
	Landau, Elaine. *Columbus Day: Celebrating a Famous Explorer*. Berkeley Heights, N.J.: Enslow Publishers, 2001. 48p. Grades: 2–5.
	Gallagher, Carole S. *Christopher Columbus and the Discovery of the New World*. Philadelphia, Penn.: Chelsea House, 2000. 63p. Grades: 4–8.
	Meltzer, Milton. *Columbus and the World around Him*. New York: Franklin Watts, 1990. 192p. Grades: 6 and up.
Halloween October 31	Poydar, Nancy. *The Perfectly Horrible Halloween*. New York: Holiday House, 2001. Unp. Grades: P–2.
	Halloween. Video. Bala Cynwyd, Penn.: Schlessinger Video Productions-Library Video Company, 1996. 25 min. Grades: K–4.
	Flanagan, Alice K. *Halloween*. Illustrated by Patrick Girouard. Minneapolis, Minn.: Compass Point Books, 2002. 32p. Grades: 1–4.
	Robinson, Fay. *Halloween: Costumes and Treats on All Hallows' Eve*. Berkeley Heights, N.J.: Enslow, 2001. 48p. Grades: 2–5.
	Halloween Tales: Spooky Pack. CD. Newark, N.J.: Peter Pan, 2001. Grades: 4 and up.
	Barth, Edna. *Witches, Pumpkins, and Grinning Ghosts: The Story of the Halloween Symbols*. Illustrated by Ursula Arndt. New York: Houghton Mifflin, 2001, 1972. 96p. Grades: 5 and up.
	The Haunted History of Halloween. DVD and video. South Burlington, Va.: A & E Television Networks, 1997. 50 min. Grades: 6 and up.

NOVEMBER

Veterans Day November 11	Cotton, Jacqueline S. *Veterans Day*. New York: Children's Press, 2002. 32p. Grades: P–2.
	Memorial Day/Veterans Day. Video. Bala Cynwyd, Penn.: Schlessinger Video Productions-Library Video Company, 2003. 23 min. Grades: K–4.
	Landau, Elaine. *Veterans Day: Remembering Our War Heroes*. Berkeley Heights, N.J.: Enslow, 2002. 48p. Grades: 2–5.
Election Day First Tuesday after the first Monday	Murphy, Patricia J. *Voting and Elections*. Minneapolis, Minn.: Compass Point Books, 2002. 24p. Grades: K–2.
	Election Day. Video. Bala Cynwyd, Penn.: Schlessinger Video Productions-Library Video Company, 1996. 25 min. Grades: K–4.
	Pascoe, Elaine. *The Right to Vote*. Brookfield, Conn.: The Millbrook Press, 1997. 48p. Grades: 3–6.On the Campaign Trail. Win/Mac CD-ROM. Watertown, Maine: Tom Snyder Productions. Grades: 5–10.

Thanksgiving Fourth Thursday	*Thanksgiving*. Video. Bala Cynwyd, Penn.: Schlessinger Video Productions-Library Video Company, 1994. 25 min. Grades: K–4.
	Anderson, Laurie Halse. *Thank You, Sarah!!!: The Woman Who Saved Thanksgiving*. Illustrated by Matt Faulkner. New York: Simon & Schuster, 2002. 40p. Grades: 1–4.
	Landau, Elaine. *Thanksgiving Day: A Time to Be Thankful*. Berkeley Heights, N.J.: Enslow, 2001. 47p. Grades: 2–4.
	Kamma, Anne. *If You Were At...the First Thanksgiving*. Illustrated by Bert Dodson. New York: Scholastic, 2001. 64p. Grades: 2–5.
	Grace, Catherine O'Neill, and Margaret M. Bruchac. With Plimoth Plantation. *1621: A New Look at Thanksgiving*. Photographs by Sisse Brimberg and Cotton Coulson. Washington, D.C.: National Geographic Society, 2001. 48p. Grades: 3–6.
	Barth, Edna. *Turkeys, Pilgrims, and Indian Corn: The Story of the Thanksgiving Symbols*. Illustrated by Ursula Arndt. New York: Houghton Mifflin, 2001, 1975. 96p. Grades: 5 and up.
	Home for the Holidays: The History of Thanksgiving. Video and DVD. South Burlington, Va.: A & E Television Networks, 1997. 50 min. Grades: 6 and up.

DECEMBER

Christmas December 25	Riley, Linnea Asplind. *The 12 Days of Christmas*. New York: Simon & Schuster Books for Young Readers, 1995. Unp. Grades: P–2.
	Dr. Seuss. How the Grinch Stole Christmas. New York: Random House, 1957. Unp. Grades: P–3.
	Moore, Clement C. *The Night before Christmas*. Illustrated by Jan Brett. New York: G.P. Putnam's Sons, 1998. Unp. Grades: P–3.
	First Christmas Record for Children. CD. New York: Sony, 1999. Grades: P–4.
	Van Allsburg, Chris. *The Polar Express*. Boston: Houghton Mifflin, 1985. Unp. Grades: P–4.
	Fradin, Dennis Brindell. *Christmas*. Berkeley Heights, N. J.: Enslow, 2002. 48p. Grades: 2–5.
	Robinson, Barbara. *The Best Christmas Pageant Ever*. Illustrated by Judith Gwyn Brown. New York: HarperCollins, 1972. 90p. Grades: 3–5.
	Barth, Edna. Holly, *Reindeer, and Colored Lights: The Story of the Christmas Symbols*. Illustrated by Ursula Arndt. New York: Houghton Mifflin, 2000, 1971. 96p. Grades: 5 and up.
	Christmas Unwrapped: The History of Christmas. Video and DVD. South Burlington, Va.: A & E Television Networks, 1997. 50 min. Grades: 6 and up.
	Dickens, Charles. *A Christmas Carol*. Illustrated by Lisbeth Zwerger. New York: North South Books, 2001. 67p. Grades: 7 and up.

Kwanzaa December 26 to January 1	Grier, Ella. *Seven Days of Kwanzaa: A Holiday Step Book*. Illustrated by John Ward. New York: Viking, 1997. Unp. Grades: P–3.
	Kwanzaa. Video. Bala Cynwyd, Penn.: Schlessinger Video Productions-Library Video Company, 1994. 25 min. Grades: K–4.
	Kwanzaa for Young People (and Everyone Else!). CD. Gardena, Calif.: Charphelia,1999. Grades: K–6.
	Goss, Linda, and Clay Goss. *It's Kwanzaa Time!* Illustrated by Ashley Bryan, Carole Byard, Floyd Cooper, Leo Dillon, Diane Dillon, Jan Spivey Gilchrist, Jonathan Green, and Jerry Pinkney. New York: G.P. Putnam's Son's, 2002. 71p. Grades: 4–7.
	Karenga, Maulana. *Kwanzaa: A Celebration of Family, Community, and Culture*. Los Angeles, Calif.: University of Sankore Press, 1998. 143p. Grades: 7 and up.

JANUARY

New Year's Day January 1	Marx, David F. *New Year's Day*. New York: Children's Press, 2000. 32p. Grades: P–2.
	Rattigan, Jama Kim. *Dumpling Soup*. Illustrated by Lillian Hsu-Flanders. Boston: Little, Brown, 1993. Unp. Grades: P–3.
	Ziefert, Harriet. *Amanda Dade's New Years Parade*. Illustrated by S. D. Schindler. New York: Penguin Putnam Books for Young Readers, 2001. Unp. Grades: P–3.
	Rau, Dana Meachen. *New Year's Day*. New York: Children's Press, 2000. 47p. Grades: K–2.
Martin Luther King, Jr. Day Third Monday	Rappaport, Doreen. *Martin's Big Words: The Life of Dr. Martin Luther King, Jr*. Illustrated by Bryan Collier. New York: Hyperion Books for Children, 2001. Unp. Grades: P–4.
	Martin Luther King, Jr. Day. Video. Bala Cynwyd, Penn.: Schlessinger Video Productions-Library Video Company, 2003. 23 min. Grades: K–4.
	Farris, Christine King. *My Brother Martin: A Sister Remembers Growing Up with the Rev. Dr. Martin Luther King, Jr*. Illustrated by Chris Soentpiet. New York: Simon & Schuster books for Young Readers, 2003. Unp. Grades: 1–5.
	Gnojewski, Carol. *Martin Luther King, Jr., Day: Honoring a Man of Peace*. Berkeley Heights, N.J.: Enslow, 2002. 48p. Grades: 2–5.
	Martin Luther King, Jr.: The Man and the Dream. Video. South Burlington, Va.: A & E Television Networks, 1998. 50 min. Grades: 6 and up.

FEBRUARY

Groundhog Day February 2	Koscielniak, Bruce. *Geoffrey Groundhog Predicts the Weather*. Boston: Houghton Mifflin, 1995. Unp. Grades: P–3.
	Levine, Abby. *Gretchen Groundhog, It's Your Day*. Illustrated by Nancy Cote. Morton Grove, Ill.: Albert Whitman, 2002. Unp. Grades: K–3.
	The Story of Punxsutawney Phil: Fearless Forecaster. Video. St. Louis, Mo.: Coronet, 1991. 10 min. Grades: K–6.
	McMullan, Kate. *Fluffy Meets the Groundhog*. Illustrated by Mavis Smith. New York: Scholastic, 2001. Unp. Grades: 1–2.
Valentine's Day February 14	de Groat, Diane. *Roses Are Pink, Your Feet Really Stink*. New York: Morrow Junior Books, 1996. Unp. Grades: P–3.
	Poydar, Nancy. *Rhyme Time Valentine*. New York: Holiday House, 2003. Unp. Grades: P–3.
	Rau, Dana Meachen. *Valentine's Day*. New York: Children's Press, 2001. 47p. Grades: 1–3.
	Flanagan, Alice K. *Valentine's Day*. Illustrated by Shelley Dieterichs. Minneapolis, Minn.: Compass Point Books, 2002. 32p. Grades: 2–4.
	Bulla, Robert Clyde. *The Story of Valentine's Day*. Illustrated by Susan Estelle Kwas. New York: HarperCollins, 1999, 1965. Unp. Grades: 2–5.
	Landau, Elaine. *Valentine's Day: Candy, Love, and Hearts*. Berkeley Heights, N.J.: Enslow, 2002. 48p. Grades: 2–5.
	Barth, Edna. *Hearts, Cupids, and Red Roses: The Story of the Valentine Symbols*. Illustrated by Ursula Arndt. New York: Houghton Mifflin, 2001, 1972. 96p. Grades: 5 and up.

Presidents' Day Third Monday	*Presidents Day*. Video. Bala Cynwyd, Penn.: Schlessinger Video Productions-Library Video Company, 2003. 23 min. Grades: K–4.
	MacMillan, Dianne M. *Presidents Day*. Berkeley Heights, N.J.: Enslow, 1997. 48p. Grades: 2–5.
	Sandler, Martin W. *Presidents*. New York: HarperCollins, 1995. 94p. Grades: 4–8.
	St. George, Judith. *So You Want to Be President?* Illustrated by David Small. New York: Philomel Books, 2000. 52p. Grades: 4 and up.

MARCH

Easter Date and month varies	Wells, Rosemary. *Max's Chocolate Chicken*. New York: Penguin Putnam Books for Young Readers, 1989. Unp. Grades: P–1.
	Berlin, Irving. *Easter Parade*. Illustrated by Lisa McCue. New York: HarperCollins, 2003. Unp. Grades: P–2.
	DJ's Choice: Easter Bunny's Favorite Songs. CD. Kenilworth, N.J.: Turn Up the Music, 2002. Grades: P–3.
	Merrick, Patrick. *Easter Bunnies*. Chanhassen, Minn.: The Child's World, 2000. 32p. Grades: K–3.
	Hague, Michael, comp. *Michael Hague's Family Easter Treasury*. New York: Henry Holt, 1999. 134p. Grades: K and up.
	Barth, Edna. *Lilies, Rabbits, and Painted Eggs: The Story of the Easter Symbols*. Illustrated by Ursula Arndt. New York: Houghton Mifflin,1998, 1970. 64p. Grades: 4–8.

St. Patrick's Day March 17	de Paola, Tomie. *Patrick: Patron Saint of Ireland.* New York: Holiday House, 1992. Unp. Grades: P–2.
	Gibbons, Gail. *St. Patrick's Day.* New York: Holiday House, 1994. Unp. Grades: K–3.
	St. Patrick's Day. Video. Bala Cynwyd, Penn.: Schlessinger Video Productions-Library Video Company, 1996. 25 min. Grades: K–4.
	Landau, Elaine. *St. Patrick's Day.* Berkeley Heights, N.J.: Enslow, 2002. 48p. Grades: 2–5.
	Barth, Edna. *Shamrocks, Harps, and Shillelaghs: The Story of St. Patrick's Day Symbols.* Illustrated by Ursula Arndt. New York: Houghton Mifflin, 2001. 96p. Grades: 6–8.
	Celebrating the Green: The History of St. Patrick's Day. Video. South Burlington, Va.: A & E Television Networks, 1998. 50 min.

APRIL

April Fools' Day April 1	Minarik, Else Holmelund. *April Fools!* Illustrated by Chris Hahner. New York: HarperCollins, 2002. 24p. Grades: P–1.
	Ruelle, Karen Gray. *April Fool!* New York: Holiday House, 2002. 32p. Grades: K–3.
	Stevenson, James. *Mud Flat April Fool.* New York: Greenwillow Books, 1998. 48p. Grades: K–2.

Earth Day April 22	*Environmental Songs for Kids*. CD. Washington, D.C.: Smithsonian Folkways Recordings, 1999. Grades: K–3.
	Wallace, Nancy Elizabeth. *Recycle Every Day!* New York: Marshall Cavendish, 2003. Unp. Grades: K–3.
	Crunch, Smash, Trash!: Monster Machines that Recycle. Video. Bala Cynwyd, Penn.: Schlessinger Video Productions-Library Video Company, 1994. 30 min. Grades: K–4.
	Maass, Robert. *Garbage*. New York: Henry Holt and Company, 2000. Unp.Grades: K–4.
	Kids & the Environment. Win/Mac CD-ROM. Watertown, Maine: Tom Snyder Productions. Grades: 2–6.
	Chandler, Gary, and Kevin Graham. *Recycling*. New York: Henry Holt, 1996. 64p. Grades: 5–8.
	Gardner, Robert. *Celebrating Earth Day: A Sourcebook of Activities and Experiments*. Illustrated by Sharon Lane Holm. Brookfield, Conn.: The Millbrook Press, 1992. 96p. Grades: 6–10.
Arbor Day Date and month varies	Bennet, Kelly. *Arbor Day*. New York: Children's Press, 2003. 32p. Grades: P–2.
	Arbor Day. Video. Bala Cynwyd, Penn.: Schlessinger Video Productions-Library Video Company, 1994. 30 min. Grades: K–4.
	Warrick, Karen Clemens. *John Chapman: The Legendary Johnny Appleseed*. Springfield, N.J.: Enslow, 2001. 128p. Grades: 4–8.

MAY

Mother's Day Second Monday	French, Vivian. *A Present for Mom*. Illustrated by Dana Kubick. Camridge, Mass.: Candlewick Press, 2002. Unp. Grades: P–2.
	Leuck, Laura. *My Monster Mama Loves Me So*. Illustrated by Mark Buehner. New York: HarperCollins, 1999. Unp. Grades: P–3.
	Mora, Pat, ed. *Love to Moma: A Tribute to Mothers*. Illustrated by Paula S. Barragan M. New York: Lee & Low Books, 2001. Unp. Grades: P–4.
Memorial Day Last Monday	*Memorial Day/Veterans Day*. Video. Bala Cynwyd, Penn.: Schlessinger Video Productions-Library Video Company, 2003. 23 min. Grades: K–4.
	Polacco, Patricia. *Pink and Say*. New York: Putnam, 1994. Unp. Grades: 3 and up.
	Kuhn, Betsy. *Angels of Mercy: The Army Nurses of World War II*. New York: Atheneum Books for Young Readers, 1999. 114p. Grades: 5 and up.

JUNE

Father's Day Third Sunday	Clements, Andrew. *Secret Father's Day Present: A Lift-the-Flap Story*. Illustrated by Varda Livney. New York: Simon & Schuster, 2000. 16p. Grades: P–1.
	Bunting, Eve. *A Perfect Father's Day*. Illustrated by Susan Meddaugh. New York: Houghton Mifflin, 1993. 32p. Grades: P–3.
	Wood, Douglas. *What Dads Can't Do*. Illustrated by Doug Cushman. New York: Simon and Schuster Books for Young Readers, 2000. Unp. Grades: P–3.
	Smalls, Irene. *Father's Day Blues: What Do You Do about Father's Day When All You Have are Mothers?* Illustrated by Kevin McGovern. Stamford, Conn.: Longmeadow Press, 1995. Unp. Grades: K–3.
	Steptoe, Javaka. *In Daddy's Arms I Am Tall: African Americans Celebrating Fathers*. New York: Lee & Low Books, 2000. Unp. Grades: 3 and up.
Flag Day June 14	Herman, John. *Red, White and Blue: The Story of the American Flag*. Illustrated by Robin Roraback. East Rutherford, N. J.: Putnam Publishing Group, 1998. 48p. Grades: K–3.
	America! A Celebration of Freedom from Our Nation's Finest. CD. Nashville, Tenn.: Coker & McCree, 1999. Grades: K and up.
	Old Glory. Video. Raleigh, N.C.: Rainbow Educational Media, 1994. 10 min. Grades: 2–5.
	Ryan, Pam Muñoz. *The Flag We Love*. Illustrated by Ralph Masiello. Watertown, Mass.: Charlesbridge, 1996. Unp. Grades: 2 and up.

JULY

Fourth of July July 4	Ziefert, Harriet. *Hats Off for the Fourth of July!* Illustrated by Gustaf Miller. New York: Puffin Books, 2000. Unp. Grades: P–2.
	Wong, Janet S. *Apple Pie 4th of July*. Illustrated by Margaret Chodos-Irvine. San Diego, Calif.: Harcourt, 2002. Unp. Grades: P–3.
	Independence Day. Video. Bala Cynwyd, Penn.: Schlessinger Video Productions-Library Video Company, 1994. 25 min. Grades: K–4.
	Merrick, Patrick. *Fourth of July Fireworks*. Chanhassen, Minn.: The Child's World, 2000. 32p. Grades: 1–4.
	Landau, Elaine. *Independence Day—Birthday of the United States*. Berkeley Heights, N.J.: Enslow Publishers, 2001. 48p. Grades: 2–5.
	Giblin, James Cross. *Fireworks, Picnics, and Flags: The Story of the Fourth of July Symbols*. Illustrated by Ursula Arndt. New York: Clarion Books, 1983. 90p. Grades: 4 and up.
	Independence Day: History of July 4th. Video. South Burlington, Va.: A & E Television Networks, 1998. 50 min. Grades: 6 and up.

AUGUST

Women's Equality Day August 26	Corey, Shana. *You Forgot Your Skirt, Amelia Bloomer*. Illustrated by Chesley McLaren. New York: Scholastic Press, 2000. Unp. Grades: K–4.
	Equality: A History of the Women's Movement in America. Video. Bala Cynwyd, Penn.: Schlessinger Video Productions-Library Video Company, 1996. 30 min. Grades: K–4.
	Fritz, Jean. *You Want Women to Vote, Lizzie Stanton?* Illustrated by DyAnne DiSalvo-Ryan. New York: G.P. Putnam's Sons, 1995. 88p. Grades: 3–6.
	Bohannon, Lisa Frederiksen. *Failure is Impossible: The Story of Susan B. Anthony*. Greensboro, N.C.: Morgan Reynolds, 2002. 112p. Grades: 6–9

ASIAN CELEBRATIONS AND HOLIDAYS

This chart contains selected books and media for studying celebrations and holidays observed in Asia, South Asia, Southeast Asia, and China. Information on the celebrations and holidays, as well as annotations for a wide variety of books and media, can be found in the individual book chapters noted in the chart.

Fall Chapter 1	Diwali (Festival of Lights)	Gardeski, Christina Mia. *Diwali*. New York: Children's Press, 2001. 32p. Grades: P–2.
		MacMillan, Dianne M. *Diwali*. Berkeley Heights, N.J.: Enslow Publishers, 1997. 48p. Grades: 2–5.
		Kadodwala, Dilip. *Divali*. Austin, Tex.: Steck-Vaughn, 1998. 31p. Grades: 4–8.
	Ramadan	Marx, David F. *Ramadan*. New York: Scholastic, 2002. 32p. Grades: K–2.
		Ghazi, Suhaib Hamid. *Ramadan*. Illustrated by Omar Rayyan. New York: Holiday House, 1996. Unp. Grades: K–3.
		Ramadan. Video. Bala Cynwyd, Penn.: Schlessinger Video Productions-Library Video Company, 1996. 25 min. Grades: K–4.
		MacMillan, Dianne M. *Ramadan and Id al-Fitr*. Berkeley Heights, N.J.: Enslow Publishers, 1995. 48p. Grades: 2–5.
		Hoyt-Goldsmith, Diane. Celebrating *Ramadan*. Photographs by Lawrence Migdale. New York: Holiday House, 2001. Unp. Grades: 3–6.

	Id-Ul-Fitr	Kerven, Rosalind. *Id-Ul-Fitr*. Chicago, Ill.: Raintree Publishers, 1997. 32p. Grades: 2–5.
		Marchant, Kerena. *Id-Ul-Fitr*. Brookfield, Conn.: The Millbrook Press, 1996. 32p. Grades: 2–5.
	Zhongqiu Jie (Mid-Autumn Moon Festival)	Russell, Ching Yeung. *Moon Festival*. Christopher Zhong-Yuan Zhang. Honesdale, Penn.: Boyds Mills Press, 1997. Unp. Grades: K–4.
		Chinese Shadow Puppet Theater. Win/Mac CD. Seattle, Wash.: Pentewa Interactive, 1999. Grades: 4–8.
September Chapter 2	Chongyang Jie (Double Nine Festival)	Lin, Grace. *Kite Flying*. New York: Alfred A. Knopf, 2002. Unp. Grades: P–1.
		Demi. *Kites: Magic Wishes That Fly Up to the Sky*. New York: Crown, 1999. Unp. Grades: 1–4.
Winter Chapter 5	TET Nguyen-Dan (Vietnamese New Year)	MacMillan, Dianne M. *Tet: Vietnamese New Year*. Berkeley Heights, N.J.: Enslow, 1994. 48p. Grades: 2–5.
		Hoyt-Goldsmith, Diane. Hoang Anh: *A Vietnamese-American Boy*. Photographs by Lawrence Migdale. New York: Holiday House, 1992. 32p. Grades: 3–8.

	Xin Nian and Deng Jie (Chinese Lunar New Year and Lantern Festival)	Wong, Janet S. *This Next New Year.* Illustrated by Yangsook Choi. New York: Farrar, Straus and Giroux, 2000. Unp. Grades: P–2.
		Chinese New Year. Video. Bala Cynwyd, Penn.: Schlessinger Video Productions-Library Video Company, 1994. 25 min. Grades: K–4.
		Demi. *Happy New Year!/Kung-his fa-ts'ai!* New York: Crown, 1997. Unp. Grades: 1–6.
		Robinson, Fay. *Chinese New Year: A Time for Parades, Family, and Friends.* Berkeley Heights, N.J.: Enslow, 2001. 48p. Grades: 2–5.
		Hoyt-Goldsmith, Diane. *Celebrating Chinese New Year.* Photographs by Lawrence Migdale. New York: Holiday House, 1998. 32p. Grades: 3–6.
	Eid-Al-Adha	*The Hajj: One American's Pilgrimage to Mecca.* Video. Bala Cynwyd, Penn.: Schlessinger Video Productions-Library Video Company, 1997. 22 min. Grades: 7 and up.
Spring Chapter 9	Holi (Festival of Color)	Krishnaswami, Uma. *Holi.* New York: Children's Press, 2003. 32p. Grades: P–2.
		Kadodwala, Dilip. *Holi.* Chicago, Ill.: Raintree: 1997. 32p. Grades: 2–5.
March Chapter 10	Hina Masuri (Doll Festival)	MacMillan, Dianne M. *Japanese Children's Day and the Obon Festival.* Berkeley Heights, N.J.: Enslow, 1997. 48p. Grades: 2–5.
April Chapter 11	Hana Matsuri (Buddha's Birthday)	Demi. *Buddha.* New York: Henry Holt, 1996. Unp. Grades: 2–4.

May Chapter 12	Tango-no-sekku (Boys' Day)	Riehecky, Janet. *Japanese Boys' Festival*. Illustrated by Krystyna Stasiak. Chicago: Children's Press, 1994. 32p. Grades: K–4.
	Kodomono-Hi (Children's Day)	Kroll, Virginia. *A Carp for Kimiko*. Illustrated by Katherine Roundtree. Watertown, Mass.: Charlesbrigdge Publishing, 1993. Unp. Grades: P–3.
Summer Chapter 13	Obon Festival	McCoy, Karen Kawamoto. *Bon Odori Dancer*. Illustrated by Carolina Yao. Chicago, Ill.: Polychrome Publishing, 1998. Unp. Grades: 1–3.
		Come Celebrate with Me: Obon—Japanese Festival of Spirits. Video. Morris Plains, N.J.: Lucerne Media, 2001. 10 min. Grades: 3–6.
July Chapter 15	Tanabata (Star Festival) (Festival of the Milky Way)	Kitada, Shin. *The Story of Tanabata. Oaktag Cards*. Illustrated by Yukihiko Mitani. New York: Kamishibai for Kids, 1995. Grades: P–4.
		Birdseye, Tom. *A Song of Stars*. Illustrated by Ju-Hong Chen. New York: Holiday House, 1990. Unp. Grades: K–3.

August Chapter 16	Hiroshima Day	Coerr, Eleanor. *Sadako*. Illustrated by Ed Young. New York: G.P. Putnam's Sons, 1993. Unp. Grades: 1–4.
		Sadako and the Thousand Paper Cranes. Video. Santa Cruz, Calif.: Informed Democracy, 1991. 30 min. Grades: 4–7.
		Coerr, Eleanor. *Sadako and the Thousand Paper Cranes*. New York: Penguin, 2002. 80p. Grades: 4–7.
		Hamanaka, Sheila, compiler. *On the Wings of Peace: In Memory of Hiroshima and Nagasaki*. New York: Houghton Mifflin, 1995. 144p. Grades: 6 and up.

CENTRAL AMERICAN AND HISPANIC CELEBRATIONS AND HOLIDAYS

This chart contains selected books and media for studying celebrations and holidays observed in Central America and Mexico. Information on the celebrations and holidays, as well as annotations for a variety of books and media, can be found in the individual book chapters noted in the chart.

September Chapter 2	Mexican Independence Day	MacMillan, Dianne M. *Mexican Independence Day and Cinco de Mayo.* Berkley Heights, N.J.: Enslow, 1997. 47p. Grades: 2–5.
November Chapter 3	Dia de los Muertos (Day of the Dead)	Johnston, Tony. *Day of the Dead.* Illustrated by Jeanette Winter. San Diego: Harcourt Brace, 1997. Unp. Grades: P–2.
		Amado, Elisa. *Barrilete: A Kite for Day of the Dead.* Photographs by Joya Hairs. Toronto, Ont.: Groundwood Books, 1999. Unp. Grades: 2–4.
		Hoyt-Goldsmith, Diane. *Day of the Dead: A Mexican-American Celebration.* Photographs by Lawrence Migdale. New York: Holiday House, 1998. Unp. Grades: 3–6.
		Mexico's Day of the Dead. Win/Mac CD. Seattle, Wash.: Pentewa Interactive, 1999. Grades: 4–8.
December Chapter 6	Our Lady of Guadelupe	de Paola, Tomie. *The Lady of Guadalupe.* New York: Holiday House, 1980. Unp. Grades: K–3.

	Las Posadas	de Paola, Tomie. *The Night of Las Posadas*. New York: Penguin Putnam Books for Young Readers, 1999. Unp. Grades: P–3.
		Ciavonne, Jean. *Carlos, Light the Farolito*. Illustrated by Donna Clair. New York: Clarion Books, 1995. Unp. Grades: K–4.
		Hoyt-Goldsmith, Dianne. *Las Posadas: A Hispanic Christmas Celebration*. Photographs by Lawrence Migdale. New York: Holiday House, 1999. Unp. Grades: 4–6.
January Chapter 7	El Dia de los Reyes (Epiphany)	de Paola, Tomie. *The Legend of Old Befana*. New York: Harcourt Brace Jovanovich, 1980. Unp. Grades: P–3.
		de Paola, Tomie. *The Story of the Three Wise Kings*. San Diego: G.P. Putnam's Sons, 1983. Unp. Grades: P–3.
		Slate, Joseph. *The Secret Stars*. Illustrated by Felipe Davalos. Tarrytown, N.Y.: Marshall Cavendish, 1998. Unp. Grades: K–3.
		Carlson, Lori Marie. *Hurray for Three Kings' Day*. Illustrated by Ed Martinez. New York: Morrow Junior Books, 1999. Unp. Grades: K–4.

May Chapter 12	Cinco de Mayo	Wade, Mary Dodson. *Cinco de Mayo*. New York: Children's Press, 2003. 32p. Grades: P–2.
		Cristina, Maria Urrutia. *Cinco de Mayo: Yesterday and Today*. Toronto, Ont.: Groundwood Books, 2002. Unp. Grades: K–3.
		Cinco de Mayo. Video. Bala Cynwyd, Penn.: Schlessinger Video Productions-Library Video Company, 1994. 25 min. Grades: K–4.
		Gnojewski, Carol. *Cinco de Mayo: Celebrating Hispanic Pride*. Berkeley Heights, N.J.: Enslow, 2002. 48p. Grades: 2–5.
		Palacios, Argentina. *Viva Mexico! The Story of Benito Juarez and Cinco de Mayo*. Illustrated by Howard Berelson. Austin, Texas: Raintree, 1992. 32p. Grades: 2–8.

JEWISH CELEBRATIONS AND HOLIDAYS

This chart contains selected books and media for learning about Jewish celebrations and holidays. Information on the celebrations and holidays, as well as annotations for a wide variety of books and media, can be found in the individual book chapters noted in the chart.

Fall Chapter 1	Rosh Hashanah and Yom Kippur	Marx, David F. *Rosh Hashanah and Yom Kippur*. New York: Children's Press, 2001. 32p. Grades: P–1.
		Kimmelman, Leslie. *Sound the Shofar! A Story for Rosh Hashanah and Yom Kippur*. Illustrated by John Himmelman. New York: HarperCollins, 1998. Unp. Grades: P–2.
		Fishman, Cathy Goldberg. *On Rosh Hashanah and Yom Kippur*. Illustrated by Melanie W. Hall. New York: Simon & Schuster Children's Publishing, 1998. Unp. Grades: K–4.
		Rosh Hashanah/Yom Kippur. Bala Cynwyd, Penn.: Schlessinger Video Productions-Library Video Company, 1994. 25 min. Grades: K–4.
	Sukkot and Simchat Torah	Gellman, Ellie. *Tamar's Sukkah*. Illustrated by Shauna Mooney Kawasaki. Rockville, Md.: Kar-Ben, 1999. Unp. Grades: P–1.
		Zalben, Jane Breskin. *Leo & Blossom's Sukkah*. New York: Henry Holt, 1990. Unp. Grades: P–3.
		Goldin, Barbara Diamond. *Night Lights: A Sukkot Story*. Illustrated by Louise August. New York: Harcourt Brace, 1995. Unp. Grades: P–4.

Winter Chapter 5	Hanukkah	Winne, Joanne. *Let's Get Ready for Hanukkah*. New York: Children's Press, 2001. 23p. Grades: P–1.
		Rosen, Michael J. *Chanukah Lights Everywhere*. Illustrated by Melissa Iwai. San Diego: Gulliver Books, 2001. Unp. Grades: P–2.
		Kimmel, Eric A. *Zigazak! A Magical Hanukkah Night*. Illustrated by Jon Goodell. New York: A Doubleday Book for Young Readers, 2001. Unp. Grades: P–4.
		A Child's Hanukkah. CD and Audiocassette. Garberville, Calif.: Music for Little People, 1998. Grades: K–3.
		Hanukkah/Passover. Video. Bala Cynwyd, Penn.: Schlessinger Video Productions-Library Video Company, 1996. 25 min. Grades: K–4.
		Bunting, Eve. *One Candle*. Illustrated by K. Wendy Popp. New York: Joanna Cotler Books, 2002. 30p. Grades: 1–5.
		Erlbach, Arlene. *Hanukkah: Celebrating the Holiday of Lights*. Berkeley Heights, N.J.: Enslow, 2002. 48p. Grades: 2–5.
		Cohn, Janice. *The Christmas Menorahs: How a Town Fought Hate*. Illustrated by Bill Farnsworth. Morton Grove, Ill.: Albert Whitman and Company, 1995. 39p. Grades: 2–6.
		Hoyt-Goldsmith, Diane. *Celebrating Hanukkah*. Photographs by Lawrence Migdale. New York: Holiday House, 1996. 32p. Grades: 3–6.

	Tu Bi-Shevat (Arbor Day)	Zalben, Jane Breskin. *Pearl Plants a Tree.* New York: Simon & Schuster Books for Young Readers, 1995. Unp. Grades: K–3.
		Alexander, Sue. *Behold the Trees.* Illustrated by Leonid Gore. New York: Scholastic, 2001. Unp. Grades: 3–6.
Spring Chapter 9	Purim	Fishman, Cathy Goldberg. *On Purim.* Illustrated by Melanie W. Hall. New York: Atheneum Books for Young Readers, 2000. Unp. Grades: P–3.
		Wolkstein, Diane. *Esther's Story.* Illustrated by Juan Wijngaard. New York: Morrow Junior Books, 1996. Unp. Grades: 1–6.
	Passover	Manushkin, Fran. *The Matzah That Papa Brought Home.* Illustrated by Ned Bittinger. New York: Scholastic, 1995. Unp. Grades: P–3.
		Manushkin, Fran. *Miriam's Cup: A Passover Story.* Illustrated by Bob Dacey. New York: Scholastic, 1998. Unp. Grades: K–4.
		Simon, Norma. *The Story of Passover.* Illustrated by Erika Weihs. New York: HarperCollins, 1997, 1965. Unp. Grades: 2–5.
		Hoyt-Goldsmith, Diane. *Celebrating Passover.* Photographs by Lawrence Migdale. New York: Holiday House, 2000. 32p. Grades: 3–6.
		Goldin, Barbara Diamond. *The Passover Journey: A Seder Companion.* Illustrated by Neil Waldman. New York: Puffin Books, 1994. 55p. Grades: 4 and up.

Summer Chapter 13	Shauvot	Goldin, Barbara Diamond. *A Mountain of Blintzes*. Illustrated by Anik McGrory. San Diego: Gulliver Books, 2001. Grades: P–2.
Chapter 18	Bat Mitzvah	Goldin, Barbara Diamond. *Bat Mitzvah: A Jewish Girl's Coming of Age*. Illustrated by Erika Weihs. New York: Viking, 1995. 139p. Grades: 5 and up.

NATIVE AMERICAN CELEBRATIONS

This chart contains books and media for learning about selected Native American celebrations, including Itse Selu, Powwow, Potlatch, and Buffalo Days. Information on the celebrations, as well as annotations for a variety of books and media, can be found in chapter 2 and chapter 18. When teaching about Native Americans, it is important to avoid stereotypes and to present information about the different tribes and their unique cultures and contributions to American life (Reese, 1996; Franklin, Roach, and Snyder, 1993).

Itse Selu (Green Corn Festival) Chapter 2	Pennington, Daniel. *Itse Selu: Cherokee Harvest Festival*. Illustrated by Don Stewart. Watertown, Mass.: Charlesbridge Publishing, 1994. Unp. Grades: K–4.
Powwow Chapter 18	Kalman, Bobbie. *Celebrating the Powwow*. New York: Crabtree Publishing, 1997. 32p. Grades: 2–4.
	Ancona, George. *Powwow*. San Diego: Harcourt Brace Jovanovich, 1993. Unp. Grades: 2–6.
	Come Celebrate with Me: Native American Powwow. Video. Morris Plains, N.J.: Lucerne Media, 2001. 10 min. Grades: 3–6.
	Into the Circle: An Introduction to Native American Powwows. Video. Bala Cynwyd, Penn.: Schlessinger Video Productions-Library Video Company, 1992. 60 min. Grades: 7 and up.

Buffalo Days Chapter 18	Hoyt-Goldsmith, Diane. *Buffalo Days*. Photographs by Lawrence Migdale. New York: Holiday House, 1997. 32p. Grades: 3–6.
Potlach Chapter 18	Hoyt-Goldsmith, Diane. *Potlatch: A Tsimshian Celebration*. Photographs by Lawrence Migdale. New York: Holiday House, 1997. 32p. Grades: 3–6.

SPECIAL CELEBRATIONS

This chart contains books and media for special celebrations observed throughout the year. These are celebrations that occur on different days and are usually observed with family and friends. Information on the celebrations, as well as annotations for a wide variety of books and media, can be found in Chapter 18.

Bar Mitzvahs and Bat Mitzvahs	Goldin, Barbara Diamond. *Bat Mitzvah: A Jewish Girl's Coming of Age*. Illustrated by Erika Weihs. New York: Viking, 1995. 139p. Grades: 5 and up.
Birthdays	*Birthday Party Singalongs*. CD. Redway, Calif.: Music for Little People, 2001. Grades: P–2.
	Knight, Margy Burns. *Welcoming Babies*. Illustrated by Anne Sibley O'Brien. Gardiner, Maine: Tilbury House, 1994. Unp. Grades: P–2.
	de Groat, Diane. *Happy Birthday to You, You Belong in a Zoo*. New York: Morrow Junior Books, 1999. Unp. Grades: P–4.
	Lankford, Mary D. *Birthdays around the World*. Illustrated by Karen Dugan. New York: Harper Collins, 2002. 32p. Grades: K–4.
	Erlbach, Arlene. *Happy Birthday, Everywhere!* Illustrated by Sharon Lane Holm. Brookfield, Conn.: The Millbrook Press, 1997. 48p. Grades: 4–6.

Circuses, Fairs, Fiestas, and Jamborees	*Circus* Magic. CD and Audiocassette. Huntington, Calif.: Youngheart Music, 1999. Grades: P–2.
	Greene, Rhonda Gowler. *Jamboree Day*. Illustrated by Jason Wolff. New York: Scholastic, 2001. Unp. Grades: P–2.
	Ancona, George. *Fiesta Fireworks*. New York: Lothrop, Lee & Shepard Books, 1998. Unp. Grades: 1–4.
	Lewin, Ted. *Fair*. New York: Lothrop, Lee & Shepard, 1997. Unp. Grades: 1–4.
Graduations	*Dr. Seuss. Oh, the Places You'll Go!* New York: Random House, 1990. Unp. Grades: K–8.
	Park, Barbara. *Junie B. Jones is a Graduation Girl*. Illustrated by Denise Brunkus. New York: Random House, 2001. 69p. Grades: 1–3.
	Anderson, Janet S. *Going through the Gate*. New York: Dutton Children's Books, 1997. 134p. Grades: 5–8.
Quinceañeras	Hoyt-Goldsmith, Diane. *Celebrating a Quinceañera: A Latina's 15th Birthday Celebration*. Photographs by Lawrence Migdale. New York: Holiday House, 2002. 32p. Grades: 3–6.
	King, Elizabeth. *Quinceañera: Celebrating Fifteen*. New York: Dutton Children's Books, 1998. 40p. Grades: 6–9.
Snow Days	Plourde, Lynn. *Snow Day*. Illustrated by Hideko Takahashi. New York: Simon & Schuster, 2001. Unp. Grades: P–1.
	Lakin, Patricia. *Snow Day!* Illustrated by Scott Nash. New York: Penguin Putnam Books for Young Readers, 2002. Unp. Grades: P–2.
	Joosse, Barbara M. *Snow Day!* Illustrated by Jennifer Plecas. New York: Clarion Books, 1995. Unp. Grades: P–3.

Tooth Fairy Visits	Bourgeois, Paulette. *Franklin and the Tooth Fairy*. Illustrated by Brenda Clark. New York: Scholastic, 1996. Unp. Grades: P–2.
	Jay, Betsy. *Jane vs. the Tooth Fairy*. Illustrated by Lori Osiecki. Flagstaff, Ariz.: Rising Moon, 2000. Unp. Grades: K–3.
	O'Connor, Jane. *Dear Tooth Fairy*. Illustrated by Joy Allen. New York: Grosset & Dunlap, 2002. 48p. Grades: 1–2.
	Beeler, Selby B. *Throw Your Tooth on the Roof: Tooth Traditions from Around the World*. Illustrated by G. Brian Karas. New York: Houghton Mifflin, 1998. Unp. Grades: 1–4.
Weddings	Cox, Judy. *Now We Can Have a Wedding!* Illustrated by DyAnne DiSalvo-Ryan. New York: Holiday House, 1998. Unp. Grades: P–3.
	Schick, Eleanor. *Navajo Wedding: A Diné Marriage Ceremony*. Tarrytown, N.Y.: Marshall Cavendish, 1999. 40p. Grades: K–4.
	Soto, Gary. *Snapshots from the Wedding*. Illustrated by Stephanie Garcia. New York: G.P. Putnam's Sons, 1997. Unp. Grades: 2–5.
	Compton, Anita. *Marriage* Customs. New York: Thomson Learning, 1993. Grades: 3–6.
Visiting Days	Woodson, Jacqueline. *Visiting Day*. Illustrated by James E. Ransome. New York: Scholastic Press, 2002. 30p. Grades: 1–8.

REFERENCES

Reese, Debbie. 1996. *Multicultural Holidays in the Classroom*. (February 2002) Available: http://npin.org/pnews/1996/pnewd96/pnewd96k.html.

Franklin, Mary R., Patricia B. Roach, and Juanita K. Snyder. 1993. "Beyond Feathers and Tomahawks: Lessons from Literature." *Social Studies and the Young Learner 6*, no.2 (November/December): 13-17

KEY TITLES FOR INTEGRATING CELEBRATIONS AND HOLIDAYS INTO THE SOCIAL STUDIES CURRICULUM

2

Social studies curriculum guides from several states were examined to find broad themes taught in kindergarten through eighth grade. Some curriculum guides include the study of religious, secular, and national patriotic holidays. In some states, starting in kindergarten students are expected to recognize patriotic symbols, understand why there are national patriotic holidays, and identify religious and secular symbols associated with holidays. As students in the upper elementary grades and middle school study United States history and world history, they learn about different religions and how religious beliefs have shaped history. Throughout the grade levels students learn about the importance of being good citizens, how to take care of their environment, and about the cultures of the world. The broad themes found in the curriculum guides formed the basis for grouping holidays and celebrations by grade levels in the chart below. The charts present these themes with holidays and celebrations, accompanied by suggested books and media. References are given for the chapters that contain additional information on the holidays and celebrations and annotations for the books and media listed in the chart. These charts include only some of the holidays and celebrations contained in this book.

KINDERGARTEN AND FIRST GRADE

Students in kindergarten and first grade learn about their families, begin to learn about their role in the community, begin to develop an understanding of citizenship, and participate in holidays and celebrations. The families theme below encompasses a multicultural collection of holidays and celebrations that are observed at home with family and friends. As students learn about these holidays and celebrations they compare and contrast their family's observances with those of other families. Community holidays and celebrations are those that are most likely to be recognized in specific locales throughout the United States, such as St. Patrick's Day. The citizenship theme includes holidays that help students focus on the rights and responsibilities associated with being good citizens. Patriotic holidays and celebrations are those that help students develop an appreciation of the beliefs, the customs, and the symbols that enhance our national identity.

Theme	Holidays and Celebrations	Books and Media
Families	Holiday Collections Chapter 17	Updike, John. *A Child's Calendar.* Illustrations by Trina Schart Hyman. New York: Scholastic, 1999. Unp. Grades: P–2.
		Hubbell, Patricia. *Rabbit Moon: A Book of Holidays and Celebrations.* Illustrated by Wendy Watson. New York: Marshall Cavendish, 2002. Unp. Grades: P–3.
	Rosh Hashanah and Yom Kippur Fall Chapter 1	Marx, David F. *Rosh Hashanah and Yom Kippur.* New York: Children's Press, 2001. 32p. Grades: P–1.
		Kimmelman, Leslie. *Sound the Shofar! A Story for Rosh Hashanah and Yom Kippur.* Illustrated by John Himmelman. New York: HarperCollins, 1998. Unp. Grades: P–2.
		Rosh Hashanah/Yom Kippur. Bala Cynwyd, Penn.: Schlessinger Video Productions-Library Video Company, 1994. 25 min. Grades: K–4.

	Ramadan Fall Chapter 1	Marx, David F. *Ramadan.* New York: Scholastic, 2002. 32p. Grades: K–2.
		Ghazi, Suhaib Hamid. *Ramadan.* Illustrated by Omar Rayyan. New York: Holiday House, 1996. Unp. Grades: K–3.
		Ramadan. Video. Bala Cynwyd, Penn.: Schlessinger Video Productions-Library Video Company, 1996. 25 min. Grades: K–4.
	Chongyang Jie (Double Nine Festival) September Chapter 2	Lin, Grace. *Kite Flying.* New York: Alfred A. Knopf, 2002. Unp. Grades: P–1.
	Grandparents Day September Chapter 2	Rotner, Shelley, and Sheila Kelly. *Lots of Grandparents.* Photographs by Shelley Rotner. Brookfield, Conn.: The Millbrook Press, 2001. Unp. Grades: P–2.
		Shields, Carol Diggory. *Lucky Pennies and Hot Chocolate.* Illustrated by Hiroe Nakata. New York: Dutton Children's Books, 2000. Unp. Grades: P–3.
		Carlson, Nancy L. *Hooray for Grandparents' Day.* New York: Viking, 2000. Unp. Grades: P–3.

	Halloween October Chapter 3	Rex, Michael. *Brooms Are For Flying!* New York: Henry Holt, 2000. Unp. Grades: P–1.
		Poydar, Nancy. *The Perfectly Horrible Halloween.* New York: Holiday House, 2001. Unp. Grades: P–2.
		Gibala-Broxholm, Scott. *Scary Fright, Are You All Right?* New York: Dial Books for Young Readers, 2002. Unp. Grades: P–3.
	Thanksgiving Day November Chapter 4	Cowley, Joy. *Gracias, the Thanksgiving Turkey.* Illustrated by Joe Cepeda. New York: Scholastic, 1996. Unp. Grades: P–1.
		Ziefert, Harriet. *What is Thanksgiving?* Illustrated by Claire Schumacher. New York: Harper-Collins, 1992. Unp. Grades: P–1.
		Bunting, Eve. *A Turkey for Thanksgiving.* Illustrated by Diane de Groat. New York: Clarion Books, 1991. Unp. Grades: P–4.
	Hanukkah Winter Chapter 5	Stone, Tanya Lee. *D is for Dreidel: A Hanukkah Alphabet Book.* Illustrated by Dawn Apperley. New York: Penguin Putnam Books for Young Readers, 2002. Unp. Grades: P–1.
		Winne, Joanne. *Let's Get Ready for Hanukkah.* New York: Children's Press, 2001. 23p. Grades: P–1.
		Rosen, Michael J. Chanukah Lights Everywhere. Illustrated by Melissa Iwai. San Diego: Gulliver Books, 2001. Unp. Grades: P–2.

	Xin Nian (Chinese New Year) Winter Chapter 5	Wong, Janet S. *This Next New Year.* Illustrated by Yangsook Choi. New York: Farrar, Straus and Giroux, 2000. Unp. Grades: P–2.
	Christmas December Chapter 6	Maccarone, Grace. *A Child Was Born: A First Nativity Book.* Illustrated by Sam Williams. New York: Scholastic, 2000. 24p. Grades: P–2.
		Riley, Linnea Asplind. *The 12 Days of Christmas.* New York: Simon & Schuster Books for Young Readers, 1995. Unp. Grades: P–2.
		Dr. Seuss. *How the Grinch Stole Christmas.* New York: Random House, 1957. Unp. Grades: P–3.
		Moore, Clement C. *The Night before Christmas.* Illustrated by Jan Brett. New York: G.P. Putnam's Sons, 1998. Unp. Grades: P–3.
		First Christmas Record for Children. CD. New York: Sony, 1999. Grades: P–4.
	New Year's Day January Chapter 7	Marx, David F. *New Year's Day.* New York: Children's Press, 2000. 32p. Grades: P–2.
		Ziefert, Harriet. *Amanda Dade's New Years Parade.* Illustrated by S. D. Schindler. New York: Penguin Putnam Books for Young Readers, 2001. Unp. Grades: P–3.

	Easter Spring Chapter 9	Henkes, Kevin. *Owen's Marshmallow Chick.* New York: HarperCollins, 2002. Unp. Grades: P–K.
		Parker, Toni Tent. *Painted Eggs and Chocolate Bunnies.* Photographs by Earl Anderson. New York: Scholastic, 2002. Unp. Grades: P–K.
		Gibbons, Gail. *Easter.* New York: Holiday House, 1989. Unp. Grades: P–2.
		Wildsmith, Brian. *The Easter Story.* Grand Rapids, Mich.: Eerdmans Books for Young Readers, 2000. Unp. Grades: P–3.
	Passover Spring Chapter 9	*My First Passover Board Book.* New York: DK Publishing, 2002. Unp. Grades: P–K.
		Hildebrandt, Ziporah. *This Is Our Seder.* Illustrated by Robin Roraback. New York: Holiday House, 1999. Unp. Grades: P–2.
	Holi Spring Chapter 9	Krishnaswami, Uma. *Holi.* New York: Children's Press, 2003. 32p. Grades: P–2.
	Valentine's Day February Chapter 8	Roth, Carol. *My Little Valentine.* Illustrated by Jennifer Beck Harris. New York: HarperFestival, 2003. 18p. Grades: P–K.
		Carr, Jan. *Sweet Hearts.* Illustrated by Dorothy Donohue. New York: Holiday House, 2003. 26p. Grades: P–1.
		Jackson, Alison. *The Ballad of Valentine.* Illustrated by Tricia Tusa. New York: Dutton Children's Books, 2002. 30p. Grades: P–2.

	Kodomono-Hi Children's Day May Chapter 12	Kroll, Virginia. *A Carp for Kimiko*. Illustrated by Katherine Roundtree. Watertown, Mass.: Charlesbrigdge Publishing, 1993. Unp. Grades: P–3.
	Mother's Day May Chapter 12	Bauer, Marion Dane. *My Mother is Mine*. Illustrated by Peter Elwell. New York: Simon & Schuster Books for Young Readers, 2001. Unp. Grades: P–1.
		Baker, Liza. *I Love You Because You're You*. Illustrated by David McPhail. New York: Scholastic, 2001. Unp. Grades: P–2.
		French, Vivian. *A Present for Mom*. Illustrated by Dana Kubick. Cambridge, Mass.: Candlewick Press, 2002. Unp. Grades: P–2.
	Father's Day June Chapter 14	Clements, Andrew. *Secret Father's Day Present: A Lift-the-Flap Story*. Illustrated by Varda Livney. New York: Simon & Schuster, 2000. 16p. Grades: P–1.
		Alden, Laura. *Father's Day*. Illustrated by Linda Hohag. Chicago: Children's Press, 1994. 31p. Grades: P–2.
		Smalls, Irene. *Kevin and His Daddy*. Illustrated by Michael Hays. Boston: Little, Brown, 1999. Unp. Grades: P–2.

	Birthdays Chapter 18	*Birthday Party Singalongs.* CD. Redway, Calif.: Music for Little People, 2001. Grades: P–2.
		Knight, Margy Burns. *Welcoming Babies.* Illustrated by Anne Sibley O'Brien. Gardiner, Maine: Tilbury House, 1994. Unp. Grades: P–2.
		Selkowe, Valrie M. *Happy Birthday to Me!* Illustrated by John Sandford. New York: HarperCollins, 2001. Unp. Grades: P–3.
	Circus, Fairs, Fiestas, Jamborees Chapter 18	*Circus Magic.* CD and Audiocassette. Huntington, Calif.: Youngheart Music, 1999. Grades: P–2.
		Greene, Rhonda Gowler. *Jamboree Day.* Illustrated by Jason Wolff. New York: Scholastic, 2001. Unp.Grades: P–2.
		Stoeke, Janet Morgan. *Minerva Louise at the Fair.* New York: Dutton Children's Books, 2000. Unp. Grades: P–2.
	Snow Days Chapter 18	Plourde, Lynn. *Snow Day.* Illustrated by Hideko Takahashi. New York: Simon & Schuster, 2001. Unp. Grades: P–1.
		Lakin, Patricia. *Snow Day!* Illustrated by Scott Nash. New York: Penguin Putnam Books for Young Readers, 2002. Unp. Grades: P–2.

	Weddings Chapter 18	Furgang, Kathy. *Flower Girl*. Illustrated by Harley Jessup. New York: Viking Children's Books, 2003. Unp. Grades: P–3.
		Schick, Eleanor. *Navajo Wedding: A Diné Marriage Ceremony.* Tarrytown, N.Y.: Marshall Cavendish, 1999. 40p. Grades: K–4.
	Kwanzaa December Chapter 6	Grier, Ella. *Seven Days of Kwanzaa: A Holiday Step Book.* Illustrated by John Ward. New York: Viking, 1997. Unp. Grades: P–3.
		Kwanzaa. Video. Bala Cynwyd, Penn.: Schlessinger Video Productions-Library Video Company, 1994. 25 min. Grades: K–4.
	St. Patrick's Day March Chapter 10	de Paola, Tomie. *Patrick: Patron Saint of Ireland.* New York: Holiday House, 1992. Unp. Grades: P–2.
		MacGill-Callahan, Sheila. *The Last Snake in Ireland: A Story about St. Patrick.* Illustrated by Will Hillenbrand. New York: Holiday House, 1999. Unp. Grades: P–3.
	Cinco de Mayo May Chapter 12	Wade, Mary Dodson. *Cinco de Mayo.* New York: Children's Press, 2003. 32p. Grades: P–2.
		Cinco de Mayo. Video. Bala Cynwyd, Penn.: Schlessinger Video Productions-Library Video Company, 1994. 25 min. Grades: K–4.
	Junteenth June Chapter 14	Welsey, Valerie Wilson. *Freedom's Gifts: A Juneteenth Story.* Illustrated by Sharon Wilson. New York: Simon & Schuster, 1997. 32p. Grades: K–3.

Citizenship	Citizenship Day September Chapter 2	*United States Constitution.* Video. Bala Cynwyd, Penn.: Schlessinger Video Productions-Library Video Company, 1996. 25 min. Grades: K–4.
	Martin Luther King, Jr. Day January Chapter 7	Rappaport, Doreen. *Martin's Big Words: The Life of Dr. Martin Luther King, Jr.* Illustrated by Bryan Collier. New York: Hyperion Books for Children, 2001. Unp. Grades: P–4.
		Adler, David A. *A Picture Book of Martin Luther King, Jr.* Illustrated by Robert Casilla. New York: Holiday House, 1991. Unp. Grades: K–2.
		Martin Luther King, Jr. Day. Video. Bala Cynwyd, Penn.: Schlessinger Video Productions-Library Video Company, 2003. 23 min. Grades: K–4.
	Election Day November Chapter 14	Murphy, Patricia J. *Voting and Elections.* Minneapolis, Minn.: Compass Point Books, 2002. 24p. Grades: K–2.
		Election Day. Video. Bala Cynwyd, Penn.: Schlessinger Video Productions-Library Video Company, 1996. 25 min. Grades: K–4.
Patriotic	Holiday Collections Chapter 17	Murphy, Patricia J. *Our National Holidays.* Minneapolis, Minn.: Compass Point Books, 2002. 24p. Grades: P–2.
	Labor Day September Chapter 2	Bredeson, Carmen. *Labor Day.* New York: Children's Press, 2003. 32p. Grades: P–2.
		Rockwell, Anne. *Career Day.* Illustrated by Lizzy Rockwell. New York: HarperCollins, 2000. Unp. Grades: P–3.

	Veterans Day November Chapter 4	Cotton, Jacqueline S. *Veterans Day.* New York: Children's Press, 2002. 32p. Grades: P–2.
	Presidents' Day February Chapter 8	*Presidents Day.* Video. Bala Cynwyd, Penn.: Schlessinger Video Productions-Library Video Company, 2003. 23 min. Grades: K–4.
	Memorial Day May Chapter 12	*Memorial Day/Veterans Day.* Video. Bala Cynwyd, Penn.: Schlessinger Video Productions-Library Video Company, 2003. 23 min. Grades: K–4
	Fourth of July July Chapter 15	Ziefert, Harriet. *Hats Off for the Fourth of July!* Illustrated by Gustaf Miller. New York: Puffin Books, 2000. Unp. Grades: P–2.
		Berlin, Irving. *God Bless America.* Illustrated by Lynn Munsinger. New York: Harper Collins, 2002. Unp. Grades: P–3.
		Wong, Janet S. *Apple Pie 4th of July.* Illustrated by Margaret Chodos-Irvine. San Diego, Calif.: Harcourt, 2002. Unp. Grades: P–3.
	Earth Day April Chapter 11	Asch, Frank. *The Earth and I.* San Diego: Harcourt Brace, 1994. Unp. Grades: P–1.
		Garbage. Video. Bala Cynwyd, Penn.: Schlessinger Video Productions-Library Video Company, 1994. 25 min. Grades: P–2.
		Gibbons, Gail. *Recycle: A Handbook for Kids.* Boston: Little, Brown, 1992. Unp. Grades: P–3.

	Arbor Day April Chapter 11	Bennet, Kelly. *Arbor Day.* New York: Children's Press, 2003. 32p. Grades: P–2.
		Bulla, Clyde Robert. *A Tree Is a Plant.* Illustrated by Stacey Schuett. New York: HarperCollins, 2001. 33p. Grades: P–2.
		Arbor Day. Video. Bala Cynwyd, Penn.: Schlessinger Video Productions-Library Video Company, 1994. 30 min. Grades: K–4.

SECOND GRADE AND THIRD GRADE

Students in second and third grade learn about their roles in the neighborhood and community. They begin to develop an understanding of the cultural similarities and differences found in families, neighborhoods, and communities. The families theme below encompasses a multicultural collection of holidays and celebrations that are observed at home with family and friends. Community holidays and celebrations are those that are most likely to be recognized in specific locales throughout the United States, such as St. Patrick's Day. The citizenship theme includes holidays that help students focus on the rights and responsibilities associated with being good citizens, such as participating in elections. Patriotic holidays and celebrations include public observances that help students develop an understanding of the beliefs, the customs, and the symbols that enhance our national identity.

Theme	Holidays and Celebrations	Books and Media
Families	Holiday Collections Chapter 17	Updike, John. *A Child's Calendar.* Illustrations by Trina Schart Hyman. New York: Scholastic, 1999. Unp. Grades: P–2.
		Hubbell, Patricia. *Rabbit Moon: A Book of Holidays and Celebrations.* Illustrated by Wendy Watson. New York: Marshall Cavendish, 2002. Unp. Grades: P–3.

	Rosh Hashanah and Yom Kippur Fall Chapter 1	Kimmel, Eric A. *Gershon's Monster: A Story for the Jewish New Year.* Illustrated by Jon J. Muth. New York: Scholastic, 2000. Unp. Grades: P–4.
		Fishman, Cathy Goldberg. *On Rosh Hashanah and Yom Kippur.* Illustrated by Melanie W. Hall. New York: Simon & Schuster Children's Publishing, 1998. Unp. Grades: K–4.
		Rau, Dana Meachen. *Rosh Hashanah and Yom Kippur.* New York: Children's Press, 2001. 48p. Grades: 1–3.
		Rosh Hashanah/Yom Kippur. Bala Cynwyd, Penn.: Schlessinger Video Productions-Library Video Company, 1994. 25 min. Grades: K–4.
	Ramadan Fall Chapter 1	Ghazi, Suhaib Hamid. *Ramadan.* Illustrated by Omar Rayyan. New York: Holiday House, 1996. Unp. Grades: K–3.
		Ramadan. Video. Bala Cynwyd, Penn.: Schlessinger Video Productions-Library Video Company, 1996. 25 min. Grades: K–4.
		Matthews, Mary. Magid *Fasts for Ramadan.* Illustrated by Earl B. Lewis. New York: Clarion, 1996. 48p. Grades: 1–5.
	Chongyang Jie (Double Nine Festival) September Chapter 2	Demi. *Kites: Magic Wishes That Fly Up to the Sky.* New York: Crown, 1999. Unp. Grades: 1–4.

	Grandparents Day September Chapter 2	Carlson, Nancy L. *Hooray for Grandparents' Day.* New York: Viking, 2000. Unp. Grades: P–3.
		Plourde, Lynn. *Thank You, Grandpa.* Illustrated by Jason Cockroft. New York: Penguin Putnam, 2003. Unp. Grades: K–3.
		Koutsky, Jan Dale. *Pen Pals.* Honesdale, Penn.: Boyds Mills Press, 2002. Unp. Grades: K–5.
	Halloween October Chapter 3	Greene, Carol. *The 13 Days of Halloween.* Illustrated by Tim Raglin. Mahwah, N.J.: Bridgewater Books, 2000. Unp. Grades: P–3.
		Gibbons, Gail. *Halloween Is...* New York: Holiday House, 2002. 26p. Grades: K–3.
		Bunting, Eve. *The Bones of Fred McFee.* Illustrated by Kurt Cyrus. San Diego: Harcourt, 2002. Unp. Grades: K–4.
	Thanksgiving Day November Chapter 4	Kimmelman, Leslie. *Round the Turkey: A Grateful Thanksgiving.* Illustrated by Nancy Cote. Morton Grove, Ill.: Albert Whitman, 2002. Unp. Grades: K–2.
		Harness, Cheryl. *Three Young Pilgrims.* New York: Simon and Schuster, 1995. 32p. Grades: K–3.
		Lakin, Patricia. *Fat Chance Thanksgiving.* Illustrated by Stacey Schuett. Morton Grove, Ill.: Albert Whitman, 2001. Unp. Grades: K–4.
		Thanksgiving. Video. Bala Cynwyd, Penn.: Schlessinger Video Productions-Library Video Company, 1994. 25 min. Grades: K–4.

	Hanukkah Winter Chapter 5	Kimmel, Eric A. *Zigazak! A Magical Hanukkah Night.* Illustrated by Jon Goodell. New York: A Doubleday Book for Young Readers, 2001. Unp. Grades: P–4.
		A Child's Hanukkah. CD and Audiocassette. Garberville, Calif.: Music for Little People, 1998. Grades: K–3.
		Silverman, Maida. *Festival of Lights: The Story of Hanukkah.* Illustrated by Carolyn S. Ewing. New York: Aladdin Paperbacks, 1999. Unp. Grades: K–3.
		Hanukkah/Passover. Video. Bala Cynwyd, Penn.: Schlessinger Video Productions-Library Video Company, 1996. 25 min. Grades: K–4.
	TET (Vietnamese New Year) Winter Chapter 5	MacMillan, Dianne M. *Tet: Vietnamese New Year.* Berkeley Heights, N.J.: Enslow, 1994. 48p. Grades: 2–5.
	Xin Nian (Chinese New Year) Winter Chapter 5	Chinn, Karen. *Sam and the Lucky Money.* Illustrated by Cornelius Van Wright and Ying-Hwa Hu. New York: Lee & Low Books, 1997. Unp. Grades: P–3.
		Chinese New Year. Video. Bala Cynwyd, Penn.: Schlessinger Video Productions-Library Video Company, 1994. 25 min. Grades: K–4.

	Christmas December Chapter 6	*First Christmas Record for Children.* CD. New York: Sony, 1999. Grades: P–4.
		Grimes, Nikki. *Under the Christmas Tree.* Illustrated by Kadir Nelson. New York: HarperCollins, 2002. Unp. Grades: P–4.
		Van Allsburg, Chris. *The Polar Express.* Boston: Houghton Mifflin, 1985. Unp. Grades: P–4.
		Ahlberg, Janet, and Allan Ahlberg. *The Jolly Christmas Postman.* Boston: Little, Brown, 1991. Unp. Grades: K–3.
		Knowlton, Laurie. *The Nativity: Mary Remembers.* Illustrated by Kasi Kubiak. Honesdale, Penn.: Boyds Mills Press, 1998. Unp. Grades: K–4.
		Tazewell, Charles. *The Littlest Angel.* Illustrated by Paul Micich. Nashville, Tenn.: Ideals Children's Books, 1991, 1974, 1946. Unp. Grades: 1–3.
	New Year's Day January Chapter 7	Rau, Dana Meachen. *New Year's Day.* New York: Children's Press, 2000. 47p. Grades: K–2.
		Carrier, Roch. *A Happy New Year's Day.* Illustrated by Gilles Pelletier. Plattsburgh, N.Y.: Tundra Books, 1991. Unp. Grades: 2–5.

	Easter Spring Chapter 9	*DJ's Choice: Easter Bunny's Favorite Songs.* CD. Kenilworth, N.J.: Turn Up the Music, 2002. Grades: P–3.
		Gibbons, Gail. *Easter.* New York: Holiday House, 1989. Unp. Grades: P–3.
		French, Fiona. *Easter: With Words from the King James Bible.* New York: HarperCollins, 2002. 24p. Grades: P–4.
		Easter. Video. Bala Cynwyd, Penn.: Schlessinger Video Productions-Library Video Company, 1994. 25 min.Grades: K–4.
		Thompson, Lauren. *Love One Another: The Last Days of Jesus.* Illustrated by Elizabeth Uyehara. New York: Scholastic, 2000. Unp. Grades: 1–3.
	Passover Spring Chapter 9	Manushkin, Fran. *The Matzah That Papa Brought Home.* Illustrated by Ned Bittinger. New York: Scholastic, 1995. Unp. Grades: P–3.
		Schotter, Roni. *Passover Magic.* Illustrated by Marylin Hafner. Boston: Little, Brown, 1995. Unp. Grades: P–3.
		Hanukkah/Passover. Video. Bala Cynwyd, Penn.: Schlessinger Video Productions-Library Video Company, 1996. 25 min. Grades: K–4.
	Holi Spring Chapter 9	Kadodwala, Dilip. *Holi.* Chicago, Ill.: Raintree: 1997. 32p. Grades: 2–5.

	Valentine's Day February Chapter 8	Cazet, Denys. *Minnie and Moo: Will You Be My Valentine?* New York: HarperCollins, 2003. 48p. Grades: P–3.
		Park, Barbara. *Junie B. Jones and the Mushy Gushy Valentine.* Illustrated by Denise Brunkus. New York: Random House, 1999. 69p. Grades: 1–2.
		Rau, Dana Meachen. *Valentine's Day.* New York: Children's Press, 2001. 47p. Grades: 1–3.
	Kodomono-Hi Children's Day May Chapter 12	MacMillan, Dianne M. *Japanese Children's Day and the Obon Festival.* Berkeley Heights, N.J.: Enslow, 1997. 48p. Grades: 2–5.
	Mother's Day May Chapter 12	Glassman, Peter. *My Working Mom.* Illustrated by Tedd Arnold. New York: HarperCollins, 1994. Unp. Grades: P–3.
		Leuck, Laura. *My Monster Mama Loves Me So.* Illustrated by Mark Buehner. New York: HarperCollins, 1999. Unp. Grades: P–3.
		Ziefert, Harriet. *31 Uses for a Mother.* Illustrated by Rebecca Doughty. New York: Penguin Putnam Books for Young Readers, 2003. Unp. Grades: P–3.
		Mora, Pat, ed. *Love to Moma: A Tribute to Mothers.* Illustrated by Paula S. Barragan M. New York: Lee & Low Books, 2001. Unp. Grades: P–4.

	Father's Day June Chapter 14	Bunting, Eve. *A Perfect Father's Day.* Illustrated by Susan Meddaugh. New York: Houghton Mifflin, 1993. 32p. Grades: P–3.
		Wood, Douglas. *What Dads Can't Do.* Illustrated by Doug Cushman. New York: Simon and Schuster Books for Young Readers, 2000. Unp. Grades: P–3.
		Smalls, Irene. *Father's Day Blues: What Do You Do about Father's Day When All You Have are Mothers?* Illustrated by Kevin McGovern. Stamford, Conn.: Longmeadow Press, 1995. Unp. Grades: K–3.
	Birthdays Chapter 18	*Birthday Party Singalongs.* CD. Redway, Calif.: Music for Little People, 2001. Grades: P–2.
		Selkowe, Valrie M. *Happy Birthday to Me!* Illustrated by John Sandford. New York: HarperCollins, 2001. Unp. Grades: P–3.
		Hopkins, Lee Bennett, selector. *Happy Birthday.* Illustrated by Hilary Knight. New York: Simon & Schuster, 1991. 26p. Grades: K–3.
		Lankford, Mary D. *Birthdays around the World.* Illustrated by Karen Dugan. New York: Harper Collins, 2002. 32p. Grades: K–4.
	Circus, Fairs, Fiestas, Jamborees Chapter 18	Ancona, George. *Fiesta Fireworks.* New York: Lothrop, Lee & Shepard Books, 1998. Unp. Grades: 1–4.
		Lewin, Ted. *Fair.* New York: Lothrop, Lee & Shepard, 1997. Unp. Grades: 1–4.

	Graduation Chapter 18	Park, Barbara. *Junie B. Jones is a Graduation Girl.* Illustrated by Denise Brunkus. New York: Random House, 2001. 69p. Grades: 1–3.
	Snow Days Chapter 18	George, Lindsay Barrett. *Who's Been Here?* New York: William Morrow, 1995. Unp. Grades: P–3.
		Joosse, Barbara M. *Snow Day!* Illustrated by Jennifer Plecas. New York: Clarion Books, 1995. Unp. Grades: P–3.
	Tooth Fairy Visits Chapter 18	Olson, Mary W. *Nice Try Tooth Fairy.* Illustrated by Katherine Tillotson. New York: Simon & Schuster Books for Young Readers, 2000. Unp. Grades: P–2.
		Jay, Betsy. *Jane vs. the Tooth Fairy.* Illustrated by Lori Osiecki. Flagstaff, Ariz.: Rising Moon, 2000. Unp. Grades: K–3.
		O'Connor, Jane. *Dear Tooth Fairy.* Illustrated by Joy Allen. New York: Grosset & Dunlap, 2002. 48p. Grades: 1–2.
	Kwanzaa December Chapter 6	*Kwanzaa.* Video. Bala Cynwyd, Penn.: Schlessinger Video Productions-Library Video Company, 1994. 25 min. Grades: K–4.
		Porter, A. P. *Kwanzaa.* Illustrated by Janice Lee Porter. Minneapolis, Minn.: Carolrhoda Books, 1991. 56p. Grades: 1–3.
		Kwanzaa for Young People and Everyone Else!. CD. Gardena, Calif.: Charphelia,1999. Grades: K–6.

	St. Patrick's Day March Chapter 10	Tucker, Kathy. *The Leprechaun in the Basement.* Illustrated by John Sandford. Morton Grove, Ill.: Albert Whitman, 1999. Unp. Grades: P–3.
		Gibbons, Gail. *St. Patrick's Day.* New York: Holiday House, 1994. Unp. Grades: K–3.
		St. Patrick's Day. Video. Bala Cynwyd, Penn.: Schlessinger Video Productions-Library Video Company, 1996. 25 min. Grades: K–4.
	Cinco de Mayo May Chapter 12	Wade, Mary Dodson. *Cinco de Mayo.* New York: Children's Press, 2003. 32p. Grades: P–2.
		Cristina, Maria Urrutia. *Cinco de Mayo: Yesterday and Today.* Toronto, Ont.: Groundwood Books, 2002. Unp. Grades: K–3.
		Cinco de Mayo. Video. Bala Cynwyd, Penn.: Schlessinger Video Productions-Library Video Company, 1994. 25 min. Grades: K–4.
	Junteenth June Chapter 14	Welsey, Valerie Wilson. *Freedom's Gifts: A Juneteenth Story.* Illustrated by Sharon Wilson. New York: Simon & Schuster, 1997. 32p. Grades: K–3.
		Branch, Muriel Miller. *Juneteenth: Freedom Day.* Photographs by Willis Branch. New York: Cobblehill/Dutton, 1998. 54p. Grades: 2–8.

Citizenship	Citizenship Day September Chapter 2	*United States Constitution.* Video. Bala Cynwyd, Penn.: Schlessinger Video Productions-Library Video Company, 1996. 25 min. Grades: K–4.
		Sachar, Louis. *Marvin Redpost: Class President.* Illustrated by Amy Wummer. New York: Random House, 1999. 67p. Grades: 2–4.
	Martin Luther King, Jr. Day January Chapter 7	*Martin Luther King, Jr. Day.* Video. Bala Cynwyd, Penn.: Schlessinger Video Productions-Library Video Company, 2003. 23 min. Grades: K–4.
		Farris, Christine King. *My Brother Martin: A Sister Remembers Growing Up with the Rev. Dr. Martin Luther King, Jr.* Illustrated by Chris Soentpiet. New York: Simon & Schuster Books for Young Readers, 2003. Unp. Grades: 1–5.
		Gnojewski, Carol. *Martin Luther King, Jr., Day: Honoring a Man of Peace.* Berkeley Heights, N.J.: Enslow, 2002. 48p. Grades: 2–5.
	Election Day November Chapter 14	*Election Day.* Video. Bala Cynwyd, Penn.: Schlessinger Video Productions-Library Video Company, 1996. 25 min. Grades: K–4.
		Sisulu, Elinor Batezat. *The Day Gogo Went to Vote.* Illustrated by Sharon Wilson. Boston: Little, Brown, 1996. Unp. Grades: K–4.

Citizenship	Election Day November Chapter 14	*Election Day.* Video. Bala Cynwyd, Penn.: Schlessinger Video Productions-Library Video Company, 1996. 25 min. Grades: K–4.
		Sisulu, Elinor Batezat. *The Day Gogo Went to Vote.* Illustrated by Sharon Wilson. Boston: Little, Brown, 1996. Unp. Grades: K–4.
Patriotic	Labor Day September Chapter 2	Rockwell, Anne. *Career Day.* Illustrated by Lizzy Rockwell. New York: HarperCollins, 2000. Unp. Grades: P–3.
		Mora, Pat. *Tomás and the Library Lady.* Illustrated by Raul Colon. New York: Alfred A. Knopf, 1997. Unp. Grades: K–4.
	Veterans Day November Chapter 4	Landau, Elaine. *Veterans Day: Remembering Our War Heroes.* Berkeley Heights, N.J.: Enslow, 2002. 48p. Grades: 2–5.
	Presidents' Day February Chapter 8	*Presidents Day.* Video. Bala Cynwyd, Penn.: Schlessinger Video Productions-Library Video Company, 2003. 23 min. Grades: K–4.
		MacMillan, Dianne M. *Presidents Day.* Berkeley Heights, N.J.: Enslow, 1997. 48p. Grades: 2–5.
	Memorial Day May Chapter 12	*Memorial Day/Veterans Day.* Video. Bala Cynwyd, Penn.: Schlessinger Video Productions-Library Video Company, 2003. 23 min. Grades: K–4.
		Ray, Deborah Kogan. *My Daddy Was a Soldier: A World War II Story.* New York: Holiday House, 1990. Unp. Grades: 2–4.

	Fourth of July July Chapter 15	*Independence Day.* Video. Bala Cynwyd, Penn.: Schlessinger Video Productions-Library Video Company, 1994. 25 min. Grades: K–4.
		Merrick, Patrick. *Fourth of July Fireworks.* Chanhassen, Minn.: The Child's World, 2000. 32p. Grades: 1–4.
		Catrow, David. *We the Kids: The Preamble to the Constitution of the United States.* New York: Dial Books for Young Readers, 2002. Unp. Grades: 1–5.
	Earth Day April Chapter 11	*Environmental Songs for Kids.* CD. Washington, D.C.: Smithsonian Folkways Recordings, 1999. Grades: K–3.
		McLeod, Elaine. *Lessons from Mother Earth.* Illustrated by Colleen Wood. Toronto, Can.: Groundwood Books, 2002. Unp. Grades: K–3.
		Wallace, Nancy Elizabeth. *Recycle Every Day!* New York: Marshall Cavendish, 2003. Unp. Grades: K–3.
		Crunch, Smash, *Trash!: Monster Machines that Recycle.* Video. Bala Cynwyd, Penn.: Schlessinger Video Productions-Library Video Company, 1994. 30 min. Grades: K–4.
	Arbor Day April Chapter 11	*Arbor Day.* Video. Bala Cynwyd, Penn.: Schlessinger Video Productions-Library Video Company, 1994. 30 min. Grades: K–4.

FOURTH GRADE

In fourth grade, students typically learn about their own state and the regions of the United States. They learn about the first inhabitants of their state, Native Americans. Then, they explore the contributions of the different racial, ethnic, and religious groups that have settled in their state. Hence, the themes in this section include Native American celebrations and cultural holidays and celebrations reflecting the various racial, ethnic, and religious groups that have settled in the United States. Although not part of this chart, the chapters in this book include a variety of books and media appropriate for helping fourth graders understand and observe a wide variety of holidays throughout the year.

Native American	Itse Selu Chapter 2	Pennington, Daniel. Itse *Selu: Cherokee Harvest Festival.* Illustrated by Don Stewart. Watertown, Mass.: Charlesbridge Publishing, 1994. Unp. Grades: K–4.
	Powwow Chapter 18	Kalman, Bobbie. *Celebrating the Powwow.* New York: Crabtree Publishing, 1997. 32p. Grades: 2–4.
		Come Celebrate with Me: Native American Powwow. Video. Morris Plains, N.J.: Lucerne Media, 2001. 10 min. Grades: 3–6.
	Buffalo Days Chapter 18	Hoyt-Goldsmith, Diane. *Buffalo Days.* Photographs by Lawrence Migdale. New York: Holiday House, 1997. 32p. Grades: 3–6.
	Potlatch Chapter 18	Hoyt-Goldsmith, Diane. *Potlatch: A Tsimshian Celebration.* Photographs by Lawrence Migdale. New York: Holiday House, 1997. 32p. Grades: 3–6.

Asian	Holiday Collections Chapter 18	Viesti, Joe, and Diane Hall. *Celebrate! In South Asia.* Photographs by Joe Viesti. New York: Lothrop, Lee and Shepard Books, 1996. 32p. Grades: 2–5.
		Viesti, Joe, and Diane Hall. *Celebrate! In Southeast Asia.* Photographs by Joe Viesti. New York: Lothrop, Lee and Shepard Books, 1996. 32p. Grades: 2–5.
		Simonds, Nina, Leslie Swartz, and The Children's Museum, Boston. *Moombeams, Dumplings, and Dragon Boats: A Treasury of Chinese Holiday Tales, Activities, and Recipes.* Illustrated by Meilo So. San Diego: Harcourt, 2002. 74p. Grades: 3–7.
		Krasno, Rena. *Floating Lanterns and Golden Shrines: Celebrating Japanese Festivals.* Illustrated by Toru Sugita. Berkeley, Calif.: Pacific View Press, 2000. 49p. Grades: 4–8.
	Ramadan Fall Chapter 1	*Ramadan.* Video. Bala Cynwyd, Penn.: Schlessinger Video Productions-Library Video Company, 1996. 25 min. Grades: K–4.
		Hoyt-Goldsmith, Diane. *Celebrating Ramadan.* Photographs by Lawrence Migdale. New York: Holiday House, 2001. Unp. Grades: 3–6.
	Chongyang Jie September Chapter 2	Demi. Kites: *Magic Wishes That Fly Up to the Sky.* New York: Crown, 1999. Unp. Grades: 1–4.

	TET Nguyen-Dan January Chapter 7	MacMillan, Dianne M. *Tet: Vietnamese New Year.* Berkeley Heights, N.J.: Enslow, 1994. 48p. Grades: 2–5.
		Hoyt-Goldsmith, Diane. *Hoang Anh: A Vietnamese-American Boy.* Photographs by Lawrence Migdale. New York: Holiday House, 1992. 32p. Grades: 3–8.
	Holi Spring Chapter 9	Kadodwala, Dilip. *Holi.* Chicago, Ill.: Raintree: 1997. 32p. Grades: 2–5
	Tanabata July Chapter 15	Kitada, Shin. *The Story of Tanabata. Oaktag Cards.* Illustrated by Yukihiko Mitani. New York: Kamishibai for Kids, 1995. Grades: P–4.
	Hiroshima Day August Chapter 16	*Sadako and the Thousand Paper Cranes.* Video. Santa Cruz, Calif.: Informed Democracy, 1991. 30 min. Grades: 4–7.
		Coerr, Eleanor. *Sadako and the Thousand Paper Cranes.* New York: Penguin, 2002. 80p. Grades: 4–7.
Central American and Hispanic	Holiday Collections Chapter 17	Orozco, José-Luis. *Fiestas: A Year of Latin American Songs of Celebration.* Illustrated by Eliza Kleven. New York: Dutton Children's Books, 2002. 48p. Grades: K–4.
		Harris, Zoe, and Suzanne Williams. *Piñatas & Smiling Skeletons: Celebrating Mexican Festivals.* Illustrated by Yolanda Garfias Woo. Berkeley, Calif.: Pacific View Press, 1998. 48p. Grades: 4–6.
		Ancona, George. *The Fiestas.* Tarrytown, N.Y. Marshall Cavendish, 2002. 48p. Grades: 4–8.

Central American and Hispanic	Mexican Independence Day September Chapter 2	MacMillan, Dianne M. *Mexican Independence Day and Cinco de Mayo.* Berkley Heights, N.J.: Enslow, 1997. 47p. Grades: 2–5.
	Cinco de Mayo May Chapter 12	*Cinco de Mayo.* Video. Bala Cynwyd, Penn.: Schlessinger Video Productions-Library Video Company, 1994. 25 min. Grades: K–4.
		Gnojewski, Carol. *Cinco de Mayo: Celebrating Hispanic Pride.* Berkeley Heights, N.J.: Enslow, 2002. 48p. Grades: 2–5.
Jewish	Holiday Collections Chapter 17	Musleah, Rahel, and Michael Klayman. *Sharing Blessings: Children's Stories for Exploring the Spirit of the Jewish Holidays.* Illustrated by May O'Keefe Young. Woodstock, Vt.: Jewish Lights Publishing, 1997. 64p. Grades: 3–6.
		Berger, Gilda. *Celebrate! Stories of the Jewish Holidays.* Paintings by Peter Catalanotto. New York: Scholastic, 1998. 114p. Grades: 4–8.
		Cooper, Ilene. *Jewish Holidays All Year Round: A Family Treasury.* Illustrated by Elivia Savadier. New York: Harry N. Abrams, 2002. 80p. Grades: 4–8.
	Rosh Hashanah and Yom Kippur Fall Chapter 1	Fishman, Cathy Goldberg. *On Rosh Hashanah and Yom Kippur.* Illustrated by Melanie W. Hall. New York: Simon & Schuster Children's Publishing, 1998. Unp. Grades: K–4.
		Rosh Hashanah/Yom Kippur. Bala Cynwyd, Penn.: Schlessinger Video Productions-Library Video Company, 1994. 25 min. Grades: K–4.

Jewish	Hanukkah Winter Chapter 5	*Hanukkah/Passover*. Video. Bala Cynwyd, Penn.: Schlessinger Video Productions-Library Video Company, 1996. 25 min. Grades: K–4.
		Bunting, Eve. *One Candle.* Illustrated by K. Wendy Popp. New York: Joanna Cotler Books, 2002. 30p. Grades: 1–5.
		Erlbach, Arlene. *Hanukkah: Celebrating the Holiday of Lights.* Berkeley Heights, N.J.: Enslow, 2002. 48p. Grades: 2–5.
		Cohn, Janice. *The Christmas Menorahs: How a Town Fought Hate.* Illustrated by Bill Farnsworth. Morton Grove, Ill.: Albert Whitman and Company, 1995. 39p. Grades: 2–6.
		Hoyt-Goldsmith, Diane. *Celebrating Hanukkah.* Photographs by Lawrence Migdale. New York: Holiday House, 1996. 32p. Grades: 3–6.
	Passover Spring Chapter 9	Manushkin, Fran. *Miriam's Cup: A Passover Story.* Illustrated by Bob Dacey. New York: Scholastic, 1998. Unp. Grades: K–4.
		Simon, Norma. *The Story of Passover.* Illustrated by Erika Weihs. New York: HarperCollins, 1997, 1965. Unp. Grades: 2–5.
		Hoyt-Goldsmith, Diane. *Celebrating Passover.* Photographs by Lawrence Migdale. New York: Holiday House, 2000. 32p. Grades: 3–6.

FIFTH GRADE

In the fifth grade, the focus of the social studies curriculum is United States history. Students learn about the diverse cultural heritage of the Native Americans and explore the contributions of the different racial, ethnic, and religious groups that have settled in America. They learn about the United States government and what it means to be a good citizen. They develop an understanding of the customs, symbols, holidays, and celebrations that represent our belief systems and identify us as American citizens. They also learn about the importance of the environment and what they can do to preserve the environment for future generations. Several, but not all, of the holidays and celebrations of different racial, ethnic, and religious groups described in this book are included in the chart below.

Theme	Holidays and Celebrations	Books and Media
Traditional American Holidays	Holiday Collections Chapter 17	Gilchrist, Cherry. *A Calendar of Festivals.* Illustrated by Helen Cann. Bristol, United Kingdom: Barefoot Books, 1998. 80p. Grades: K–8.
		Spies, Karen. *Our National Holidays.* Brookfield, Conn.: The Millbrook Press, 1992. 47p. Grades: 3–6.
		Penner, Lucille Recht. Celebration: *The Story of American Holidays.* Illustrated by Ib Ohlsson. New York: Macmillan Publishing, 1993. 79p. Grades: 4–8.
	Labor Day September Chapter 2	Gourley, Catherine. *Good Girl Work: Factories, Sweatshops, and How Women Changed Their Role in the American Workforce.* Brookfield, Conn.: The Millbrook Press, 1999. 96p. Grades: 4 and up.
		Roberts-Davis, Tanya. *We Need to Go to School: Voices of the Rugmark Children.* Toronto, Ont.: Groundwood Books, 2001. 48p. Grades: 5–8.

	Veterans Day November Chapter 4	Landau, Elaine. *Veterans Day: Remembering Our War Heroes.* Berkeley Heights, N.J.: Enslow, 2002. 48p. Grades: 2–5.
	Election Day November Chapter 4	Pascoe, Elaine. *The Right to Vote.* Brookfield, Conn.: The Millbrook Press, 1997. 48p. Grades: 3–6.
		On the Campaign Trail. Win/Mac CD-ROM. Watertown, Maine: Tom Snyder Productions. Grades: 5–10.
	Thanksgiving Day November Chapter 4	Kamma, Anne. *If You Were At...the First Thanksgiving.* Illustrated by Bert Dodson. New York: Scholastic, 2001. 64p. Grades: 2–5.
		MacMillan, Dianne M. *Thanksgiving Day.* Berkeley Heights, N.J.: Enslow, 1997. 48p. Grades: 2–5.
		Cohen, Barbara. *Molly's Pilgrim.* Illustrated by Danie Mark Duffy. New York: HarperCollins, 1998. 28p. Grades: 2–6.
		Grace, Catherine O'Neill, and Margaret M. Bruchac. *With Plimoth Plantation. 1621: A New Look at Thanksgiving.* Photographs by Sisse Brimberg and Cotton Coulson. Washington, D.C.: National Geographic Society, 2001. 48p. Grades: 3–6.

	Christmas December Chapter 7	Fradin, Dennis Brindell. *Christmas.* Berkeley Heights, N. J.: Enslow, 2002. 48p. Grades: 2–5.
		Bierhorst, John, translator. *Spirit Child: A Story of the Nativity.* Illustrated by Barbara Cooney. New York: North-South Books, 2001, 1984. Unp. Grades: 2–6.
		Rollins, Charlemae Hill. *Christmas Gif': An Anthology of Christmas Poems, Songs, and Stories Written By and About African Americans.* Illustrated by Ashley Bryan. New York: Morrow Junior Books, 1993, 1963. 106p. Grades: 4 and up.
		Barth, Edna. Holly, Reindeer, and Colored Lights: The Story of the Christmas Symbols. Illustrated by Ursula Arndt. New York: Houghton Mifflin, 2000, 1971. 96p. Grades: 5 and up.
	Kwanzaa Christmas December Chapter 7	Jones, Amy Robin. *Kwanzaa.* Chanhassen, Minn.: The Child's World, 2001. 40p. Grades: 3–6.
		Goss, Linda, and Clay Goss. *It's Kwanzaa Time!* Illustrated by Ashley Bryan, Carole Byard, Floyd Cooper, Leo Dillon, Diane Dillon, Jan Spivey Gilchrist, Jonathan Green, and Jerry Pinkney. New York: G.P. Putnam's Son's, 2002. 71p. Grades: 4–7.
	New Year's Day January Chapter 8	Carrier, Roch. *A Happy New Year's Day.* Illustrated by Gilles Pelletier. Plattsburgh, N.Y.: Tundra Books, 1991. Unp. Grades: 2–5.

	Martin Luther King, Jr. Day January Chapter 7	Gnojewski, Carol. *Martin Luther King, Jr., Day: Honoring a Man of Peace.* Berkeley Heights, N.J.: Enslow, 2002. 48p. Grades: 2–5.
		Summer, L. S. The March on Washington. Chanhassen, Minn.: The Child's World, 2001. 40p. Grades: 4–8.
	Valentine's Day February Chapter 8	Barth, Edna. *Hearts, Cupids, and Red Roses: The Story of the Valentine Symbols.* Illustrated by Ursula Arndt. New York: Houghton Mifflin, 2001, 1972. 96p. Grades: 5 and up.
	Presidents' Day February Chapter 8	MacMillan, Dianne M. *Presidents Day.* Berkeley Heights, N.J.: Enslow, 1997. 48p. Grades: 2–5.
		Sandler, Martin W. *Presidents.* New York: HarperCollins, 1995. 94p. Grades: 4–8.
	Easter Spring Chapter 9	Chambers, Catherine. *Easter.* Austin, Tex.: Raintree Steck-Vaughn, 1998. 31p. Grades: 2–5.
		Barth, Edna. *Lilies, Rabbits, and Painted Eggs: The Story of the Easter Symbols.* Illustrated by Ursula Arndt. New York: Houghton Mifflin, 1998, 1970. 64p. Grades: 5 and up.

	St. Patrick's Day March Chapter 10	Landau, Elaine. *St. Patrick's Day.* Berkeley Heights, N.J.: Enslow, 2002. 48p. Grades: 2–5.
		Nolan, Janet. The St. Patrick's Day Shillelagh. Illustrated by Ben F. Stahl. New York: Albert Whitman, 2002. Unp. Grades: 2–5.
		Barth, Edna. Shamrocks, Harps, and Shillelaghs: The Story of St. Patrick's Day Symbols. Illustrated by Ursula Arndt. New York: Houghton Mifflin, 2001. 96p. Grades: 5 and up.
	Earth Day April Chapter 11	*Kids & the Environment.* Win/Mac CD-ROM. Watertown, Maine: Tom Snyder Productions. Grades: 2–6.
		Landau, Elaine. *Earth Day: Keeping Our Planet Clean.* Berkeley Heights, N.J.: Enslow, 2002. 48p. Grades: 2–5.
		Chandler, Gary, and Kevin Graham. *Recycling.* New York: Henry Holt, 1996. 64p. Grades: 5–8.
	Mother's Day May Chapter 12	Myers, Walter Dean. *Angel to Angel: A Mother's Gift of Love.* New York: HarperCollins, 1999. 40p. Grades: 4 and up.
	Memorial Day May Chapter 12	Haskins, Jim. *Black, Blue & Gray: African Americans in the Civil War.* New York: Simon & Schuster Books for Young Readers, 1998. 154p. Grades: 5 and up.
		Kuhn, Betsy. *Angels of Mercy: The Army Nurses of World War II.* New York: Atheneum Books for Young Readers, 1999. 114p. Grades: 5 and up.

	Graduation Special Celebrations Chapter 18	Anderson, Janet S. *Going through the Gate.* New York: Dutton Children's Books, 1997. 134p. Grades: 5–8.
	Father's Day June Chapter 14	Steptoe, Javaka. *In Daddy's Arms I Am Tall: African Americans Celebrating Fathers.* New York: Lee & Low Books, 2000. Unp. Grades: 3 and up.
	Juneteenth June Chapter 14	McKissack, Patricia C., and Frederick L. McKissack. *Days of Jubilee: The End of Slavery in the United States.* Illustrated by Diane Dillon and Leo Dillon. New York: Scholastic, 2003. 144p. Grades: 4 and up.
		Taylor, Charles. *Juneteenth: A Celebration of Freedom.* Greensboro, N.C.: Open Hand Publishing, 2002. Unp. Grades: 5–8.
	Fourth of July July Chapter 15	Landau, Elaine. *Independence Day—Birthday of the United States.* Berkeley Heights, N.J.: Enslow Publishers, 2001. 48p. Grades: 2–5.
		Bateman, Teresa. *Red, White, Blue and Uncle Who?: The Stories behind Some of America's Patriotic Symbols.* Illustrated by John O'Brien. New York: Holiday House, 2001. 64p. Grades: 4 and up.
		Statue of Liberty. DVD and video. Alexandria, Va.: Public Broadcasting Service, 2002. 60 min. Grades: 4 and up.

	Women's Equality Day August Chapter 16	Levin, Pamela. *Susan B. Anthony: Fighter for Women's Rights.* Philadelphia: Chelsea House, 1993. 79p. Grades: 5–9.
		Salisbury, Cynthia. *Elizabeth Cady Stanton: Leader of the Fight for Women's Rights.* Berkeley Heights, N.J.: Enslow, 2002. 128p. Grades: 5–9.
Native American	Powwow Chapter 18	*Come Celebrate with Me: Native American Powwow.* Video. Morris Plains, N.J.: Lucerne Media, 2001. 10 min. Grades: 3–6.
	Buffalo Days Chapter 18	Hoyt-Goldsmith, Diane. *Buffalo Days.* Photographs by Lawrence Migdale. New York: Holiday House, 1997. 32p. Grades: 3–6.
	Potlatch Chapter 18	Hoyt-Goldsmith, Diane. *Potlatch: A Tsimshian Celebration.* Photographs by Lawrence Migdale. New York: Holiday House, 1997. 32p. Grades: 3–6.

Asian	Potlatch Chapter 18	Viesti, Joe, and Diane Hall. *Celebrate! In South Asia.* Photographs by Joe Viesti. New York: Lothrop, Lee and Shepard Books, 1996. 32p. Grades: 2–5.
		Viesti, Joe, and Diane Hall. *Celebrate! In Southeast Asia.* Photographs by Joe Viesti. New York: Lothrop, Lee and Shepard Books, 1996. 32p. Grades: 2–5.
		Simonds, Nina, Leslie Swartz, and The Children's Museum, Boston. *Moombeams, Dumplings, and Dragon Boats: A Treasury of Chinese Holiday Tales, Activities, and Recipes.* Illustrated by Meilo So. San Diego: Harcourt, 2002. 74p. Grades: 3–7.
		Krasno, Rena. *Floating Lanterns and Golden Shrines: Celebrating Japanese Festivals.* Illustrated by Toru Sugita. Berkeley, Calif.: Pacific View Press, 2000. 49p. Grades: 4–8.
	Ramadan Fall Chapter 1	Hoyt-Goldsmith, Diane. *Celebrating Ramadan.* Photographs by Lawrence Migdale. New York: Holiday House, 2001. Unp. Grades: 3–6.
	Holi Spring Chapter 9	Kadodwala, Dilip. *Holi.* Chicago, Ill.: Raintree: 1997. 32p. Grades: 2–5
	Hiroshima Day August Chapter 16	*Sadako and the Thousand Paper Cranes.* Video. Santa Cruz, Calif.: Informed Democracy, 1991. 30 min. Grades: 4–7.
		Coerr, Eleanor. *Sadako and the Thousand Paper Cranes.* New York: Penguin, 2002. 80p. Grades: 4–7.

Central American and Hispanic	Holiday Collections Chapter 17	Orozco, José-Luis. *Fiestas: A Year of Latin American Songs of Celebration.* Illustrated by Eliza Kleven. New York: Dutton Children's Books, 2002. 48p. Grades: K–4.
		Harris, Zoe, and Suzanne Williams. *Piñatas & Smiling Skeletons: Celebrating Mexican Festivals.* Illustrated by Yolanda Garfias Woo. Berkeley, Calif.: Pacific View Press, 1998. 48p. Grades: 4–6.
		Ancona, George. *The Fiestas.* Tarrytown, N.Y. Marshall Cavendish, 2002. 48p. Grades: 4–8.
	Mexican Independence Day September Chapter 2	MacMillan, Dianne M. *Mexican Independence Day and Cinco de Mayo.* Berkley Heights, N.J.: Enslow, 1997. 47p. Grades: 2–5.
	Cinco de Mayo May Chapter 12	Gnojewski, Carol. *Cinco de Mayo: Celebrating Hispanic Pride.* Berkeley Heights, N.J.: Enslow, 2002. 48p. Grades: 2–5.

Jewish	Holiday Collections Chapter 17	Musleah, Rahel, and Michael Klayman. *Sharing Blessings: Children's Stories for Exploring the Spirit of the Jewish Holidays.* Illustrated by May O'Keefe Young. Woodstock, Vt.: Jewish Lights Publishing, 1997. 64p. Grades: 3–6.
		Berger, Gilda. *Celebrate! Stories of the Jewish Holidays.* Paintings by Peter Catalanotto. New York: Scholastic, 1998. 114p. Grades: 4–8.
		Cooper, Ilene. *Jewish Holidays All Year Round: A Family Treasury.* Illustrated by Elivia Savadier. New York: Harry N. Abrams, 2002. 80p. Grades: 4–8.d
	Hanukkah Winter Chapter 5	Erlbach, Arlene. *Hanukkah: Celebrating the Holiday of Lights.* Berkeley Heights, N.J.: Enslow, 2002. 48p. Grades: 2–5.
		Cohn, Janice. *The Christmas Menorahs: How a Town Fought Hate.* Illustrated by Bill Farnsworth. Morton Grove, Ill.: Albert Whitman and Company, 1995. 39p. Grades: 2–6.
		Hoyt-Goldsmith, Diane. *Celebrating Hanukkah.* Photographs by Lawrence Migdale. New York: Holiday House, 1996. 32p. Grades: 3–6.
	Passover Spring Chapter 9	Hoyt-Goldsmith, Diane. *Celebrating Passover.* Photographs by Lawrence Migdale. New York: Holiday House, 2000. 32p. Grades: 3–6.

SIXTH GRADE

Sixth grade is a time for learning about world history, exploring the regions of the world, and studying the cultures of the world. Students develop an understanding of the similarities and differences between the cultures. They learn about the major religions and their impact on world history. As students learn about the different religions, they also discover the significance of holidays and celebrations such as Christmas and Passover. The chart below includes some of the holidays and celebrations from these cultures: Asian, Central American and Hispanic, Jewish, and European. Additional holidays and celebrations from a variety of cultures are included throughout the chapters in this book.

Theme	Holidays and Celebrations	Books and Media
Asian	Holiday Collections Chapter 17	Simonds, Nina, Leslie Swartz, and The Children's Museum, Boston. *Moombeams, Dumplings, and Dragon Boats: A Treasury of Chinese Holiday Tales, Activities, and Recipes.* Illustrated by Meilo So. San Diego: Harcourt, 2002. 74p. Grades: 3–7.
		Krasno, Rena. *Floating Lanterns and Golden Shrines: Celebrating Japanese Festivals.* Illustrated by Toru Sugita. Berkeley, Calif.: Pacific View Press, 2000. 49p. Grades: 4–8.
		Stepanchuk, Carol. *Red Eggs & Dragon Boats: Celebrating Chinese Festivals.* Berkeley, Calif.: Pacific View Press, 1994. 48p. Grades: 4–8.
	Ramadan Fall Chapter 1	Hoyt-Goldsmith, Diane. *Celebrating Ramadan.* Photographs by Lawrence Migdale. New York: Holiday House, 2001. Unp. Grades: 3–6.

	TET Nguyen-Dan January Chapter 7	Hoyt-Goldsmith, Diane. *Hoang Anh: A Vietnamese-American Boy.* Photographs by Lawrence Migdale. New York: Holiday House, 1992. 32p. Grades: 3–8.
	Hiroshima Day August Chapter 16	*Sadako and the Thousand Paper Cranes.* Video. Santa Cruz, Calif.: Informed Democracy, 1991. 30 min. Grades: 4–7.
		Coerr, Eleanor. *Sadako and the Thousand Paper Cranes.* New York: Penguin, 2002. 80p. Grades: 4–7.
		Grant, R. G. *Hiroshima and Nagasaki.* Austin, Tex.: Steck-Vaughn, 1998. 64p. Grades: 6–9.
Central American and Hispanic	Holiday Collections Chapter 17	Harris, Zoe, and Suzanne Williams. *Piñatas & Smiling Skeletons: Celebrating Mexican Festivals.* Illustrated by Yolanda Garfias Woo. Berkeley, Calif.: Pacific View Press, 1998. 48p. Grades: 4–6.
		Ancona, George. *The Fiestas.* Tarrytown, N.Y. Marshall Cavendish, 2002. 48p. Grades: 4–8.
		Presilla, Maricel E. *Feliz Nochebuena, Feliz Navidad: Christmas Feasts of the Hispanic Caribbean.* Illustrated by Ismael Espinosa Ferrer. New York: Henry Holt, 1994. Unp. Grades: 4–8.
	Quinceañeras Chapter 18	Hoyt-Goldsmith, Diane. *Celebrating a Quinceañera: A Latina's 15th Birthday Celebration.* Photographs by Lawrence Migdale. New York: Holiday House, 2002. 32p. Grades: 3–6.
		King, Elizabeth. *Quinceañera: Celebrating Fifteen.* New York: Dutton Children's Books, 1998. 40p. Grades: 6–9.

	Cinco de Mayo May Chapter 12	Palacios, Argentina. *Viva Mexico! The Story of Benito Juarez and Cinco de Mayo.* Illustrated by Howard Berelson. Austin, Texas: Raintree, 1992. 32p. Grades: 2–8.
Jewish	Holiday Collections Chapter 17	Cooper, Ilene. *Jewish Holidays All Year Round: A Family Treasury.* Illustrated by Elivia Savadier. New York: Harry N. Abrams, 2002. 80p. Grades: 4–8.
	Hanukkah Winter Chapter 5	Cohn, Janice. *The Christmas Menorahs: How a Town Fought Hate.* Illustrated by Bill Farnsworth. Morton Grove, Ill.: Albert Whitman and Company, 1995. 39p. Grades: 2–6.
		Hoyt-Goldsmith, Diane. *Celebrating Hanukkah.* Photographs by Lawrence Migdale. New York: Holiday House, 1996. 32p. Grades: 3–6.
		Koss, Amy Goldman. *How I Saved Hanukkah.* Illustrated by Diane de Groat. New York: Dial Books for Young Readers, 1998. 88p. Grades: 3–6.
		Zalben, Jane Breskin. *The Magic Menorah: A Modern Chanukah Tale.* Illustrated by Donna Diamond. New York: Simon & Schuster Books for Young Readers, 2001. 56p. Grades: 4–8.

	Passover Spring Chapter 9	Hoyt-Goldsmith, Diane. *Celebrating Passover.* Photographs by Lawrence Migdale. New York: Holiday House, 2000. 32p. Grades: 3–6.
		Goldin, Barbara Diamond. *The Passover Journey: A Seder Companion.* Illustrated by Neil Waldman. New York: Puffin Books, 1994. 55p. Grades: 4 and up.
European	Guy Fawkes Day November Chapter 4	Ashworth, Leon. *Guy Fawkes.* Berkshire, England: Cherrytree Press, 1997. 32p. Grades: 4–8.
	Bastille Day July Chapter 15	Plain, Nancy. *Louis XVI, Marie-Antoinette and the French Revolution.* New York: Marshall Cavendish, 2002. 88p. Grades: 6 and Up.

SEVENTH GRADE AND EIGHTH GRADE

Students in seventh and eighth grade learn more about the state in which they live, or explore United States history in greater depth than in fifth grade. Students learn about the diverse cultural heritage of the Native Americans and explore the contributions of the different racial, ethnic, and religious groups that have settled in America. They learn about the United States government and what it means to be a good citizen. They develop an understanding of the customs, symbols, holidays, and celebrations that represent our belief systems and identify us as American citizens. They also learn about the importance of the environment and what they can do to preserve the environment for future generations. Several, but not all, of the holidays and celebrations of different racial, ethnic, and religious groups described in this book are included in the chart below.

Theme	Holidays and Celebrations	Books and Media
Traditional American Holidays	Holiday Collections Chapter 17	Gilchrist, Cherry. *A Calendar of Festivals.* Illustrated by Helen Cann. Bristol, United Kingdom: Barefoot Books, 1998. 80p. Grades: K–8.
		Penner, Lucille Recht. *Celebration: The Story of American Holidays.* Illustrated by Ib Ohlsson. New York: Macmillan Publishing, 1993. 79p. Grades: 4–8.
	Labor Day September Chapter 2	Gourley, Catherine. *Good Girl Work: Factories, Sweatshops, and How Women Changed Their Role in the American Workforce.* Brookfield, Conn.: The Millbrook Press, 1999. 96p. Grades: 4 and up.
		Roberts-Davis, Tanya. *We Need to Go to School: Voices of the Rugmark Children.* Toronto, Ont.: Groundwood Books, 2001. 48p. Grades: 5–8.

	Veterans Day November Chapter 4	Antle, Nancy. *Lost in the War*. New York: Penguin Putnam Books for Young Readers, 1998. 137p. Grades: 5–8.
		Slate, Joseph. *Crossing the Tressle*. Tarrytown, N.Y.: Marshall Cavendish, 1999. 144p. Grades: 5–8.
		Gay, Kathlyn, and Martin Gay. *Vietnam War*. New York: Twenty-First Century Books, 1996. 64p. Grades: 6 and up.
	Election Day November Chapter 4	*On the Campaign Trail*. Win/Mac CD-ROM. Watertown, Maine: Tom Snyder Productions. Grades: 5–10.
	Thanksgiving Day November Chapter 4	Bial, Raymond. *The Powhatan*. New York: Marshall Cavendish, 2002. 128p. Grades: 4–9.
		Barth, Edna. *Turkeys, Pilgrims, and Indian Corn: The Story of the Thanksgiving Symbols*. Illustrated by Ursula Arndt. New York: Houghton Mifflin, 2001, 1975. 96p. Grades: 5 and up.
		Home for the Holidays: The History of Thanksgiving. Video and DVD. South Burlington, Va.: A & E Television Networks, 1997. 50 min. Grades: 6 and up.

	Christmas December Chapter 7	Rollins, Charlemae Hill. *Christmas Gif': An Anthology of Christmas Poems, Songs, and Stories Written By and About African Americans.* Illustrated by Ashley Bryan. New York: Morrow Junior Books, 1993, 1963. 106p. Grades: 4 and up.
		Barth, Edna. *Holly, Reindeer, and Colored Lights: The Story of the Christmas Symbols.* Illustrated by Ursula Arndt. New York: Houghton Mifflin, 2000, 1971. 96p. Grades: 5 and up.
		Christmas Unwrapped: The History of Christmas. Video and DVD. South Burlington, Va.: A & E Television Networks, 1997. 50 min. Grades: 6 and up.
		Dickens, Charles. *A Christmas Carol.* Illustrated by Lisbeth Zwerger. New York: North South Books, 2001. 67p. Grades: 7 and up.
		Walsh, Joseph J. *Were They Wise Men or Three Kings?*: Book of Christmas Questions. Louisville, Ky.: Westminister John Knox Press, 2001. 127p. Grades: 7 and up.

L.W. Nixon Library
Butler County Community College
901 South Haverhill Road
El Dorado, Kansas 67042-3280

	Kwanzaa Christmas December Chapter 7	Goss, Linda, and Clay Goss. *It's Kwanzaa Time!* Illustrated by Ashley Bryan, Carole Byard, Floyd Cooper, Leo Dillon, Diane Dillon, Jan Spivey Gilchrist, Jonathan Green, and Jerry Pinkney. New York: G.P. Putnam's Son's, 2002. 71p. Grades: 4–7.
		Karenga, Maulana. *Kwanzaa: A Celebration of Family, Community, and Culture.* Los Angeles, Calif.: University of Sankore Press, 1998. 143p. Grades: 7 and up.
		McClester, Cedric. *Kwanzaa: Everything You Always Wanted to Know But Didn't Know Where to Ask.* New York: Gumbs & Thomas, 1994. 44p. Grades: 7 and up.
	Martin Luther King, Jr. Day January Chapter 7	Summer, L. S. *The March on Washington.* Chanhassen, Minn.: The Child's World, 2001. 40p. Grades: 4–8.
		Pettit, Jayne. *Martin Luther King, Jr.: A Man with a Dream.* New York: Franklin Watts, 2001. 112p. Grades: 6 and up.
		Martin Luther King, Jr.: The Man and the Dream. Video. South Burlington, Va.: A & E Television Networks, 1998. 50 min. Grades: 6 and up.
	Valentine's Day February Chapter 8	Barth, Edna. *Hearts, Cupids, and Red Roses: The Story of the Valentine Symbols.* Illustrated by Ursula Arndt. New York: Houghton Mifflin, 2001, 1972. 96p. Grades: 5 and up.

	Presidents' Day February Chapter 8	Sandler, Martin W. *Presidents.* New York: HarperCollins, 1995. 94p. Grades: 4–8.
		Foster, Genevieve, and Joanna Foster. *George Washington's World, Expanded Edition.* Sandwich, Mass.: Beautiful Feet Books, 1997. 356p. Grades: 5 and up.
	Easter Spring Chapter 9	Barth, Edna. *Lilies, Rabbits, and Painted Eggs: The Story of the Easter Symbols.* Illustrated by Ursula Arndt. New York: Houghton Mifflin, 1998, 1970. 64p. Grades: 5 and up.
	St. Patrick's Day March Chapter 10	Barth, Edna. *Shamrocks, Harps, and Shillelaghs: The Story of St. Patrick's Day Symbols.* Illustrated by Ursula Arndt. New York: Houghton Mifflin, 2001. 96p. Grades: 5 and up.
		Dunlop, Eileen. *Tales of St. Patrick.* New York: Holiday House, 1997. 125p.Grades: 6–8.
		Celebrating the Green: The History of St. Patrick's Day. Video. South Burlington, Va.: A & E Television Networks, 1998. 50 min. Grades: 6 and up.

	Earth Day April Chapter 11	Chandler, Gary, and Kevin Graham. *Recycling.* New York: Henry Holt, 1996. 64p. Grades: 5–8.
		Gardner, Robert. *Celebrating Earth Day: A Sourcebook of Activities and Experiments.* Illustrated by Sharon Lane Holm. Brookfield, Conn.: The Millbrook Press, 1992. 96p. Grades: 6–10.
		Garbage. Video. The History Channel, A & E Television Networks, 1999. 25 min. Grades: 7 and up.
	Mother's Day May Chapter 12	Myers, Walter Dean. *Angel to Angel: A Mother's Gift of Love.* New York: HarperCollins, 1999. 40p. Grades: 4 and up.
	Memorial Day May Chapter 12	Haskins, Jim. *Black, Blue & Gray: African Americans in the Civil War.* New York: Simon & Schuster Books for Young Readers, 1998. 154p. Grades: 5 and up.
		Kuhn, Betsy. *Angels of Mercy: The Army Nurses of World War II.* New York: Atheneum Books for Young Readers, 1999. 114p. Grades: 5 and up.
		Gaeddert, Louann. *Friends and Enemies.* New York: Atheneum Books for Young Readers, 2000. 177p. Grades: 6–10.
		Anderson, Janet S. *Going through the Gate.* New York: Dutton Children's Books, 1997. 134p. Grades: 5–8.

	Father's Day June Chapter 14	Steptoe, Javaka. *In Daddy's Arms I Am Tall: African Americans Celebrating Fathers*. New York: Lee & Low Books, 2000. Unp. Grades: 3 and up.
	Juneteenth June Chapter 14	McKissack, Patricia C., and Frederick L. McKissack. *Days of Jubilee: The End of Slavery in the United States*. Illustrated by Diane Dillon and Leo Dillon. New York: Scholastic, 2003. 144p. Grades: 4 and up.
		Taylor, Charles. *Juneteenth: A Celebration of Freedom*. Greensboro, N.C.: Open Hand Publishing, 2002. Unp. Grades: 5–8.
	Fourth of July July Chapter 15	Bateman, Teresa. *Red, White, Blue and Uncle Who?: The Stories behind Some of America's Patriotic Symbols*. Illustrated by John O'Brien. New York: Holiday House, 2001. 64p. Grades: 4 and up.
		Statue of Liberty. DVD and video. Alexandria, Va.: Public Broadcasting Service, 2002. 60 min. Grades: 4 and up.
	Women's Equality Day August Chapter 16	Levin, Pamela. *Susan B. Anthony: Fighter for Women's Rights*. Philadelphia: Chelsea House, 1993. 79p. Grades: 5–9.
		Salisbury, Cynthia. *Elizabeth Cady Stanton: Leader of the Fight for Women's Rights*. Berkeley Heights, N.J.: Enslow, 2002. 128p. Grades: 5–9.

Native American	Powwow Chapter 18	*Into the Circle: An Introduction to Native American Powwows.* Video. Bala Cynwyd, Penn.: Schlessinger Video Productions-Library Video Company, 1992. 60 min. Grades: 7 and up.
Asian	Holiday Collections Chapter 17	Simonds, Nina, Leslie Swartz, and The Children's Museum, Boston. *Moombeams, Dumplings, and Dragon Boats: A Treasury of Chinese Holiday Tales, Activities, and Recipes.* Illustrated by Meilo So. San Diego: Harcourt, 2002. 74p. Grades: 3–7.
		Krasno, Rena. *Floating Lanterns and Golden Shrines: Celebrating Japanese Festivals.* Illustrated by Toru Sugita. Berkeley, Calif.: Pacific View Press, 2000. 49p. Grades: 4–8.
		Stepanchuk, Carol. *Red Eggs & Dragon Boats: Celebrating Chinese Festivals.* Berkeley, Calif.: Pacific View Press, 1994. 48p. Grades: 4–8.
	Hiroshima Day August Chapter 16	Hoyt-Goldsmith, Diane. *Hoang Anh: A Vietnamese-American Boy.* Photographs by Lawrence Migdale. New York: Holiday House, 1992. 32p. Grades: 3–8.
		Sadako and the Thousand Paper Cranes. Video. Santa Cruz, Calif.: Informed Democracy, 1991. 30 min. Grades: 4–7.
		Coerr, Eleanor. *Sadako and the Thousand Paper Cranes.* New York: Penguin, 2002. 80p. Grades: 4–7.
		Grant, R. G. *Hiroshima and Nagasaki.* Austin, Tex.: Steck-Vaughn, 1998. 64p. Grades: 6–9.

Central American and Hispanic	Holiday Collections Chapter 17	Ancona, George. *The Fiestas.* Tarrytown, N.Y.: Marshall Cavendish, 2002. 48p. Grades: 4–8.
		Presilla, Maricel E. *Feliz Nochebuena, Feliz Navidad: Christmas Feasts of the Hispanic Caribbean.* Illustrated by Ismael Espinosa Ferrer. New York: Henry Holt, 1994. Unp. Grades: 4–8.
		Menard, Valerie. *The Latino Holiday Book: From Cinco de Mayo to Dia de los Muertos—The Celebrations and Traditions of Hispanic Americans.* New York: Marlowe, 2000. 174p. Grades: 7 and up.
Jewish	Holiday Collections Chapter 17	Berger, Gilda. *Celebrate! Stories of the Jewish Holidays.* Paintings by Peter Catalanotto. New York: Scholastic, 1998. 114p. Grades: 4–8.
		Cooper, Ilene. Jewish Holidays All Year Round: A Family Treasury. Illustrated by Elivia Savadier. New York: Harry N. Abrams, 2002. 80p. Grades: 4–8.
		The Jewish Holidays Video Guide. Bala Cynwyd, Penn.: Schlessinger Video Productions-Library Video Company, 1990. 75 min. Grades: 7 and up.
European	Guy Fawkes Day November Chapter 4	Ashworth, Leon. *Guy Fawkes.* Berkshire, England: Cherrytree Press, 1997. 32p. Grades: 4–8.
	Bastille Day July Chapter 15	Plain, Nancy. *Louis XVI, Marie-Antoinette and the French Revolution.* New York: Marshall Cavendish, 2002. 88p. Grades: 6 and Up.

PART II. AUTUMN

Autumn Celebrations and Holidays with Moveable Dates

1

After the summer heat, the cool, crisp days of fall bring a welcome change. As plants and animals prepare to rest, crops are harvested and leaves fall from the trees. The crops provide the bounty for harvest feasts and family gatherings. In some areas, leaves turn brilliant colors before falling, providing glorious feasts for the eyes. Fall holidays with moveable dates include Diwali (Festival of Lights), Rosh Hashanah, Yom Kippur, Sukkot, Simchat Torah, Ramadan, Id-Ul-Fitr, and Zhongqiu Jie (Mid-Autumn Moon Festival). Diwali is a Hindu holiday celebrated in late October or early November. Rosh Hashanah, Yom Kippur, Sukkot, and Simchat Torah are Jewish holidays. Rosh Hashanah begins in September or early October. Rosh Hashanah ends with Yom Kippur, which is followed by Sukkot and then Simchat Torah. Ramadan is a month-long fast observed by Muslims during the ninth month of the Islamic calendar; Id-Ul-Fitr celebrates the end of the fast. The Chinese celebrate Zhongqiu Jie on the fifteenth day of the eighth month of the Chinese lunar calendar.

DIWALI (FESTIVAL OF LIGHTS)

For Hindus the new moon in late October or early November signals Diwali (Divali), or the Festival of Lights (Barkin and James, 1994), which lasts for five days. This festival celebrates the triumph of good over evil (Kadodwala, 1998). During Diwali, the goddess Lakshmi visits homes, bringing good fortune and wealth. New clothes and gold jewelry are bought and worn (MacMillan, 1997). As with other celebrations, traditions vary from place to place, but commonly include lighting divas (lamps), feasting, cleaning houses inside and out, gathering with family members and friends, and stringing lights on houses and buildings. Each day of the festival has a special significance (Kadowala, 1998). The first day, Dhana-Trayodashi, reminds Hindus that death is a part of life. On the second day, Narak Chaturdashi, Hindus recall that good can come from evil, and tell the story of the god Krishna defeating the demon Narakasur. The third day is Lakshmi Pujan, when Hindus welcome the goddess Lakshmi into their homes to bring good fortune, health, and happiness. The new year begins on the fourth day of Diwali, and is celebrated by worshipping, wearing new clothes, sharing gifts, visiting, feasting, and lighting fireworks. The fifth day is Sister's Day, when men visit their sisters, who prepare special meals for them. (See Hanukkah and Christmas for other Festivals of Light; see Chinese New Year, TET, New Year's Day, Rosh Hashanah, and Yom Kippur for other New Year's celebrations.)

BOOK AND MEDIA CHOICES

Gardeski, Christina Mia. *Diwali*. New York: Children's Press, 2001. 32p.
Grades: P–2. Colorful, lively photographs and simple text tell the story of this Hindu holiday. Houses decorated with strings of lights, carnival rides, and a plate of cookies look familiar to young readers. A picture glossary and an index are included. This book is from the Rookie Read-About Holidays series.

MacMillan, Dianne M. *Diwali*. Berkeley Heights, N.J.: Enslow Publishers, 1997. 48p.
Grades: 2–5. The book begins with an introduction to Hinduism, which describes it as more than a religion. Lakshima, the goddess of good fortune and wealth, is honored during Diwali with offerings of fruit, flowers, and sweets. As the sun goes down, lights shine and families gather to feast. A glossary and an index conclude the book. This book is from the Best Holiday Books series.

Kadodwala, Dilip. *Divali*. Austin, Tex.: Steck-Vaughn, 1998. 31p.
Grades: 4–8. Color photographs and clear, concise text describe this important Hindu celebration. The author presents just enough details to give students an understanding of the religious significance of the holiday and an appreciation of the culture and traditions surrounding it. Readers learn the importance of each of the five days of the holiday. A glossary, a list of books for further reading, and an index are included. This book is from the World of Holidays series.

EXPLORATIONS

1. Before reading *Diwali* (Gardeski, 2001), share the pictures in the book with the students and help them make connections between Diwali and celebrations they are familiar with, such as Hanukkah or Christmas. Students discover that making cookies, giving presents, displaying lights, and holding religious ceremonies are common to all of these celebrations.

2. After reading *Divali* (Kadodwala, 1998), have the students return to the chapter "Holiday Fun." The author briefly mentions the henna designs, mehndi, that women have painted on their hands, and includes a photograph. Mehndi enhances women's beauty and is commonly applied for weddings, Divali, and other celebrations. Students from India or Pakistan may come to school with these elaborate designs painted on their hands after celebrations, and they may be willing to share this piece of their culture with their classmates.

ROSH HASHANAH AND YOM KIPPUR

Rosh Hashanah, the beginning of the Jewish New Year, occurs on the first and second days of the Jewish month of Tishri (Cooper, 2002). It falls sometimes in September, sometimes in October. Rosh Hashanah lasts for two days and begins ten days of repentance (Days of Awe) that end with Yom Kippur. Rosh Hashanah and Yom Kippur are High Holy Days, times for reflecting on one's life and making changes (Moehn, 2000). During morning synagogue services on Rosh Hashanah, the shofar, a trumpet made from a ram's horn, is blown to remind Jews to reflect on their actions during the past year (Burghardt, 2001). On the first day of Rosh Hashanah Jewish people gather by the sea, lakes, or rivers for the ceremony of tashlikh, when they say prayers and throw bread crumbs on the water to symbolize the casting-off of their sins (Kimmel, 2000). On the eve of Yom Kippur a large meal is shared; adults and children over thirteen then fast until sundown on Yom Kippur. Yom Kippur ends with Kil Nidre services at the synagogue, when the shofar is blown again (Moehn, 2000). Just as many people make resolutions for changing their lives on New Year's Day, Jews use Rosh Hashanah to reflect and make decisions on how to become a better person in the coming year

(Cooper, 2002). On the eve of Yom Kippur a yahrzeit candle is lit in remembrance of those who have died (Rau, 2001). The souls of the departed are also remembered on the eighth day of Sukkot, the second day of Shavuot, and the last day of Passover (Scharfstein, 1999). (See All Souls' Day, All Saints' Day, Qing Ming, Dia de los Muertos, Id-Ul-Fitr, and TET Nguyen-Dan for other holidays that include commemorations of the dead.)

BOOK AND MEDIA CHOICES

Marx, David F. *Rosh Hashanah and Yom Kippur*. New York: Children's Press, 2001. 32p.
Grades: P–1. The prayers and thoughtful reflections of Rosh Hashanah and Yom Kippur are briefly introduced in this book for young children, which contains color photographs and large print. Unfamiliar words are defined in the text and pronunciation guides are included. A picture glossary and an index conclude the book. This book is from the Rookie Read-About Holidays series.

Kimmelman, Leslie. *Sound the Shofar! A Story for Rosh Hashanah and Yom Kippur*. Illustrated by John Himmelman. New York: HarperCollins, 1998. Unp.
Grades: P–2. In this story, a young girl whose Uncle Jake will blow the shofar during Rosh Hashanah and Yom Kippur services describes how her family observes the Days of Awe. These special days include sharing challah, apples, and honey during the Rosh Hashanah family meal, fasting on Yom Kippur, gathering food for the poor, and reflecting on the past year's behavior to become a better person in the year ahead. Simple text in a large font and colorful illustrations encourage young students to read this book on their own.

Zalben, Jane Breskin. *Happy New Year, Beni*. New York: Henry Holt, 1993. Unp.
Grades: P–2. Students are sure to relate to Cousin Max, who almost spoils the family Rosh Hashanah celebration. A lesson from Grandpa about tashlikh helps get Max's new year off to a new start. The warm pastel illustrations and the description of the family gathering introduce the holiday and its traditions. A recipe for Tante Rose's Round Raisin Challah and a glossary conclude the book.

Weilerstein, Sadie Rose. *K'tonton's Yom Kippur Kitten*. Illustrated by Joe Boddy. Philadelphia, Penn.: The Jewish Publication Society, 1995. Unp.

Grades: P–3. K'tonton is a thumb-size little boy, who persuades his mother to feed a stray cat the day after Rosh Hashanah. When K'tonton accidentally knocks over a cup of honey, he lets his mother believe the cat made the mess. On the next day, his mother refuses to feed the cat. When he fasts for Yom Kippur, he begins to understand how the hungry kitten must feel and confesses to his mother that he was the one who spilled the honey. Black-and-white line drawings illustrate the story. A glossary concludes the book.

Kimmel, Eric A. *Gershon's Monster: A Story for the Jewish New Year*. Illustrated by Jon J. Muth. New York: Scholastic, 2000. Unp.
Grades: P–4. During Rosh Hashanah, rather than make amends for his "selfishness and thoughtless deeds" and try to change his ways, Gershon simply stuffed them all in a sack and tossed them in the sea. A rabbi warns him to mend his ways or his children will suffer. On their fifth birthday, Gershon's twins are threatened by a sea monster covered with scales created from Gershon's misdeeds. Gershon repents and his children are saved. Full-page watercolor illustrations beautifully capture the tone of the story. An author's note explains the origin of the legend and the Jewish ceremony called tashlikh.

Fishman, Cathy Goldberg. *On Rosh Hashanah and Yom Kippur*. Illustrated by Melanie W. Hall. New York: Simon & Schuster Children's Publishing, 1998. Unp.
Grades: K–4. When summer turns to fall and the mail brings New Year's cards, the High Holy Days are coming. Rosh Hashanah and Yom Kippur traditions and symbols are explained by a young girl as she and her family begin a new year. The muted illustrations convey the somber, serious nature of these observances. A glossary concludes the book.

Rosh *Hashanah/Yom Kippur*. Bala Cynwyd, Penn.: Schlessinger Video Productions-Library Video Company, 1994. 25 min.
Grades: K–4. Viewers learn that the Jewish High Holy Days mark the end of one year and the beginning of the next. This is a time to ask for forgiveness for past behaviors and think about ways to become a better person. Prayers, ceremonies, songs, and a folktale help students understand the deep religious significance of these days. This video is part of the Holidays for Children series.

Rau, Dana Meachen. *Rosh Hashanah and Yom Kippur*. New York: Children's Press, 2001. 48p.

Grades: 1–3. Being kind to others, remembering the dead, making atonement, saying prayers, and fasting are all a part of Rosh Hashanah and Yom Kippur. The easy-to-read text presents a clear overview of the observances and captioned color photographs provide additional information. A Hebrew calendar, resources for learning more, a glossary, and an index are included. This book is from A True Book series.

Pushker, Gloria Teles. *Toby Belfer and the High Holy Days*. Illustrated by Judith Hierstein. New Orleans: Pelican Publishing, 2001. Unp.
Grades: 2–4. Thinking about Rosh Hashanah and Yom Kippur, Toby Belfer explains the customs and traditions to her non-Jewish friend Donna. Toby learns some things about herself while explaining the holy days to Donna. Hierstein's illustrations add to the meaning of the text. The book ends with a recipe for honey cake.

EXPLORATIONS

1. Before reading *Rosh Hashanah and Yom Kippur* (Marx, 2001), give students an opportunity to dip a piece of sliced apple into honey. Explain that apples dipped in honey are eaten to ensure a sweet and bountiful year. Share with the students any regional traditions for ensuring a good year, such as eating black-eyed peas and cabbage on New Year's Day.

2. After reading *Sound the Shofar! A Story for Rosh Hashanah and Yom Kippur* (Kimmelman, 1998), discuss the idea of reflecting on past behaviors and deciding on changes to make in the next year. Students might think about classroom or library behaviors that have caused problems, such as talking out of turn or pushing in line. The students can then pick one behavior that the whole class will work on changing during the next month.

3. While reading *K'tonton's Yom Kippur Kitten* (Weilerstein, 1995), ask the students how they think K'tonton feels at different points in the story, such as when his mother feeds the kitten, when he knocks over the honey, when he fasts, when he confesses to his mother, and when the kitten is fed again.

4. Before reading *Gershon's Monster: A Story for the Jewish New Year* (Kimmel, 2000), talk to the students about the importance of apologizing when they lose their temper, tell a lie, are selfish, or thoughtlessly say something mean.

5. After reading *Gershon's Monster: A Story for the Jewish New Year* (Kimmel, 2000), ask the students why they think Gershon shoved his "selfishness and thoughtless deeds" in a sack and dropped them in the sea rather than make changes in his behavior.

6. In the video Rosh Hashanah/Yom Kippur children write "good deeds lists" to help them become better persons. Discuss the good deeds the children in the video mention and then have the students create their own "good deeds list." The class may decide to create one list that they can all focus on during the rest of the school year.

7. After reading *Rosh Hashanah and Yom Kippur* (Rau, 2001), have students discuss times when others have done something kind for them. Then have the students discuss and write about ideas they have for being kind to others. Allow them to share their writings with each other.

SUKKOT AND SIMCHAT TORAH

Sukkot begins five days after Yom Kippur (Scharfstein, 1999). Reform Jews celebrate for seven days, Conservative and Orthodox Jews for eight days (Burghardt, 2001). Sukkot is also called the Feast of Tabernacles (Moehn, 2000) and the Harvest Festival (Scharfstein, 1999). A sukkah (outdoor shelter) is built and decorated with fruit and flowers. This shelter reminds Jews of the huts the Israelites built in the desert during the Exodus and the temporary huts farmers built in the fields to provide shelter as they harvested their crops (Burghardt, 2001). Meals are eaten in the sukkah, and some families sleep in the sukkah. Simchat Torah (Rejoicing in the Law) follows Sukkot. On this day, the reading of the Torah is completed with the last verses of Deuteronomy; the Torah is rewound, and the reading begins again with the first verses of Genesis (Burghardt, 2001; Scharfstein, 1999). This is a day for rejoicing and merriment as the Torah is carried in a procession around the synagogue. (See Zhongqiu Jie, Itse Selu, and Thanksgiving for information on other harvest festivals.)

BOOK AND MEDIA CHOICES

Gellman, Ellie. *Tamar's Sukkah*. Illustrated by Shauna Mooney Kawasaki. Rockville, Md.: Kar-Ben, 1999. Unp.
Grades: P–1. Tamar has a sukkah, but something is missing. This begins a story in which Tamar's friends arrive and help her decorate her sukkah. The story ends with all of the children sitting in the sukkah eating and visiting.

Zalben, Jane Breskin. *Leo & Blossom's Sukkah*. New York: Henry Holt, 1990. Unp.
Grades: P–3. When Leo and Blossom see Papa building the family sukkah, they decide to build one of their own. The children's friends join in and soon the other children's parents are helping with the project. The book closes with the family spending the night in the sukkah. Detailed illustrations help tell the story of this community effort and celebration of the harvest.

Goldin, Barbara Diamond. *Night Lights: A Sukkot Story*. Illustrated by Louise August. New York: Harcourt Brace, 1995. Unp.
Grades: P–4. As the family works together to build and decorate their sukkah, Daniel does not share Naomi's excitement about spending the night alone in the sukkah. Last year, their grandfather spent the night with them and sang Daniel to sleep. This year they will be sleeping in the sukkah alone. Together they overcome their fears as they look through the thatched roof into the dark sky and see the same night lights that comforted their ancestors.

EXPLORATIONS

1. Read and discuss *Tamar's Sukkah* (Gellman, 1999) with the students. Then, read Leo & Blossom's Sukkah (Zalben, 1990), and help students make connections between the two books. Both of these books include children working together to build a sukkah.

2. Before reading *Night Lights: A Sukkot Story* (Goldin, 1995), ask students if they have ever camped out overnight. Let them briefly talk about their experiences. Then, explain that the children in the story will be sleeping in their backyard.

3. *Night Lights: A Sukkot Story* (Goldin, 1995) and Barrilete: A Kite for Day of the Dead (Amado, 1999) are both about children celebrating a holiday after the death of a grandfa-

ther. The first book is fiction, the second nonfiction. They provide an interesting contrast to show children how the same theme is explored in both genres.

4. Students can see pictures of sukkahs built in backyards around the globe at www.torah.org/learning/yomtov/sukkos/succospictures.html.

RAMADAN

Ramadan commemorates the prophet Muhammad receiving the Koran or Qur'an, the Islamic holy book, from the archangel Gabriel. Ramadan is celebrated in the ninth month of the Islamic calendar, which is based on the phases of the moon without adjustments for the solar cycle (Moehn, 2000). This causes the holiday to occur about ten days earlier each year. The Asian and African continents are home to the largest number of Muslims; however, many Muslims also live in Europe and the United States (Ahsan, 1987). Ramadan is a month-long fast during which Muslims do not eat or drink anything between sunup and sundown. The sick, elderly, travelers, small children, and pregnant women are exempt from fasting. Muslims fast to demonstrate their faith in God, Allah, and their obedience to his commands (Hoyt-Goldsmith, 2001). Ramadan is a time for praying, studying the Koran, and making amends. Id-Ul-Fitr celebrates the end of Ramadan. (See Lent, Rosh Hashanah, and Yom Kippur for other holidays of fasting and contemplation.)

BOOK AND MEDIA CHOICES

Marx, David F. *Ramadan*. New York: Scholastic, 2002. 32p.
Grades: K–2. Color photographs, large print, and simple text explain Ramadan to the youngest students. A picture glossary and an index are included. This book is from the Rookie Read-About Holiday series.

Ghazi, Suhaib Hamid. *Ramadan*. Illustrated by Omar Rayyan. New York: Holiday House, 1996. Unp.
Grades: K–3. Hakeem and his family rise before daybreak for Suhur, an early meal that has to sustain them through their daylong fast. At school, Hakeem and his friends play outside while the other children eat lunch. However, they try not to play so hard that they become thirsty. At sunset, the fast is broken by a meal called Iftar, which begins with eating dates and saying prayers. The story describes

Hakeem's feelings of hunger as he goes through the day without food. Although Hakeems's story is not the central focus of the book, it is the part that young children relate to as the book is read. The book provides information on Islam and the month-long fast of Ramadan. Beautiful, detailed watercolor illustrations portray the rich Islamic heritage and the American Muslim culture.

Ramadan. Video. Bala Cynwyd, Penn.: Schlessinger Video Productions-Library Video Company, 1996. 25 min.
Grades: K–4. Viewers learn about the history and beliefs of Muslims and their month of fasting, Ramadan. Live-action sequences, animation, and still photographs explain the religious significance and traditions associated with this holiday. This video is part of the Holidays for Children series.

Matthews, Mary. *Magid Fasts for Ramadan*. Illustrated by Earl B. Lewis. New York: Clarion, 1996. 48p.
Grades: 1–5. Eight-year-old Magid wants to fast during Ramadan, even though he is told he is too young. He fasts in secret until his sister discovers what he is doing and tells his parents. His parents and grandfather reprimand him, but also come to understand his desires and allow him to fast for half of the day. Watercolor illustrations with Arabic border motifs complement the text. A glossary concludes the book.

MacMillan, Dianne M. *Ramadan and Id al-Fitr*. Berkeley Heights, N.J.: Enslow Publishers, 1995. 48p.
Grades: 2–5. The book begins with an introduction to the religion of Islam, including information on the prophet Muhammad, the five "Pillars of Islam" (duties), mosques, and the Koran. It then describes the observances of Ramadan and Id al-Fitr. By fasting during Ramadan, Muslims strengthen their faith and develop an empathy for poor people who do not have enough to eat. Id al-Fitr is a time when the entire Muslim community comes together to celebrate the end of the fast. A glossary and an index conclude the book. This book is from the Best Holiday Books series.

Hoyt-Goldsmith, Diane. *Celebrating Ramadan*. Photographs by Lawrence Migdale. New York: Holiday House, 2001. Unp.
Grades: 3–6. Readers experience Ramadan with Ibraheem, a Muslim fourth grader living in Princeton, New Jersey, in this photo-essay. They follow along as he prays and fasts, goes to school, and participates in the other traditions associated with Ramadan. His family traditions blend those of his mother, who is from Egypt, and his father,

who is from Bosnia. Background information on Islam is contained in sidebars and woven into the text to introduce a religion that may be unfamiliar to the students. A glossary and an index conclude the book.

EXPLORATIONS

1. In the evening, the Prophet Muhammad broke his fast by eating a few dates. When Muslims break their fast during Ramadan, they eat dates as Muhammad did. Before learning about Ramadan, offer the students dates to sample. Students may be unfamiliar with dates, and this is a way for them to learn about a new food.

2. After reading *Ramadan* (Ghazi, 1996), ask students about how Hakeem must feel when the other children are eating lunch and lining up at the water fountain. Ask them for suggestions of ways they could make it easier for Hakeem.

3. After reading *Magid Fasts for Ramadan* (Matthews, 1996), have students discuss why Magid wants to fast. Then, engage them in a discussion about why his parents changed their minds and allowed him to fast for half of the day.

4. After reading *Magid Fasts for Ramadan* (Matthews, 1996), students can create their own picture glossary of terms related to this celebration. *Ramadan* (Marx, 2002) concludes with a brief picture glossary that students can use as a model and expand on. Students can draw pictures to accompany the terms or write definitions in their own words.

5. While reading *Celebrating Ramadan* (Hoyt-Goldsmith, 2001), have students record similarities between their lives and Ibraheem's life. The book contains photographs of Ibraheem and his friends and family wrapping presents, making cookies, eating meals together, reading, playing basketball, and working on the computer. Then, have the students write about the similarities.

6. In *Celebrating Ramadan* (Hoyt-Goldsmith, 2001), students learn that Ibraheem's mother was born in Egypt and his father came from Bosnia. Students can ask their parents about unique traditions and rituals surrounding their own holiday celebrations and find out where they originated. Students may discover that the angel on top of their Christmas tree was once on their grandmother's tree.

ID-UL-FITR

Id-Ul-Fitr (Eid-Al-Fitr) celebrates the end of Ramadan, the good things resulting from fasting, and the gift of the Koran (Marchant, 1996). The new moon at the end of Ramadan signals the beginning of this three-day festival (Henderson and Thompson, 2002). Id-Ul-Fitr begins with prayers at the mosque, followed by family feasts and the giving of presents. Each family donates money or food to the poor; this gift is called Zakat-ul-Fitr. Celebrations of Id-Ul-Fitr vary around the world and may include horse races, camel races, polo matches, festive markets, Koran-reciting competitions, and special foods (Marchant, 1996). In Pakistan, parents give their children new clothes, money, and gifts (Viesti and Hall, 1996). This is also a time to visit cemeteries and clean graves. (See Yom Kippur, All Souls' Day, All Saints' Day, Dia de los Muertos, Qing Ming, and TET for other holidays that include commemorations of the dead.)

BOOK AND MEDIA CHOICES

Kerven, Rosalind. *Id-Ul-Fitr*. Chicago, Ill.: Raintree Publishers, 1997. 32p.
Grades: 2–5. Color photographs and lively text explain the customs and traditions associated with this joyous celebration. Prayers, feasts with special foods, and gatherings with families and friends are all part of this observance. Information on Islamic art is also included.

Marchant, Kerena. *Id-Ul-Fitr*. Brookfield, Conn.: The Millbrook Press, 1996. 32p.
Grades: 2–5. The origins and traditions of Islam and Id-Ul-Fitr are introduced in clear, succinct text accompanied by colorful photographs. This is a time of celebration and happiness, which is reflected in the smiling faces and the joyous celebrations in the photographs. However, it is also a time for remembering the dead, which includes visits to the cemetery. The author describes the different ways this festival is celebrated in different Muslim communities around the world. A glossary, a bibliography, and an index are included. This book is from the Festivals series.

EXPLORATIONS

1. Before reading *Id-Ul-Fitr* (Marchant, 1996), engage students in a discussion of when they receive presents throughout the year. Make a list of their responses. After

reading the book, return to the list and help students make connections between the giving of gifts and holiday celebrations.

2. After reading *Id-Ul-Fitr* (Marchant, 1996), help students make connections between this celebration and other celebrations that include remembering ancestors, such as Yom Kippur, All Saints' Day, All Souls' Day, Dia de los Muertos, Qing Ming, and TET Nguyen-Dan.

3. After reading *Id-Ul-Fitr* (Marchant, 1996), return to the text and remind students that the author states there are variations in the celebration of this festival in different countries. Have the students offer ideas about why there are variations, and have them make connections between the variations in holiday celebrations in the United States.

4. While reading *Id-Ul-Fitr* (Kerven, 1997), have students write questions that come to mind about Id-Ul-Fitr on sticky notes and place the notes in the book. After reading the book, these questions can be used to spark classroom discussions and provide ideas for research reports.

ZHONGQIU JIE (MID-AUTUMN MOON FESTIVAL)

Chinese celebrate Zhongqiu Jie (Mid-Autumn Moon Festival or Harvest Moon Festival) on the fifteenth day of the eighth month of the Chinese lunar calendar, when the moon is bright and round. This is a time to give thanks for a good harvest and ask for a good harvest next year (Winchester, 1996). The festival honors the Moon Goddess, Chang E, and women make offerings to the moon of fruits and moon cakes. Round fruits symbolizing the shape of the moon, such as apples, pomegranates, and grapes, are used for the offering. Moon cakes are made from a flaky pastry and have a variety of fillings, such as fruit, coconut, date paste, and smashed beans (Stepanchuk and Wong, 1991). Families and friends gather outdoors for activities such as looking at the moon and watching puppet shows (Stepanchuk and Wong, 1991). A favorite puppet show is the story of Chang E and her husband Hou Yi, which can be found in *Moonbeams, Dumplings, & Dragon Boats: A Treasury of Chinese Holiday Tales, Activities and Recipes* (Simonds, Swartz, and The Children's Museum, Boston, 2002). Additional information about this festival can be found at www.chinapage.com/festival/festival.html. (See Itse Selu, Sukkot, and Thanksgiving for other harvest festivals.)

BOOK AND MEDIA CHOICES

Russell, Ching Yeung. *Moon Festival*. Illustrated by Christopher Zhong-Yuan Zhang. Honesdale, Penn.: Boyds Mills Press, 1997. Unp.
Grades: K–4. As the author remembers her childhood celebrations of the Moon Festival she invites readers to see, hear, smell, and taste the festivities. Descriptive text and dramatic oil paintings draw the readers into this family reunion. At the end of the book, the girl wishes that her parents were with her and that her family will soon be reunited.

Chinese Shadow Puppet Theater. Win/Mac CD. Seattle, Wash.: Pentewa Interactive, 1999.
Grades: 4–8. This program enables students to visit a puppet theater and attend a puppet play. Then, they write a play, create shadow puppets, and build a puppet theater for staging their own performance.

EXPLORATIONS

1. After reading *Moon Festival* (Russell, 1997), have students make inferences about why the girl in the story is not living with her parents. Where are her parents? Why did they not come home for the celebration as the uncle did?

2. After students learn about the Harvest Moon Festival and hear the story of Chang E and Hou Yi, they can create their own shadow puppet show using the *Chinese Shadow Puppet Theater* software program.

3. Directions for creating shadow puppets and a puppet theater can be found in *Moonbeams, Dumplings, & Dragon Boats: A Treasury of Chinese Holiday Tales, Activities and Recipes* (Simonds, Swartz, and The Children's Museum, Boston, 2002). Students enjoy writing their own plays and creating a variety of shadow puppets to perform them. This activity provides students with opportunities to be creative and learn to work together with their classmates. (See Asian Holidays.)

REFERENCES

Ahsan, M. M. 1987. *Muslim Festivals*. Vero Beach, Fla.: Rourke Enterprises.

Amado, Elisa. 1999. *Barrilete: A Kite for Day of the Dead*. Toronto, Ont.: Groundwood Books.

Barkin, Carol, and Elizabeth James. 1994. *The Holiday Handbook*. New York: Clarion Books.

Burghardt, Linda. 2001. *Jewish Holiday Traditions: Joyful Celebrations from Rosh Hashanah to Shavuot*. New York: Kensington Publishing.

Cooper, Ilene. 2002. *Jewish Holidays All Year Round: A Family Treasury*. New York: Harry N. Abrams.

Henderson, Helene, and Sue E. Thompson. 2002. *Holidays, Festivals, and Celebrations of the World Dictionary*, 3rd ed. Detroit, Mich.: Omnigraphics.

Hoyt-Goldsmith, Diane. 2001. *Celebrating Ramadan*. New York: Holiday House.

Kadodwala, Dilip. 1998. *Divali*. Austin, Tex.: Steck-Vaughn.

Kimmel, Eric A. 2000. *Gershon's Monster: A Story for the Jewish New Year*. New York: Scholastic.

MacMillan, Dianne M. 1997. *Diwali*. Berkeley Heights, N.J.: Enslow Publishers.

Marchant, Kerena. 1996. *Id-Ul-Fitr*. Brookfield, Conn.: The Millbrook Press.

Moehn, Heather. 2000. *World Holidays: A Watts Guide for Children*. New York: Franklin Watts.

Rau, Dana Meachen. 2001. *Rosh Hashanah and Yom Kippur*. New York: Children's Press.

Scharfstein, Sol. 1999. *Understanding Jewish Holidays and Customs: Historical and Contemporary*. Hoboken, N.J.: KTAV Publishing House.

Simonds, Nina, Leslie Swartz, and The Children's Museum, Boston. 2002. *Moonbeams, Dumplings, & Dragon Boats: A Treasury of Chinese Holiday Tales, Activities and Recipes*. San Diego: Harcourt.

Stepanchuk, Carol, and Charles Wong. 1991. *Mooncakes and Hungry Ghosts: Festivals of China*. San Francisco: China Books & Periodicals.

Viesti, Joe, and Diane Hall. 1996. *Celebrate! In South Asia*. Photographs by Joe Viesti. New York: Lothrop, Lee and Shepard Books.

Winchester, Faith. 1996. *Asian Holidays*. Mankato, Minn.: Capstone Press.

SEPTEMBER HOLIDAYS AND CELEBRATIONS 2

September marks the start of a new school year, with back-to-school clothes, crisp notebooks, shiny crayons, and sharp new pencils. September holidays include Chongyang Jie (Double Nine Festival), Labor Day, Grandparents Day, Mexican Independence Day, Citizenship Day, and Itse Selu. In China Chongyang Jie is celebrated on the ninth by sending kites aloft into clear blue skies. In the United States and Canada, the first Monday of the month is designated Labor Day, which honors workers and officially marks the end of summer. Grandparents Day is celebrated on the first Sunday after Labor Day to honor grandparents and recognize their importance in their grandchildren's lives. Mexican Independence Day, on September 16, commemorates the beginning of Mexico's fight for independence. The seventeenth is Citizenship Day, a time for reflecting on the roles of citizens in a democracy and the importance of the Constitution. September is also the month for the Cherokee Itse Selu (Green Corn Festival), which is a time to give thanks for the harvest and celebrate the start of a new year. In the Northern Hemisphere the autumn equinox, when the day and night are equal in length, falls on the twentieth, twenty-first, or twenty-second of September (Leslie and Gerace, 2000).

CHONGYANG JIE (DOUBLE NINE FESTIVAL)

Chongyang Jie (Double Nine Festival) is celebrated in China on the ninth day of the ninth month of the Chinese lunar calendar. On this day kites soar into the heavens, sending wishes and messages to the spirits or carrying away bad luck. Kites come in all shapes, sizes, and colors. The shapes of the kites symbolize the traits the owners wish to possess (Lin, 2002). Kites representing bad luck are flown high into the sky; then the strings are cut, and the kites sail away, taking the bad luck with them. Over the years, the flying of kites has spread to Japan, Thailand, India, and Mexico. Each of these countries has its own customs, traditions, and festivals associated with kite flying. (See Dia de los Muertos to learn about the elaborate kites made in Santiago Sacatepéquez, Guatemala.)

BOOK AND MEDIA CHOICES

Lin, Grace. *Kite Flying*. New York: Alfred A. Knopf, 2002. Unp.
Grades: P–1. A strong wind is blowing, so the family works together with paper, glue, and sticks to make a dragon kite. They add bamboo strips to make their dragon kite talk to the wind as it flies. Colorful illustrations with Chinese designs fill the pages of the book, and one short sentence on each two-page spread tells the story. The book concludes with information about the Double Nine Festival and kite flying.

Compestine, Ying Chang. *The Story of Kites.* Illustrated by Yong Sheng Xuan. New York: Holiday House, 2003. Unp.
Grades: K–4. Part of the duties of the Kang boys, Ting, Pan, and Kuai, was to bang nosily on pots and pans and blow whistles to keep the birds away from the family's rice fields. At first this was fun, but eventually it just became tiring, so the boys looked for other ways to drive the birds away. They tried to make wings and jump off a high hill to scare the birds, but they only crashed into the tall grass. After several failed attempts, they finally made kites with colorful, scary pictures on them that frightened the birds away. The Kang family had the first kite factory ever. The book concludes with an author's note, instructions for making a kite, hints for kite safety, and directions for flying a kite.

Demi. *Kites: Magic Wishes That Fly Up to the Sky*. New York: Crown, 1999. Unp.
Grades: 1–4. Part fact and part fiction, this book tells the story of the Double Nine Festival in China. A mother wishing for wealth, wisdom, power, and nobility for her son has a painter create a dragon kite to symbolize her wishes. Together mother and son fly the kite, so the gods in heaven will see the wishes and grant them. The pages of the book are filled with colorful kites painted with animals, flowers, gods,

and Buddhas, all representing wishes. Illustrated instructions for making a kite conclude the book.

Farndon, John. *Flight*. Tarrytown, N.Y.: Marshall Cavendish, 2002. 32p. Grades: 4–8. Students who are fascinated with kites and wonder about how they stay aloft will find answers to their questions in this book. Color photographs, labeled diagrams, sidebars, and clear, concise text explain the mysteries of flight to students. The book includes simple science experiments with step-by-step instructions and diagrams to ensure students understand the concepts of flight presented in the book. One of the experiments includes simple directions for making a kite from a plastic garbage bag. A glossary and an index are included. This book is from the Science Experiments series.

EXPLORATIONS

1. After reading *Kite Flying* (Lin, 2002), return to the book with the students and work with them to make a list of the items the family used to make their kite. Creating lists is one type of informal writing activity that helps students organize their thoughts and think about their reading.

2. After reading *Kite Flying* (Lin, 2002), return to the book and have students focus on the repeated patterns in the wallpaper, the kite, and the characters' clothing. Provide the students with ink and stamps to create their own repeating patterns. Tempra paints and stamps carved from potatoes can also be used. Calling the students' attention to the patterns and having them create their own helps make them aware of patterns and structures in their environment. Patterning is an important core curriculum concept that crosses curriculum areas (Shaw and Blake, 1998).

3. Before reading *Kites: Magic Wishes That Fly Up to the Sky* (Demi, 1999), have students contribute to a classroom list of wishes that they would like to fly up to the sky. Then, have students create construction paper kites and write their wishes on them.

4. Older students enjoy creating and flying their own kites. *Flight* (Farndon, 2002) provides simple instructions for making a kite, accompanied by color photographs and a diagram. A kite-making center could be established in the

room with these materials: plastic garbage bag, adhesive tape, string, scissors, paper clips, and bamboo skewers.

LABOR DAY

The first Monday in September, Labor Day, is recognized in the United States, Canada, Puerto Rico, and the Virgin Islands as the day to honor workers (Moehn, 2000). This holiday, conceived by Peter J. McGuire and Matthew Maguire in 1882, commemorates the achievements of labor unions and their workers (Henderson and Thompson, 2002). Workers of all ages are found in the books and media annotated below. Over the years, this holiday has come to denote the end of summer and the beginning of the school year for schoolchildren and their families. Additional information on Labor Day can be found on the U.S. Department of Labor Web site at www.dol.gov/opa/aboutdol/laborday.htm.

BOOK AND MEDIA CHOICES

Bredeson, Carmen. *Labor Day*. New York: Children's Press, 2003. 32p. Grades: P–2. Easy-to-read text with few words on the page tells about the harsh treatment that led workers to demand changes in their working conditions. They joined unions and campaigned to pass laws to protect workers. A picture glossary is included. This book is from the Rookie Read-About Holidays series.

Rockwell, Anne. *Career Day*. Illustrated by Lizzy Rockwell. New York: HarperCollins, 2000. Unp. Grades: P–3. Mrs. Madoff's class meets people with a variety of occupations on Career Day. Students are introduced to a culturally diverse group, from the mother who is a judge, to the father who plays the bass in an orchestra at night and cares for a baby during the day, to the sanitation truck driver, to the manager of the local grocery store. This book is a wonderful introduction to careers for young readers.

Mora, Pat. *Tomás and the Library Lady*. Illustrated by Raul Colon. New York: Alfred A. Knopf, 1997. Unp. Grades: K–4. Each summer Tomás and his family leave their home in Texas to pick crops in Iowa. In the afternoons, Papa Grande tells the children stories in the shade of a tree. When he runs out of stories, he encourages Tomás to go to the library to read and discover new stories. There a librarian offers him a drink of water and brings him stacks of books to read. He gets lost in the stories and reads them to his family in the evenings. A note at the end of the book tells readers about the true story of migrant worker Tomás Rivera's love of reading, and a librarian in Iowa who encouraged him to read. Rivera grew up to become an author and educator; when he died, he was the chancellor of the University of California at Riverside, and a campus library bears his name.

Hoyt-Goldsmith, Diane. *Migrant Worker: A Boy from the Rio Grande Valley*. Photographs by Lawrence Migdale. New York: Holiday House, 1996. 32p.
Grades: 3–6. Eleven-year-old Ricardo and his family tell readers about their life as migrant farm workers. During the school year, Ricardo lives with his mother and siblings in Rio Grande City, Texas, while his father works in Chicago and sends money home. In the summer, the whole family travels around to farms harvesting crops. Federal labor laws, including the child labor laws, do not cover migrant workers, so they work long hours in often-hazardous situations. A brief biography of César Chavez and his work in organizing the United Farm Workers of America Union is included. A glossary, an index, and a map conclude the book.

Collins, David R. Farmworker's *Friend: The Story of César Chavez*. Minneapolis, Minn: Carolrhoda Books, 1996. 80p.
Grades: 4–8. Chavez selflessly devoted his life to improving migrant workers' lives. He first organized his own community of Mexican Americans to enable them to make changes in their lives. Then, he began to organize farm workers and helped them form a union to increase their wages and improve their working conditions. He used the nonviolent tactics of Mohandas Gandhi and staged peaceful protests. Black-and-white photographs accompany this powerful story. A bibliography and an index conclude the book.

Gourley, Catherine. *Good Girl Work: Factories, Sweatshops, and How Women Changed Their Role in the American Workforce*. Brookfield, Conn.: The Millbrook Press, 1999. 96p.
Grades: 4 and up. Primary source documents, including diaries and letters, tell the stories of women and girl factory workers in the late 1800s and early 1900s. Twelve-hour days, deplorable working conditions, and lower wages than their male counterparts spurred revolts and protests that slowly changed their working conditions. Black-and-white photographs and reproductions offer testimony to

the harsh lives of these women and girls. The book includes an index.

Freedman, Russell. *Kids at Work*. Photographs by Lewis Hines. New York: Houghton Mifflin, 1994. 104p.
Grades: 5–8. Lewis Hines traveled across America in the early twentieth century photographing child laborers. This former schoolteacher realized that his photographs would convince people that child labor was child slavery. Russell Freedman has written the text to accompany these compelling black-and-white photographs. A bibliography, picture credits, and an index conclude the book.

Roberts-Davis, Tanya. *We Need to Go to School: Voices of the Rugmark Children*. Toronto, Ont.: Groundwood Books, 2001. 48p.
Grades: 5–8. This book examines the impact of Rugmark, an organization that works to end the exploitation of child labor, on the lives of Nepalese children. Black-and-white photographs and the children's own stories, poetry, and drawings tell of their harsh early years making rugs and how their lives changed when they were given the opportunity to leave the factories and attend school. Resources for learning more and an index are included.

Ryan, Pam Muñoz. *Esperanza Rising*. New York: Scholastic, 2000. 262p.
Grades: 6–9. Leaving behind a life of wealth and privilege in Mexico, thirteen-year-old Esperanza and her mother become migrant farm workers in California after her father dies and her uncle takes over their ranch. The story is set in the 1930s, and the Mexican migrant workers fight for their jobs as families escaping the Dust Bowl in Oklahoma arrive looking for work. When her mother becomes ill and is hospitalized, Esperanza must take responsibility for supporting them and running the household. The book is also available on audiocassette.

Labor Day: Celebrating the Work We Do. Video. Bala Cynwyd, Penn.: Schlessinger Video Productions-Library Video Company, 1999. 44 min.
Grades: 6 and up. From family-owned businesses to America's child laborers to everyday workers, students learn about the variety of jobs Americans hold and how we celebrate the end of summer on Labor Day. This video is part of the Picture This America series.

Bartoletti, Susan Campbell. *Kids on Strike!* Boston, Mass.: Houghton Mifflin, 1999. 208p.
Grades: 6 and up. As America grew into an industrial nation and the need for more workers arose, children, with their boundless energy, were employed in factories and coal mines. They sold newspapers on street corners, kept weaving looms running, sorted coal, and undertook a variety of other jobs to help support their families. These children worked long hours in unsafe environments for low pay. Eventually, they organized and began the fight for better working conditions and higher wages. Black-and-white photographs and the young workers' own words tell their compelling stories. The book includes a timeline of federal child labor laws, a bibliography, and an index.

EXPLORATIONS

1. After reading *Career Day* (Rockwell, 2000), have the students talk to their parents about their occupations. Then, have the students draw pictures of their parents at work or write about their parents' jobs. Provide space in the classroom to display their work and give them an opportunity to talk about different jobs and consider which ones they might like to pursue.

2. Before reading *Tomás and the Library Lady* (Mora, 1997), ask students to share examples of how librarians have helped them.

3. After reading *Migrant Worker: A Boy from the Rio Grande Valley* (Hoyt-Goldsmith, 1996), have students discuss why they think federal labor laws do not cover migrant workers.

4. As students read *Farmworker's Friend: The Story of César Chavez* (Collins, 1996), have them write down their personal responses to events in his life in a two-column format similar to the one below. Reflecting on a person's life and writing down their responses helps students to better understand that person's contributions (Harvey and Goudvis, 2000).

5. After reading *Farmworker's Friend: The Story of César Chavez* (Collins, 1996), have students read about Martin Luther King, Jr. and his work. Both of these men used Gandhi's nonviolent tactics to work for change. (See Martin Luther King, Jr. Day.)

Personal Responses	
Facts from the Text	Responses
César's family lost their store and land in the Great Depression and became migrant farm workers.	
César's was jailed for sitting in the white's section of the movie theater.	
Ross showed César how Mexican-Americans could help themselves and have a say in their lives.	
César organized the National Farm Workers Association.	
The public supported his grape boycott.	
César fasted to call attention to the high cancer rates of the farm workers exposed to pesticides.	
Twenty-five thousand people attended his funeral.	

Figure 2-1. Writing personal responses to events in a person's life helps students focus on the contributions of the individual and the impact of these contributions on society.

6. After reading *Good Girl Work: Factories, Sweatshops, and How Women Changed Their Role in the American Workforce* (Gourley, 1999), have students return to the text and reread some of the excerpts from the primary source documents. Why do they think the author included the women's own words in the book? What impact did the women's words have on their understanding of the material in the book?

7. After reading *We Need to Go to School: Voices of the Rugmark Children* (Roberts-Davis, 2001), have students discuss the reasons the children give for needing to go to school. Then, have the students discuss why they need to go to school. Help students make connections between their lives and the lives of the children in the book.

8. After reading *We Need to Go to School: Voices of the Rugmark Children* (Roberts-Davis, 2001), students can learn more about the Rugmark Foundation and read about the lives of the Rugmark children at www.rugmark.org.

9. While watching *Labor Day: Celebrating the Work We Do*, have students make a list of all the occupations depicted in the film. After watching the film, have them work in small groups to consolidate their lists and add occupations that they might be interested in pursuing that were not mentioned in the film. Students can each pick an occupation to research and find out the responsibilities, the average salary, and the education required for the job. One source of information on different careers can be found at www.bls.gov/k12/html/edu_over.htm. Students can then write about the occupation and contribute it to a class book on careers. Having students research careers while in middle school helps them begin to think about the courses they will need to take in high school to help them achieve their goals.

10. While reading *Esperanza Rising* (Ryan, 2000), have students note the changes in Esperanza during the course of the story. After reading the book, provide them with questions to discuss about the character. What kind of person is Esperanza? How does she change over the course of the story? Are the changes believable? What caused the biggest change in Esperanza?

GRANDPARENTS DAY

Grandparents Day is celebrated on the first Sunday after Labor Day. What began with Marian McQuade's concern for West Virginia's shut-ins—many of whom were senior citizens—eventually became this national holiday. She recognized that many shut-ins were only visited on Christmas and their birthdays, and she wanted a way to make people aware of the need to visit shut-ins more frequently. In 1972, President Richard Nixon proclaimed October 15 National Shut-in Day. Later, McQuade began to lobby for a National Grandparents Day. In September 1978, President Jimmy Carter designated the first Sunday after Labor Day as National Grandparents Day. The purpose of this day is not only to honor grandparents, but also to give them an opportunity to express their love for their grandchildren and help children develop an appreciation of all that older people have to offer. This is a day for honoring the elderly and remembering to visit the shut-ins and those in nursing homes throughout the year. Additional information on this holiday can be found at www.grandparents-day.com. The books annotated below help children recognize all that they have learned from their grandparents and all that their grandparents have to offer them.

BOOK AND MEDIA CHOICES

Rotner, Shelley, and Sheila Kelly. *Lots of Grandparents*. Photographs by Shelley Rotner. Brookfield, Conn.: The Millbrook Press, 2001. Unp.
Grades: P–2. Smiling grandparents, both young and old, appear on the pages of this book. This book dispels the stereotypes of grandparents as old and in need of assistance. Grandparents of a variety of ages and from different ethnic backgrounds are shown working, having fun, sharing treasures, loving, being proud of their grandchildren, and spending time with their grandchildren.

Shields, Carol Diggory. *Lucky Pennies and Hot Chocolate*. Illustrated by Hiroe Nakata. New York: Dutton Children's Books, 2000. Unp.
Grades: P–3. A grandfather and grandson spend a wonderful weekend together picking up lucky pennies, riding in a convertible with the top down, stuffing lots of marshmallows in hot chocolate, and sharing knock-knock jokes. Charming illustrations and the amusing surprise ending add to the appeal of the book.

Carlson, Nancy L. *Hooray for Grandparents' Day*. New York: Viking, 2000. Unp.
Grades: P–3. Arnie has no grandparents to bring to school for Grandparents' Day, so he decides to invite his neighbors, but then discovers they are out of town. He mentions his plight to adults he sees on his way to and from school. The next day Arnie arrives at school to find a classroom filled with his classmates' proud grandparents. Then, in through the door come the neighborhood bakery owners, the dress shop owner, the school custodian, the librarian, and the coach, all claiming Arnie as their grandson.

McCaughrean, Geraldine. *My Grandmother's Clock*. Illustrated by Stephen Lambert. New York: Clarion Books, 2002. Unp.
Grades: P–3. In an idyllic house by the seashore, Grandmother and Grandfather live without clocks, except for the broken grandfather clock whose base holds an umbrella, a walking stick, and a picture of King Zog. When their granddaughter asks why they have no working clocks, her grandmother patiently explains how she uses nature and everyday events to tell the time. For example, it takes an hour

for her grandfather to read the paper or for them to walk the dog. The shadows of the magnolia tree tell her the time of day, clanking garbage cans mean it is Wednesday, and leaves aflame with color mean it is autumn.

Kessler, Christina. *My Great-Grandmother's Gourd*. Illustrated by Walter Lyon Drudop. New York: Orchard Books, 2000. Unp.
Grades: K–1. When a water pump is installed in a Sudanese village, the people rejoice because they will not need to store rainwater in the baobab tree this year. However, one very wise grandmother prepares her baobab tree to store water captured during the rainy season. When the villagers begin to make fun of her work, her granddaughter helps her. When the pump breaks, the grandmother volunteers to share her water with the villagers until the pump is fixed. This wise grandmother concludes that it is best to mix the old and the new. An author's note explains that the book is based on a true story.

Plourde, Lynn. *Thank You, Grandpa*. Illustrated by Jason Cockroft. New York: Penguin Putnam, 2003. Unp.
Grades: K–3. This is a loving tribute to a very special relationship between a young girl and her grandfather. When she was a toddler, they began their walks in the woods, where he helped her discover the wonders of nature and taught her about saying goodbye. Throughout the years their walks continued, until one day the girl walked alone, remembering all the lessons her grandfather taught her.

Koutsky, Jan Dale. *Pen Pals*. Honesdale, Penn.: Boyds Mills Press, 2002. Unp.
Grades: K–5. The story unfolds through a scrapbook filled with the pictures and correspondence that a grandmother and granddaughter exchanged over the years. Their loving, supportive relationship sustained them both, though they were separated by time and distance. An author's note at the end of the book encourages readers to talk to important elders in their lives to learn about them and to share common experiences.

Hoyt-Goldsmith, Diane. *Pueblo Storyteller*. Photographs by Lawrence Migdale. New York: Holiday House, 1991. 28p.
Grades: 3–8. April's grandparents and uncle teach her about her rich Pueblo heritage by having her help them make bread in outdoor ovens, craft a pottery storyteller from clay, and make a Cochiti drum. Color photographs depict a loving family preserving and passing on their heritage. The book includes contact information for learning

more about the Storytellers, Cochiti drums, and the Pueblo dance group. The book concludes with a glossary and an index.

EXPLORATIONS

1. Before reading the book *Lots of Grandparents* (Rotner and Kelly, 2001), have students brainstorm a list of things they do with their grandparents. After reading the book, have students add to the list. Then, help them organize the list into categories such as work, play, outdoors, and indoors.

2. After reading *Hooray for Grandparents' Day* (Carlson, 2000), help students make a list of all the "grandparents" they have in their lives. Carlson believes children should be encouraged to reach out to all the potential grandparents in their lives, as grandparents have so much to share.

3. After reading *My Grandmother's Clock* (McCaughrean, 2002), have students think about ways they tell time. Many young children keep track of time by television shows. They may also know that sounds in their houses indicate time; for example, hearing water running in the shower in the morning means a parent is getting up.

4. Introduce seasonal changes to children by reading *My Grandmother's Clock* (McCaughrean, 2002). Start a class log to record the seasonal changes they observe on the playground when they go out for recess.

5. Before reading *Thank You, Grandpa* (Plourde, 2003), read the students the title of the book and show them the pictures. Ask them why they think the title of the book is *Thank You, Grandpa*. Then, ask them what they think the girl is thanking her grandfather for doing.

6. *Thank You, Grandpa* (Plourde, 2003) and *When I Go Camping with Grandma* (Bauer, 1995) are both stories about grandparents who introduced their grandchildren to nature's sights and sounds. Students can easily make comparisons between the two books. (See Summer Excursions.)

7. The students can explore the National Grandparents Day Web site at www.grandparents-day.com for ideas about how to remember shut-ins and those in nursing homes.

The class can discuss the ideas and decide on one for a class project.

8. At the beginning of the book *My Great-Grandmother's Gourd* (Kessler, 2000) is a list of Arabic words with pronunciation guides and definitions. Before reading the book, write the words on the board and pronounce them for the students. Share the definitions of the words with the students and explain that the words are used in the book and that knowing the definitions will help them understand the story.

9. After reading *My Great-Grandmother's Gourd* (Kessler, 2000), point out to students how the author uses descriptive, sensory words to help paint pictures in their minds—for example, "the shimmering blue sky met the earth's baking red clay." Have students explore the text for other examples. Then provide older students the time to work with a partner and use sensory words to describe things in the classroom or outside on the playground.

10. After reading *Pen Pals* (Koutsky, 2002), have students share experiences they have had with their grandparents. Ask them about pictures they may have or letters they may have received from their grandparents. Older students might want to become pen pals with residents in nursing homes.

11. After reading *Pueblo Storyteller* (Hoyt-Goldsmith, 1991), have students practice their letter-writing skills by writing letters requesting additional information about the Storytellers, Cochiti drums, or the Pueblo dance group. These addresses are available in the book. Once they receive the information, students can work in groups to make multimedia presentations of their information using *HyperStudio* or *Microsoft PowerPoint* software.

12. After learning about Grandparents Day, have students discuss ways they can honor their grandparents and let them know that they appreciate them. Then, provide students with time to create cards for their grandparents or write them letters. Students who do not have grandparents can be encouraged to think about other older adults in their lives.

MEXICAN INDEPENDENCE DAY

Mexican Independence Day, celebrated on September 16, marks the beginning, rather than the end, of Mexico's fight for independence. For three hundred years Mexico was under Spanish rule. On September 16, 1810, a Catholic priest, Father Miguel Hidalgo, rang the church bells in the small town of Dolores to call the Mexicans from the fields and mines (MacMillan, 1997). He convinced the people that the only way to have better lives was to overthrow the Spanish government and rule themselves. This fight for independence lasted eleven years. (See Cinco de Mayo.)

BOOKS AND MEDIA CHOICES

MacMillan, Dianne M. *Mexican Independence Day and Cinco de Mayo*. Berkley Heights, N.J.: Enslow, 1997. 47p.
Grades: 2–5. This book examines the history of these important Mexican holidays, and makes distinctions between two days that are often confused with each other. The book also discusses the roles of Father Miguel Hidalgo and Benito Juarez in these holidays. Customs and traditions associated with the celebrations provide an interesting look at this colorful country. A glossary and an index conclude the book. This book is from the Best Holiday Books series.

EXPLORATIONS

1. Before reading *Mexican Independence Day and Cinco de Mayo* (MacMillan, 1997), have students create a two-column chart. In the first column, ask them to list all of the things they do to celebrate the Fourth of July. As they are reading, have them write down comparable things that they read about Mexican Independence Day celebrations.

2. As students study Mexico's fight for independence, challenge them to find answers to a variety of questions and think of their own questions to research. What did independence mean to the Mexican people? Why was it important for them to gain their independence? How did independence change their lives? How did independence affect Mexico's economy?

Independence Day Traditions		
	Fourth of July	Mexican Independence Day
Date:		
Activities:		
Foods:		
Typical Weather:		
Other:		

Figure 2-2. Recording Independence Day traditions helps students make connections between Americans and Mexicans celebrations.

CITIZENSHIP DAY

Citizenship Day is celebrated on September 17. On this day in 1787, the Constitution of the United States was signed, so the holiday was originally called Constitution Day. In 1952, Constitution Day was combined with "I Am an American Day," and the holiday was renamed Citizenship Day (Henderson and Thompson, 2002). "I Am an American Day" was proposed by the American Legion as a day to honor foreigners who had become United States citizens. Citizenship Day is set aside for thinking about the rights and duties of citizenship and commemorating the signing of the Constitution (Moehn, 2000). Parades, patriotic programs, and naturalization ceremonies are some of the ways this day is celebrated. Additional information about Constitution Day, lesson plans, and activities can be found on the National Archives and Records Administration (NARA) Web site at www.archives.gov/digital_classroom/lessons/constitution_day/constitution_day.html.

Book and Media Choices

United States Constitution. Video. Bala Cynwyd, Penn.: Schlessinger Video Productions-Library Video Company, 1996. 25 min.
Grades: K–4. Viewers attend the Constitutional Convention in 1787 and learn about the conflicts and discussions that arose as the delegates set out to write the Constitution. Washington talks about his role at the convention and students hear about Benjamin Franklin's concerns, both of which provide personal glimpses into behind-the-scenes activities. Still photographs, animation, and live-action footage work together to tell the story and hold students' attention. This video is part of the American History for Children series.

Sachar, Louis. *Marvin Redpost: Class President.* Illustrated by Amy Wummer. New York: Random House, 1999. 67p.
Grades: 2–4. Marvin, his classmates, the teachers, and the principal are all wearing clothes with holes in them for "hole day" when the president of the United States makes a surprise visit to the school, accompanied by television crews. In Marvin's classroom, the president makes a statement about citizenship and what it takes to be a good citizen. When Marvin asks about how to become president, he winds up on the evening news. This is A Stepping Stone Book.

Fritz, Jean. *Shh! We're Writing the Constitution.* Illustrated by Tomie de Paola. New York: Putnam Publishing, 1998. 64p.
Grades: 2–5. Readers slip behind closed doors to join the Constitutional Convention in 1787 and discover firsthand how the Constitution was written. Anecdotes about the founding fathers catch young readers' interest, as do de Paola's quirky illustrations. The text of the Constitution is included for older students to read and discuss. This book is also available as a thirty-one minute video and a computer CD.

De Capua, Sarah. *Serving on a Jury.* New York: Children's Press, 2002. 47p.
Grades: 3–5. Glossy color photographs and large, easy-to-read text provide students with an introduction to the jury process in America. Readers learn that our system of trial by jury comes from the ancient Greeks. They also learn about the jury selection process and what it is like to serve on a jury. Resources for learning more, a glossary, and an index are included. This book is from A True Book series.

Isler, Claudia. *The Right to Free Speech*. New York: The Rosen Publishing Group, 2001. 128p.
Grades: 4–6. The First Amendment protects citizens' right to free speech, but what exactly does that mean, and when are citizens' rights violated? Specific court cases and biographical information help students understand this complex issue and provide interesting reading. The Bill of Rights, a glossary, resources for learning more, books for further reading, and an index are included. This book is from the Individual Rights and Civic Responsibility series.

Leebrick, Kristal. *The United States Constitution*. Mankato, Minn.: Capstone Press, 2002. 48p.
Grades: 4–8. Easy-to-understand text, reproductions, photographs, and fact-filled sidebars help students develop an appreciation and an understanding of the Constitution. In order to maintain secrecy about the Constitutional Convention, the delegates worked in the summer heat with the windows closed. Several delegates stayed near Benjamin Franklin for the duration of the convention, as he was known to be a talker, especially at parties. The delegates were afraid that Franklin might slip and talk about their meetings. A map of the United States in 1787, a timeline, a glossary, books for further reading, places of interest, Internet sites, and an index conclude the book. This book is from the Let Freedom Ring series.

Multimedia Collections: United States Constitution. Win/Mac CD. Bala Cynwyd, Penn.: Schlessinger Video Productions-Library Video Company, 2001.
Grades: 4 and up. Digital photos, clip art, audio clips, video clips, and documents make this a rich resource for library and classroom collections. These resources can be incorporated into a multimedia presentation. This CD is from the Multimedia Collections Series.

Klee, Sheila. *Volunteering for a Political Campaign*. New York: Children's Press, 2000. 57p.
Grades: 5 and up. While written for teens interested in doing community-service hours, this book is also a useful resource for students wanting to learn about political campaigns and candidates. Students are encouraged to learn as much as they can about a candidate, talk about the candidate to others, and consider the candidate's pros and cons. A glossary, resources for learning more, and an index are included. This book is from the Service Learning series.

The Constitution. Win/Mac CD-ROM. Watertown, Maine: Tom Snyder Productions.
Grades: 5–10. In this simulation, students discover the dilemmas, compromises, and problems that were involved in writing the Constitution. This software is from the *Decisions, Decisions 5.0* software series.

The U.S. Constitution & the Bill of Rights. Video. Bala Cynwyd, Penn.: Schlessinger Video Productions-Library Video Company, 2002. 23 min.
Grades: 5 and up. Viewers learn that the Constitution is a dynamic document that scholars from around the world continue to study and interpret. Students gain an understanding of the compromises and decisions that were made as the Constitution and the Bill of Rights were drafted and signed. A teacher's guide is included. This video is one of the United States Government Video Series.

Collier, Christopher, and James Lincoln Collier. *Creating the Constitution, 1787*. Tarrytown, N.Y.: Benchmark Books, 1999. 92p.
Grades: 6 and up. The excitement, confusion, frustration, and intrigue surrounding the creation of the Constitution are captured in the pages of this book, actively engaging readers in learning about this historic document. The book provides enough details for students to understand what happened, but not so many that they will be overwhelmed. Reproductions, photographs, and maps highlight key points in the text and aid in understanding. An epilogue, a bibliography, and an index are included. This book is from The Drama of American History series.

EXPLORATIONS

1. To help students understand how the members of the Constitutional Convention felt, have them participate in a simulation called "The Constitution Game," which can be found on the National Archives and Records Administration Web site at www.archives.gov/digital_classroom/lessons/constitution_day/game.html.

2. Before reading *Marvin Redpost: Class President* (Sachar, 1999), brainstorm ideas about what it takes to be a good citizen. After reading the book, ask students if they have read about anything that they need to add to their list.

3. Have students select one of the court cases in *The Right to Free Speech* (Isler, 2001) that they would like to discuss and do research to learn more about the issues involved in the case. These court cases make for provocative, interesting discussions.

4. After reading *Volunteering for a Political Campaign* (Klee, 2000), have students go to the Project Vote Smart Web site at www.vote-smart.org, enter their nine-digit zip code in the "Find Your Representative" box, and learn about the politicians who represent them. Then, provide students with an opportunity to discuss what they have learned.

5. At ConstitutionFacts.com, students can find the text of the Constitution, fascinating facts about it, and information on the men who signed it. This fact-filled Web site is located at www.constitutionfacts.com/cons.shtml.

ITSE SELU (GREEN CORN FESTIVAL)

Itse Selu (Green Corn Festival) is a Cherokee harvest festival that occurs at the time of the Harvest Moon in September. This four-day celebration is a time of giving thanks for the new crop of corn and marks the beginning of a new year. In preparation for the festival, houses are cleaned and old fires are put out. During the festival, the priest starts a new fire and prays that there will be plentiful food in the new year and that old quarrels will be forgotten (Pennington, 1994). Additional information about the Cherokee Nation can be found on their Web site at www.cherokee.org. (See Native American Holidays in Chapter 18.)

BOOK AND MEDIA CHOICES

Pennington, Daniel. *Itse Selu: Cherokee Harvest Festival*. Illustrated by Don Stewart. Watertown, Mass.: Charlesbridge Publishing, 1994. Unp.
Grades: K–4. As children learn about this harvest festival, they also learn about the Cherokee people and their customs by spending the day with Little Wolf. A Cherokee word, pronunciation, key, and definition are found at the bottom of each page of text. An introduction contains background information on the Cherokee people. The book concludes with a Cherokee syllabary, and explains that it was creat-

ed by Sequoyah, the only individual to single-handedly devise a written language.

Roop, Connie. ...*If You Lived with the Cherokee.* Illustrated by Peter Roop. New York: Scholastic, 1998. 80p.
Grades: 2–5. The question-and-answer format of the book enables students to quickly find the information they are interested in reading about. Students learn about Cherokee celebrations, clothing, and food, the Trail of Tears, and other interesting details about the lives of these Native Americans. A Cherokee syllabary concludes the book.

Claro, Nicole. *The Cherokee Indians.* Philadelphia, Penn.: Chelsea House, 1992. 80p.
Grades: 5–8. The southeastern United States was the original home of the Cherokee. In 1838, the American government forced them to relocate to Oklahoma. Tragically, many of the Cherokee died during this forced relocation, known as the Trail of Tears. The book includes a glossary, a chronology, and an index. This book is from The Junior Library of American Indians series.

EXPLORATIONS

1. After reading *Itse Selu: Cherokee Harvest Festival* (Pennington, 1994), call students' attention to the colors used in the illustrations. The illustrations contain warm shades of green, brown, and yellow that let the reader know this book is set in the fall. Developing an appreciation and understanding of the illustrations in books enables students to gain additional meanings from them.

2. The book *Itse Selu: Cherokee Harvest Festival* (Pennington, 1994) contains a Cherokee tale about a clever rabbit and the foolish wildcat. Readers familiar with Joel Chandler Harris's tale of "Brer Rabbit and the Tar Baby" will recognize the similarities in the stories. If students are not familiar with Harris's story, share the story with them, and then have them make comparisons between the two stories.

3. After reading *Itse Selu: Cherokee Harvest Festival* (Pennington, 1994) or *If You Lived with the Cherokee* (Roop, 1998), students who are interested in the Cherokee syllabary can try out the interactive lesson at www.cherokee.org/Culture/KidsGames.asp. When students click on a

symbol, they hear the sound for the symbol, see the symbol used in a word, and see the word written in a sentence.

REFERENCES

Bauer, Marion Dane. 1995. *When I Go Camping with Grandma*. Memphis, Tenn.: Troll Associates.

Harvey, Stephanie, and Anne Goudvis. 2000. *Strategies That Work: Teaching Comprehension to Enhance Understanding*. Portland, Maine: Stenhouse Publishers.

Henderson, Helene, and Sue E. Thompson. 2002. *Holidays, Festivals, and Celebrations of the World Dictionary*, 3rd ed. Detroit, Mich.: Omnigraphics.

HyperStudio 4.0. 2003. Boston, Mass.: Sunburst Technology.

Leslie, Clare Walker, and Frank E. Gerace. 2000. *The Ancient Celtic Festivals and How We Celebrate Them Today*. Illustrated by Clare Walker Leslie. Rochester, Vt.: Inner Traditions.

Lin, Grace. 2002. *Kite Flying*. New York: Alfred A. Knopf.

MacMillan, Dianne M. 1997. *Mexican Independence Day and Cinco de Mayo*. Berkley Heights, N.J.: Enslow.

Microsoft PowerPoint. Redmond, Wash.: Microsoft Corporation.

Moehn, Heather. 2000. *World Holidays: A Watts Guide for Children*. New York: Franklin Watts.

Pennington, Daniel. 1994. *Itse Selu: Cherokee Harvest Festival*. Watertown, Mass.: Charlesbridge Publishing.

Shaw, Jean M., and Sally S. Blake. 1998. *Mathematics for Young Children*. Upper Saddle River, N.J.: Prentice-Hall.

OCTOBER HOLIDAYS AND CELEBRATIONS 3

In some regions of the United States, leaves are turning glorious colors and floating to the ground. The first hints of cooler weather are in the air. October is the month for celebrating Columbus Day, United Nations Day, and Halloween. On the second Monday in October we remember Columbus's exploits and their impact on indigenous people. October 24 is United Nations Day, when we pause to reflect on the peacekeeping efforts of the United Nations (UN) around the globe. The last day of the month is reserved for Halloween, with costumes, trick-or-treating, and parties. It is fitting to note that in this month we celebrate both Columbus's expansion of the known world and an organization that tries to keep all of the nations of the world living in harmony.

COLUMBUS DAY

On October 12, 1492, Columbus landed in the West Indies. His arrival in the "New World" was an inspiration to other explorers. In the United States, the second Monday in October is a federal holiday in honor of Columbus and his explorations. Puerto Rico, Canada, Central America, South America, Italy, and Spain also honor this skilled navigator and explorer (Spies, 1992). In some places in the United States and in Latin America, rather than celebrate Columbus Day, they celebrate the diverse people who inhabit the land discovered by Columbus (Gardeski, 2001). This holiday is also known as El Dia de la Raza or "Day of the Race," honoring the mestizo race created by the intermarriage of the Europeans and native Central and South Americans (Menard, 2000; Viesti and Hall, 1996).

BOOK AND MEDIA CHOICES

Gardeski, Christina Mia. *Columbus Day*. New York: Children's Press, 2001. 32p.
Grades: P–2. "Are you an explorer?" This query sets young readers' minds to thinking as the book describes what an explorer does, using both words and pictures of youngsters exploring. The book contains a brief introduction of Columbus and his voyages and concludes by telling readers that Columbus Day reminds us of the importance of taking time to explore. A picture glossary and an index are included. This book is from the Rookie Read-About Holidays series.

Landau, Elaine. *Columbus Day: Celebrating a Famous Explorer*. Berkeley Heights, N.J.: Enslow Publishers, 2001. 48p.
Grades: 2–5. This concise biography of Columbus helps children understand why we celebrate Columbus Day. Colorful pictures, maps, and sidebars help readers understand the importance of Columbus's explorations and discoveries. Although the continents of North and South America were named for another explorer, Amerigo Vespucci, many cities on both continents and a South American country were named for Columbus. The book briefly mentions that not all Americans consider him a hero because of his cruel treatment of the Native Americans. A craft project, a glossary, resources for learning more, and an index conclude the book. This book is from the Finding Out About Holidays series.

Gallagher, Carole S. *Christopher Columbus and the Discovery of the New World*. Philadelphia, Penn.: Chelsea House, 2000. 63p.
Grades: 4–8. Columbus's life was one of hard work, frustration, and long days at sea. His persistence and determination led to discoveries and settlements that changed the course of history. Rich color photographs and reproductions enhance the text and invite readers to discover Columbus and learn about life during this age of exploration. A chronology, a glossary, a bibliography, and an index are included. This book is from the Explorers of the New Worlds series.

Meltzer, Milton. *Columbus and the World around Him*. New York: Franklin Watts, 1990. 192p.
Grades: 6 and up. Meltzer presents the facts to readers and lets them draw their own conclusions about Columbus. Readers learn that Columbus lacked a formal education and was self-taught. His treasured books traveled on his voyages with him, and today scholars can view his books with his handwritten notes in the margins.

Meltzer shares some of these notes with his readers. This is an award-winning biography of a remarkable man, and one students enjoy reading. Illustrations, maps, document reproductions, and drawings are included.

EXPLORATIONS

1. Prior to reading *Columbus Day* (Gardeski, 2001), have students brainstorm about what the word "explorer" means. After reading the book, have the students refine their definition.

2. After reading *Columbus Day: Celebrating a Famous Explorer* (Landau, 2001), provide students with an opportunity to discuss the book and then write about what they learned.

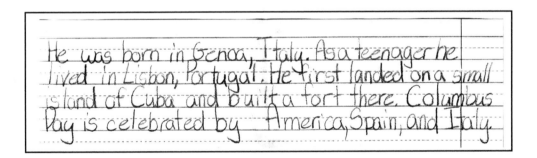

He was born in Genoa, Italy. As a teenager he lived in Lisbon, Portugal. He first landed on a small island of Cuba and built a fort there. Columbus Day is celebrated by America, Spain, and Italy.

3. "The Medieval Sourcebook: Christopher Columbus: Extracts from Journal," at http://www.fordham.edu/halsall/source/columbus1.html, has excerpts from Columbus's journal. Reading the entries from September ninth through September seventeenth, students discover that Columbus accurately reported the distance his ship traveled in his journal, but recorded fewer leagues in the ship's log; his journal states why he did this. After visiting the site, have students write about why he recorded fewer leagues in the log. These excerpts also describe how the crew determined that land was near. Have students examine the clues the crew used and write about why this information indicated land was near.

4. During his lifetime, no portraits were painted of Christopher Columbus. The Web page "Looks Are Deceiving: the Portraits of Christopher Columbus," at http://comm faculty.fullerton.edu/lester/writings/Admiral.html, examines portraits of Columbus, which reflect his personality as well as the cultural influences of the times when they were painted. Written descriptions of Columbus's appearance are included in the article. Have students discuss the discrepancies in the written accounts and then create their own portrait of Columbus based on the descriptions.

5. Provide students with opportunities to talk about their favorite books and which ones they would take with them if they were traveling. Create a class list of favorites to help students select books to check out of the library.

6. The celebration of Columbus Day has evolved over time. While originally established to honor Christopher Columbus's landing in the New World, it now also calls attention to the fact that his landing forever altered the lives of the indigenous people (Menard, 2000). *The Latino Holiday Book: From Cinco de Mayo to Dia de los Muertos—The Celebrations and Traditions of Hispanic Americans* (Menard, 2000) contains information on El Dia de la Raza that helps students understand how holidays have different meanings in different cultures. (See Central American and Hispanic Holidays in Chapter 17.)

UNITED NATIONS DAY

On October 24, 1945, representatives from the United States, Great Britain, the Soviet Union, and Nationalist China established the United Nations (Henderson and Thompson, 2002). The charter for the UN includes these aims: keeping the peace between nations, encouraging nations to be just with one another, promoting international cooperation, and providing a means for nations to work together (Stein, 1994). When disputes arise between nations, the UN attempts to negotiate peaceful solutions. When negotiations fail, the UN steps in to provide humanitarian aid to the victims (Stein, 1994). United Nations Day celebrations include parades and international festivals to help the participants develop an understanding and appreciation of each other's cultures.

BOOK AND MEDIA CHOICES

Stein, R. Conrad. *The United Nations*. Chicago, Ill.: The Children's Press, 1994. 32p.
Grades: 4–6. Beginning with a gripping description of the role of the UN in the Cuban Missile Crisis, this book grabs and holds readers' attention. They learn about the history of the UN and its mission in the world today. Photographs, illustrations, and an index are included. This book is from the Cornerstones of Freedom series.

Melvern, Linda. *United Nations*. New York: Franklin Watts, 2001. 32p.
Grades: 4–8. Captioned photographs, text, and sidebars create a kaleidoscope of information on the United Nations and its peacekeeping operations throughout the world. At the end of the book, readers are encouraged to visit the United Nations Web site at www.un.org to learn more and to contribute to its vital work. The book includes a glossary, resources for learning more, and an index. This book is from the World Organizations series.

Kramer, Barbara. *Madeleine Albright: First Woman Secretary of State*. Berkeley Heights, N.J.: Enslow Publishers, 2000. 112p.
Grades: 6 and up. This biography of Madeleine Albright contains a great deal of information on her work as the United States' twenty-first ambassador to the United Nations. Reading about this time in her life provides students with a deeper understanding of the work of the United Nations and the difficult role of an ambassador. The book concludes with a chronology, chapter notes, resources for learning more, and an index. This book is from the People to Know series.

EXPLORATIONS

1. Create a concept map using *Inspiration* software as children brainstorm what they know about the United Nations. After reading about the UN, have the students return to the concept map and add, delete, and rearrange items based on what they have learned.

2. Have students visit the United Nations home page at www.un.org. Here they can find out more about the UN, learn about the issues on the UN agenda, and view Web casts of meetings, conferences, and events. After visiting the site, have students write a brief description of one of

the events taking place at the UN on the day they visited the site.

3. The captions accompanying illustrations in nonfiction books are a frequently-overlooked resource that can provide additional information to help students comprehend the material in the text. *United Nations* (Melvern, 2001) has captioned illustrations that can be used to reinforce the usefulness of this practice. Before reading the book, have students read just the captions and then discuss what they think they will learn from the book.

4. After learning about the United Nations, have students research one of the member nations. Let the students decide which of several topics they will research. Possible topics include geography, products, imports, exports, ethnic groups, political system, or interesting holidays. Then, let the students decide how they will share the information with their classmates. Providing choices helps students take ownership of the project.

5. While reading *Madeleine Albright: First Woman Secretary of State* (Kramer, 2000), have students develop a character sketch. Lead the students in a discussion of things to include in their character sketches. One class decided on these elements: physical appearance, personality and interest, education and/or intellectual pursuits, childhood and family life, experiences that made an impact, and the impact of surrounding events and times (Harvey, 1998).

HALLOWEEN

Halloween is celebrated on October 31. For the ancient Celts, this day marked the end of the year and a time when witches and ghosts roamed the land (Barkin and James, 1994). Halloween can be traced from the Celtic harvest festival of Samhain, the Roman harvest festival of Pomona, and the Roman day to honor the dead, Feralia (Moehn, 2000). From Ireland came the customs of carving jack-o'-lanterns and trick-or-treating (Moehn, 2000). The Irish went door to door collecting food for a community feast (Barkin and James, 1994). With the spread of Christianity in the ninth century came the November first celebration of All Saints' Day. The evening before was called "All Hallows' Even," which eventually became Halloween (Zalben, 1999). Some African Americans celebrate Harambee, "unity," instead of Halloween (Winchester, 1996). This is a time for them to come together to celebrate and learn about African American art and culture.

BOOK AND MEDIA CHOICES

Rex, Michael. *Brooms Are For Flying!* New York: Henry Holt, 2000. Unp.

Grades: P–1. Youngsters stomp, peek, moan, and fly their way through this action-packed Halloween book. A group of friendly trick-or-treaters demonstrate these action verbs and young readers join in this rollicking celebration. Large print with only a few words on each page assures that beginning readers will discover they can soon read this book all by themselves.

Barrett, Judi. *Which Witch is Which?* Illustrated by Sharleen Collicott. New York: Atheneum Books for Young Readers, 2001. Unp. Grades: P–2. This clever concept book, with its wordplay and rhyming series of questions, introduces students to a whimsical collection of witches and a variety of words to add to their vocabularies. The details in the pictures that are needed to answer the questions are very small, so this book is best used one-on-one or with a very small group of children. Cartoon animals in colorful costumes hold young readers' attention as they attempt to answer the questions.

Poydar, Nancy. *The Perfectly Horrible Halloween*. New York: Holiday House, 2001. Unp.
Grades: P–2. Nothing could be worse than leaving your Halloween costume on the school bus and watching all of your classmates don their costumes. Arnold tries to improvise a bug costume, but when his classmates laugh he seeks refuge under a white dropcloth splattered with paint. With twists and turns and eerie sounds he becomes a ghost and wins the award for the scariest costume. Students relate to Arnold as he copes with disaster and unwittingly solves his problem.

Gibala-Broxholm, Scott. *Scary Fright, Are You All Right?* New York: Dial Books for Young Readers, 2002. Unp.
Grades: P–3. When a monster child is exposed to a human child, disastrous things begin to happen. The monster child contracts Human-i-tis. Now, she wants to keep a kitten as a pet rather than eat it for dessert as her mother suggests. She makes pizza for dinner, sings "Twinkle, Twinkle, Little Star," and covers her bedroom wall with butterflies and rainbows. When Dr. Ghastly's medicine does not return her to normal, her parents accept her as she is.

Greene, Carol. *The 13 Days of Halloween*. Illustrated by Tim Raglin. Mahwah, N.J.: Bridgewater Books, 2000. Unp.
Grades: P–3. For twelve days, a green ghoul lovingly presents his lady fair, an equally green ghoul, with a variety of Halloween surprises, beginning with a vulture in a dead tree. In the tradition of the "Twelve Days of Christmas," students eagerly begin chanting as this

cumulative tale unfolds. The twist at the end of the tale is that the lady presents her suitor with a gift on the thirteenth day that scares both him and the vulture. Readers decide what it is that has frightened the suitor and the vulture. They are given a hint: "A real, live..."

Melmed, Laura Krauss. *Fright Night Flight*. Illustrated by Henry Cole. New York: HarperCollins, 2002. Unp.
Grades: P–3. A fun-loving green witch grabs her cat and boards her super jet-fueled broomstick for a wild Halloween ride. Along the way she picks ups a ghoulish collection of passengers depicted in hilarious illustrations. The lyrical rhyming text encourages students to guess who will be the next to hop aboard the magical broom, where there is always room for one more. At the end of the ride, the ghoulish passengers announce they are going to descend on your house. Rest assured they know the street.

Gibbons, Gail. *Halloween Is...* New York: Holiday House, 2002. 26p.
Grades: K–3. Told with simple but informative text, this book describes the origins and history of Halloween traditions and festivities from ancient times to the present day. Brightly colored illustrations complement the text. This is a good introductory volume to the holiday.

Bunting, Eve. *The Bones of Fred McFee*. Illustrated by Kurt Cyrus. San Diego: Harcourt, 2002. Unp.
Grades: K–4. When the children hang a plastic skeleton in the tree, it seems to come to life as it dances in the wind. As its bones clickety-clack the dog and the rooster avoid going near the tree. The day after Halloween, when the children go to take the skeleton down from the tree, it has disappeared...but a gravesite lies at the foot of the tree. The story is told in a charming, rhyming verse. Scratchboard and watercolor illustrations set the tone for this eerie Halloween adventure.

Halloween. Video. Bala Cynwyd, Penn.: Schlessinger Video Productions-Library Video Company, 1996. 25 min.
Grades: K–4. Bring along your imaginations and a friendly ghost, entreats the host of the program, as students prepare to join in the Halloween celebration at the community center. A dramatic poetry presentation sends chills up the spine. Students learn that Halloween traditions came to America from Costa Rica, Mexico, and Ireland. This video is part of the Holidays for Children series.

Cazet, Denys. *Minnie and Moo Meet Frankenswine.* New York: HarperCollins, 2001. 48p.
Grades: 1–3. When lightning strikes the barn, all the animals run out, screaming that there is a monster inside. Since Olga the pig is not with them, they are convinced the monster has eaten her. Minnie and Moo, two cows who are camping under a tree, watch as the animals hide behind the farmhouse. When a light comes on in the farmhouse, the animals believe the monster has eaten the farmer and his wife, and they run to Minnie and Moo for help. Minnie and Moo solve the mystery, and everyone settles back down to sleep until the next scream in the night. This humorous, engaging mystery is an I Can Read Book.

Robinson, Fay. *Halloween: Costumes and Treats on All Hallows' Eve.* Berkeley Heights, N.J.: Enslow, 2001. 48p.
Grades: 2–5. The history of Halloween is traced from the Celts to the Romans to the Roman Catholic Church. Readers find out how these groups all influenced the celebration of Halloween. The book explains the origins of Halloween symbols such as the jack-o-lantern, ghosts, and witches. In the last chapter readers find rules for staying safe on Halloween. The book includes a glossary, resources for learning more, and an index. This book is from the Finding Out About Holidays series.

Wisniewski, David. *Halloweenies.* New York: HarperCollins, 2002. 72p.
Grades: 2–5. This outrageously funny book is a collection of five "scary"—well, not really "scary," but hilarious stories about a "werewuss," Frankenstein's hamster, space toupees, the abominable showman, and something terrible that happened last summer. The slapstick humor is just right for children who think that "gross" is really "cool." Black-and-white ink drawings accompany the text, just right for Halloween fun.

Jones, Diana Wynne. *Witch's Business.* New York: HarperCollins, 2002. 201p.
Grades: 3–7. When Frank and Jess break a new chair, their father decides to withhold their allowance for four months to pay for it. In need of money, they establish Own Back Ltd. to help customers exact revenge for their wrongs. When their business becomes too successful, the neighborhood witch intervenes, because Frank and Jess are stealing her customers. The inventive, humorous story is filled with surprises.

Halloween Tales: Spooky Pack. CD. Newark, N.J.: Peter Pan, 2001.
Grades: 4 and up. Three CDs of spooky tales ensure that everyone
will find a tale or two just right for Halloween listening.

Barth, Edna. *Witches, Pumpkins, and Grinning Ghosts: The Story of
the Halloween Symbols*. Illustrated by Ursula Arndt. New York:
Houghton Mifflin, 2001, 1972. 96p.
Grades: 5 and up. Discover the ancient history of Halloween and the
origins of the traditions and rituals practiced today as we celebrate
this spooky festival. Readers learn how goblins, witches, bats, toads,
broomsticks, ghosts, jack-o-lanterns, rattling bones, and Halloween
foods became associated with this pagan festival. Line drawings
illustrate the concise, fact-filled text.

The Haunted History of Halloween. DVD and video. South
Burlington, Va.: A & E Television Networks, 1997. 50 min.
Grades: 6 and up. Step back in time with narrator Harry Smith to
uncover the origins of pagan Halloween traditions, including the origins of the jack-o-lantern. Included is information on how Christians
tried to transform this pagan holiday into All Saints' Day. This video
is part of the History of the Holidays series.

EXPLORATIONS

1. While reading *Brooms Are For Flying!* (Rex, 2000), pause
   to let students act out the action verbs used in the story.

2. After reading *Which Witch is Which?* (Barrett, 2001), write
   one or two of the unfamiliar words on the board. Return to
   the book and help children determine the meaning of the
   word. This is a book that students want to hear repeatedly, and a few vocabulary words at a time can be introduced
   each time the story is read.

3. After reading *The Perfectly Horrible Halloween* (Poydar,
   2001), invite students to brainstorm ideas for other ways
   Arnold could have solved his problem. Then, let them
   share similar experiences they may have had.

4. While reading *Scary Fright, Are You All Right?* (Gibala-
   Broxholm, 2002), have older students complete a chart
   noting differences between human children and monster
   children. Young children can complete the chart with
   teacher assistance after reading the book.

Comparison Chart	
Monster Child	Human Child
Keeps bats and spiders as pets	Keeps kittens as pets
Eats spider web soup	Eats pizza
Howls at the moon	Wishes on stars
Draws dragons and ghosts	Draws rainbows and butterflies

Figure 3-1. Completing a comparison chart such as this one helps children make connections between their lives and the lives of children they encounter in books.

5. Before guessing what the gift to the suitor is in *The 13 Days of Halloween* (Greene, 2000), have the students look back through the books at the gifts he gave the lady. Since none of those gifts seem to scare them, what could the gift be that scares the ghoul and the vulture? Once students have decided on possible gifts, have them write down their reasons for their selections.

6. After reading *Fright Night Flight* (Melmed, 2002), return to the text and have students list the order in which the ghoulish creatures climbed aboard the broom.

7. After learning about Halloween, have students create a wall mural of Halloween traditions and customs, indicating the country of origin for each one. This activity will help students see the historical origins of the holiday and enable them to recognize the cultural origins of the traditions and customs associated with Halloween. Possible resources to use include *The Haunted History of Halloween* (video) and *Halloween: Costumes and Treats on All Hallows' Eve* (Robinson, 2001).

8. Before reading *The Bones of Fred McFee* (Bunting, 2002), tell the students about the information on the back flap of the book, where the author shares how the idea for the poem came as she was driving along a road and saw a

plastic skeleton hanging from a tree in a yard she passed. Then, ask the students to brainstorm a list of personal experiences that they might use as ideas for their own writing. When they have completed their lists, ask them to place the lists in their writing folders.

9. After reading *The Bones of Fred McFee* (Bunting, 2002), have students come up with explanations for what really happened in the story. For example, ask them, why do they think the dog avoided the tree? What happened to the skeleton after Halloween? Who dug the grave that appeared under the tree?

10. Before students begin reading *Witch's Business* (Jones, 2002), explain that the author used a cause-and-effect organizational pattern. For example, when the children broke the chair, their father withheld their allowance. While reading the book, have the students look for and record other cause-and-effect patterns that they see. They may recognize cause-and-effect chains, causes with more than one effect, or one effect with several causes. Have students briefly sketch the patterns they uncover.

11. To help children stay safe on Halloween, have them play the *Official Halloween Safety Game* located at www.halloweenmagazine.com/play2.html. Students first read the *Safety Guidelines for Halloween*, and then begin making choices as they journey through the neighborhood trick-or-treating.

12. The students can write a scary Halloween story by starting with "It was a dark and stormy night and I was lost." First, have them brainstorm a list of scary words to include in the story. Have the students work with a partner or in a small group. Each student writes one sentence and then passes the story on to another student to write the next sentence. Remind the students to read what the last person wrote down before they add their sentence. Once the story is finished, the students can share it with their classmates. They may want to use puppets to tell the story and locate props such as candy wrappers, wooden blocks, and aluminum foil to create spooky sound effects.

REFERENCES

Barkin, Carol, and Elizabeth James. 1994. *The Holiday Handbook*. New York: Clarion Books.

Gardeski, Christina Mia. 2001. *Columbus Day*. New York: Children's Press.

Harvey, Stephanie. 1998. *Nonfiction Matters: Reading, Writing, and Research in Grades 3–5*. York, Maine: Stenhouse Publishers.

Henderson, Helene, and Sue E. Thompson. 2002. *Holidays, Festivals, and Celebrations of the World Dictionary*, 3rd ed. Detroit, Mich.: Omnigraphics.

Inspiration Ver. 7.0. Inspiration Software, Portland, Ore.

Menard, Valerie. 2000. *The Latino Holiday Book: From Cinco de Mayo to Dia de los Muertos—The Celebrations and Traditions of Hispanic Americans*. New York: Marlowe.

Moehn, Heather. 2000. *World Holidays: A Watts Guide for Children*. New York: Franklin Watts.

Spies, Karen. 1992. *Our National Holidays*. Brookfield, Conn.: The Millbrook Press.

Stein, R. Conrad. 1994. *The United Nations*. Chicago, Ill.: The Children's Press.

Viesti, Joe, and Diane Hall. 1996. *Celebrate! In Central America*. Photographs by Joe Viesti. New York: Lothrop, Lee and Shepard Books.

Winchester, Faith. 1996. *African-American Holidays*. Mankato, Minn.: Bridgestone Books.

Zalben, Jane Breskin. 1999. *To Every Season: A Family Holiday Cookbook*. New York: Simon & Schuster Books for Young Readers.

NOVEMBER HOLIDAYS AND CELEBRATIONS 4

As plants become dormant and animals prepare to hibernate, nature in the Northern Hemisphere rests. November holidays are All Saints' Day, All Souls' Day, Dia de los Muertos, National Sandwich Day, Guy Fawkes Day, Veterans Day, Election Day, and Thanksgiving. November 1 and 2 are for remembering the dead, as Christians observe All Saints' Day, All Souls' Day, and Dia de los Muertos (Day of the Dead). November 3 is National Sandwich Day, in honor of a favorite way to fix food. Guy Fawkes Day, celebrated on November 5, commemorates a failed plot to blow up the English king James I and the Parliament. Veterans Day, on November 11, is for pausing to reflect on the courage of veterans who have gone to war to protect Americans. The Tuesday after the first Monday in November is United States Election Day, for voting on public officials. Thanksgiving is celebrated on the fourth Thursday in November, and commemorates the first harvest celebration of the Pilgrims and Native Americans. November is a time for remembering the dead, honoring veterans' sacrifices, participating in elections, and feasting on the bounty the earth provides.

ALL SAINTS' DAY AND ALL SOULS' DAY

Roman Catholics, Anglicans, and Orthodox Christians recognize November first as All Saints' Day and November second as All Souls' Day (Moehn, 2000). All Saints' Day is for remembering Christians who spent their lives serving God, some of whom died for their beliefs (Thompson, 1997). All Souls' Day is for visiting cemeteries, cleaning graves, and decorating graves with flowers, crosses, and wreaths as a remembrance of relatives and friends who have died (Dues, 2000). (See Dia de los Muertos, Yom Kippur, Obon Festival, Qing Ming, Id-Ul-Fitr, and TET for other holidays that commemorate the dead.)

BOOK AND MEDIA CHOICES

Chambers, Catherine. *All Saints, All Souls, and Halloween*. Austin, Tex.: Raintree Steck-Vaughn, 1997. 31p.
Grades: 3–6. Color photographs from around the world show how these three holidays span the globe, from Europe to Africa to Latin America to the United States. Lighting candles, holding parades, dancing, praying, visiting, wearing costumes, and preparing special food are ways these holidays are celebrated. A glossary, books for further reading, and an index are included. This book is from the World of Holidays series.

Sanderson, Ruth. *Saints: Lives and Illuminations*. Grand Rapids, Mich.: Eerdmans, 2003. Unp.
Grades: 4–6. These one-page biographies of forty saints, accompanied by pencil and oil illustrations, include some recognized by the Roman Catholic Church and some recognized by the Eastern Orthodox Church. The author notes what the saints are patrons of, but does not provide sources for the information contained in the biographies. The book concludes with an index.

Mulvihill, Margaret. *The Treasury of Saints and Martyrs*. New York: Viking, 1999. 80p.
Grades: 4–8. Brief biographies of forty-five saints are enhanced by reproductions of paintings, tapestries, manuscripts, and stained glass. The entries focus on four key periods: the early days, the Roman Empire, the Middle Ages to the Reformation, and the modern era. A glossary, index, and calendar of saints are included.

EXPLORATIONS

1. After reading some of the entries in *Saints: Lives and Illuminations* (Sanderson, 2003) or *The Treasury of Saints and Martyrs* (Mulvihill, 1999), have students discuss the saints' character traits. To get their discussions started, provide a list of traits such as caring for others, personal courage, self-sacrifice, perseverance, and resourcefulness.

2. Students can role-play the life of one of the saints by first looking for key events in the saint's life to dramatize. Then, they can write a short script and locate appropriate props. After rehearsing, they can present their dramatizations to their classmates.

DIA DE LOS MUERTOS

Mexico, Latin America, and some areas of the United States remember the dead on November first and second. This holiday is Dia de los Muertos (Day of the Dead). Often, the first day of November is reserved for honoring children who have died and the second day for adults who have died. In Mexico, this commemoration celebrates death as a part of life, not something strange or frightening (Andrade, 1999). It is a time for cleaning and decorating graves, visiting family, and feasting together. Bright golden marigolds decorate the graves and guide the spirits who return to earth for the celebration (Johnston, 1997). Special foods are associated with this holiday, such as pan de merutos (bread of the dead), tamales, chicken with mole sauce, and calaveras de azucar (sugar skulls). Additionally, the favorite foods of the deceased are prepared. (See All Saints' Day, All Souls' Day, Yom Kippur, Obon Festival, Qing Ming, Id-Ul-Fitr, and TET for other holidays that commemorate the dead.)

BOOK AND MEDIA CHOICES

Johnston, Tony. *Day of the Dead*. Illustrated by Jeanette Winter. San Diego: Harcourt Brace, 1997. Unp.
Grades: P–2. The excitement is mounting as the family prepares to celebrate the Day of the Dead. The children are trying to see what papa has brought home and asking to sample the tamales, sugarcane, and mole sauce. Finally, the day arrives, and the family gathers all the food and makes their way to the graveyard, dropping bright yellow marigold petals to guide the spirits. Bowls of salt and water are placed on the graves to symbolize ongoing life. Now is the time to feast, sing, dance, and remember the dead. An author's note with additional information on the Day of the Dead concludes the book.

Joosse, Barbara M. *Ghost Wings*. Illustrated by Giselle Potter. San Francisco: Chronicle Books, 2001. Unp.
Grades: P–3. In this loving tribute to the importance of a grandmother in her granddaughter's life, readers learn about the never-ending cycle of life. In the spring, when the monarch butterflies left the Mexican forest and flew north, the grandmother died. Before she died, she told her granddaughter that when the butterflies return in autumn, they carry the souls of the old ones. During Days of the Dead, her family sets up an altar with remembrances of her grandmother and goes to the cemetery to clean and decorate the grave.

In the autumn sunlight, a butterfly tickles the girl's arm and she remembers her grandmother's words. A glossary, information on monarch butterflies, and activities for extending the book are included. (*The Christmas Thingamajig* by Lynn Manuel and *Bluebird Summer* by Deborah Hopkinson are other books that deal with the death of a grandmother.)

Krull, Kathleen. *Maria Molina and the Day of the Dead*. Illustrated by Enrique O. Sanchez. New York: Macmillan Publishing, 1994. Unp.
Grades: K–3. On the evening of October thirty-first, Maria Molina and her family are in the cemetery remembering her baby brother. She wonders what it would be like if she lived in the United States and was going trick-or-treating instead. On the evening of November first, they return to the cemetery and honor her grandmother. Two years later, she is in the United States trick-or-treating and wondering who will honor the spirits of her grandmother and baby brother. Her parents set up an ofrenda (altar) in the house filled with remembrances of her grandmother and brother. As they read the story, students learn about the traditions and rituals associated with this holiday and how immigrants bring their traditions with them to America. Earth-toned illustrations capture the spirit of Mexico.

Amado, Elisa. *Barrilete: A Kite for Day of the Dead*. Photographs by Joya Hairs. Toronto, Ont.: Groundwood Books, 1999. Unp.
Grades: 2–4. In the Guatemalan village of Santiago Sacatepéquez, the Day of the Dead is celebrated by flying large, elaborate, handmade kites. Juan and his brothers used to help their grandfather make kites to fly. Now, their grandfather is dead, and Juan, his brothers, and his friends are determined to make a kite in his honor. Photographs bring to life this ancient town and its people who are known for their spectacular kites. (See Chongyang Jie for another celebration that includes kites.)

Hoyt-Goldsmith, Diane. *Day of the Dead: A Mexican-American Celebration*. Photographs by Lawrence Migdale. New York: Holiday House, 1998. Unp.
Grades: 3–6. Ten-year-old twins living in Sacramento, California, share their celebration of the Day of the Dead. Hoyt-Goldsmith explains how this celebration combines Aztec beliefs and Catholic rituals. Wearing colorful papier-mâché or plaster masks, the people walk in a procession to the cemetery, where they place flowers on the graves of departed loved ones. The procession ends at the local

church, where mass is said, followed by dancing and music. The book includes a glossary and an index.

Lasky, Kathryn. *Days of the Dead*. Photographs by Christopher G. Knight. New York: Hyperion Books for Children, 1994. 48p.
Grades: 3–8. Just as the monarch butterflies return to Mexico for Days of the Dead, so do the spirits of the deceased. Bright golden marigold petals and candles mark paths for the returning spirits, and tables are filled with offerings for them. Graves are weeded, cleaned, and decorated with flowers and candles. Some family members will spend the night in the cemetery praying and singing. The color photographs contain images that may be unfamiliar to readers, and these images can be used as a starting place for classroom discussions. The book concludes with additional information about Days of the Dead and a glossary.

Mexico's Day of the Dead. Win/Mac CD. Seattle, Wash.: Pentewa Interactive, 1999.
Grades: 4–8. This interactive software program enables students to explore the history and cultural context of this holiday. Craft projects, visits with folk artists, a tour of a Mexican village, and a visit to a home preparing for the festival immerse children in this unique celebration. Students can write and illustrate a book with this software program. Students can also choose to have the program narrated in either Spanish or English.

Andrade, Mary J. *Through the Eyes of the Soul, Day of the Dead in México*. San Jose, Calif.: La Oferta Review Newspaper, 1999. 84p.
Grades: 6 and up. This book focuses on Day of the Dead celebrations of the people in the Mexican state of Michoacan de Ocampo, which include prayers, food, visiting, and remembering the dead. The text is written in both Spanish and English. Photographs, recipes, and first person narrative beautifully portray this celebration of life and death. Descriptions of rituals and traditions associated with the different towns reveal the uniqueness of each town's celebration.

EXPLORATIONS

1. Before reading *Day of the Dead* (Johnston, 1997), ask students to think about special holiday foods that they look forward to eating each year, such as turkey and dressing on Thanksgiving. Then, introduce the foods mentioned in the book.

2. After reading *Ghost Wings* (Joosse, 2001), have students think about the characteristics of the grandmother that made her so special to the girl. Create a class list of the characteristics. Then, help students make connections to their own lives by having them share the special characteristics of their grandparents or other older adults in their lives.

3. In *Barrilete: A Kite for Day of the Dead* (Amado, 1999), Juan's grandfather has taught him to make kites for Day of the Dead. Ask students about things that their grandparents have taught them. Younger students can draw a picture of themselves learning from a grandparent; older students can write several paragraphs about their experiences, which they can then share with their grandparents.

4. Before reading *Days of the Dead* (Lasky, 1994), show students the picture on page thirteen of the woman placing flowers inside a small fenced enclosure containing a white cross. This marks the spot where her brother and his friend died in a car crash. Students may have seen similar white crosses along a roadside near where they live and may not realize what the crosses represent.

5. Using the software program *Mexico's Day of the Dead*, have the students write a book about what they have learned about celebrating Day of the Dead.

6. Students can learn more about *Day of the Dead* in Mexico by visiting this Web site: www.dayofthedead.com. Mary J. Andrade, author of Through the Eyes of the Soul, Day of the Dead in México, maintains the site. Pages of photographs, recipes, and poems, as well as a list of books about traditions and rituals in different regions of Mexico, provide a wealth of information about how this holiday is observed throughout the country.

NATIONAL SANDWICH DAY

November 3 celebrates National Sandwich Day. The Fourth Earl of Sandwich, an Englishman named John Montagu, is credited with inventing the sandwich. Unwilling to leave his gambling, he had his servant bring him some meat sandwiched between two slices of bread (Barkin and James, 1994). Students are familiar with sandwiches and each has their own personal favorite; however, few know the origin of sandwiches or that they have their own holiday.

BOOK AND MEDIA CHOICES

Lord, John Vernon, and Janet Burroway. *The Giant Jam Sandwich*. Boston: Houghton Mifflin, 1987. Unp.
Grades: K–3. In this delightful nonsense tale, the residents of Itching Down create a giant strawberry jam sandwich in order to trap the four million wasps that have flown into their village. Rhyming couplets and whimsical illustrations tell the story of these clever villagers.

Robbins, Ken. *Make Me a Peanut Butter Sandwich (and a Glass of Milk)*. New York: Scholastic, 1992. Unp.
Grades: K–4. From peanuts to peanut butter, from wheat to bread, and from cow to milk carton, this book tells the story of all the work that goes into making an after-school snack. Brief text and large color photographs help students understand just what it takes to make a peanut butter sandwich and a glass of milk.

EXPLORATIONS

1. While reading *The Giant Jam Sandwich* (Vernon and Burroway, 1987), young students find plenty of opportunities to actively participate in this lively story by acting it out and making noises. For example, there is thumping, bumping, and banging going on while mixing the dough for the bread. Older students enjoy finding the absurdities portrayed in the pictures.

2. After reading *The Giant Jam Sandwich* (Vernon and Burroway, 1987), provide students an opportunity to make their own jam sandwiches. Offering a variety of jams lets them taste jams they may not have tried before.

3. Before reading *Make Me a Peanut Butter Sandwich (and a Glass of Milk)* (Robbins, 1992), have students write down what they think are the ingredients for making peanut butter. After reading the book, have the students make peanut butter by combining peanuts, a small amount of peanut oil, and a pinch of salt in a food processor. Spread the peanut butter on bread and serve it to the students.

4. Introduce students to surveying and graphing by taking a class survey to determine their favorite sandwiches. Have the students create a graph to display their findings and then interpret the findings. Once they have finished this exercise with their classmates, students will be ready to survey other students in the school during lunch or recess and compile their results. Students can create their graphs with paper and pencil or by using the software program *The Graph Club 2.0* or *Graph Master*.

GUY FAWKES DAY

In England, November fifth commemorates the failure of the Gunpowder Plot in 1605, when Guy Fawkes and his friends attempted to blow up the king of England and the Parliament. The Catholics in England had suffered under the rule of the Protestant King James I. Fawkes was part of a group that plotted to get rid of James I and the Parliament, and then help James's Catholic daughter, Elizabeth, become queen (Ashworth, 1997). The conspirators rented a cellar under one of the Houses of Parliament and filled it with gunpowder, which they planned to ignite to blow up the Parliament and the king (Ashworth, 1997). Guy Fawkes was chosen to light the gunpowder, but the plot was discovered, and he was arrested on the eve of November fifth, the day Parliament was to open. This event is commemorated by lighting bonfires and burning straw dummies called "guys"; hence, another name for this holiday is Bonfire Night (Moehn, 2000).

BOOK AND MEDIA CHOICES

Guy, John. *Tudor and Stuart Life.* Kent, Great Britain: *Ticktock*, 1997. 33p.
Grades: 4–6. Color illustrations with captions describe the lives of ordinary and famous people in sixteenth- and seventeenth-century England during the reign of the Tudors and Stuarts. This brief history provides background information to help students understand the Gunpowder Plot. A glossary and an index are included.

Ashworth, Leon. *Guy Fawkes.* Berkshire, England: Cherrytree Press, 1997. 32p.

Grades: 4–8. This is a concise, well-written text that contains a brief biography of Guy Fawkes, the background information needed to understand his actions, and a detailed description of failed plot and its aftermath. Ashworth notes that the gunpowder was stacked and ready on New Year's Eve for the February opening of Parliament. When the opening of Parliament was delayed from February to October due to the plague, the gunpowder decayed, so it may not have exploded even if Fawkes had had the chance to light it. Reproductions, photographs, and sidebars complement the text. The book concludes with a glossary, a list of places to visit, and an index. This book is from the British History Makers series.

EXPLORATIONS

1. Before learning about Guy Fawkes Day, ask the students for examples of terrorist attacks. Then, explain to the students that the Gunpowder Plot was a failed terrorist attack and its purpose was to overthrow the government of England.

2. After reading *Guy Fawkes* (Ashworth, 1997), ask students to return to the text and create a list of the reasons why Guy Fawkes and the other traitors believed what they were doing was right. What things in their pasts led them to believe that their actions were justified?

VETERANS DAY

November 11 is set aside to honor veterans, those who have served in the armed forces and those who have died fighting in the armed forces. On November 11, 1918, World War I ended with the signing of the armistice agreement at 11:00 a.m. (Barkin and James, 1994). This holiday was originally called Armistice Day, but the name was changed to Veterans Day to honor veterans not only of World War I, but of all wars. On Veterans Day at the National Cemetery in Arlington, Virginia, a solemn ceremony is held and a wreath is laid on the Tomb of the Unknown (Spies, 1992). This tomb contains the remains of unidentified soldiers from World War I, World War II, the Korean War, and the Vietnam War. People who donate to the Disabled American Veterans receive red poppies to wear on Veterans Day. Parades, speeches, programs honoring veterans, and placing flowers and flags on veterans' graves are ways to observe this holiday. (See Memorial Day.)

BOOK AND MEDIA CHOICES

Cotton, Jacqueline S. *Veterans Day*. New York: Children's Press, 2002. 32p.
Grades: P–2. This book is a warm tribute to the veterans who worked hard to keep our country safe. Concise text defines the term "veteran" and explains why we honor veterans in terms that even the youngest students can understand. Colorful pictures of veterans and people who honor them help students understand the importance of what veterans have done. A picture glossary and an index are included. This book is from the Rookie Read-About Holidays series.

Memorial Day/Veterans Day. Video. Bala Cynwyd, Penn.: Schlessinger Video Productions-Library Video Company, 2003. 23 min.
Grades: K–4. Songs, stories, and interviews with veterans help students understand why we honor veterans on these very special days. Visiting Arlington National Cemetery, with its rows of white headstones, is a dramatic sight that stays with viewers long after the video ends. A teacher's guide is available. This video is part of the Holidays for Children series.

Landau, Elaine. *Veterans Day: Remembering Our War Heroes*. Berkeley Heights, N.J.: Enslow, 2002. 48p.
Grades: 2–5. Many men and women have fought over the years for the freedoms all Americans enjoy. One of the ways Americans show gratitude and respect for our service men and women is to honor them on Veterans Day. This book describes how the holiday originated and how it is celebrated in different parts of our country. Marginal notes and pictures add information and appeal to this book. It closes with a craft project, a glossary, a bibliography, a list of Internet addresses, and an index. This book is from the Finding Out about Holidays series.

Hest, Amy. *Love You, Soldier*. New York: Penguin, 1991. 47p.
Grades: 3–6. When Katie is seven, she and her mother take her father to the train station in New York City as he leaves to join the soldiers fighting in World War II. Her mother's pregnant friend, whose husband is also fighting in the war, moves in with them. Together, they become a family and welcome baby Rosie into the

world. Katie's father dies in the war. Rosie's father comes back and takes his family to their home in Massachusetts. Once again, Katie's family is shattered. Her mother begins to build a relationship with her friend Sam, but Katie does not want another father.

Antle, Nancy. *Lost in the War*. New York: Penguin Putnam Books for Young Readers, 1998. 137p.
Grades: 5–8. Even though it is 1982, twelve-year-old Lisa lives with the Vietnam War daily. Her father died fighting in the war, and her mother was a nurse in Vietnam. Lisa wants a normal life, but her mother's nightmares and flashbacks and talk of Vietnam keep interfering. This gripping story reminds readers that when we think of veterans, we must also remember the women who served in the armed forces, and that war has a lasting impact on people's lives. (See *Red, White, Blue and Uncle Who?: The Stories behind Some of America's Patriotic Symbols* by Teresa Bateman for information on the Vietnam Veterans Memorial.)

Slate, Joseph. *Crossing the Tressle*. Tarrytown, N.Y.: Marshall Cavendish, 1999. 144p.
Grades: 5–8. Set in West Virginia in 1944, this is the story of fourteen-year-old Loni, who lost an eye in the car accident that killed her father. As Loni struggles to decide between an eye patch and a glass eye, her eleven-year-old brother, Petey, wrestles with his fear of crossing the train tressle alone next year to get to school. Stone, an artist, befriends the family and begins giving Loni art lessons. Stone is a former prisoner of war, who is battling mental demons as he tries to rebuild his life. Readers learn about the challenges faced by veterans who return from war with mental problems as well as physical disabilities.

Gay, Kathlyn, and Martin Gay. *Vietnam War*. New York: Twenty-First Century Books, 1996. 64p.
Grades: 6 and up. As the authors describe the reasons for the war, the war itself, and the impact of the war, they weave in the words of the participants. Color and black-and-white photographs portray the grim realities of this war. Resources for learning more and an index are included. The book is from the Voices of the Past, which features books on American wars from the Revolutionary War to the Persian Gulf War.

EXPLORATIONS

1. After reading *Veterans Day* (Cotton, 2002), have students examine the picture glossary at the end of the book. Talk to them about the words and pictures. Ask them to define the words based on what they see in the pictures.

2. To help students learn about this holiday, there is a Veterans Day Play under the classroom projects and activities link on the Veterans Day home page at www.va.gov/vetsday. The play was written by a teacher and involves a group of fifth grade students doing research on Veterans Day.

3. While watching *Memorial Day/Veterans Day*, ask the students to take notes or draw pictures. Then, have the students use the notes or pictures as they discuss the video in small groups.

4. Authors use dialogue, actions, and narration to develop characters (Rothlein and Meinbach, 1996). Students can use the character Katie in *Love You, Soldier* (Hest, 1993) to understand how the author revealed the character by completing a chart similar to the one below.

Character Analysis				
Qualities	Actions	Dialogue	Narration	Comments of Others
caring strong and determined helpful	visited with the widow Mrs. Leitstein	"You are just like family."	And I wanted to ask, Are you lonely, Mrs. Leitstein?	"Just like family …I like the way that sounds."

Figure 4-1. Creating a character analysis helps students see how authors use dialogue, actions, and narration to develop characters. Completing the first entry with the students provides them with a model to use as they fill out the rest of the chart.

5. In the course of the story *Lost in the War* (Antle, 1998), the characters change as they deal with the feelings they have about the impact of the Vietnam War on their lives. Put the students in small groups and have them discuss the characters in the story and the changes they undergo as the story progresses. What events in the story bring about changes in the characters?

6. *Crossing the Tressle* (Slate, 1999) is a good book for reading aloud to the class, perhaps reading one chapter a day before they begin their work. When you stop reading, ask students to make predictions about what will happen in the book. Remind them to make their predictions based on what they know about the characters and what has happened so far in the story.

7. Before studying Veterans Day, have students brainstorm a list of questions they have about the holiday. Then have them look at the list of frequently asked questions (FAQs) on the Veterans Day home page at www.va.gov/vetsday to see if any of their questions are answered. FAQs are an often-overlooked resource on Web sites, and this activity shows students the potential usefulness of this resource.

ELECTION DAY

In the United States, Election Day is the Tuesday after the first Monday in November. A truly democratic society must allow all of its citizens to vote, but it was a long time after the signing of the Constitution before all American citizens were given this right (Pascoe, 1997). In 1870, the Fifteenth Amendment gave male African Americans the right to vote. It was not until 1920 that women received the right to vote with the signing of the Nineteenth Amendment. The Twenty-sixth Amendment, signed in 1971, lowered the voting age from twenty-one years to eighteen years. (See Women's Equality Day to learn more about the Nineteenth Amendment.)

BOOK AND MEDIA CHOICES

Murphy, Patricia J. *Voting and Elections*. Minneapolis, Minn.: Compass Point Books, 2002. 24p.
Grades: K–2. This book introduces students to the voting process, what it means to vote, how to register, what a candidate is, and other

basic information on voting and elections. Each two-page spread contains a full-page photograph and a page of easy-to-read text. The book concludes with a brief glossary, facts about voting, resources for learning more, and an index. This book is from the Let's See Library-Our Nation series.

Election Day. Video. Bala Cynwyd, Penn.: Schlessinger Video Productions-Library Video Company, 1996. 25 min.
Grades: K–4. The community center is preparing for Election Day by having a candidate debate and a get-out-the-vote rally. Students learn a variety of terms related to elections as they watch this informative video. Still pictures, animation, and live-action video are used to present the information. This video is part of the Holidays for Children series.

Sisulu, Elinor Batezat. *The Day Gogo Went to Vote*. Illustrated by Sharon Wilson. Boston: Little, Brown, 1996. Unp.
Grades: K–4. Thembi, a six-year-old South African girl, tells the story of Gogo, her grandmother, who has not left the house in many years. When Gogo learns that for the first time blacks will be allowed to vote in an election, she announces she is going to town to vote. The family is upset and does not want her to make the long, hard journey to town. Gogo insists that she must go, because blacks in South Africa have fought for this right for many years. A rich man in town hears that Gogo plans to vote and volunteers to send his car for her. Accompanied by her granddaughter, Gogo rides to town and casts her vote. Rich pastel illustrations portray the solemnity and importance of this date in South African history. A glossary and pronunciation guide are found at the beginning of the book.

Pascoe, Elaine. *The Right to Vote*. Brookfield, Conn.: The Millbrook Press, 1997. 48p.
Grades: 3–6. Readers learn the history of voting in America. They learn about the importance of voting and the changes in the voting process over the years. Special sections contain descriptions of the different kinds of elections, the Electoral College, and the "Motor Voter Law." The book concludes with an explanation of the Bill of Rights, a glossary, a bibliography, and an index. This book is from the Land of the Free series.

On the Campaign Trail. Win/Mac CD-ROM. Watertown, Maine: Tom Snyder Productions.

Grades: 5–10. In this simulation, students join the campaign trail as they run for president. Along the trail, they learn about party politics. This software is from the *Decisions, Decisions 5.0* software series.

EXPLORATIONS

1. After reading *The Day Gogo Went to Vote* (Sisulu, 1996), have students talk about the feelings and emotions experienced by Gogo, Thembi, and her parents on this historic day. Then, help the students make connections between voting in America and voting in South Africa.

2. Prior to watching *Election Day*, provide students with a three-column chart with words they will hear in the video in the first column. In the second column, have the students write down what they think the words mean. As they watch the video, have them listen for the words and determine if they have written down the correct definitions. They can use the third column to write down any new meanings that they learn as they watch. A sample chart is below.

3. After reading *The Right to Vote* (Pascoe, 1997), have students work in small groups to create a timeline depicting the history of voting in America. Students can draw their timelines on blank paper or create multimedia timelines using Tom Snyder's *Timeliner5.0*. This software is appropriate for grades one and up and is available from Tom

Vocabulary Chart		
Words	Meaning before watching video	Meaning after watching video
candidate		
debate		
Get-out-the-vote rally		

Figure 4-2. Vocabulary charts activate students' prior knowledge before watching a video and give them a focus as they watch the video.

Snyder Productions on CD-ROM for both Macintosh and Windows computers.

4. Create an Election Day bulletin board and encourage students to bring information they find on the candidates, including newspaper articles, flyers placed on their front doors, and bumper stickers. Provide students opportunities to discuss the information they have learned about the candidates.

THANKSGIVING DAY

Long before the First Thanksgiving was celebrated in America, ancient Romans, Chinese, and Jewish people gave thanks with harvest festivals. The ancient Romans celebrated Cerelia, the Chinese celebrate Zhongqiu Jie (Mid-Autumn Moon Festival), and the Jews celebrate Sukkot (Landau, 2001). November 16, 1789, was proclaimed a day for prayers and thanksgiving by George Washington (Barkin and James, 1994). However, Thanksgiving was not celebrated yearly, nor was it always celebrated on the same day. In the 1800s, Sara Josepha Hale began campaigning for a national day of thanksgiving (Spies, 1992). Her tireless efforts paid off in 1863, when President Abraham Lincoln proclaimed the last Thursday in November a national holiday. In 1941, the date was officially changed to the fourth Thursday in November. Thanksgiving commemorates the successful harvest in 1621, when the Wampanoag and the Pilgrims came together to celebrate the bounty. Reese (1996) suggests providing information about present-day Native Americans in order to avoid presenting stereotypical images of Native Americans at Thanksgiving. Chapter 18, Special Celebrations, contains book annotations for Native American celebrations, and these books contain background information on Native Americans. The Fourth World Documentation Project Web site (www.2020tech.com/thanks/temp.html) includes information and resources for librarians and teachers about the myths and stereotypes associated with the First Thanksgiving celebration. Today, Thanksgiving celebrations include family gatherings, feasts, football games, and parades. In Canada, Thanksgiving is celebrated on the second Monday in October (Flanagan, 2002). The books and media annotated below contain information on current and past celebrations of Thanksgiving, and include books about Native Americans. (See Itse Selu, Zhongqiu Jie, and Sukkot.)

BOOK AND MEDIA CHOICES

Cowley, Joy. *Gracias, the Thanksgiving Turkey*. Illustrated by Joe Cepeda. New York: Scholastic, 1996. Unp.
Grades: P–1. Miguel, a young Puerto Rican boy who lives in New York City, receives a live turkey to fatten up for Thanksgiving. He names the turkey Gracias, which means "thanks," and becomes fast friends with it. Miguel devises a number of schemes to prevent Gracias from being eaten. One day, the turkey follows Miguel to church and is blessed by the priest. Miguel's grandmother declares that a blessed turkey cannot be served for dinner, so Gracias is saved. Spanish words are interspersed throughout the story and defined in a glossary at the end of the book.

Ziefert, Harriet. *What is Thanksgiving?* Illustrated by Claire Schumacher. New York: HarperCollins, 1992. Unp.

Grades: P–1. In this lift-the-flap story, Little Mouse helps as her family prepares for Thanksgiving. As the family shops, cooks, and feasts with relatives, Little Mouse learns about giving thanks. The story progresses as the flaps are lifted and ends with a tired, sleeping Little Mouse.

Bunting, Eve. *A Turkey for Thanksgiving*. Illustrated by Diane de Groat. New York: Clarion Books, 1991. Unp.
Grades: P–4. Mr. and Mrs. Moose have invited their friends to share Thanksgiving dinner with them. Mrs. Moose would really like to have a turkey for Thanksgiving, so Mr. Moose sets off through the woods in search of one. He is joined by their friends, who have sighted a turkey nesting by the river. They push the reluctant turkey back to the house to join in the Thanksgiving Feast. Students will be as surprised as Turkey to discover that he is to be seated at the head of the table, rather than on the table. Diane de Groat's lively, funny illustrations of these animal antics vividly depict the story.

Kimmelman, Leslie. *Round the Turkey: A Grateful Thanksgiving*. Illustrated by Nancy Cote. Morton Grove, Ill.: Albert Whitman, 2002. Unp.
Grades: K–2. Readers spend Thanksgiving Day with Jesse and his family as they use rhyming verses to reflect on their year and tell what they are thankful for this year. A family tree at the beginning of the book introduces the family members, and Jesse provides a running commentary in the corners of the pages. Lively illustrations depict the family members' thoughts and help readers as they decipher the text.

Harness, Cheryl. *Three Young Pilgrims*. New York: Simon and Schuster, 1995. 32p.
Grades: K–3. Blending fact and fiction, Harness tells the story of the Allerton family, who sailed to America on the Mayflower. The children, Bartholemew, Remember, and Mary, along with their father, survived the harsh winter, but their mother and the new baby did not. Richly detailed paintings help to tell the story of the hardships endured by the Pilgrims and the celebration of the First Thanksgiving. The book includes a timeline, a list of events happening in other parts of the world during the time of the Pilgrims, information on the individual Pilgrims who sailed on the Mayflower, and a bibliography.

Lakin, Patricia. *Fat Chance Thanksgiving*. Illustrated by Stacey Schuett. Morton Grove, Ill.: Albert Whitman, 2001. Unp.
Grades: K–4. A fire destroys the apartment where Carla lives with her mother, and the only possession Carla salvages is her book, *A Pilgrim Thanksgiving*. Carla and her mother move into a tiny new apartment two weeks before Thanksgiving. Carla dreams of a Thanksgiving feast, but her mother's reply is "fat chance." They do not have enough money, and their friends live far away. However, Carla and her new friend Julio decide to organize a Thanksgiving feast in a different way. Mr. Lewis, the apartment manager, volunteers the lobby and some tables. Some of the neighbors agree to bring one dish to share, and on Thanksgiving they all gather together for a very special feast.

Rael, Elsa Okon. *Rivka's First Thanksgiving*. Illustrated by Maryann Kovalski. New York: Simon & Schuster, 2001. Unp.
Grades: K–4. When Rivka learns about Thanksgiving in school, she tries to convince her Jewish family, immigrants from Poland, that they need to celebrate the holiday. Unsure of what to do, Rivka's grandmother takes her to talk to the rabbi about Thanksgiving. Since the holiday has to do with Pilgrims and Native Americans, the rabbi decides that Jews should not celebrate it. Rivka then writes him a letter explaining that the Pilgrims came to America to escape from "mean, wicked people," which is also the reason the Jews came to America. The rabbi reconsiders and becomes a guest at the family's Thanksgiving feast. The book concludes with a glossary.

Thanksgiving. Video. Bala Cynwyd, Penn.: Schlessinger Video Productions-Library Video Company, 1994. 25 min.
Grades: K–4. Highlights of the video include a visit to Plimoth Plantation to view a reenactment of the First Thanksgiving and learn about Native American harvest celebrations, including the Abenaki myth about origin of corn and the Nanticoke tribal dancers. Shots of the Macy's Thanksgiving Parade are also shown. A teacher's guide is included. This video is from the Holidays for Children series.

Jackson, Garnet. *The First Thanksgiving*. Illustrated by Carolyn Croll. New York: Scholastic, 2000. 32p.
Grades: 1–2. This story of the First Thanksgiving, the Pilgrims' hardships, and their friendship with the Native Americans is accompanied by pastel illustrations and easy-to-read text. This book is from the Hello Readers series.

Corey, Shana. *Milly and the Macy's Parade*. Illustrated by Brett Helquist. New York: Scholastic, 2002. 36p.
Grades: 1–3. Milly and her parents emigrated from Poland to the United States. Her papa worked for the big department store, Macy's. Milly loved Macy's and went there after school every day. She found out that other immigrants who worked for the store were very homesick for their homelands during this holiday season. She went to Mr. Macy with her idea for a parade that would celebrate all the cultures, becoming a truly American celebration. It was first called a Christmas Parade, but has long been known as the Macy's Thanksgiving Day Parade.

Anderson, Laurie Halse. *Thank You, Sarah!!!: The Woman Who Saved Thanksgiving*. Illustrated by Matt Faulkner. New York: Simon & Schuster, 2002. 40p.
Grades: 1–4. Sarah Hale realized that Thanksgiving was dying out and did not want this important day to be lost to history, so she began a campaign to have Thanksgiving proclaimed a national holiday. Thirty-eight years of writing letters to four different presidents finally resulted in Lincoln proclaiming Thanksgiving a national holiday. Lively writing with an irreverent tone and humorous caricatures tell the story of this persistent woman and the relentless barrage of letters she wrote for a cause she knew was important. The book concludes with a "Feast of Facts" about Thanksgiving.

Donnelly, Judy. *The Pilgrims and Me*. Illustrated by Maryann Cocca-Leffler. New York: Grosset & Dunlap, 2002. 32p.
Grades: 1–4. When assigned to a report about something that happened a long time ago, Carrie Rosen decides to write about Plimoth Plantation, Massachusetts. The photographs from her family trip are included, along with brief paragraphs and childlike drawings. This unique format is a clever way to help students learn about the Pilgrims.

Landau, Elaine. *Thanksgiving Day: A Time to Be Thankful*. Berkeley Heights, N.J.: Enslow, 2001. 47p.
Grades: 2–4. Feasts, parades, football games, and traveling are all part of the present-day celebration of Thanksgiving. Sarah Josepha Hale, a writer, was convinced that our celebration should be a national one, and finally President Abraham Lincoln decreed that it should be. Marginal notes, color photographs, and reproductions add information and appeal to this book. Readers are reminded that Thanksgiving is about giving thanks and caring, and they are

challenged to include these ideals in their celebration. The book concludes with a glossary, resources for learning more, and an index. This book is from the Finding Out about Holidays series.

Osborne, Mary Pope. *Thanksgiving on Thursday*. Illustrated by Sal Murdocca. New York: Random House, 2002. 76p.
Grades: 2–4. The magic tree house transports Jack and Annie back to 1621 and the First Thanksgiving feast. Catching eels, digging clams, and retrieving a turkey from an open fire prove challenging chores for the time-traveling duo. This book has short chapters and is illustrated by black-and-white line drawings. The book includes information about Thanksgiving and the Pilgrims. This book is from the Magic Tree House series. (See *Summer Reading is Killing Me* by Jon Scieszka for another book with time travel.)

Kamma, Anne. *If You Were At...the First Thanksgiving*. Illustrated by Bert Dodson. New York: Scholastic, 2001. 64p.
Grades: 2–5. Students learn that children their ages were at the First Thanksgiving, and the book describes their daily lives. The question-and-answer format of the book provides students with interesting basic facts about the First Thanksgiving. The somber brown, gray, and green colors used in the illustrations portray the bleak fall days and the simple lives of the Pilgrims.

MacMillan, Dianne M. *Thanksgiving Day*. Berkeley Heights, N.J.: Enslow, 1997. 48p.
Grades: 2–5. The beginnings of Thanksgiving date back to the arrival of people called Pilgrims from England. They were unprepared for the hard times of disease and near-starvation. A group of Native Americans taught the Pilgrims how to hunt, fish, and grow crops that would thrive in the area they settled. This book describes this first Thanksgiving and ways in which the holiday has changed over the years to the present day. The book concludes with a glossary and index. This book is from the Best Holiday Books series.

Cohen, Barbara. *Molly's Pilgrim*. Illustrated by Danie Mark Duffy. New York: HarperCollins, 1998. 28p.
Grades: 2–6. Teased and tormented by her classmates because she is different, Molly, a Jewish Russian immigrant, teaches her classmates about modern-day pilgrims. Students learn that pilgrims still come to American in search of freedom. This book is also available on video.

Dorris, Michael. *Guests*. New York: Hyperion Paperbacks for Children, 1999. 119p.

Grades: 3–6. When Moss's father invites strangers to their harvest feast, the young Native American refuses to help get ready for the visitors and leaves the village. Moss does not want outsiders at the feast, as this is a time for families and clans. Eventually, Moss comes to realize that his father is not happy about having the strangers come, but he invited them because they are hungry and he knows it is the right thing to do.

Grace, Catherine O'Neill, and Margaret M. Bruchac. With Plimoth Plantation. *1621: A New Look at Thanksgiving*. Photographs by Sisse Brimberg and Cotton Coulson. Washington, D.C.: National Geographic Society, 2001. 48p.

Grades: 3–6. Thanksgiving is presented from the perspective of the Wampanoag people, who were living on the land settled by the Pilgrims. The celebration of Thanksgiving grew from one paragraph written in a letter in 1621. The photographs accompanying the text were taken during a reenactment at Plimoth Plantation. Also included in the book are information on the reenactment, a chronology, an index, and a bibliography. The bibliography includes a section with materials for teachers.

Bial, Raymond. *The Powhatan*. New York: Marshall Cavendish, 2002. 128p.

Grades: 4–9. The Powhatans' peaceful existence was tragically altered when the colonists arrived. In this book, their lives and customs are explained. The book includes a timeline, brief biographies of notable Powhatans, a glossary, resources for further information, and an index. This book is from the Lifeways series.

Barth, Edna. *Turkeys, Pilgrims, and Indian Corn: The Story of the Thanksgiving Symbols*. Illustrated by Ursula Arndt. New York: Houghton Mifflin, 2001, 1975. 96p.

Grades: 5 and up. Brief chapters provide information on the Pilgrim fathers, mothers, children, faces, animals and houses. The chapters contain interesting anecdotes about individual Pilgrims and their daily lives. At first, the only animals the Pilgrims had were two dogs that dug up the corn seeds because they smelled the dead fish planted with the corn. Chapters are also included on Thanksgiving dinner, some of the foods associated with the feast, and the origins of the horn of plenty. The book includes a bibliography and an index.

Home for the Holidays: The History of Thanksgiving. Video and DVD. South Burlington, Va.: A & E Television Networks, 1997. 50 min. Grades: 6 and up. Follow along and trace the development of Thanksgiving from the ancient harvest celebrations to the First Thanksgiving to the present-day celebrations of food, family, football, and parades. Learn why Abraham Lincoln decided in 1863 to make the day a national holiday. This video is part of the History of the Holidays series.

EXPLORATIONS

1. After reading *Round the Turkey: A Grateful Thanksgiving* (Kimmelman, 2002), have the students jot down things that happened to their family in the past year for which they are thankful. Using one of the students' ideas, model how to write a short free-verse poem. Ask the students for suggestions about what to include in the poem. Then, have the students create their own short poems.

2. Ask the children what they think their parents are thankful for this year. Then, have the students create a Thanksgiving card for their parents and write what they think their parents are thankful for on the inside of the card.

3. Students can learn more about Thanksgiving at the An American Thanksgiving for Kids and Families Web site at www.night.net/thanksgiving. There are links to information on the First Thanksgiving, Thanksgiving foods, and Thanksgiving games and poetry. Under the Thanksgiving foods links, students can visit the Cranberry Expo in Wisconsin and learn about this traditional Thanksgiving food.

4. Before reading *Three Young Pilgrims* (Harness, 1995), share the background information at the end of the book with the students to help them understand the story. The information is about the children who traveled on the Mayflower, and knowing this information will help children make personal connections to what they hear in the story.

5. While reading *Fat Chance Thanksgiving* (Lakin, 2001), pause after some of the events in the story and record students' thoughts about the characters' feelings on a chart such as the one below. Feeling charts help students

Feelings Chart		
Events	Characters	
	Carla	Julio
Julio ran past Carla and her mother in the lobby of the apartment building.		
Carla said her Thanksgiving plans included a big feast. Mr. Lewis told them they had to get ten people to agree to the feast.		
Mrs. Li said she would bring something, but would not stay.		
Mr. Lewis said he would share his folding tables.		
Everyone was seated at the feast.		

Figure 4-4. Developing a feelings chart enables students to analyze character's feelings about events in the story, and can help students develop empathy for the characters.

analyze the reactions of the characters to events in the story (Yopp and Yopp, 2001).

6. In *Rivka's First Thanksgiving* (Rael, 2001), her letter to the rabbi is an example of persuasive writing. Project a copy of the letter on the wall for the students and have them examine the letter. Ask them why they think the letter succeeded in convincing the rabbi to change his mind. What parts of the letter were the most convincing? Work with students to make a list of the things to include in a persuasive letter. Let them brainstorm topics for a persuasive letter and then have them write one. They might want to write a letter to the teacher explaining why they need a longer recess or

less homework, or they might want to write a letter to the principal asking for a longer lunch period. Students may also have a civic concern that they want to write about to a local politician.

7. After reading *Rivka's First Thanksgiving* (Rael, 2001), return to Rivka's letter in the book. Call students' attention to the fact that her letter convinced the rabbi that Jews needed to celebrate Thanksgiving. Letters have convinced presidents to proclaim that certain days be declared national holidays. For example, Sara Josepha Hale convinced President Lincoln to proclaim Thanksgiving a national holiday. Her story is found in *Thank You, Sarah!!!: The Woman Who Saved Thanksgiving* (Anderson, 2002).

8. After reading *Thanksgiving on Thursday* (Osborne, 2002), have the students discuss the things that were strange to the twins, such as catching eels. Then, have the students make a list of things that the Pilgrims or Wampanoag would find strange if they showed up at students' houses on Thanksgiving.

9. Before reading *If You Were At...the First Thanksgiving* (Kamma, 2001), explain to students that nonfiction books are often read just to locate specific information, rather than read from cover to cover. Show them the table of contents and explain that they may just want to read the parts of the book that answer questions of interest to them.

10. While reading *1621: A New Look at Thanksgiving* (Grace and Bruchac, 2001), have students make a comparison chart of the myths and facts surrounding Thanksgiving. Then have the students visit Plimoth-on-the Web at www.plimoth.org/Library/Thanksgiving/firstT.htm to discover more information about the myths and facts surrounding Thanksgiving.

11. When students make comparisons between what they already know and the new information they are learning, they develop a deeper understanding of the content and are more likely to remember what they learn. Using a three-column chart, students can think about what they know about Thanksgiving foods and what they learn. In the first column, students write down the foods they eat at Thanksgiving, and in the second column they write down the foods that they think were eaten at the First

Thanksgiving. Then, have the students conduct research to find out what foods were served at the First Thanksgiving and write those in the third column. The following resources can be used in their research: *1621: A New Look at Thanksgiving* (Grace and Bruchac, 2001); the video *Home for the Holidays: The History of Thanksgiving*; and the Web page "A 'First Thanksgiving' Dinner for Today," maintained by Plimoth Plantation at www.plimoth.org/Library/Thanksgiving/afirst.htm. When they have completed their charts, have the students write a summary of their findings.

12. Throughout time, people all over the world have held harvest celebrations. Small groups of students can research other harvest celebrations and share what they learn with their classmates. Other harvest celebrations included in this book are Itse Selu (Green Corn Festival), Zhongqiu Jie, and Sukkot.

REFERENCES

Andrade, Mary J. 1999. *Through the Eyes of the Soul, Day of the Dead in México*. San Jose, Calif.: La Oferta Review Newspaper.

Barkin, Carol, and Elizabeth James. 1994. *The Holiday Handbook*. New York: Clarion Books.

Bateman, Teresa. 2001. *Red, White, Blue and Uncle Who?: The Stories behind Some of America's Patriotic Symbols*. New York: Holiday House.

Dues, Greg. 2000. *Catholic Customs and Traditions*. Mystic, Conn.: Twenty-Third Publications.

Flanagan, Alice K. 2002. *Thanksgiving*. Minneapolis, Minn.: Compass Point Books.

The Graph Club 2.0. (Mac/Win CD-ROM). Tom Snyder Productions, Watertown, Mass.

Graph Master. (Mac/Win CD-ROM). Tom Snyder Productions, Watertown, Mass.

Hopkinson, Deborah. 2001. *Bluebird Summer*. New York: Greenwillow Books.

Johnston, Tony. 1997. *Day of the Dead*. Illustrated by Jeanette Winter. San Diego: Harcourt Brace.

Landau, Elaine. 2001. *Thanksgiving Day: A Time To Be Thankful*.

Berkeley Heights, N.J.: Enslow Publishers.

Manuel, Lynn. 2002. *The Christmas Thingamajig*. New York: Dutton Children's Books.

Moehn, Heather. 2000. *World Holidays: A Watts Guide for Children*. New York: Franklin Watts.

Pascoe, Elaine. 1997. *The Right to Vote*. Brookfield, Conn.: The Millbrook Press.

Reese, Debbie. 1996. "Teaching Young Children about Native Americans." ERIC Digest, ED394744.

Spies, Karen. 1992. *Our National Holiday*. Brookfield, Conn.: The Millbrook Press.

Thompson, Jan. 1997. *Christian Festivals*. Crystal Lake, Ill.: Heinemann.

TimeLiner 5.0. (Mac/Win CD-ROM). Tom Snyder Productions, Watertown, Mass.

Rothlein, Liz, and Anita Meyer Meinbach. 1996. *Legacies: Using Children's Literature in the Classroom*. New York: HarperCollins.

Scieszka, Jon. 1998. *Summer Reading is Killing Me*. New York: Viking.

Yopp, Ruth Helen, and Hallie Kay Yopp. 2001. *Literature-Based Reading Activities*, 3rd ed. Boston: Allyn and Bacon.

PART III. WINTER

i

Winter Celebrations and Holidays with Moveable Dates

5

The cold, gray days of winter are broken by celebrations including Hanukkah, TET Nguyen-Dan (Vietnamese New Year), Xin Nian (Chinese Lunar New Year), Deng Jie (Lantern Festival), Tu Bi-Shevat (Jewish Arbor Day), and Eid-Al-Adha. Hanukkah begins between November 25 and December 26 and commemorates the Maccabee army's defeat of the Syrians and the rededication of the temple in Jerusalem. Between the twentieth of January and the twentieth of February, the three-day celebration of TET Nguyen-Dan begins, as does the fifteen-day celebration of Xin Nian. Deng Jie (Lantern Festival) is celebrated on the last day of Xin Nian. Tu Bi-Shevat is celebrated on the fifteenth day of the Jewish month of Shevat, between January 16 and February 13. On the tenth day of the twelfth Islamic month, Eid-Al-Adha marks the end of the Islamic pilgrimage to Mecca. The winter months are for celebrating new beginnings with candles, fireworks, special foods, and parades.

HANUKKAH

Hanukkah (Chanukah) lasts eight days and begins on the twenty-fifth day of the Jewish month of Kislev, between November 25 and December 26 (Moehn, 2000). Hanukkah (Festival of Lights) commemorates the Maccabee army's defeat of the Syrians and the rededication of the temple in Jerusalem. When the victorious Jews marched into Jerusalem, they discovered that their temple had been defiled and began to clean it (Scharfstein, 1999). There was only enough purified oil in the temple to rekindle the Eternal Light for one day, yet it burned for eight days (Burghardt, 2001; Scharfstein, 1999). This event is commemorated by lighting the menorah (candelabrum). The menorah holds one candle for each of the eight days, as well as a ninth or shammash (helper candle), which is used to light the other candles. Hanukkah foods include latkes (potato pancakes) and sufganiyot (jelly doughnuts). Children receive gelt (money) that they use to play dreidel (a four-sided top). Often on one night of Hanukkah, family and friends gather for a party, and gifts may be exchanged.

BOOK AND MEDIA CHOICES

Stone, Tanya Lee. *D is for Dreidel: A Hanukkah Alphabet Book.* Illustrated by Dawn Apperley. New York: Penguin Putnam Books for Young Readers, 2002. Unp.
Grades: P–1. This alphabet book uses brief rhymes to explain the Hanukkah symbols to young children. Colorful illustrations, many with yellow backgrounds, glow with the spirit and joy of Hanukkah. The book concludes with the story of Hanukkah.

Winne, Joanne. *Let's Get Ready for Hanukkah.* New York: Children's Press, 2001. 23p.
Grades: P–1. The focus of this book is the rituals associated with Hanukkah, rather than the religious significance. This small book is just the right size for small hands. Large print with only one or two short sentences on each page and full-page color photographs make this a good book for introducing Hanukkah rituals to young readers. A glossary, resources for further learning, and an index are included.

Ziefert, Harriet. *What is Hanukkah?* Illustrated by Rick Brown. New York: HarperCollins, 1994. Unp.
Grades: P–1. Basic questions about Hanukkah are explained in this introductory book. Readers learn that Hanukkah is a time to remember miracles, a shammash is a helper candle, a dreidel is a spinning top, and the celebrations include serving potato latkes and sharing presents. This book is a Lift-the-Flap Story.

Rosen, Michael J. *Chanukah Lights Everywhere.* Illustrated by Melissa Iwai. San Diego: Gulliver Books, 2001. Unp.
Grades: P–2. Each night, as the family lights one more candle on the menorah, a young boy sees lights all around him. For example, on the third night he sees three lights on the front porch welcoming guests, and on the fourth night he see four flames under the pots on the stove.

Newman, Lesléa. *Runaway Dreidel!* Illustrated by Kyrsten Brooker. New York: Henry Holt, 2002. Unp.
Grades: P–3. A boy spinning his shiny new dreidel is surprised when it suddenly takes off on its own. Rhyming verse leads readers on a merry chase as the dreidel spins out the door, through the streets of the neighborhood, and into the sky. Readers recognize elements of *The Night before Christmas* and the story of the Gingerbread Boy in this tale. Oil paint and paper collage add a three-dimensional quality to illustrations that almost seem to be in motion. (See *Runaway Rice Cake* by Ying Chang Compestine in the Xin Nian section in this chapter.)

Podwal, Mark. *The Menorah* Story. New York: Greenwillow Books, 1998. 22p.
Grades: P–3. This story of the menorah takes the reader from the time of Moses, through the trials of the Jewish people under the evil King Antiochus, to the leadership of Judah Maccabee, and on to the present day. Readers learn the difference between the ancient seven-candle menorah and the eight-candle menorah used today. There is an author's note at the beginning of the book with explanatory information.

Kimmel, Eric A. *Zigazak! A Magical Hanukkah Night*. Illustrated by Jon Goodell. New York: A Doubleday Book for Young Readers, 2001. Unp.
Grades: P–4. Two hilarious devils full of mischief descend on a town one evening during Hanukkah and set dreidels dancing, latkes flying, and candles exploding. The worried townsfolk hurry to the rabbi's house to ask his help. Seeing goodness in the evil, he turns the mayhem into a magical, festive Hanukkah celebration unlike any other.

Chanukah at Home. CD and Audiocassette. Cambridge, Mass.: Rounder Records, 1988.
Grades: K–3. Several different artists sing Chanukah songs, including "Chanukah Oh Chanukah," "Kindle a Candle of Light," and "Eight Candles."

A Child's Hanukkah. CD and audiocassette. Garberville, Calif.: Music for Little People, 1998.
Grades: K–3. This is a lively collection of original songs for celebrating Hanukkah accompanied by dialogue that ties the songs together.

Silverman, Maida. *Festival of Lights: The Story of Hanukkah*. Illustrated by Carolyn S. Ewing. New York: Aladdin Paperbacks, 1999. Unp.
Grades: K–3. This story of the first Hanukkah tells how Judah led the Maccabees against King Antiochus IV and his soldiers and reclaimed their temple. Included in the book are the legend of the menorah, instructions for making a dreidel, and the song "Rock of Ages."

Hanukkah/Passover. Video. Bala Cynwyd, Penn.: Schlessinger Video Productions-Library Video Company, 1996. 25 min.
Grades: K–4. Stories, puppets, games, and songs explain the significance of the Jewish holidays of Hanukkah and Passover. A traditional Seder meal, a visit to a matzo bakery, a presentation by Jewish folk singers, and the making of a dreidel involve children in exploring and learning about the traditions associated with these holidays. This video is part of the Holidays for Children series.

Adler, David. *One Yellow Daffodil: A Hanukkah Story*. Illustrated by Lloyd Bloom. San Diego: Harcourt Brace, 1995. Unp.
Grades: 1–4. Dark, haunting pictures portray this somber story of a Holocaust survivor who lost his family and his home. One day in a prison camp he spotted a single yellow daffodil blooming and decided that if the flower could survive, so could he. When he returned to his home, he discovered another family living in his family's house and claiming their belongings. This family returned only a small box of his family's belongings, including a menorah. Years later he shares the menorah with a Jewish family he meets in his flower shop.

Pushker, Gloria Teles. *Toby Belfer Never Had a Christmas Tree*. Illustrated by Judith Hierstein. Gretna, La.: Pelican Publishing, 1991. Unp.
Grades: 1–4. This is the story of the only Jewish family in a small rural community. While Toby loved to help her friends decorate their Christmas trees, she never had one in her house. One winter evening she invites her friends to join her family as they celebrate the first night of Hanukkah. In the end, Toby's friends are glad she never had a Christmas tree and that she invited them to share Hanukkah. The book includes a recipe for latkes, rules for playing dreidel, and instructions for building a menorah. This book is also available on audiocassette.

Bunting, Eve. *One Candle*. Illustrated by K. Wendy Popp. New York: Joanna Cotler Books, 2002. 30p.

Grades: 1–5. This beautiful story of how one particular family cele-brates Hanukkah revolves around the family members who survived the Holocaust. Grandma and Great Aunt Rose were children when they were sent to Buchenwald during World War II. Their bravery and the way they were able to celebrate Hanukkah in their barracks became a bright light of love and courage to their descendants. One particularly moving illustration depicts the Holocaust victims looking on as the family celebrates Hanukkah.

Rosen, Michael J. *Our Eight Nights of Hanukkah*. Illustrated by DyAnne DiSalvo-Ryan. New York: Holiday House, 2000. Unp.
Grades: 1–5. Readers join a Jewish family as they celebrate the eight nights of Hanukkah. Each of the eight nights has a different activity, including a temple Hanukkah party, a family dinner, deliver-ing gifts to a shelter, and bringing their menorah to their friends' house, where they help them decorate their Christmas tree. The book concludes with a pronunciation guide for the Hebrew words in the story.

Erlbach, Arlene. *Hanukkah: Celebrating the Holiday of Lights*. Berkeley Heights, N.J.: Enslow, 2002. 48p.
Grades: 2–5. This book begins with an explanation of who the Jewish people are. It describes how Hanukkah became a holiday, what a menorah is, and talks about parties, gelt, and gifts. Marginal notes and pictures add information and appeal to this book. It closes with a craft project, a timeline, a glossary, a bibliography, a list of Internet addresses, and an index. This book is from the Finding Out about Holidays series.

Cohn, Janice. *The Christmas Menorahs: How a Town Fought Hate*. Illustrated by Bill Farnsworth. Morton Grove, Ill.: Albert Whitman and Company, 1995. 39p.
Grades: 2–6. This book is based on the true story of how the people of Billings, Montana responded to an act of hate against a Jewish family. A rock was thrown through the bedroom window of a young boy, knocking over his electric Menorah. This hate crime, reported on television stations, came to the attention of the boy's teacher and his classmates. They drew Menorahs and placed them on their houses and in their windows. The newspaper learned of this and printed a full-page Menorah, asking the citizens of Billings to hang it in their windows, which they did. The book includes an introduction describing the actual events.

Hoyt-Goldsmith, Diane. *Celebrating Hanukkah*. Photographs by Lawrence Migdale. New York: Holiday House, 1996. 32p.
Grades: 3–6. Eleven-year-old Leora and her family invite readers into their home as they celebrate Hanukkah. This informative photo-essay explains the origins of Hanukkah and describes the holiday traditions, including lighting the menorah, eating latkes, playing driedel, receiving gelt, and exchanging gifts. A glossary, a list of suggestions for doing something special each night of Hanukkah, and an index conclude the book.

Koss, Amy Goldman. *How I Saved Hanukkah*. Illustrated by Diane de Groat. New York: Dial Books for Young Readers, 1998. 88p.
Grades: 3–6. What do you do for Hanukkah when you are the only Jewish girl in your fourth grade classroom, your mother is too busy to make latkes, your father is out of town, and your best friend celebrates Christmas? If you are Marla Feinstein, you enlist the help of your best friend, Lucy, and involve your family, friends, and neighbors in a splendid Hanukkah celebration. Readers learn about friendship and self-acceptance as well as Hanukkah traditions.

Zalben, Jane Breskin. *The Magic Menorah: A Modern Chanukah Tale*. Illustrated by Donna Diamond. New York: Simon & Schuster Books for Young Readers, 2001. 56p.
Grades: 4–8. In the midst of her Chanukah preparations, Stanley's mother realizes she does not have cinnamon for the applesauce. As she rushes out to the store, she asks Stanley to locate the box Grandpa Abe wants taken down from the attic. Inside the box is an old, tarnished brass menorah, which Stanley begins to shine. Suddenly, an old man in a moth-eaten overcoat and a black felt hat appears and grants Stanley three wishes. Stanley's first two wishes are for fame and fortune, but his ideas of fame and fortune do not exactly match the genie's idea of what they mean. His third wish is for happiness. This is a story that helps us all recognize what is important in life. A glossary is included to explain the Yiddish words sprinkled throughout the text.

EXPLORATIONS

1. Before reading *What is Hanukkah?* (Ziefert, 1994), write the words "shammash," "dreidel," and "potato latkes" on the board. Say the words aloud and ask the children what they think the words mean. After reading the story return to the words, and help the children refine their definitions based on what they learned in the story.

2. As you read *Chanukah Lights Everywhere* (Rosen, 2001), have the students find and count the lights in the illustrations.

3. The paintings in *The Menorah Story* (Podwal, 1998) can be used by students as models when they paint pictures. The artwork fills the pages and the backgrounds have been painted, rather than being left white. The paintings are not large, and students can be given a half sheet of paper and use the paintings in the book as models.

4. After reading *One Candle* (Bunting, 2002), have students reflect on the family's special ritual for remembering those who died in the Holocaust. This is an example of how one family has included a special ritual in their holiday celebration. Ask students about any special rituals that their family has incorporated into their holiday celebrations.

5. While reading *Our Eight Nights of Hanukkah* (Rosen, 2000), have the students write down what happens on each of the eight nights or sketch what happens. Then, have them use their notes or sketches to retell the story to a partner.

6. Use *The Christmas Menorahs: How a Town Fought Hate* (Cohn, 1995) to begin a class discussion about prejudice and hate crimes.

7. In *How I Saved Hanukkah* (Koss, 1998), Marla is the only Jewish student in her fourth grade class. When others in the class make red and green construction paper Christmas decorations, she is given white and blue construction paper to make Hanukkah decorations. Use the story to start a discussion with the students about what it feels like to be different. Ask them to think about a time when they were singled out or felt different from others. What could other people have done to make them feel comfortable and help them become a part of the group?

8. Before reading *The Magic Menorah: A Modern Chanukah Tale* (Zalben, 2001), tell students that in the story, Stanley is granted three wishes, and he asks for fame, fortune, and happiness. Ask the students to write down their definitions of fame, fortune, and happiness. While reading the story, have the students write down the genie's definitions of these terms. After reading the story, provide the students with time to discuss the different definitions.

Comparing Definitions		
	My Definition	Genie's Definition
Fame		
Fortune		
Happiness		

Figure 5-1. Students discover in this exercise that people have different definitions for words depending on their backgrounds.

TET NGUYEN-DAN (VIETNAMESE NEW YEAR)

TET Nguyen-Dan is a three-day celebration of the Vietnamese New Year, which has been influenced by Chinese culture because the Chinese ruled Vietnam for nearly three centuries (Hoyt-Goldsmith, 1992). The celebration begins on the first day of the first month of the lunar year according to the Chinese lunar calendar, which means it falls between January 21 and February 20. The events of these three days dictate what the rest of the year will be like, so people forgive one another, buy new clothes, and exchange gifts; broken things are fixed; and visitors are considered very important (Viesti and Hall, 1996). Children receive red envelopes containing a few dollars. This is a day for remembering ancestors and spending time with family members (Winchester, 1996). Additional information about TET can be found at www.limsi.fr/Recherche/ CIG/etet1.htm. (See Yom Kippur, All Souls' Day, All Saints' Day, Dia de los Muertos, Id-Al-Fitr, and Qing Ming for other holidays that commemorate the dead.)

BOOK AND MEDIA CHOICES

MacMillan, Dianne M. *Tet: Vietnamese New Year*. Berkeley Heights, N.J.: Enslow, 1994. 48p.
Grades: 2–5. Tet (Vietnamese New Year) is celebrated in both Vietnam and in the United States. It is like a birthday, Thanksgiving, Christmas, and New Year's all celebrated during one holiday. Tet

begins on the first day of the lunar year, which happens sometime between late January and early February. The book concludes with a glossary, a note to parents, teachers, and librarians, and an index. This book is from the Best Holiday Books series.

Hoyt-Goldsmith, Diane. *Hoang Anh: A Vietnamese-American Boy*. Photographs by Lawrence Migdale. New York: Holiday House, 1992. 32p.
Grades: 3–8. Hoang Anh Chau, a Vietnamese-American, and his family came to America as refugees, and now live in San Rafael, California. In the first part of the book, Hoang Anh talks about the problems his family has faced since they came to America. In the second part of the book readers learn about the Vietnamese New Year, TET. The book includes a legend about the origin of the rice cakes eaten during TET. In San Jose, California, TET is celebrated with a festival, complete with games of skill, sideshows, music, special foods, booths with crafts and plants, and temples, where people burn incense and say prayers for their ancestors.

EXPLORATIONS

1. In *Hoang Anh: A Vietnamese-American Boy* (Hoyt-Goldsmith, 1992), Hoang Anh talks about the adjustments he and his family have made to their lives since coming to America. Students in the classroom from other countries may welcome the opportunity to discuss Hoang Anh's problems and then make comparisons to their own lives.

2. Students can make connections between their lives and the lives of children they meet in books such as *Hoang Anh: A Vietnamese-American Boy* (Hoyt-Goldsmith, 1992). Students can first discuss similarities and differences in small groups. Then, working together, the students can write down their thoughts. Discussion helps them to reflect and organize their thoughts. Then, they can complete sentences such as these:

Hoang Anh is like me because: _____, _____, and _____.

Hoang Anh is not like me because: _____, _____, and _____.

XIN NIAN AND DENG JIE (CHINESE LUNAR NEW YEAR AND LANTERN FESTIVAL)

Xin Nian (Chinese New Year) is based on the lunar calendar and is celebrated for fifteen days, beginning between late January and late February. It marks the end of winter and the beginning of spring. The Chinese have celebrated New Year's for over four thousand years (Hoyt-Goldsmith, 1998). In preparation for this holiday, they clean their houses, buy new clothes, prepare food, and care for the graves of their ancestors. One week before the New Year begins, the family smears honey on the lips of the picture of the Chinese Kitchen God so it will say kind things about the family (Compestine, 2001). Then, the picture is burned so the Kitchen God can report to the Emperor of Heaven (Compestine, 2001). During the celebration, people visit relatives, give away red envelopes filled with money, and light fireworks to scare away evil spirits. Dancers in colorful costumes perform the Dragon Dance, accompanied by drums and cymbals. The New Year's Eve feast includes noodles, a whole chicken, a whole fish, dumplings, rice, vegetables, and a rice cake or niangao. The holiday ends with Deng Jie (Lantern Festival), when families carrying lighted paper lanterns join a parade with clowns, musicians, dancers, and a Chinese dragon (Spies, 1992).

Book and Media Choices

Brown, Tricia. *Chinese New Year*. Photographs by Fran Ortiz. New York: Henry Holt, 1987. Unp.
Grades: P–2. Travel to Chinatown in San Francisco and join in the joyous celebration of Chinese New Year. As one year ends, it is time to sweep out the old and welcome the new with house cleaning, lucky characters, special foods, and prayers. The climax of the holiday is the Golden Dragon Parade. The twisting, swirling dragon is joined by floats, marching bands, and beauty queens. Black and white photographs accompany the succinct text.

Wong, Janet S. *This Next New Year*. Illustrated by Yangsook Choi. New York: Farrar, Straus and Giroux, 2000. Unp.
Grades: P–2. As this poem tells readers, Chinese New Year is for everyone, no matter what their background. The family is busy cleaning the house and taking baths in order to "soak up good luck." This is the day for scaring away evil spirits and making a "fresh start."

Bright, colorful illustrations fill the pages of the book, and they are a delight to linger over so as not to miss a single detail.

Chinn, Karen. *Sam and the Lucky Money*. Illustrated by Cornelius Van Wright and Ying-Hwa Hu. New York: Lee & Low Books, 1997. Unp.
Grades: P–3. For Chinese New Year Sam received four red envelopes, each containing one crisp new dollar bill. Sam and his mother travel to crowded Chinatown and Sam searches for ways to spend his money. He soon discovers that four dollars will not buy much, but then he realizes that, to the barefoot stranger he accidentally steps on, four dollars is a fortune. This is a gentle story about the importance of charity. Detailed watercolor illustrations capture the excitement and frenzy of Chinatown. This book is available on videocassette.

Compestine, Ying Chang. *The Runaway Rice Cake*. Illustrated by Tungwai Chau. New York: Simon & Schuster Books for Young Readers, 2001. Unp.
Grades: P–4. Due to a drought, food was scarce and Momma had only enough flour to make one rice cake to celebrate the New Year. When she opened the steamer, the rice cake ran away. It ran past the family, past the chickens, past the pigs, and past the other people in the town. They finally captured it when it ran into an old woman. When she commented that she had not had much to eat lately, the parents graciously offered her their rice cake. She ate the whole cake and the hungry family sadly returned home. Their neighbors heard of the family's generosity, and each brought some of their own food to share with them. There was not much food, but it magically multiplied and the family had enough to eat. (See *Runaway Dreidel!* by Lesléa Newman in the Hanukkah section of this chapter.)

Waters, Kate, and Madeline Slovenz-Low. *Lion Dancer: Ernie Wan's Chinese New Year*. Photographs by Martha Cooper. New York: Scholastic, 1990. Unp.
Grades: K–3. Readers join the Wan family in New York's Chinatown as they celebrate Chinese New Year. Six-year-old Ernie Wan explains the customs, traditions, and foods associated with the holiday. This is a special celebration for him, as he will perform the Dragon Dance in the parade through the streets of New York City. Color photographs beautifully portray the family as they welcome the new year. The book concludes with a Chinese lunar calendar and a Chinese horoscope.

Chinese New Year. Video. Bala Cynwyd, Penn.: Schlessinger Video Productions-Library Video Company, 1994. 25 min.
Grades: K–4. Viewers attend a Chinese New Year's parade, complete with drums and fireworks to chase away evil spirits. A feast follows the parade and introduces students to a variety of Chinese foods. Chinese customs such as sweeping away from the door in order to avoid sweeping out good luck provide students with an intriguing examination of this ancient holiday celebration. This video is from the Holidays for Children series.

Demi. *Happy New Year!/Kung-his fa-ts'ai!* New York: Crown, 1997. Unp.
Grades: 1–6. Delicate, colorful, detailed illustrations help explain the significance of sweeping, planting, gifts, firecrackers, and prayers in Chinese New Year's celebrations. This is a time for sweeping out the old and celebrating new beginnings. Readers learn that gifts of food and plants are given, and discover that the different foods, trees, and flowers each represent special wishes and happiness for the New Year. A feast on New Year's Eve includes special foods that symbolize wishes for the coming year.

MacMillan, Dianne M. *Chinese New Year.* Berkeley Heights, N.J.: Enslow, 1994. 48p.
Grades: 2–5. One of the oldest holidays still celebrated today is the Chinese New Year. The Chinese use twelve different animals to represent each year: the rat, ox, tiger, rabbit, dragon, snake, horse, sheep or ram, monkey, rooster, dog and pig. People born in one of these animal years are said to be like the animal. The holiday is celebrated with parades and fireworks. The book contains a note, a glossary, and an index. This book is from the Best Holiday Books series.

Robinson, Fay. *Chinese New Year: A Time for Parades, Family, and Friends.* Berkeley Heights, N.J.: Enslow, 2001. 48p.
Grades: 2–5. The Dragon Parade is one way the Chinese have celebrated the New Year over the last two thousand years. This parade is especially popular in the Chinatown areas of U.S. cities. This book starts with the holiday's beginnings, describes the symbols and beliefs connected with Chinese New Year, and closes with ways the day is celebrated. Marginal notes and pictures add information and appeal to this book. It closes with a craft project, a glossary, a bibliography, a list of Internet addresses, and an index. This book is from the Finding Out about Holidays series.

Hoyt-Goldsmith, Diane. *Celebrating Chinese New Year*. Photographs by Lawrence Migdale. New York: Holiday House, 1998. 32p.
Grades: 3–6. Readers discover the two-week-long celebration of Chinese New Year through the eyes of ten-year-old Ryan Leong. Ryan shops with his father for the special ingredients needed for the traditional dishes, such as shark fin soup. He helps his father honor their ancestors by cleaning the gravestones and placing flowers and fruit on the graves. The Lion Dancers and the snaking dragon are the highlights of the Chinese New Year's parade. Vibrant color photographs depict the New Year's festivities and lively prose describes the many different traditions associated with the ancient celebration. The book ends with a glossary and an index. (See TET, Yom Kippur, All Saints' Day, All Souls' Day, Dia de los Muertos, Qing Ming, and Id-Ul-Fitr for other holidays that remember the dead.)

Explorations

1. *This Next New Year* (Wong, 2000) makes the point that you do not have to be Chinese to celebrate Chinese New Year. Celebrations are shared between cultures, and many things Americans have adopted as their own come from the celebrations of other countries. For example, firecrackers come to us from China and the piñata comes from Mexico. Helping children see the connections between the holidays and the countries helps them develop an appreciation of other cultures.

2. Before reading *Sam and the Lucky Money* (Chinn, 1997), tell them the title of the book and ask them what they think "Lucky Money" means. After reading the book, discuss why the money was lucky for Sam even though he did not get to keep it.

3. Before reading *The Runaway Rice Cake* (Compestine, 2001), ask a volunteer to tell what happened in the story about the runaway gingerbread boy. Tell them that the story they are going to hear is about a runaway rice cake, and they are to listen carefully because at the end of the story the class will work together to remember all of the characters the runaway rice cake encounters.

4. Before children watch the video *Chinese New Year*, have them write down a list of the things they do to celebrate New Year's. As they watch the video, tell them to circle anything on their list that is the same in the Chinese New

Year celebration. Also, have them write down anything that is in the Chinese New Year celebration that is not on their list. After watching the video, have the students discuss the similarities and differences and use their lists to write a summary of their discussion.

5. After reading *Happy New Year!/Kung-his fa-ts'ai!* (Demi, 1997), provide students with red paper to write down their own wishes or poems about happiness, good fortune, and wishes for their classmates. Display these happy messages around the room for them to share with their classmates.

6. Students can find a variety of links to resources for learning more about Chinese New Year at www.chinapage.com/newyear.html. There are links to pictures of dragons, animated fireworks displays, a New Year's card, and a printable Chinese calendar.

7. As students learn about the Chinese New Year, have them complete a comparison chart to determine the similarities and differences between parades they have seen and the Chinese New Year parade using a chart such as the one below. In the first column, have them list things they remember seeing in other parades that are not in a Chinese New Year parade. In the second column, have them list things that are in both parades. In the third column, have them list things they have seen or learned are in Chinese New Year parades that are not in other parades they have seen.

Comparing Parades		
Parades I have seen:	Things that are in both parades:	Chinese New Year's Parade:

Figure 5-2. This activity enables students to compare parades they have seen with the Chinese New Year's parade described in the book.

TU BI-SHEVAT (JEWISH ARBOR DAY)

Tu Bi-Shevat (Jewish Arbor Day) is celebrated on the fifteenth day of the Jewish month of Shevat, between January 16 and February 13 (Moehn, 2000). This is a day for honoring trees and planting new trees. Jews recognize that trees provide shelter and food, as well as keep the soil fertile. The Jewish National Fund collects donations from Jews around the world to buy trees to plant in Israel (Scharfstein, 1999). Trees planted in the Forest of the Martyrs in Israel will one day total six million, one for each person killed in the Holocaust (Scharfstein, 1999). The books annotated below tell about the importance of planting trees. (See Arbor Day and Earth Day.)

BOOK AND MEDIA CHOICES

Zalben, Jane Breskin. *Pearl Plants a Tree*. New York: Simon & Schuster Books for Young Readers, 1995. Unp.
Grades: K–3. Pearl and her grandfather travel back to his old neighborhood to see the apple tree he planted during his first spring in America. Then, Pearl plants an apple seed that sprouts into a tree. In the spring, Pearl and her grandfather plant the tiny tree outdoors. The book closes with information on tree-planting holidays, Tu B'Shavat, and instructions on growing a tree from a seed.

Alexander, Sue. *Behold the Trees*. Illustrated by Leonid Gore. New York: Scholastic, 2001. Unp.
Grades: 3–6. Over many years, the trees of Canaan were destroyed in wars and cut down for construction, but no new trees were planted. Black goats finished off the roots of the trees, the animals left, and the land became barren. However, people moved back to the land and planted trees, and gradually the land is being reclaimed. The book begins with an acknowledgement of the Jewish National Fund's efforts to replant the land and the book ends with an author's note about Tu B'Shevat (Tu Bi-Shevat). Lush acrylic paintings of trees include additional images that help tell this story.

EXPLORATIONS

1. The text of *Behold the Trees* (Alexander, 2001) contains the names of a variety of trees that use to grow in Canaan, including fig, terebinth, acacia, and tamarisk. The students can research information on the trees and create booklets with pictures and information about the different varieties

of trees. These booklets can be created by hand or by using a desktop publishing software.

2. In *Behold the Trees* (Alexander, 2001), students read the names of a variety of currencies, including pence, guilders, florins, and centavos, that are contributed to the Jewish National Fund to purchase trees. Students can use the encyclopedia or online resources to match country names to the currencies. Students may have examples of the currencies at home that they can bring to class to show their classmates.

EID-AL-ADHA

Eid-Al-Adha and Id-Ul-Fitr are the only two festivals officially recognized by the Islamic faith. Eid-Al-Adha is held on the tenth day of the twelfth Islamic month, Zul-hiffa, and marks the end of the Hajj, the pilgrimage to Mecca. The pilgrimage to Mecca is an obligation of Muslim men and women who can afford to make the trip, and is undertaken during the last month of the Islamic calendar (Ahsan, 1987). It is also called the Feast of Sacrifice, as it commemorates Abraham's faith in Allah and his willingness to sacrifice his son to obey Allah's command (Moehn, 2000). Allah then stopped Abraham from sacrificing his son and instead provided him with a ram to sacrifice. In some Muslim countries, the sacrificed animal is divided into three portions: one for the poor, one for a feast with family and friends, and one for the family only.

BOOK AND MEDIA CHOICES

The Hajj: One American's Pilgrimage to Mecca. Video. Bala Cynwyd, Penn.: Schlessinger Video Productions-Library Video Company, 1997. 22 min.
Grades: 7 and up. Michael Wolfe, an ABC News reporter, takes viewers on a journey of discovery as they explore the origins and meanings of the Muslim traditions and rituals associated with the Hajj. This video is from the ABC News Special series.

EXPLORATIONS

1. Preview *The Hajj: One American's Pilgrimage to Mecca* and create a study guide for students to complete as they watch the video.

2. After watching *The Hajj: One American's Pilgrimage to Mecca*, have the students visit a Web site for making travel arrangements and estimate how much it would cost to make a pilgrimage to Mecca.

REFERENCES

Ahsan, M. M. 1987. *Muslim Festivals*. Vero Beach, Fla.: Rourke Enterprises.

Burghardt, Linda. 2001. *Jewish Holiday Traditions: Joyful Celebrations from Rosh Hashanah to Shavuot*. New York: Kensington Publishing.

Compestine, Ying Chang. 2001. *The Runaway Rice Cake*. New York: Simon & Schuster Books for Young Readers.

Hoyt-Goldsmith, Diane. 1992. *Hoang Anh: A Vietnamese-American Boy*. New York: Holiday House.

Hoyt-Goldsmith, Diane. 1998. *Celebrating Chinese New Year*. New York: Holiday House.

Inspiration, Ver. 7.0. Inspiration Software, Inc., Portland, Ore.

Moehn, Heather. 2000. *World Holidays: A Watts Guide for Children*. New York: Franklin Watts.

Newman, Lesléa. 2002. *Runaway Dreidel!* Illustrated by Kyrsten Brooker. New York: Henry Holt.

Scharfstein, Sol. 1999. *Understanding Jewish Holidays and Customs: Historical and Contemporary*. Hoboken, N.J.: KTAV Publishing House.

Spies, Karen. 1992. *Our National Holidays*. Brookfield, Conn.: The Millbrook Press.

Viesti, Joe, and Diane Hall. 1996. *Celebrate! In Southeast Asia*. Photographs by Joe Viesti. New York: Lothrop, Lee and Shepard Books.

Winchester, Faith. 1996. *Asian Holidays*. Mankato, Minn.: Capstone Press.

DECEMBER HOLIDAYS AND CELEBRATIONS 6

December is filled with excitement and celebrations, including St. Nicholas Day, Our Lady of Guadalupe Day, Santa Lucia Day, Las Posadas, Advent, Christmas, and Kwanzaa. These celebrations are a time to reflect and pray, but they are also associated with giving and sharing. The month starts with St. Nicholas Day on December 6. St. Nicholas is believed to be the model for Santa Claus. On December 12, the patron saint of Mexico, Our Lady of Guadalupe, is honored. December 13 is Santa Lucia Day, a celebration of light to brighten dark, gloomy winter days. The nine-day celebration of Las Posadas begins on December fifteenth. This celebration is a reenactment of Mary and Joseph's arrival in Bethlehem. Advent begins on the fourth Sunday before Christmas, and for Christians marks a time of preparation for the birth of Jesus (Moehn, 2000). Christians throughout the world celebrate the birth of Jesus on December 25. This is also the day to open presents from Santa Claus and to exchange presents with friends and relatives. The books and media annotated below are grouped into those that commemorate the religious event of Christmas and those that focus on the secular celebration. Gelb (1987) cautions librarians and teachers about the unintended negative consequences of organizing their December curriculum around the celebration of Christmas. These consequences include reinforcing the commercialism of Christmas, emphasizing rewards for behavior, and isolating children of minority faiths (Gelb, 1987). December 26 marks the start of the seven-day celebration of Kwanzaa, a time for African Americans to reflect on and celebrate their heritage. The Winter Solstice occurs on December 20 or 21 and is the shortest, darkest day of the year (Leslie and Gerace, 2000).

ST. NICHOLAS DAY

St. Nicholas Day is celebrated on December 6. St. Nicholas was a fourth-century bishop who gave gifts to children and helped the poor (Moehn, 2000). Upon hearing that a poverty-stricken father was going to force his daughters into slavery, St. Nicholas dropped gold coins down their chimney, some of which landed in the stockings drying beside the fireplace (Henderson and Thompson, 2002). There are many stories about St. Nicholas's generosity and about miracles credited to him (Carus, 2002). Some believe he served as the model for the present-day Santa Claus.

BOOK AND MEDIA CHOICES

Shepard, Aaron. *The Baker's Dozen: A Saint Nicholas Tale.* Illustrated by Wendy Edelson. New York: Aladdin Paperbacks, 1995. Unp.
Grades: P–3. This story is set in a Dutch settlement in colonial America as the people are preparing to celebrate St. Nicholas Day. An old woman comes into a baker's shop and requests a dozen St. Nicholas cookies. When the baker gives her twelve, she tells him that a dozen is thirteen cookies. She refuses to buy the cookies, and after her visit his bakery fails. In a dream one night, he sees St. Nicholas giving out presents, and realizes that his sack of presents never seems to empty no matter how many he gives away. The baker awakens the next morning, bakes more cookies, and resolves to make a dozen thirteen; and once again, his business prospers. Lavish, detailed illustrations make readers want to step into the pictures and examine them in more detail.

Carus, Louise, editor and translator. *The Real St. Nicholas: Tales of Generosity and Hope from around the World.* Wheaton, Ill.: Quest Books, 2002. 214p.
Grades: 1–8. This book contains a collection of St. Nicholas tales for reading aloud. Many of the tales have notes about their origins, and recipes follow some. Aaron Shepard's dramatization, which can be found at www.aaronshep.com, is included in this book. Sources, books for further reading, and a selected bibliography conclude the book.

Tompert, Ann. *St. Nicholas.* Illustrated by Michael Garland. Honesdale, Penn.: Boyds Mills Press, 2000. Unp.

Grades: 2–5. Nicholas's generous spirit and kind heart caused him to be remembered at Christmas by various names, including Santa Claus. This picture-book biography tells of his selflessness and his strong faith. Mixed-media illustrations in a mosaic style beautifully complement the text. An author's note is included.

EXPLORATIONS

1. After reading *The Baker's Dozen: A Saint Nicholas Tale* (Shepard, 1995), discuss with the students how the baker's generosity benefited him. When he stopped worrying about getting his money's worth, he was richly rewarded.

2. A reader's theater script of *The Baker's Dozen: A Saint Nicholas Tale* (Shepard, 1995) can be downloaded on the author's Web site at www.aaronshep.com. Students can rehearse this script and then perform it for other classes during those long afternoons before Christmas when the students are restless and looking forward to winter vacation.

OUR LADY OF GUADALUPE DAY

Our Lady of Guadalupe is the patron saint of Mexico, and she is honored on December 12 in Mexico and in Mexican American communities (Goring, 1995). The Virgin Mary, Mother of Jesus, appeared to Juan Diego on the hill of Tepeyac in Mexico City and told him to have the Catholic bishop build a church on the place where she stood (Harris and Williams, 1998). The bishop told Juan Diego to bring a sign from the Virgin Mary. She directed Juan Diego to go to a cold, rocky hillside to pick roses and return to her with them. She rearranged the roses in his tilma (cloak), and when he went to show them to the bishop an image of the Virgin Mary appeared on the tilma (Harris and Williams, 1998). Juan Diego's tilma is still on display in the Basilica of the Virgin of Guadalupe. It was made of a coarse fabric that usually deteriorates in about ten years; but over four hundred years have gone by and Juan Diego's tilma has not deteriorated, nor has the image of the Virgin Mary faded (de Paola, 1980).

BOOK AND MEDIA CHOICES

de Paola, Tomie. *The Lady of Guadalupe*. New York: Holiday House, 1980. Unp.

Grades: K–3. This is a beautifully told story of Juan Diego's devotion, faith, and persistence. Our Lady of Guadalupe chose him to deliver her message about having a church built on the hill of Tepeyac. It took three visits to the bishop and a special sign before he was believed. The earth-tone illustrations done in pencil, inks, and watercolors capture the look and mood of the Mexican countryside.

EXPLORATIONS

1. In *The Lady of Guadalupe* (de Paola, 1980), students see that Juan Diego's persistence was rewarded in the end. Take the time to talk to the students about being persistent. *Thank You, Sarah!!!: The Woman Who Saved Thanksgiving* (Anderson, 2002) is another book with an example of persistence. Sarah Hale spent thirty-eight years working to have Thanksgiving recognized as a national holiday. (See Thanksgiving.)

2. Have students examine the earth tones used in the illustrations in *The Lady of Guadalupe* (de Paola, 1980). Then, call their attention to the bright yellow, pink, blue, and green colors of Our Lady of Guadalupe herself. Ask students why they think de Paola used those colors for Our Lady of Guadalupe. What is the impact of the bright colors in the illustrations?

SANTA LUCIA DAY

In Sweden, Denmark, Finland, and Norway, as well as Scandinavian communities in America, Santa Lucia Day is commemorated on December thirteenth, and, for many, marks the beginning of the Christmas season (Thompson, 1997). St. Lucy blinded herself on the winter solstice rather than marry a nobleman, and because of her faith God restored her sight (Moehn, 2000). Later in life, she was stabbed in the throat. She is the patron saint of the blind and she guards against throat infections (Moehn, 2000). As the darkness of winter sets in, Santa Lucia is a beacon of light. Traditionally, the oldest girl in the family dresses in a white gown tied with a red sash, wearing a wreath of evergreen lingonberry and candles on her head (Henderson and Thompson, 2002). She awakens the family members and serves them Lussekatts, which are saffron-flavored buns with raisins (Kindersley, 1997).

BOOK AND MEDIA CHOICES

Peterson, Melissa. *Hanna's Christmas*. Illustrated by Melissa Iwai. New York: Harper Festival, 2001. 26p.
Grades: 1–3. After Hanna's family moved from Sweden to America, Hanna was terribly homesick. Even when a large wooden crate from Mormor arrived filled with gifts, Hanna only missed her grandmother more. The crate also held a beautiful white dress with a red sash for Hanna to wear on Santa Lucia Day. However, her mother said that there was no time to make Hanna a crown and to bake Lucia buns. But there is something else in the crate that makes everything work out just right. This is a good fictional introduction to Santa Lucia Day for children.

EXPLORATIONS

1. After learning about Santa Lucia Day or after reading *Hanna's Christmas* (Peterson, 2001), help the students create a simple concept map such as the one below to record what they learned.

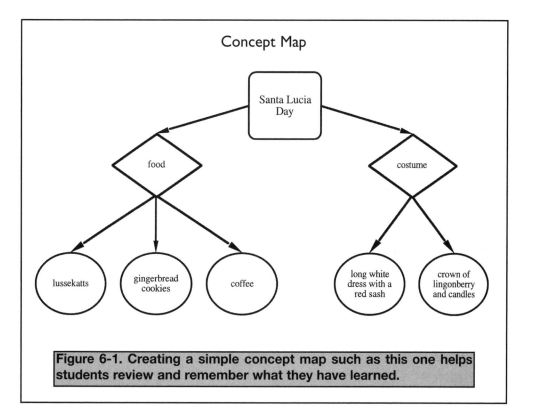

Figure 6-1. Creating a simple concept map such as this one helps students review and remember what they have learned.

2. While *Hanna's Christmas* (Peterson, 2001) introduces children to Santa Lucia Day, it can also be used as a starting point for a discussion on moving and leaving behind friends and loved ones. This can be particularly difficult during holidays. Children need opportunities to share their feelings about the loss and separation they have experienced.

LAS POSADAS

From December 15 to December 23, reenactments of Mary and Joseph's visit to Bethlehem take place in Mexico, Latin America, and parts of the United States. During these nine days the focus is on the birth of Jesus, rather than on gifts and Santa Claus. This celebration began in Spain four hundred years ago at a time when many people could not read. Dramatizing the Biblical journey during a nine-day novena was one way to teach people the story. This celebration helps people focus on the real meaning of Christmas. Communities come together and open their homes, as everyone has a part to play in these reenactments. Each night the holy couple travels to different houses and asks for a place to stay (Moehn, 2000). After being initially turned down, the couple is admitted and the community enjoys good food, music, and dancing.

BOOK AND MEDIA CHOICES

de Paola, Tomie. *The Night of Las Posadas*. New York: Penguin Putnam Books for Young Readers, 1999. Unp.
Grades: P–3. Sister Angie has staged the town's celebration of Las Posadas for many years, and this year her niece, Lupe, and her husband, Roberto, are going to be Mary and Joseph. However, Sister Angie is home sick and Lupe and Roberto are stranded in a snowstorm. A young couple appears from out of the darkness to take the places of Lupe and Roberto. No one knows who they are, but when Sister Angie goes to the church later in the evening to light a candle, she notices that the carving of Mary and Joseph is dusted with snow. At the beginning of the book are a brief glossary and an introduction.

Ciavonne, Jean. Carlos, *Light the Farolito*. Illustrated by Donna Clair. New York: Clarion Books, 1995. Unp.
Grades: K–4. On this the last night of Las Posadas, the peregrinos (pilgrims) will stop at Carlos's home and be welcomed. When his

parents and grandfather are late returning from an errand and darkness falls, Carlos's aunt has him light the farolito (lantern) to light the way for the peregrinos. When the procession arrives at Carlos's house and his grandfather is not there to respond to their cries for "a place to rest," it is up to Carlos to respond. A detailed note at the end of the book explains that communities celebrate Las Posadas in slightly different ways. The colorful acrylic paintings capture Carlos's Mexican heritage and his warm, loving family.

Hoyt-Goldsmith, Dianne. *Las Posadas: A Hispanic Christmas Celebration*. Photographs by Lawrence Migdale. New York: Holiday House, 1999. Unp.
Grades: 4–6. Kristen Lucero and her family host readers as they join a Mexican American community on December fifteenth to begin the nine-day celebration of Las Posadas. This religious celebration reenacts Mary and Joseph's journey through Bethlehem on the night of Christ's birth. Colorful photographs portray the heritage and rituals that accompany this celebration. A glossary and index are included at the end of the book.

EXPLORATIONS

1. After reading *The Night of Las Posadas* (de Paola, 1999), have the students work in small groups to create a story map showing the sequence of events.

2. After reading *The Night of Las Posadas* (de Paola, 1999) and Carlos, Light the Farolito (Ciavonne, 1995), have students work in groups to write their own script to reenact the travels of Mary and Joseph. Remind them that each community has its own variation of the performance, so you do not expect theirs to be exactly like the ones in the books.

ADVENT

Advent begins on the fourth Sunday before Christmas and lasts until Christmas Day. This is a time for praying and reading the Bible to prepare for the coming of Christ (Thompson, 1997). Children count the days until Christmas using an advent calendar. Each day, the children open a door on the calendar to reveal a Christmas scene. Behind the door for Christmas Eve is a Nativity scene (Moehn, 2000). Many churches and families have advent wreaths made of evergreens with four candles. Each Sunday of Advent another candle is lit until, on the last Sunday before Christmas, all four candles are burning.

CHRISTMAS—RELIGIOUS

On December 25 Christians celebrate the birth of Jesus in Bethlehem. Before Jesus was born, Caesar Augustus ordered his people to return to the city where they were born to be counted and taxed. When Joseph and Mary arrived in Bethlehem, all the inns were filled and the only place they could find to stay was the stable of an inn. Jesus was born that night in the stable. Angels announced his birth to shepherds, who came to pay homage to the new king. A bright star appeared over Bethlehem announcing his birth, leading three Wise Men to seek him (Moehn, 2000). The books annotated below tell of the birth of Jesus.

BOOK AND MEDIA CHOICES

Maccarone, Grace. *A Child Was Born: A First Nativity Book*. Illustrated by Sam Williams. New York: Scholastic, 2000. 24p.
Grades: P–2. Told in simple verse form, this book is an excellent introduction to the Christmas story for very young children. The charming illustrations will have children returning to the story again and again.

Hogrogian, Nonny. *The First Christmas*. New York: Greenwillow Books, 1995. Unp.
Grades: P–3. Text from the King James Version of the Bible tells the story of the First Christmas, with small ink drawings of angels hovering nearby. Soft, subtle oil paintings help to tell the story of the birth of the Christ child.

The First Noel: A Child's Book of Christmas Carols to Play and Sing. New York: DK Publishing, 1998. 32p.
Grades: K–4. Thirteen beloved Christmas carols and their musical arrangements are combined with illustrations from artists past and present. The artwork represents a variety of styles and makes this a very special book of carols.

Knowlton, Laurie. *The Nativity: Mary Remembers*. Illustrated by Kasi Kubiak. Honesdale, Penn.: Boyds Mills Press, 1998. Unp.

Grades: K–4. This is the story of Christ's birth told by Mary, his mother. Throughout trying times, she knows that God is with her and she is not afraid. Glowing acrylic paintings accompany the text.

Chorao, Kay. *The Christmas Story*. New York: Holiday House, 1996. 28p.
Grades: K and up. Radiant illustrations evoke quiet, warm feelings for this adaptation of the Christmas story from the King James Version of the Bible. Readers of any age will appreciate this book.

Calhoun, Mary. *A Shepherd's Gift*. Illustrated by Raul Colon. New York: HarperCollins, 2001. Unp.
Grades: 1–3. An orphaned shepherd boy chases after his beloved lamb, which has run off in search of its mother. He follows them to a stable in the hillside, where he discovers the holy family. Basking in the peace and serenity of the stable, he offers his sheep to provide soft fleece for the baby.

Tazewell, Charles. *The Littlest Angel*. Illustrated by Paul Micich. Nashville, Tenn.: Ideals Children's Books, 1991, 1974, 1946. Unp.
Grades: 1–3. Heaven was not quite the same after the arrival of the littlest angel, who was forever getting into mischief and not acting or looking at all angelic. On the night of Christ's birth he gives the Christ child his most treasured possession, a small, shabby box containing items he had collected on earth. God recognizes the significance of the gift and transforms it into the Star of Bethlehem, announcing the Christ child's birth. The book contains glorious full-page illustrations that are easily shared when the story is read aloud to a group of children. A historical note on the story is included.

French, Fiona. *Bethlehem: With Words from the Authorized Version of the King James Bible*. New York: HarperCollins, 2001. 24p.
Grades: 1 and up. Stained-glass illustrations in bright colors add to the attraction of the story. It begins with Caesar Augustus's proclamation that citizens go to their hometown to be counted and taxed. The story ends with Joseph taking his family into Egypt to escape Herod.

The First Christmas. Video. Wyckoff, N.J.: Billy Budd Films, 1998. 20 min.
Grades: 2 and up. The story of the birth of Jesus is told using clay animation with touches of humor. Christopher Plummer narrates the video.

Hodges, Margaret. *Silent Night: The Song and Its Story*. Illustrated by Tim Ladwig. Grand Rapids, Mich.: Eerdmans Books for Young Readers, 1997. 34p.

Grades: 2 and up. This story of the origin of the world's most famous Christmas carol is accompanied by exquisite illustrations. While most people have heard the story before, few realize that Joseph Mohr and Franz Gruber were unintentionally separated from their creation until after Mohr died. In a monastery many years later, Gruber was asked if he knew the origins of the song and was able to relate the story. Known today in many countries and languages, Silent Night is the most sung of all the Christmas carols.

Bierhorst, John, translator. *Spirit Child: A Story of the Nativity*. Illustrated by Barbara Cooney. New York: North-South Books, 2001, 1984. Unp.

Grades: 2–6. This story of Christ's birth combines Nativity elements from medieval folklore, the gospels of Matthew and Luke, and Aztec tradition. Originally, the Aztec people chanted this story to the accompaniment of drums. Cooney's illustrations capture the land and culture of the Aztecs. A note at the end of the book explains that this tale was translated from Psalmodia Christiana, one of the first books published in the New World. It was written in the Aztec language in 1583.

The First Christmas. Illustrated with paintings from the National Gallery, London. New York: Simon and Schuster Books for Young Readers, 1992. 29p.

Grades: 4 and up. Text from the authorized King James Version of the Bible on the birth of Jesus is illustrated with portions of paintings from the National Gallery in London. These magnificent reproductions show students how famous artists envisioned the birth of Christ. The index includes art credits beside thumbnail reproductions of the entire work of art. The credits provide information on the artists' techniques and additional information about the reproduction.

EXPLORATIONS

1. When you finish reading *A Shepherd's Gift* (Calhoun, 2001), reread the last page and ask the students what they think the author is saying. Whose voices did Matthew hear? What child were they singing about? What songs might they have been singing?

2. Children relate to the adventures of the littlest angel. After reading *The Littlest Angel* (Tazewell, 1991), ask children which of his antics remind them of themselves and which ones do not.

3. Before reading *The Littlest Angel* (Tazewell, 1991), ask students what gifts they would bring the Christ child and why they selected the gifts they did. Remind the students that there is no right or wrong answer and that everyone's ideas for gifts will be respected.

4. Before reading *Silent Night: The Song and Its Story* (Hodges, 1997), have students listen to a recording of the song. Ask them what the song means to them. After reading the book, play the song again and have the children sing along.

5. After reading *Silent Night: The Song and Its Story* (Hodges, 1997), ask the students what their favorite part of the story was and why it was their favorite part.

6. While reading *Spirit Child: A Story of the Nativity* (Bierhorst, 2001), have students use small sticky notes to mark passages that they can identify from Aztec and medieval folklore.

7. After reading *The First Christmas*, have the students refer to the information in the index about the artists' techniques. The information helps students develop an appreciation of art and an understanding of techniques they can use in their own artwork.

CHRISTMAS—SECULAR

While Christmas began as a religious holiday, during the Middle Ages it also became a day for fun (Moehn, 2000). Christmas celebrations around the world vary from country to country, and some of the books and media annotated below contain information on the different ways it is celebrated. The symbols, traditions, and rituals of Christmas come from many different countries, and some date back to the Roman holiday of Saturnalia. Santa Claus, Christmas trees, wreaths, mistletoe, holly, reindeer, fruitcakes, parades, and cards are some of the symbols associated with Christmas. This is a time for families and friends to gather and celebrate with by feasting and exchanging presents. Christmas is also a time for peace, harmony, and goodwill.

BOOK AND MEDIA CHOICES

Riley, Linnea Asplind. *The 12 Days of Christmas*. New York: Simon & Schuster Books for Young Readers, 1995. Unp.
Grades: P–2. A note at the beginning of the book contains interesting information about the origins of the gifts in the song. Cut-paper artwork in lively, bright colors depicts the various gifts. Young children are able to see and count all of the gifts. The last double-page spread that folds out to provide room for all fifty-two people, twenty-three birds, and the musical arrangement of the song.

Dr. Seuss. *How the Grinch Stole Christmas*. New York: Random House, 1957. Unp.
Grades: P–3. The hard-hearted Grinch does not want to listen to the happy Who-ville Christmas celebration. He decides to steal the presents and decorations in order to keep Christmas from coming. Much to his surprise, Christmas arrives even without all the trimmings, and suddenly the Grinch realizes the real meaning of Christmas. This book is available on audiocassette and videocassette.

Moore, Clement C. *The Night before Christmas*. Illustrated by Jan Brett. New York: G.P. Putnam's Sons, 1998. Unp.
Grades: P–3. Jan Brett's distinctive, detailed illustrations provide a new look at this familiar poem. Each page is bordered in red and gold, and has Christmas decorations within the borders. In the illustrations, students find two curious stowaways from Santa's workshop who wreak havoc as Santa delivers presents.

First Christmas Record for Children. CD. New York: Sony, 1999.
Grades: P–4. Sing along with Doris Day, Rosemary Clooney, Gene Autrey, and others as they croon twelve Christmas favorites. Some of the songs included on the CD are "Here Comes Santa Claus," "Rudolph the Red-Nosed Reindeer," "Jingle Bells," and "Santa Claus Is Coming to Town."

Grimes, Nikki. *Under the Christmas Tree*. Illustrated by Kadir Nelson. New York: HarperCollins, 2002. Unp.
Grades: P–4. Twenty-three holiday poems with rich, dark illustrations capture the wonder and magic of Christmas symbols and family traditions. Readers find their favorite recollections, from relatives who leave your face tattooed with lipstick, to wild hunts through the house in search of presents, to singing Christmas carols by candlelight in a darkened church.

Van Allsburg, Chris. *The Polar Express*. Boston: Houghton Mifflin, 1985. Unp.
Grades: P–4. The Polar Express is a magical steam train that whisks children to the North Pole on Christmas Eve to see Santa begin his ride through the night. A young boy is given the chance to receive the first gift of Christmas, and he requests a silver bell from Santa's sleigh, which only those who believe in Santa Claus can hear. Exquisite, glowing, mysterious illustrations capture the magic of a very special night. This book is a Caldecott Medal winner. It is available on audiocassette.

Ahlberg, Janet, and Allan Ahlberg. *The Jolly Christmas Postman*. Boston: Little, Brown, 1991. Unp.
Grades: K–3. At this time of peace and goodwill, the postman is delivering greetings to and from familiar storybook characters as they wish one another Merry Christmas. Readers can pull the cards, games, and puzzles out of the envelopes to enjoy. The postman's last stop is the North Pole, where he gets a ride home from Santa as he makes his rounds. Charming verse, delightful pictures, and humorous cards and games make this a book to treasure and enjoy over and over again.

Ammon, Richard. *An Amish Christmas*. Illustrated by Pamela Patrick. New York: Atheneum Books for Young Readers, 1996. Unp.
Grades: K–4. The Amish Christmas is a simple celebration, without Christmas trees, elaborate decorations, and mounds of presents. The celebration begins on Christmas Eve with a school Christmas program. On the first day of Christmas, after chores and breakfast, the family exchanges simple, useful gifts. Then, the relatives gather to share a Christmas feast and visit with one another. The second day of Christmas begins with chores and includes another opportunity for visiting with relatives. Colorful, pastel illustrations beautifully depict the Amish Christmas celebration.

Bunting, Eve. *December*. Illustrated by David Diaz. San Diego: Harcourt Brace, 1997. Unp.
Grades: K–4. On Christmas Eve, a boy and his mother are huddled in their tiny cardboard house celebrating Christmas with a tiny tree and two Christmas cookies he obtained in exchange for thirty-two drink cans. On their wall is the December page from a calendar with a Christmas angel. An old woman appears at their door, and they invite her inside to get warm and share their Christmas celebration. Was the woman an apparition? Was she their Christmas angel? Did

she bring the miracle that found the boy and his mother in their own apartment the next year? Acrylic, watercolor, and gouache paintings on collage backgrounds enhance the mystery surrounding the story.

Shannon, David. *The Amazing Christmas Extravaganza*. New York: Scholastic, 1995. Unp.
Grades: K–4. It all started when Mr. Merriweather hung a single strand of Christmas lights on his house and his neighbor Mr. Clack sneered at them and promised a bigger and better display. The competition was on, and before it was over Mr. Merriweather had created a Christmas extravaganza that brought people from miles around. Cars full of sightseers jammed the streets. When his display plunged the neighborhood into darkness, the neighbors took action.

Rylant, Cynthia. *Christmas in the Country*. Illustrated by Diane Goode. New York: Scholastic, 2002. Unp.
Grades: 1–3. Even if children have never spent Christmas in the country, they can relate to the Christmas of this young girl who lives in the care of her grandparents. Hanging lights on the house, maneuvering around a too-wide or too-tall tree, unpacking Christmas ornaments, singing in church, getting just the right gifts, and gathering with family and friends are some of the memories that are shared in this first person narrative, complemented by warm, amusing pen-and-ink and watercolor illustrations.

Yin. *Dear Santa, Please Come to the 19th Floor*. Illustrated by Chris Soentpiet. New York: Philomel Books, 2002. Unp.
Grades: 1–4. Ever since the accident, Carlos has been confined to a wheelchair. Willy decides that the best thing to cheer him up would be a visit from Santa Claus. But Carlos believes that Santa will not come to his high-rise apartment in New York City, because no one ever wants to come there. Undaunted, Willy sends Santa an e-mail with instructions on how to ring the buzzer to be let into the apartment building. Santa does come, and he leaves the boys with a message of hope, telling them never to stop dreaming.

Hoffmann, Ernest Theodor Amadeus. *Nutcracker*. Illustrated by Renée Graef. Retold by Julie Paschkis. San Francisco, Calif.: Chronicle Books, 2001. 40p.
Grades: 1–5. This is an enduring Christmas tale of a toy nutcracker and a young girl who breaks a spell and changes him into a handsome prince. A CD included in the book contains an audio version of the book and Tchaikovsky's musical score.

Paterson, Katherine. *Marvin's Best Christmas Ever*. Illustrated by Jane Clark Brown. New York: HarperCollins, 1997. 48p.
Grades: 2–4. As Christmas approaches, Marvin wonders what he can give his parents this year. His older sister May always makes wonderful, lasting gifts, but Marvin thinks his are never as good. Finally he thinks of just the right thing, and it turns out to be the perfect Christmas gift. This easy-reader book challenges new readers and makes it possible for them to read on their own. This book is from the I Can Read series.

Erlbach, Arlene. *Christmas: Celebrating Life, Giving, and Kindness*. Berkeley Heights, N.J.: Enslow, 2001. 48p.
Grades: 2–5. A brief description of Christmas is followed by an explanation of how it became a holiday, who Santa Claus is and why he brings gifts to children, how the holiday grew in America, and what Christmas is like now. Marginal notes and pictures add information and appeal to this book. It closes with a craft project, a timeline, a glossary, a bibliography, a list of Internet addresses, and an index. This book is from the Finding Out about Holidays series.

Fradin, Dennis Brindell. *Christmas*. Berkeley Heights, N. J.: Enslow, 2002. 48p.
Grades: 2–5. Beginning with the birth and life of Jesus Christ, this book describes the origins and history of Christmas. Information on the way it became a holiday, the emergence of Saint Nicholas, its arrival in America, and Christmas in our time follow. The book includes a glossary and an index. This book is from A Best Holiday Book series.

Manuel, Lynn. *The Christmas Thingamajig*. Illustrated by Carol Benioff. New York: Dutton Children's Books, 2002. Unp.
Grades: 2–5. Chloe dreads spending Christmas at her grandparents' house because Grandma has died and Christmas will not be the same without her. The house is filled with memories of Grandma, and the memories are depicted in the illustrations. Her parents and her grandfather gradually help her to understand that family traditions are what make it possible to go on with celebrations and to remember those who have died. Grandma created a Christmas ornament she called a Thingamajig, and each year she and Chloe would hang it on the tree and dance. This year her grandfather joins her as she hangs the Thingamajig and dances around the tree.

Buck, Pearl S. *Christmas Day in the Morning*. Illustrated by Mark Buehner. New York: HarperCollins, 2002, 1955. 28p.
Grades: 2 and up. This beautiful old Christmas story has been recently illustrated by the talented Mark Buehner, and recreates within the hearts and minds of readers the true meaning of Christmas, which no amount of money can buy. Young Rob wants to give his father an especially nice gift this year because he has only recently realized the depth of his parents' love, but he has no money. He carefully plans something he can do for his father that will be all his to give: he will get up an hour earlier on Christmas morning and milk the cows all by himself so his father won't have to. It is a wonderful gift and one his father appreciates more than he can express.

Robinson, Barbara. *The Best Christmas Pageant Ever*. Illustrated by Judith Gwyn Brown. New York: HarperCollins, 1972. 90p.
Grades: 3–5. When the six Herdman children decide to take over the Christmas pageant they turn the church topsy-turvy, but in the process they learn about the Christmas story and remind everyone else about the true meaning of Christmas. Readers laugh out loud at the children's antics as they make the pageant one that will not be forgotten. This book is available on videocassette.

Harness, Cheryl. *Papa's Christmas Gift: Around the World on the Night before Christmas*. New York: Simon and Schuster, 1995.
Grades: 3–6. The story is set in 1822, the year the famous poem was written, and shows what was happening around the world during Christmas of that year. An introduction sets the stage for the story by describing what was going on that year, such as the Erie Canal being built, the Zulu Empire being formed, and gaslights being lit in Boston for the first time. This multicultural, historical journey includes Beethoven, the brothers Grimm, and children from diverse countries such as Mexico, Africa, and Italy. This rhyming poem has special appeal to children and the detailed illustrations provide information needed to understand what was happening around the world.

The Nutcracker Music Game. Windows CD-ROM. New York: Music Games International.
Grades: 3–6. This interactive CD-ROM features nine music games and the story of the Nutcracker.

Rollins, Charlemae Hill. *Christmas Gif': An Anthology of Christmas Poems, Songs, and Stories Written By and About African*

Americans. Illustrated by Ashley Bryan. New York: Morrow Junior Books, 1993, 1963. 106p.
Grades: 4 and up. The book begins with a note to readers about the use of the terms "Colored" and "Negro," which were considered acceptable terms when the book was first published. Rather than alter the meanings of the poems, the words have been left unchanged. The message of peace, unity, and goodwill still speaks to us all. In addition to the poems, songs, and stories there are recipes. Works by Langston Hughes, Frederick Douglass, Zora Neal Hurston, and Booker T. Washington are included.

Barth, Edna. *Holly, Reindeer, and Colored Lights: The Story of the Christmas Symbols*. Illustrated by Ursula Arndt. New York: Houghton Mifflin, 2000, 1971. 96p.
Grades: 5 and up. From flying reindeer to dangling mistletoe, this book contains interesting details on the history behind a variety of Christmas symbols. Readers discover that our Christmas traditions have come to us from many countries, and some were originally associated with pagan ceremonies. Simple illustrations in the margins add to the information about this festive celebration.

Christmas Unwrapped: The History of Christmas. Video and DVD. South Burlington, Va.: A & E Television Networks, 1997. 50 min.
Grades: 6 and up. Viewers discover that Christmas can be traced back to pagan festivals celebrating the winter solstice, how the Christmas tree became part of the celebration, and how the patron saint of children evolved into Santa Claus. This is a fascinating look at the origins and traditions associated with this favorite holiday. This video is part of the History of the Holidays series.

Davies, Valentine. *Miracle on 34th Street*. Illustrated by Tomie de Paola. San Diego: Harcourt Brace Jovanovich, 1984. 118p.
Grades: 6 and up. Debuting as a movie in 1946 and then as a book in 1947, this beloved tale of Kris Kringle, the Macy's department store Santa Claus, has been reissued to the delight of all true believers. It is a treasured holiday tradition that is enjoyed each year. This book is available on video.

Dickens, Charles. *A Christmas Carol*. Illustrated by Lisbeth Zwerger. New York: North South Books, 2001. 67p.
Grades: 7 and up. This version of the classic Christmas tale has full-page illustrations that enhance the appeal of the lengthy text to middle school and high school readers. The large picture-book format of

the book also lends an air of accessibility to the text. This book is available on video.

Walsh, Joseph J. *Were They Wise Men or Three Kings?: Book of Christmas Questions*. Louisville, Ky.: Westminister John Knox Press, 2001. 127p.

Grades: 7 and up. This book addresses questions such as: "Who really wrote 'A Visit from St. Nicholas?", "Why does Santa travel by sleigh and reindeer?", and "Is Christmas Commercialism New?" This engaging narrative is filled with fascinating details about Christmas. Readers are sure to find answers to questions they might not think to ask.

EXPLORATIONS

1. While reading *The 12 Days of Christmas* (Riley, 1995), use Inspiration software to create a diagram to record the gifts that were given each day.

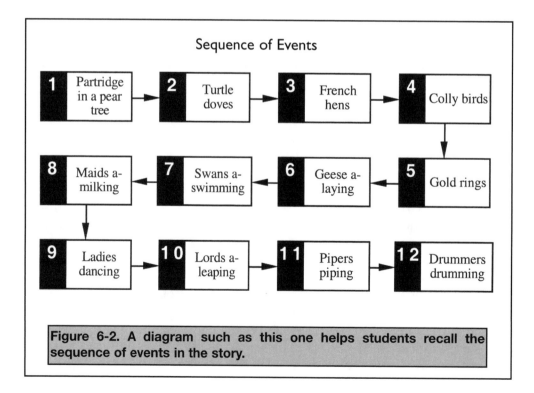

Figure 6-2. A diagram such as this one helps students recall the sequence of events in the story.

2. After reading *How the Grinch Stole Christmas* (Seuss, 1957), ask the children why Christmas came even though the Grinch took all of the Christmas decorations and gifts.

3. *The Night before Christmas* (Moore, 1998) is a story that children probably have heard before. Since they are familiar with the story, it would be a good one to use to model sequence of events.

4. After reading poems from *Under the Christmas Tree* (Grimes, 2002), call students' attention to her use of figurative language such as "faces tattooed with lipstick." Then, have them work as a class to come up with descriptions such as this one to include in their own writing.

5. Before reading *December* (Bunting, 1997), introduce the book by explaining to the students that this is a story to help us remember that Christmas is not just about getting but also about giving.

6. *The Amazing Christmas Extravaganza* (Shannon, 1995) easily lends itself to a variety of discussion topics. Why was Mrs. Merriweather worried? What did the children think of their father's actions? How did the neighbor's feel after they destroyed Mr. Merriweather's extravaganza? What did Mr. Merriweather learn? Why do you think David Shannon wrote this story? What connections can you make to the story?

7. After reading *Christmas in the Country* (Rylant, 2002), return to the text and point out some of the phrases used by Rylant to describe this Christmas celebration. Having students examine these sentences and phrases makes them aware of how words can be used to paint pictures in our heads. Model for them how to use similar phrasing in their own writing. The following are examples of text selections: "Each ornament reminded me of my whole life," "It seemed sometimes like an embarrassed guest."

8. After reading *Dear Santa, Please Come to the 19th Floor* (Yin, 2002), discuss why Santa gave Carlos a basketball and Willy a telescope.

9. After reading *Christmas: Celebrating Life, Giving, and Kindness* (Erlbach, 2001) or *Were They Wise Men or Three Kings?: Book of Christmas Questions* (Walsh, 2001) or watching *Christmas Unwrapped: The History of Christmas,*

have the students discuss in small groups what they learned that surprised them. The students can also compare the information in the different sources and take note of the contradictions or alternate ideas on where the different Christmas symbols originated.

10. Before reading *The Christmas Thingamajig* (Manuel, 2002), introduce it to the children by telling them it is about a child who is having a difficult time celebrating Christmas because her grandmother has died and will not be there this year. Children who have lost family members during the year may not want to hear this story as the memories may be too painful, and their feelings should be considered. (See *Thanksgiving Wish* by Michael J. Rosen for another book about accepting the loss of a grandmother during a holiday celebration.)

11. *The Christmas Thingamajig* (Manuel, 2002), *Bluebird Summer* (Hopkinson, 2001), and *Ghost Wings* (Joosse, 2001) focus on children dealing with the loss of their grandmother. Ask students to compare how the children in the stories coped with the loss of their grandmothers. Lessons learned from these books can help students as they cope with similar losses in their lives.

12. After reading *Christmas Day in the Morning* (Buck, 2002), have the students work in small groups to think of Christmas presents they can give a parent or loved one such as the one Rob gave his father. Then, have a class discussion of their ideas.

13. Some of the works in *Christmas Gif': An Anthology of Christmas Poems, Songs, and Stories Written By and About African Americans* (Rollins, 1993) lend themselves to dramatic interpretations. Students can work together to create presentations for their classmates.

KWANZAA

From December 26 to January 1, African Americans celebrate Kwanzaa. This harvest celebration is also a time for African Americans to celebrate their history, explore their culture, honor their ancestors, and affirm their beliefs and values (Barkin and James,

1994). Kwanzaa was started in 1966 in America by Maulana Karenga and is based on African harvest festivals (Hoyt-Goldsmith, 1993). The celebration is based on seven Kwanzaa principles, one for each day of the holiday, reflecting African family and community values. These principles are: 1) unity, 2) self-determination, 3) collective work and responsibility, 4) cooperative economics, 5) purpose, 6) creativity, and 7) faith. The principles are also associated with seven symbols derived from African culture. Kwanzaa blends elements of other holiday celebrations and includes gifts, resolutions, a harvest feast, candles, and a flag (Hintz and Hintz, 1996). The traditional colors of the celebration are black, representing black citizens around the world; red, representing their struggles; and green, representing the rewards that follow struggles. Another African American holiday is Junkanoo, which was started by slaves who were not allowed to celebrate on Christmas (Winchester, 1996). Their celebrations were held from December 26 to January 1. In the Bahamas Junkanoo is a national festival, but in some places it has been replaced by Kwanzaa.

BOOK AND MEDIA CHOICES

Grier, Ella. *Seven Days of Kwanzaa: A Holiday Step Book*. Illustrated by John Ward. New York: Viking, 1997. Unp.
Grades: P–3. This brief introduction to Kwanzaa invites students to actively participate in reading and learning about this harvest festival. The two-page spreads consist of a full-page color illustration on the left side, and on the right side the principle, the symbol, a graphic of the symbol, and a brief song or chant. Students enjoy singing and chanting as the book is read. Kente cloth designs mark the staggered pages. The book concludes with four recipes to include in a Kwanzaa festival.

Kwanzaa. Video. Bala Cynwyd, Penn.: Schlessinger Video Productions-Library Video Company, 1994. 25 min.
Grades: K–4. In this award-winning video, viewers learn that Kwanzaa is a time for African Americans to rejoice in the strength of their families and friends. Students learn about the seven principles of Kwanzaa and listen to an African folktale about conflict resolution. This video is part of the Holidays for Children series.

Porter, A. P. *Kwanzaa*. Illustrated by Janice Lee Porter. Minneapolis, Minn.: Carolrhoda Books, 1991. 56p.

Grades: 1–3. Students can read this book on their own. The glossary at the beginning of the book introduces new words they will encounter as they read. Throughout the book the illustrations provide clues students need to read and understand the text. The origins of the holiday, the symbols associated with it, and the principles to be practiced are described in easy-to-understand text. The seven principles are written across a two-page spread at the end of the book. At the conclusion of the book is a practical list of the items needed to celebrate Kwanzaa. The author considers this a basic list and encourages readers to start simply and add to their celebration each year.

Kwanzaa for Young People (and Everyone Else!). CD. Gardena, Calif.: Charphelia,1999.
Grades: K–6. Children and adults perform original songs in this joyous celebration of African American heritage.

Hintz, Martin, and Kate Hintz. *Kwanzaa: Why We Celebrate It the Way We Do*. Mankato, Minn.: Capstone Press, 1996. 48p.
Grades: 2–4. A great deal of information on the history, symbolism, and activities for celebrating Kwanzaa are in this brief chapter book. For example, readers learn that the red and green candles in the kinara are lit on alternate days as a reminder that after struggles come rewards. Often the presents children receive from their parents help the children learn about their African American heritage. The book includes a glossary, resources for learning more, and an index. This book is from the Celebrate series.

Freeman, Dorothy Rhodes, and Dianne M. MacMillan. *Kwanzaa*. Berkeley Heights, N.J.: Enslow, 1992. 48p.
Grades: 2–5. Kwanzaa is a Swahili word for "first," representing the first fruits picked at harvest time. During this celebration, people wear bright African-style clothes, eat African food, and listen to African music. The seven principles of Kwanzaa are called Nguzo Saba, and one is celebrated each of the seven days. The book closes with The Seven Principles, a glossary, a note to parents, teachers, and librarians, and an index. This book is from the Best Holiday Books series.

Medearis, Angela Shelf. *Seven Spools of Thread: A Kwanzaa Story*. Illustrated by Daniel Minter. New York: Albert Whitman, 2000. 40p.
Grades: 2–5. Seven bickering, fighting brothers are forced to work together without quarreling in order to spin seven spools of thread

into gold by the end of the day, as stipulated in their father's will. If they fail to do so, they will become beggars. The brothers succeed, and in the course of the story readers learn about the seven principles of Kwanzaa. Bright linoleum-block prints illustrate the story. At the end of the story is information about Kwanzaa, the seven principles, and instructions for creating a simple weaving loom.

Jones, Amy Robin. *Kwanzaa*. Chanhassen, Minn.: The Child's World, 2001. 40p.
Grades: 3–6. Kwanzaa is a time for remembering and reflecting. During the seven-day celebration, African Americans reflect on their accomplishments and remember their ancestors. Bright, colorful photographs depict the preparations and festivities that accompany this celebration. Glossaries, an index, and resources for learning more are included.

Hoyt-Goldsmith, Diane. *Celebrating Kwanzaa*. Photographs by Lawrence Migdale. New York: Holiday House, 1993. 32p.
Grades: 4–6. Readers join thirteen-year-old Andiey's family and learn about the seven principles and symbols of Kwanzaa. On the seventh and last day, the friends and family members participate in the Kwanzaa Karamu, or feast, complete with delectable foods, gifts, and singing. Color photographs of the festivities and family members help readers feel that they are a part of the celebration. A glossary, an index, and a map of Africa conclude the book.

Goss, Linda, and Clay Goss. *It's Kwanzaa Time!* Illustrated by Ashley Bryan, Carole Byard, Floyd Cooper, Leo Dillon, Diane Dillon, Jan Spivey Gilchrist, Jonathan Green, and Jerry Pinkney. New York: G.P. Putnam's Son's, 2002. 71p.
Grades: 4–7. The principles reflected on during the seven days of Kwanzaa are explained in delightful stories that capture students' attention and imagination. Noted illustrators have created pictures to accompany the stories. Games, recipes, crafts, and songs are included for a Karamu (feast) and accompanying festivities. Books for further reading conclude the book.

Karenga, Maulana. *Kwanzaa: A Celebration of Family, Community, and Culture*. Los Angeles, Calif.: University of Sankore Press, 1998. 143p.
Grades: 7 and up. The creator of Kwanzaa, Dr. Maulana Karanega, provides an informative look at this celebration of African culture. The book is a rich resource for information on African culture and the

history, values, and symbols of Kwanzaa. A bibliography and an index are included.

McClester, Cedric. *Kwanzaa: Everything You Always Wanted to Know But Didn't Know Where to Ask*. New York: Gumbs & Thomas, 1994. 44p.
Grades: 7 and up. The book contains information on the history and celebration of Kwanzaa, including recipes for a Kwanzaa Karamu. What makes this slim paperback unique is that it also includes information on hairstyles, fashions, gift ideas, and a shopper's guide.

EXPLORATIONS

1. After reading *Seven Days of Kwanzaa: A Holiday Step Book* (Grier, 1997), have the students work together and prepare one of the recipes at the end of the book. Date and

Figure 6-3. These students are creating Kwanzaa decorations for their classroom celebration.

Peanut Salad or Jambalaya Salad could be mixed in the classroom and each child given a small taste.

2. Write the principles of Kwanzaa on the board and ask the students what they think they mean. Using some of the books annotated above, have them work in small groups, with each group investigating one of the principles. Provide time for the groups to share their information. Then, have each child write their definition of the principle in their own words.

3. After watching *Kwanzaa*, ask students how they can apply the lesson from the folktale on conflict resolution to their own lives.

4. After learning about Kwanzaa, have students plan and create their own Kwanzaa celebration.

5. Kwanzaa is one of several harvest festivals. Others include Thanksgiving, the Jewish Sukkot, and the Chinese Mid-Autumn Moon Festival. Providing students with books on these festivals helps them make connections between the celebrations and begin to recognize the similarities between the cultures.

6. Kwanzaa is just one celebration of light. Others include Diwali, Hanukkah, Las Posadas, Bon Matsuri, and Christmas. The book *Celebrations of Light: A Year of Holidays around the World* (Luenn, 1998) describes twelve celebrations of light. (See Chapter 17.) Have the students read about the celebrations, list them, and then decide how they will group them into categories. For example, the celebrations can be grouped according to those that celebrate spring and those that use light to dispel the darkness of winter. Some of them celebrate death, while others celebrate life.

REFERENCES

Anderson, Laurie Halse. 2002. *Thank You, Sarah!!!: The Woman Who Saved Thanksgiving*. New York: Simon & Schuster.

Barkin, Carol, and Elizabeth James. 1994. *The Holiday Handbook*. New York: Houghton Mifflin.

de Paola, Tomie. 1980. *The Lady of Guadalupe*. New York: Holiday House.

Gelb, Steven A. 1987. "Christmas Programming in Schools: Unintended Consequences." (April 2003) Available: www.tolerance.org/teach/printar.jsp?p=0&ar=391&pi=apg.

Goring, Ruth. 1995. *Holidays and Celebrations*. Vero Beach, Fla.: Rourke Publications.

Harris, Zoe, and Suzanne Williams. 1998. *Piñatas & Smiling Skeletons: Celebrating Mexican Festivals*. Berkeley, Calif.: Pacific View Press.

Henderson, Helene, and Sue E. Thompson. 2002. *Holidays, Festivals, and Celebrations of the World Dictionary*, 3rd ed. Detroit, Mich.: Omnigraphics.

Hintz, Martin, and Kate Hintz. 1996. *Kwanzaa: Why We Celebrate It the Way We Do*. Mankato, Minn.: Capstone Press.

Hopkinson, Deborah. 2001. *Bluebird Summer*. New York: Greenwillow Books.

Hoyt-Goldsmith, Diane. 1993. *Celebrating Kwanzaa*. New York: Holiday House.

Inspiration Ver. 7.5. Inspiration Software, Inc., Portland, Ore.

Joosse, Barbara M. 2001. *Ghost Wings*. San Francisco: Chronicle Books.

Kindersley, Anabel. 1997. *Celebrations*. New York: DK Publishing.

Leslie, Clare Walker, and Frank E. Gerace. 2000. *The Ancient Celtic Festivals and How We Celebrate Them Today*. Rochester, Vt.: Inner Traditions.

Luenn, Nancy. 1998. *Celebrations of Light: A Year of Holidays around the World*. New York: Atheneum Books for Young Readers.

Moehn, Heather. 2000. *World Holidays: A Watts Guide for Children*. New York: Franklin Watts.

Rosen, Michael J. 1999. *Thanksgiving Wish*. New York: The Blue Sky Press.

Thompson, Jan. 1997. *Christian Festivals*. Crystal Lake, Ill.: Heinemann.

Winchester, Faith. 1996. *African-American Holidays*. Mankato, Minn.: Bridgestone Books.

January Holidays and Celebrations 7

For many people, January is a time of new beginnings and the promise of new and exciting things. New Year's Day, Epiphany (Three Kings' Day), and Martin Luther King, Jr. Day are commemorated in January. In the United States and many other countries, January first marks the start of a new year, with resolutions, parades, and football games. For Christians, January 6 is Epiphany (Three Kings' Day, Twelfth Night), which commemorates the visit of the three kings to the Christ child and officially marks the end of the Christmas season. On the third Monday in January Martin Luther King, Jr. Day is celebrated. His civil rights work provided new beginnings for African Americans and other minorities.

NEW YEAR'S DAY

January first means the start of a new year, and for many this is a time to reflect on the past year and resolve to make changes in the year ahead. Making noise on New Year's with noisemakers and fireworks dates back to ancient times, when the noise was believed to scare away evil spirits (Penner, 1993). Some people believe that eating certain foods on New Year's Day will bring good luck and wealth during the year; German-Americans serve sauerkraut and pork, while black-eyed peas and cabbage are common in the American South. In Scotland, bringing a lump of coal and a piece of bread to friends assures that they will be warm and well-fed during the year (Barkin and James, 1994). Football games and parades are other traditions associated with New Year's Day in America. For some cultures and religions, the new year begins at other times of the year. (See Xin Nian, Diwali, Rosh Hashanah, and TET.)

Book and Media Choices

Marx, David F. *New Year's Day*. New York: Children's Press, 2000. 32p.
Grades: P–2. Fireworks, a large lighted ball dropping in New York City's Times Square, the Tournament of Roses Parade, and football games are all ways we celebrate the start of a new year. Photographs and easy-to-read text make this small book appealing to young readers. A picture glossary is included. This book is from the Rookie Read-About Holidays series.

Rattigan, Jama Kim. Dumpling Soup. Illustrated by Lillian Hsu-Flanders. Boston: Little, Brown, 1993. Unp.
Grades: P–3. When a large family gets together to celebrate New Year's, their diverse cultural heritage is also celebrated. The story takes place in Hawaii, where the traditions of many cultures—Korean, Japanese, Chinese, Hawaiian, and haole (white)—all combine to make this New Year's celebration unique. This year, Marisa gets to help make dumplings for the soup. She soon learns how difficult it is to make uniform dumplings, but in the embrace of a loving family she also learns that perfection is not required for love and acceptance. A brief glossary of English, Hawaiian, Japanese, and Korean terms is included.

Ziefert, Harriet. *Amanda Dade's New Years Parade*. Illustrated by S. D. Schindler. New York: Penguin Putnam Books for Young Readers, 2001. Unp.
Grades: P–3. This lively cumulative rhyme describes the New Year's parade led by Amanda Dade. Bright, pastel illustrations capture the excitement of the parade as it moves through the town. This is a book for reading aloud again and again, as students quickly learn the rhyme and chime in as the story is read.

Rau, Dana Meachen. *New Year's Day*. New York: Children's Press, 2000. 47p.
Grades: K–2. This small book is filled with facts about New Year's Day, including the history of the holiday, religious observances of the holiday, and how it is celebrated in different countries, including the United States. One thing many of the celebrations have in common is noise. Making noise is believed to scare away evil spirits. Resources for learning more, a glossary, and an index are included. This book is from A True Book series.

Carrier, Roch. *A Happy New Year's Day*. Illustrated by Gilles Pelletier. Plattsburgh, N.Y.: Tundra Books, 1991. Unp.
Grades: 2–5. The author transports readers back to his childhood as he recounts a joyous New Year's Day celebration in a Canadian village in 1940. On this day family members visited, feasted, and sang. Bright, bold colors light up the full-page illustrations that capture this timeless celebration at the beginning of a new year.

EXPLORATIONS

1. In *Dumpling Soup* (Rattigan, 1993), students discover that the family's celebration is actually a combination of celebrations from the different cultural groups represented by the family members. In *Celebrating Ramadan* (Hoyt-Goldsmith, 2001), students also learn that Ibraheem's fam-

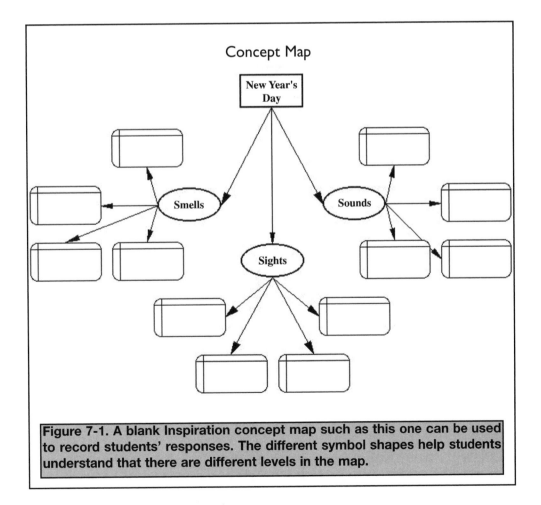

Figure 7-1. A blank Inspiration concept map such as this one can be used to record students' responses. The different symbol shapes help students understand that there are different levels in the map.

ily celebration combines traditions from his mother's homeland of Egypt and his father's homeland of Bosnia. Ask students about different cultures that are represented in their holiday traditions.

2. *New Year's Day* (Rau, 2000) describes the different ways people make noise on New Year's to scare away evil spirits, including setting off fireworks and shooting guns. This information could be used to start a class discussion on the hazards of fireworks and the danger of shooting guns into the air.

3. After reading *A Happy New Year's Day* (Carrier, 1991), have students return to the pictures in the book and use their senses to think about the smells, sounds, and tastes they would be experiencing if they were celebrating with the family.

4. Just as different countries celebrate New Year's Day in different ways, so do different families in the same culture. Inquire as to how the students' families celebrate the day. Then, provide the students time to draw pictures or write about their family's celebrations.

5. One tradition associated with New Year's Day is the making of resolutions. The problem, of course, is trying to keep the resolutions. Suggest to the students that they think up one or two resolutions that the whole class can try to keep. By working on resolutions together, they are more likely to keep them.

EPIPHANY (THREE KINGS' DAY)

January 6 is Epiphany, or El Dia de los Reyes (Three Kings' Day), in honor of the three kings who brought gifts to the baby Jesus. For Latinos, the visit of the Three Kings is similar to the Christmas Eve visit of Santa Claus. The night before Three Kings' Day, children place boxes of grass outside their doors for the kings' camels, and the next morning they discover that the grass has been replaced by gifts (Winchester, 1996). On Three Kings' Day, a cake with a tiny plastic baby baked inside is served. Whoever gets the slice of cake with the baby is named the rey or king (Carlson, 1999). In France, an almond cake with a bean hidden inside is served, and the person who gets the piece of cake with the bean is crowned a king or a queen (France, 1999). In Italy, Twelfth Night is celebrated on January 6. On this night, the kindly witch, Befana, leaves toys and candy for good children (Henderson and Thompson, 2002). For many, January 6 marks the end of the Christmas season and the time to take down the Christmas decorations and store them away until the next year.

BOOK AND MEDIA CHOICES

de Paola, Tomie. *The Legend of Old Befana*. New York: Harcourt Brace Jovanovich, 1980. Unp.
Grades: P–3. When the three kings stop to ask direction on their way to Bethlehem, Old Befana is too busy sweeping to stop and go with them. But as she thinks about what they said about the Child, she decides she should follow them. First, she makes cakes, cookies, and candy to bring to the Child. Then, she sets out searching for the Child, but cannot find the way. On Twelfth Night she still searches for the Child, leaving gifts for the children she encounters along the way.

de Paola, Tomie. *The Story of the Three Wise Kings*. San Diego: G.P. Putnam's Sons, 1983. Unp.
Grades: P–3. When they see a new star announcing the birth of a great king, three kings set out on a journey carrying gifts for the new baby. Simple, elegant verse and richly colored illustrations tell the timeless tale. An author's note at the beginning of the story provides background information on the three kings, how information about them has changed over the centuries, and how the Feast of the Epiphany commemorates their journey.

Slate, Joseph. *The Secret Stars*. Illustrated by Felipe Davalos. Tarrytown, N.Y.: Marshall Cavendish, 1998. Unp.
Grades: K–3. When an icy storm arrives, Sila and Pepe worry that the three kings will not find their way. Their grandmother wraps them in her warm quilt and takes them on a magical journey to discover the secret stars that are all around them in nature, from the icy strands of a spider's web, to the ice on the ranch pond, to the frost on the deer's horns. The story takes place in New Mexico and describes the Latino traditions associated with the holiday.

Carlson, Lori Marie. *Hurray for Three Kings' Day*. Illustrated by Ed Martinez. New York: Morrow Junior Books, 1999. Unp.

Grades: K–4. Drawing upon Venezuelan, Puerto Rican, Mexican, and Latin American traditions, Carlson creates a story of one family's celebration of Three Kings' Day. On the evening before Three Kings' Day, three siblings go out dressed as the three kings and knock on their neighbors' doors in search of the Christ child. Rich oil paintings depict a family and community celebrating. An author's note at the beginning of the book provides information on how this holiday is celebrated in different countries.

EXPLORATIONS

1. At the end of *The Secret Stars* (Slate, 1998), the children are discovering secret stars in the veins on their grandmother's cheeks and notice that the three pines on the hill have been transformed into the Three Kings. Take the students outdoors to find magical stars in nature and have them create sketches of what they see.

2. After reading Hurray for *Three Kings' Day* (Carlson, 1999), ask the students if the children's neighborhood excursion reminded them of a holiday celebrated in America. Then, have the students discuss similarities and differences between Three Kings' Day and Halloween.

3. In *Hurray for Three Kings' Day* (Carlson, 1999), Anna's older brothers complain about her and tease her. Students in the classroom can probably relate to older siblings who do similar things to them. Provide students opportunities to share their stories and help them decide on ways to deal with older siblings.

MARTIN LUTHER KING, JR. DAY

On the third Monday in January, the life of Martin Luther King, Jr. is celebrated. In the days of segregation, African Americans could not attend the same schools, eat in the same restaurants, or drink at the same water fountains as whites. Even on public buses, they were required to sit in the back and give up their seats to whites if they were asked. Dr. King was a peaceful minister who became a civil rights activist, making Americans aware of the injustices faced daily by many citizens. He led marches, made speeches, and believed that voting was the way to make changes in society (Winchester, 1996). He practiced Gandhi's philosophy of nonviolent protest, used methods such as boycotts, marches, and sit-ins to end segregation. In 1955, he led the Montgomery, Alabama bus boycott after Rosa Parks was arrested for refusing to give up her bus seat to a white person. His most famous speech, "I Have a Dream," was given in Washington, D.C. His dream was that African Americans and whites would accept and respect each other. He worked for desegregation and equal rights across the United States (Penner, 1993). In 1963, he was awarded the Nobel Peace Prize for his efforts. He was assassinated in 1968 in Memphis, Tennessee. Martin Luther King, Jr. Day is celebrated with parades and speeches. Some believe a better way to honor Dr. King's memory is to spend the day serving and helping others. (See Labor Day for information on César Chavez, who also used Gandhi's nonviolent tactics.)

BOOK AND MEDIA CHOICES

Rappaport, Doreen. *Martin's Big Words: The Life of Dr. Martin Luther King,* Jr. Illustrated by Bryan Collier. New York: Hyperion Books for Children, 2001. Unp.
Grades: P–4. An author's note and an illustrator's note tell the readers about their connections to Dr. King's life and the importance of his work. Large watercolor and paper collage illustrations beautifully depict the life and work of Martin Luther King, Jr. The illustrations enhance the sparse text that highlights Dr. King's powerful words.

Adler, David A. *A Picture Book of Martin Luther King, Jr.* Illustrated by Robert Casilla. New York: Holiday House, 1991. Unp.
Grades: K–2. Readers learn about Dr. King's family background, his leadership in the bus boycott, and the march on Washington, D.C. in 1963. Learning about his childhood helps young readers understand why he fought for racial equality. Evocative watercolor illustrations portray Dr. King's life and capture the attention of young readers. This book is also available on video and audiocassette.

Martin Luther King, Jr. Day. Video. Bala Cynwyd, Penn.: Schlessinger Video Productions-Library Video Company, 2003. 23 min.
Grades: K–4. The emphasis in this video is on honoring Martin Luther King, Jr.'s memory by serving others. Rather than taking a day off, students are encouraged to spend the day helping others with activities such as food drives. Students learn about Dr. King's

childhood and his role in the civil rights movement. A teacher's guide is available. This video is part of the Holidays for Children series.

Ringgold, Faith. *If a Bus Could Talk: The Story of Rosa Parks*. New York: Simon & Schuster Books for Young Readers, 1999. 30p.
Grades: K–4. As Marcie waits to catch the bus for school, an old bus with no driver pulls up to the bus stop. The bus begins to tell her the story of Rosa Parks, the woman who has been called the "mother" of the civil rights movement. On the bus, Marcie meets others who worked to end segregation in Alabama.

Farris, Christine King. *My Brother Martin: A Sister Remembers Growing Up with the Rev. Dr. Martin Luther King, Jr*. Illustrated by Chris Soentpiet. New York: Simon & Schuster Books for Young Readers, 2003. Unp.
Grades: 1–5. Farris shares intimate glimpses into King's childhood with readers, as she tells about his pranks, listening to family stories, and being surrounded by a loving extended family. Their parents tried to isolate the children from racism as they grew up in segregated Atlanta, Georgia. But when two white neighborhood boys suddenly announce they can no longer play with Martin and his brother because they are "Negroes," his mother tries to explain racism and segregation to young Martin. He replies that one day he "will turn this world upside down." Watercolor illustrations powerfully portray this moving story. At the end of the book is a poem by Mildred Johnson that reminds us of the potential of all children to achieve greatness. An afterword by the author and an illustrator's note conclude the book.

King, Martin Luther, Jr. *I Have a Dream*. New York: Scholastic, 1997. 40p.
Grades: 1 and up. Fifteen Coretta Scott King Award-winning artists contributed illustrations to accompany this moving speech. These evocative illustrations capture the emotions expressed in the speech. The book includes a forward by Coretta Scott King, statements from the artists about their illustrations, and a short biography of Dr. King.

Gnojewski, Carol. *Martin Luther King, Jr., Day: Honoring a Man of Peace.* Berkeley Heights, N.J.: Enslow, 2002. 48p.
Grades: 2–5. The life and teachings of Martin Luther King, Jr. are explored in this book. A civil rights leader, King believed that the laws of the United States were for everyone, regardless of their religion,

race, or gender. The reader learns of the prejudices and biases King endured while he was growing up. Marginal notes and pictures add to the reader's appreciation of the book. It includes a craft project, a glossary, a bibliography, Internet addresses, and an index. This book is from the Finding Out about Holidays series.

Summer, L. S. *The March on Washington*. Chanhassen, Minn.: The Child's World, 2001. 40p.
Grades: 4–8. On Wednesday, August 28, 1963, the March on Washington for Jobs and Freedom was led by Dr. Martin Luther King, Jr. At the end of the day, he addressed the crowd of about 250,000 protestors and delivered his "I Have a Dream" speech. Moving photographs and clear, concise text tell of the events leading up to the March on Washington, the march itself, and the far-reaching impact of the march. The book includes a timeline, a glossary, an index, and resources for learning more.

Pettit, Jayne. *Martin Luther King, Jr.: A Man with a Dream*. New York: Franklin Watts, 2001. 112p.
Grades: 6 and up. As readers learn about the life of this great man, they develop an appreciation for his nonviolent resistance and the changes he brought about by showing people how to stand up for their rights. This biography includes the text of some of Dr. King's speeches, enabling students to read his powerful words for themselves. A chronology, source notes, resources for learning more, and an index are included. This book is from A Book Report Biography series.

Martin Luther King, Jr.: The Man and the Dream. Video. South Burlington, Va.: A & E Television Networks, 1998. 50 min.
Grades: 6 and up. Dr. King's speeches and sermons, combined with interviews with his confidantes, tell the story of his struggle against injustice using nonviolent tactics. This video is part of the A & E Biography: Historical Figures Series and the A & E Biography: Black Studies Series.

EXPLORATIONS

1. Before reading *Martin's Big Words: The Life of Dr. Martin Luther King, Jr.* (Rappaport, 2001), talk to students about the denotations (literal meanings) and connotations (figurative meanings) of words.

2. After reading *Martin's Big Words: The Life of Dr. Martin Luther King, Jr.* (Rappaport, 2001), have students select their favorite quote from the book and discuss the meanings of the words. Then, have the students write their favorite quote at the top of a piece of paper and write a personal reflection on what the words mean to them.

3. Students interested in learning more about Dr. Martin Luther King, Jr. can access a hypertext version of his biography at www.stanford.edu/group/King/about_king. By clicking on the hyperlinked text in the document, students can access additional information and explanations about the terms used. For example, by clicking on the word "nonviolence," students access information on Dr. King's philosophy of nonviolence.

4. After reading *I Have a Dream* (King, 1997), return to the illustrations and share with students the illustrators' comments found at the end of the book. These comments describe what the illustrators depicted in their works.

5. After learning about Martin Luther King, Jr., students can create a timeline of events for the civil rights era. On the Web page "We Shall Overcome: Historic Places of the Civil Rights Movement," at www.cr.nps.gov/nr/travel/civil-rights/sitelist1.htm, students can access pictures and information to help them with their timeline.

6. After reading *The March on Washington* (Summer, 2001), have students return to the chapter "Free at Last" and discuss the impact of television on the civil rights movement. Why do they think that television helped accomplish the goals of the civil rights movement? Have them watch the evening news to determine the present-day impact of television on events in their lives. Provide them time to discuss their thoughts in class the next day.

7. After reading *Martin Luther King, Jr.: A Man with a Dream* (Pettit, 2001), have students visit the Web site of The Martin Luther King, Jr. Center for Nonviolent Social Change at www.thekingcenter.com. By clicking on the Dr. Martin Luther King, Jr. link on the left side of the screen, students can access an audio excerpt from his sermon "The Drum Major Instinct." Hearing his words in his own voice helps students develop a greater appreciation for him.

8. One way to honor Dr. King's memory is by serving others in the community. The Martin Luther King, Jr. Center for Nonviolent Social Change Web site at www.thekingcenter.com has information on service activities sorted by zip code.

9. After viewing *Martin Luther King, Jr.: The Man and the Dream*, engage students in a discussion of why he used nonviolence and why it worked.

REFERENCES

Barkin, Carol, and Elizabeth James. 1994. *The Holiday Handbook*. New York: Houghton Mifflin.

Carlson, Lori Marie. 1999. *Hurray for Three Kings' Day*. New York: Morrow Junior Books.

France. 1999. Danbury, Conn.: Grolier Educational.

Henderson, Helene, and Sue E. Thompson. 2002. *Holidays, Festivals, and Celebrations of the World Dictionary*, 3rd ed. Detroit, Mich.: Omnigraphics.

Hoyt-Goldsmith, Diane. 2001. *Celebrating Ramadan*. New York: Holiday House.

Inspiration Ver. 7.5. Inspiration Software, Inc., Portland, Ore.

Penner, Lucille Recht. 1993. *Celebration: The Story of American Holidays*. New York: Macmillan Publishing.

Winchester, Faith. 1996. *Hispanic Holidays*. Mankato, Minn.: Capstone Press.

FEBRUARY HOLIDAYS AND CELEBRATIONS 8

As winter lessens its grip on the land and crocuses push through the last remains of the snow, we know spring cannot be far behind—or can it? Punxsutawney Phil answers that question on February 2, Groundhog Day. Valentine's Day, on February 14, celebrates lovers and is a time to do something nice for loved ones and friends. The third Monday in February is Presidents' Day, in honor of two of our most famous presidents, George Washington and Abraham Lincoln. Just as Punxsutawney Phil awakens from his hibernation, the earth begins to emerge from its long winter dormancy.

GROUNDHOG DAY

On February 2, tourists and television reporters descend on Punxsutawney, Pennsylvania to watch a groundhog named Punxsutawney Phil poke his head out of his hole (Barkin and James, 1994). If Phil sees his shadow, winter will last for six more weeks; if he does not, then spring will arrive shortly. This celebration was brought to America by early German settlers, who in Germany watched for a badger to come out of its burrow (Henderson and Thompson, 2002). While this is not a scientific way to predict the weather, it is a well-established tradition that provides a reason for a celebration.

BOOK AND MEDIA CHOICES

Freeman, Don. Gregory's *Shadow*. New York: Penguin Putnam Books for Young Readers, 2000. Unp.
Grades: P–2. With Groundhog Day approaching, Gregory is frantic because he has lost his shadow. Young readers empathize with

Gregory and his shadow as the two search for one another. Yet, once they have found each other, they realize if they are seen together on Groundhog Day, the farmers will not be happy since it means winter will linger. Simple, uncluttered illustrations help students focus on Gregory's problem and understand his dilemma.

Koscielniak, Bruce. *Geoffrey Groundhog Predicts the Weather*. Boston: Houghton Mifflin, 1995. Unp.
Grades: P–3. When Geoffrey awakens on February second, he reports his predictions about the weather to the newspaper. The next year he awakens to discover cameras, lights, and a crowd outside of his door, and with all the lights he cannot determine if he sees his shadow or not. When the town demands an answer, he promises a response, but he is not sure what to say. He turns for help to his mother, since she checks for her shadow every Groundhog Day. Ink drawings with watercolor washes enhance the text.

Kroll, Steven. *It's Groundhog Day*. Illustrated by Jeri Bassett. New York: Scholastic, 1991. Unp.
Grades: K–3. As winter approaches, Godfrey Groundhog settles in for his long winter nap and sets his alarm for 7:30 a.m. on February second. Roland Raccoon knows that if Godfrey does not see his shadow when he wakes up there will be an early spring, which will ruin Roland's ski resort business. When Godfrey wakes up, Roland kidnaps him and stuffs him in burlap bag to keep him from going above ground. Godfrey manages to escape, and does not see his shadow. Roland's friends console him by convincing him to join them at the beach and open a hot dog stand.

Levine, Abby. *Gretchen Groundhog, It's Your Day*. Illustrated by Nancy Cote. Morton Grove, Ill.: Albert Whitman, 2002. Unp.
Grades: K–3. Great-Uncle Gus is too old to show up on Groundhog Day, so it is time for Gretchen to take over. She is too shy to appear before the crowd, and the town soon discovers that no groundhog will be emerging. The daughter of the town historian saves the day by bringing Gretchen papers from previous groundhogs, beginning with Goody Groundhog, who sailed to America on the Mayflower. As Gretchen goes through the papers she discovers that all of her ancestors were nervous about appearing in front of the crowd. Gretchen decides that she too can gather enough courage to appear.

Groundhog Day. Video. Bala Cynwyd, Penn.: Schlessinger Video Productions-Library Video Company, 2003. 23 min.

Grades: K–4. Celebrate Groundhog Day by introducing students to Punxsutawney Phil and the legend surrounding his unique weather-predicting talents. Along the way, students learn about changing seasons, hibernation, and shadows. A teacher's guide is included. This video is part of the Holidays for Children series.

The Story of Punxsutawney Phil: Fearless Forecaster. Video. St. Louis, Mo.: Coronet, 1991. 10 min.
Grades: K–6. Whether or not Phil appears on Groundhog Day really depends on his pre-hibernation preparations. This short film introduces Phil and his famous predictions.

McMullan, Kate. *Fluffy Meets the Groundhog*. Illustrated by Mavis Smith. New York: Scholastic, 2001. Unp.
Grades: 1–2. The students in Ms. Day's class decide that if a groundhog can predict the weather, so can their guinea pig, Fluffy. Three other guinea pigs are invited to join in the festivities for Groundpig Day. The students write poems making predictions based on the groundpigs' antics. On February second, the guinea pigs are turned loose on the playground so they can make predictions about the end of winter. Fluffy runs away and winds up down a groundhog's hole. Young readers are delighted to discover how Fluffy saves the day for the timid groundhog. From the Hello Reader! Level 3 series.

EXPLORATIONS

1. Before reading *Gregory's Shadow* (Freeman, 2000), explain to students that if the groundhog sees his shadow on February second, then there will be six more weeks of winter. If he does not see his shadow, winter will soon end. This explanation can be found at the beginning of the book.

2. After reading *Gregory's Shadow* (Freeman, 2000), discuss how Gregory feels safe when he has his shadow. Then, provide students with opportunities to talk about things that make them feel safe.

3. After reading *Geoffrey Groundhog Predicts the Weather* (Koscielniak, 1995), talk to students about how Geoffrey knew he could call his mother to help him with his dilemma. Ask students to think about things they know they can count on their mother to help them do. Write their responses on the board and then provide students time to write

about a time their mother helped them. These responses can be saved and the students can give them to their mothers on Valentine's Day.

4. After reading *It's Groundhog Day* (Kroll, 1991), ask students what they think of Godfrey Groundhog and Roland Raccoon. Tell them to think carefully about their responses, because they will have to provide information from the story to support their responses. They can simply write their opinion and support for the opinion on a piece of paper or complete a chart such as the one below.

Opinions		
Character	Opinion of the Character	Support for the Opinion
Godfrey Groundhog		
Roland Raccoon		

Figure 8-1. As students read they form opinions about characters in the story. This activity asks them to record their opinions and then provide support for their opinions based on the text.

5. Before reading *Gretchen Groundhog, It's Your Day* (Levine, 2002), assure students that it is natural to be afraid of appearing before an audience. After reading the book talk to students about ways to relax before having to speak, such as taking slow, deep breaths and spending a few quiet minutes alone.

6. At end of January, show the students the video *Groundhog Day*. Next, have the students make predictions on whether or not Punxsutawney Phil will see his shadow on February second. Then, have the students write their predictions on slips of paper with their names. Tally their results and place them on a chart in the classroom. An extension of this

would be to allow students to do research on the Internet and change their predictions if they can use their research to justify the changes.

7. Just as the students in Ms. Day's class in *Fluffy Meets the Groundhog* (McMullan, 2001) write poems about their class guinea pig, students can write poems about the antics of the classroom pet.

VALENTINE'S DAY

Were there one or two St. Valentines? No one knows for sure (Fradin, 1990). One story is about a priest who disobeyed the Roman emperor Claudius and performed marriage ceremonies for Roman soldiers. Claudius did not want his soldiers to marry, because married men were unwilling to leave their families and fight. Valentine was imprisoned and put to death for defying the emperor for the sake of love and marriage. Another story tells of a priest who was jailed for helping Christians. While he was imprisoned, he was befriended by children, including a blind girl. Before he was put to death on February 14, he sent her a note signed "From your

Valentine." A miracle occurred and she was able to see and read the note. Valentine's Day also has its origins in the Roman festival of Lupercalia, held on February 15 to celebrate the beginning of spring (Flanagan, 2002). Today, Valentine's Day is for sharing love and friendship (Bulla, 1999). Since this day is a celebration for lovers, it is not surprising that the books provide female readers with variety of ways to find out the name of their future husband. For example, one suggests that the first male they see on Valentine's Day will become their husband. The heart, representing love, and the color red are familiar symbols of this day.

BOOK AND MEDIA CHOICES

Capucilli, Alyssa Satin. *Biscuit's Valentine's Day*. Illustrated by Pat Schories. New York: HarperCollins, 2001. 16p.
Grades: P–K. This flap book follows all the mischief and misadventures in Biscuit's day as he tries to help his owner deliver her valentines. The brightly colored illustrations add to the attraction of this book for very young children.

Roth, Carol. *My Little Valentine*. Illustrated by Jennifer Beck Harris. New York: HarperFestival, 2003. 18p.
Grades: P–K. Rhythmic, silly text is accompanied by warm, tender illustrations to make up this comforting book about the special love between a parent and child. This board book will be especially attractive to the very young child.

Schoberle, Cecile. *Big Pig Saves Valentine's Day*. New York: HarperFestival, 2003. 20p.
Grades: P–K. Big Pig is what an older sister calls her baby brother in this flap book, because he gets into such big messes and so much trouble. After she makes valentines and cookies for all of her friends at school, Big Pig snatches them out of her backpack when she is not looking. Distraught at finding the cards missing, she believes she has lost them. But Mother and Big Pig show up and save the day.

Carr, Jan. *Sweet Hearts*. Illustrated by Dorothy Donohue. New York: Holiday House, 2003. 26p.
Grades: P–1. The collage illustrations are just perfect for this simple story of a little panda bear making and hiding valentines for his family, even the dog. The book begins with a brief history of Valentine's Day and closes with instructions on how to make simple valentines.

Jackson, Alison. *The Ballad of Valentine*. Illustrated by Tricia Tusa. New York: Dutton Children's Books, 2002. 30p.
Grades: P–2. Written in the meter of the folksong "Clementine," this delightful story of a shy suitor and his love object, Valentine, is one that young readers will want to sing-along to. Colorful illustrations with charming characters capture young readers' attention.

Rockwell, Anne. *Valentine's Day*. Illustrated by Lizzy Rockwell. New York: HarperCollins, 2001. 32p.
Grades: P–2. All of the children in school were making very special valentines to send to a student who had moved far away from their school. They used lace doilies, glitter, glue, and many other things to make these special valentines. In addition, before Valentine's Day they received a valentine from their friend Michiko in Japan, along with a photograph of her with her grandparents.

Cazet, Denys. *Minnie and Moo: Will You Be My Valentine?* New York: HarperCollins, 2003. 48p.
Grades: P–3. Donning Cupid outfits, the comic cow couple write and deliver valentine poems to all the animals in the farmyard. Unfortunately, the poems get mixed up and are delivered, by bow and arrow, to the wrong animals and to the farmer and his wife.

Cole, Babette. *Truelove*. New York: Dial Books for Young Readers, 2002. Unp.
Grades: P–3. Truelove, a warm, adorable puppy, feels neglected when a new baby arrives and gets all the attention. Everything Truelove does to try to regain the family's love leads to disaster, but in the end, he discovers that there is enough love to go around.

de Groat, Diane. *Roses Are Pink, Your Feet Really Stink*. New York: Morrow Junior Books, 1996. Unp.
Grades: P–3. This year Gilbert and his classmates are exchanging handwritten valentine cards. Gilbert has to write something nice about each of his classmates on their cards. For most of his class-mates, it is easy to think up something nice to say. But for the boy who tweaked his nose and the girl who laughed at his glasses, Gilbert cannot think of anything nice. His solution to his dilemma angers everyone in the classroom. In the end, Gilbert and his two classmates resolve their differences and Gilbert makes them each new valentine cards.

Poydar, Nancy. *Rhyme Time Valentine*. New York: Holiday House, 2003. Unp.
Grades: P–3. Ruby loves Valentine's Day, and loves making her own valentines and dressing all in red on the special day. But on the way to school, something happens to her valentines, and she arrives dressed in red but feeling blue. At recess, she tries to make more valentines, but there is no red construction paper. In the end, Ruby's ingenuity saves the day.

Maitland, Barbara. *The Bookstore Valentine*. Illustrated by David LaRochelle. New York: Dutton Children's Books, 2002. 48p.
Grades: K–3. This delightful story revolves around a bookstore owner, his cat, a ghost, and an employee hired just for the Valentine's Day sale. They discover that they seem to be perfect for each other, and with the help of Cobweb the cat and the "ghost" they discover they have similar thoughts about each other. This "love story" will appeal to young readers.

Park, Barbara. *Junie B. Jones and the Mushy Gushy Valentine*. Illustrated by Denise Brunkus. New York: Random House, 1999. 69p.
Grades: 1–2. Kindergartner Junie B. Jones discovers that Valentine's Day is about sharing special cards with your classmates. Her enthusiasm for decorating the large valentine box earns her a chance to sit in her chair and watch the other students cut and paste decorations on the box. On Valentine's Day at the bottom of the box is a large, mushy card for her from her secret admirer. In the end, she discovers who her secret admirer is and that he thinks she is what makes the classroom "sparky."

Rau, Dana Meachen. *Valentine's Day*. New York: Children's Press, 2001. 47p.
Grades: 1–3. Large print, easy-to-read text, and color photographs ensure that students can read and understand this book on their own. They learn about valentine legends, discover the meanings behind valentine symbols, and find suggestions for sharing Valentine's Day with loved ones. The book includes resources for finding out more, a glossary, and an index. This book is from A True Book series.

Flanagan, Alice K. *Valentine's Day*. Illustrated by Shelley Dieterichs. Minneapolis, Minn.: Compass Point Books, 2002. 32p.
Grades: 2–4. From the stories of Saint Valentine to paper valentines, this is a concise history of the celebration. Readers learn about

Valentine's Day traditions in different countries and why hearts, flowers, cupids, and birds are traditional symbols of this celebration. Also included in the book are ideas for celebrating the holiday, such as doing something special for someone you love. This chapter book concludes with a glossary, resources for learning more, and an index. This book is from the Holidays and Festivals series.

Stevenson, James. *A Village Full of Valentines*. New York: Greenwillow Books, 1995. 39p.
Grades: 2–4. A loving band of animals celebrates Valentine's Day in all sorts of different ways in the short chapters in this book. From the world's tiniest valentine to one that circles the whole village, these animals share an assortment of valentines.

Bulla, Robert Clyde. *The Story of Valentine's Day*. Illustrated by Susan Estelle Kwas. New York: HarperCollins, 1999, 1965. Unp.
Grades: 2–5. Bulla traces the origins of Valentine's Day back to the Roman holiday Lupercalia, "feast of Lupercus." Lupercus was a Roman god who protected farmers, their crops, and their animals. As Bulla recounts the history of this holiday, he includes customs used throughout the ages to celebrate this day of love and friendship. Colorful illustrations filled with red and pink help to tell the history. The book concludes with directions for making "pinprick" valentines, acrostic valentines, and a recipe for valentine cookies.

Landau, Elaine. *Valentine's Day: Candy, Love, and Hearts*. Berkeley Heights, N.J.: Enslow, 2002. 48p.
Grades: 2–5. When we think of Valentine's Day, we often think of cards, flowers, and candy. On this holiday everyone wants to share with loved ones, or at least with very good friends. Readers learn about the fun and interesting things they can do to celebrate this holiday, about Saint Valentine, and about early customs and stories. Margin notes and pictures make the book more attractive to youngsters. The book includes a craft project, a glossary, a bibliography, Internet addresses, and an index. This book is from the Finding Out about Holidays series.

Maguire, Gregory. *Four Stupid Cupids*. New York: HarperCollins, 2002. 183p.
Grades: 3–6. When an ancient Grecian urn arrives from her aunt, Fawn takes it to school to show her friends. When the urn breaks, four cupids emerge, unfold their wings, and begin buzzing around the classroom. Fawn and her classmates devise a plan to have the

cupids make a love match for their teacher, and in the process learn about love themselves.

Young, Ed. *Voices of the Heart*. New York: Scholastic, 1997. Unp.
Grades: 3 and up. Twenty-six Chinese characters, each containing the symbol for the heart, are each presented in collage. These characters represent a feeling or emotion of the heart, and each is explained in the words beside the collage. There are layers of meaning to uncover in the symbols, and each can be a starting point for a classroom discussion. For example, "Forgiveness—The heart accepts everything." This symbol combines the symbols for woman, mouth, and heart.

Barth, Edna. *Hearts, Cupids, and Red Roses: The Story of the Valentine Symbols*. Illustrated by Ursula Arndt. New York: Houghton Mifflin, 2001, 1972. 96p.
Grades: 5 and up. Discover the amazing stories behind the symbols associated with Valentine's Day in this fact-filled book, and learn about the history of this special day for loving and caring for others. Simple illustrations accompany the text.

EXPLORATIONS

1. After reading *Truelove* (Cole, 2002), have students make a list of ways that their family members show that they love them. Then, have them create a second list of ways they show they love their family members.

2. Before reading *Truelove* (Cole, 2002), share with students some of the sayings in the book such as "Love cures all hurt" and "Love gives you strength." Ask students what they think these statements mean. Then, give them time to illustrate their favorite saying.

3. In *Rhyme Time Valentine* (Poydar, 2003), Ruby saves her day by sharing the box of candy hearts her parents had given her that morning with her classmates. Share some candy hearts with the students as you read them aloud. Older students can be divided into small groups and each group given a small stack of candy hearts. Have the group read the sayings to each other, and then have them decide which saying best fits each person in the group and why.

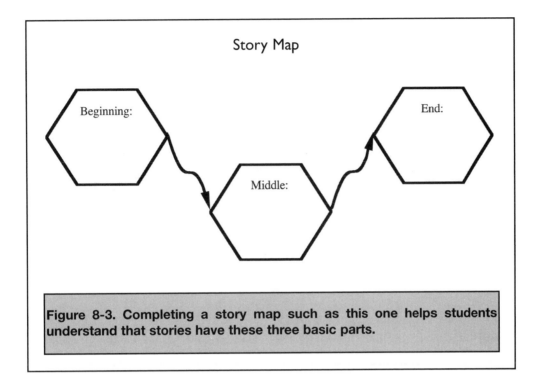

Story Map

Beginning:

Middle:

End:

Figure 8-3. Completing a story map such as this one helps students understand that stories have these three basic parts.

4. After reading *The Bookstore Valentine* (Maitland, 2002), work with the students to create a simple story map showing the beginning, middle, and end of the story.

5. After reading *Junie B. Jones and the Mushy Gushy Valentine* (Park, 1999), ask students to note which part they thought was the funniest, which part surprised them, and which part was exciting.

6. After reading *A Village Full of Valentines* (Stevenson, 1995), have students return to the text and write down all the different valentines the animals shared. Then have them rank the valentines from their favorite to their least favorite. Let them work in small groups to compare their rankings and to discuss their reasons for their rankings. Remind them that there are no right or wrong answers.

7. After reading *The Story of Valentine's Day* (Bulla, 1999), share the acrostic valentines at the end of the book with students. Then have students work together to create their own acrostic valentines.

8. After reading *Four Stupid Cupids* (Maguire, 2002), divide the students into small groups of three or four and have them discuss their favorite parts of the story and tell why it was their favorite part. Then, have them write about their favorite part, justifying their selection.

9. Provide the students with a collection of books on Valentine's Day such as *The Story of Valentine's Day* (Bulla, 1999); *Hearts, Cupids, and Red Roses: The Story of the Valentine Symbols* (Barth, 2001); and *Valentine's Day: Candy, Love, and Hearts* (Landau, 2002). Ask them to research the different ideas about the origin of the holiday.

PRESIDENTS' DAY

The third Monday in February is set aside to honor George Washington and Abraham Lincoln. These two presidents were both born in February, both led the country through war, and both believed in freedom and equality (Barkin and James, 1994). George Washington was commander in chief of the army during the Revolutionary War. When the government of the new nation was formed, he was elected the first president of the United States and served two terms. His birthday was originally celebrated by the nation with parades and balls (Spies, 1992). Abraham Lincoln was our sixteenth president, and served from 1861 to 1865. He led the nation through the Civil War and, after the Civil War, hoped to reunite the North and the South. Five days after the end of the Civil War, he was assassinated. These presidents are remembered for the leadership they provided the nation during times of crisis.

BOOK AND MEDIA CHOICES

Presidents Day. Video. Bala Cynwyd, Penn.: Schlessinger Video Productions-Library Video Company, 2003. 23 min.
Grades: K–4. Stories, songs, and crafts help children learn about Presidents' Day, President George Washington, and President Abraham Lincoln. They also learn about how Americans elect their president, the duties of the president, and about the White House. A teacher's guide is available. This video is part of the Holidays for Children series.

Gaines, Ann Graham. *George Washington: Our First President*. Chanhassen, Minn.: The Child's World, 2002. 48p.
Grades: 2–4. Gaines provides a brief, yet thorough introduction to the life of our first president, from his childhood, to his leadership of the army as the colonies fought for independence, to his presidency, and eventually his retirement at his beloved Mount Vernon. A two-page spread discusses Washington's views on slavery and his actions with regard to his own slaves. Photographs, reproductions, maps, and sidebars enhance the material presented in the text. The book includes a timeline, a glossary, a listing of the presidents, facts about presidents, resources for learning more, and an index.

Fradin, Dennis B. *Washington's Birthday*. Berkeley Heights, N.J.: Enslow, 1990. 48p.
Grades: 2–5. Illustrations, photographs, and a survey completed by George Washington fill the pages of this brief biography. Four short chapters describe why and how Washington's Birthday is celebrated. A glossary and an index are included. This book is from the Best Holiday series.

MacMillan, Dianne M. *Presidents Day*. Berkeley Heights, N.J.: Enslow, 1997. 48p.
Grades: 2–5. George Washington and Abraham Lincoln are two of our most beloved and famous presidents. Because both of them were born in February, we use this month to honor and celebrate their lives. We learn a little about their childhoods and as well as the accomplishments of their presidencies. The book includes a note to parents, teachers, and librarians, a glossary, and an index. This book is from the Best Holiday Books series.

Giblin, James Cross. *George Washington: A Picture Book Biography*. Illustrated by Michael Dooling. New York: Scholastic, 1992. 48p.
Grades: 3–5. Throughout his life, Washington faced a series of struggles and hardships. His perseverance and determination were tested as he led the colonies in their revolt against England and their struggle to form a new nation. The book concludes with a section providing additional information about Washington and his day, including a map of the colonies, important dates, the story of cherry tree, Washington's Rules of Good Behavior, information on historic sites, and an index.

Freedman, Russell. *Lincoln: A Photobiography*. New York: Scholastic, 1987. 150p.
Grades: 3–6. Carefully selected photographs and reproductions, combined with extensively researched text, make this Newbery Award-winning book an outstanding biography for students. A sample of Lincoln's words, historic sites, information on books about Lincoln, picture credits, and an index are included.

Harness, Cheryl. *Abe Lincoln Goes to Washington, 1837–1865*. Washington, D.C.: National Geographic Society, 1996. Unp.
Grades: 3–6. From his law practice in Springfield, Illinois to his years in the White House, readers are treated to an engaging account of the life of this President, who led the nation through the turmoil of the Civil War and sought a peaceful reconciliation at its end. Richly detailed, realistic illustrations fill the pages. Lincoln's words help to tell his story and help readers understand why Americans honor and respect this president.

Sullivan, George. *Abraham Lincoln*. New York: Scholastic, 2000. 128p.
Grades: 4–6. This biography includes excerpts from Lincoln's own writings and speeches, enabling readers to fully appreciate the character, wisdom, and humility of our sixteenth president. Black-and-white reproductions and photographs help to enhance readers' understanding of Lincoln's life. A chronology, a bibliography, resources for more information, and an index are included. This book is from the In Their Own Words series.

Sandler, Martin W. *Presidents*. New York: HarperCollins, 1995. 94p.
Grades: 4–8. Photographs and illustrations from the vast collection of the Library of Congress, combined with interesting snippets of information about the personal lives of the presidents, make this a wonderful resource for enticing students to learn about the presidents. A list of the presidents, information on the Library of Congress, and an index conclude the book. This is A Library of Congress book.

St. George, Judith. *So You Want to Be President?* Illustrated by David Small. New York: Philomel Books, 2000. 52p.
Grades: 4 and up. Cartoon-like illustrations accompany a variety of interesting facts and details about the men who were once president of the United States. For example, William Taft was so large that he had to have a custom-built tub installed in the bathroom. At the end

of the book, readers find brief biographical sketches of the presidents. This book is Caldecott Medal winner and is available on video.

Foster, Genevieve, and Joanna Foster. *George Washington's World*, Expanded Edition. Sandwich, Mass.: Beautiful Feet Books, 1997. 356p.
Grades: 5 and up. Each chapter focuses on a time in Washington's life, and readers learn what was happening in the world during that time. Each chapter begins with a collection of small drawings of prominent people mentioned during the time period. Explorations, discoveries, and ideas pertinent to the period are briefly described. These detailed, informative visuals enable readers to make connections between events happening in America during Washington's lifetime and in other parts of the world. A bibliography and an index are included

Marrin, Albert. *George Washington and the Founding of a Nation*. New York: Dutton Children's Books, 2001. 276p.
Grades: 6 and up. This well-researched biography of Washington provides information about his life and the events unfolding during his lifetime, but focuses on his military career. Quotes, illustrations, and maps provide additional information that helps readers understand the events examined in the text. Resources for learning more and an index conclude the book.

EXPLORATIONS

1. Introduce the video *Presidents Day* by playing the first few minutes, then stopping the video to have the students make predictions about what they will learn from it. After watching the video, discuss their predictions and have them determine which of their predictions were correct.

2. Prior to viewing *Presidents Day*, have the students brainstorm a list of things they think are the duties of the president. While watching the video, have them take notes on what they learn about the duties of the president. After watching the video, ask them about the duties that surprised them or about the duties they put on their list that were not mentioned in the video.

3. After reading about Washington's views on slavery in *George Washington: Our First President* (Gaines, 2002),

provide students an opportunity to discuss why a man who fought for liberty and justice also owned slaves. This is a complicated question, but it should start students thinking about how a country that valued freedom could allow slavery.

4. Readers interested in learning more about George Washington's home, Mount Vernon, can access information on the Internet at www.mountvernon.org.

5. At the end of *George Washington: A Picture Book Biography* (Giblin, 1992), readers find some of the Rules of Good Behavior that Washington copied from a book. Share with the students that George Washington did not have many opportunities to go to school, and that he was interested in self-improvement. Copying these rules and applying them was one of the ways he tried to improve himself. Ask the students to read over the rules and determine which ones are still applicable today.

6. Before reading *Lincoln: A Photobiography* (Freedman, 1987), have students carefully examine the photographs and take notes on what they learn about Abraham Lincoln just by looking at the pictures and reading the captions. Students may benefit from having the teacher or librarian model how to take notes from text.

7. After reading *Abe Lincoln Goes to Washington, 1837–1865* (Harness, 1996) and/or *Abraham Lincoln* (Sullivan, 2000), have students make a list of the reasons he is considered one of the greatest presidents. Remind them that they need to be able to support their responses with information from the book.

8. After reading *Abraham Lincoln* (Sullivan, 2000), have students return to page ninety-three and examine the text of Lincoln's Gettysburg address. Remind students that earlier in the biography on page six, Sullivan noted that Lincoln "used simple language to express great ideas." Have students discuss the simple words in this address that express important ideas.

9. Place the names of the presidents in a paper sack and have students randomly select one of the names. Then, using *Presidents* (Sandler, 1995) and *So You Want to Be President?* (St. George, 2000), have the students write a short report on the president to present to their classmates.

After the presentations, have the students discuss which president was the most interesting.

10. Students can use the information in *George Washington's World*, Expanded Edition (Foster and Foster, 1997) to create a large wall mural depicting Washington's life and the events going on around the world during his life time. This visual will help students make connections between what they have learned in American history and in world history.

11. After learning about the presidents, students can draw pictures of the presidents and create a Presidents' Day bulletin board.

REFERENCES

Barkin, Carol, and Elizabeth James. 1994. *The Holiday Handbook*. New York: Clarion Books.

Bulla, Robert Clyde. 1999. *The Story of Valentine's Day*. New York: HarperCollins.

Flanagan, Alice K. 2002. *Valentine's Day*. Minneapolis, Minn.: Compass Point Books.

Fradin, Dennis Brindell. 1990. *Valentine's Day*. Hillside, N.J.: Enslow Publishers.

Henderson, Helene, and Sue E. Thompson. 2002. *Holidays, Festivals, and Celebrations of the World Dictionary*, 3rd ed. Detroit, Mich.: Omnigraphics.

Spies, Karen. *Our National Holidays*. 1992. Brookfield, Conn.: The Millbrook Press.

PART IV. SPRING

SPRING CELEBRATIONS AND HOLIDAYS WITH MOVEABLE DATES

9

Following the dark, dormant, chill of winter, spring is a time of renewal and growth. Hibernating plants and animals awaken, grow, and reproduce. Seemingly overnight, trees sprout shiny, green leaves and plants explode with colorful, fragrant blossoms. The drab, gray days of winter give way to sunshine and warmth. The world over, people celebrate the rebirth and renewal of spring through Carnival, Mardi Gras, Lent, Easter, Purim, Passover, Qing Ming, and Holi. Carnival and Mardi Gras (Fat Tuesday) are times for celebrating before Ash Wednesday signals the start of the Christian holy season of Lenten fast. Palm Sunday, Holy Thursday, and Good Friday lead up to the joyous celebration of Easter. Jewish people commemorate Purim and Passover in the spring. Purim recalls Queen Esther saving the Jewish people from destruction, while Passover celebrates the Israelites' freedom from the bondage of slavery in Egypt. Qing Ming is a Chinese festival that evolved from a celebration of spring into a Festival of the Dead (Stepanchuk and Wong, 1991). In India, Holi (Festival of Color) celebrates the wheat harvest. Spring includes solemn festivals of prayer and reflection and joyous times of rebirth and renewal.

CARNIVAL AND MARDI GRAS

Carnival (Carnaval) encompasses the period from January 6, the Twelfth Night, until midnight on Mardi Gras. In anticipation of the self-denial to come, during these weeks leading up to Lent people set aside cultural restraint in favor of masked balls, parades, king cake, and celebrations. The climax of this festive time is Mardi Gras (Fat Tuesday); a day of parades, parties, and feasts before the Lenten fast begins. At midnight, Mardi Gras ends and the season of Lent begins with Ash Wednesday (Coil, 1994). Mardi Gras arrives forty-six days before Easter; depending on the liturgical calendar, it falls sometime between February third and March ninth. In Miami, the Cuban American pre-Lenten party or carnaval is called Calle Ocho (Eighth Street), named for the street that runs through the center of Little Havana (Menard, 2000). Music, food, and dancing mark this festival that revels in Cuban cultural heritage. In Brazil, people celebrate Carnaval for the five days leading up to Lent (Ancona, 1999), a period extended to two weeks in France (France, 1999).

BOOK AND MEDIA CHOICES

Coil, Suzanne M. *Mardi Gras!* Photographs by Mitchel Osborne. New York: Macmillan Publishing, 1994. 48p.
Grades: 1–4. This short book filled with color photographs contains a great deal of information on the raucous festivity of Mardi Gras. Beginning with the history of the celebration readers also learn about the krewes, the Mardi Gras Indians, the balls, the parades, the bands, the costumes, and the marching clubs. This brief book presents a very thorough discussion of the holiday, complete with an index.

Dorros, Arthur. *Tonight is Carnaval*. New York: Puffin Unicorn Books, 1991. Unp.
Grades: 1–4. High in the Andes Mountains a young boy prepares for Carnaval, which is a time for visiting with friends, wearing costumes, playing music, and dancing. Arpilleras sewn by the Club de Madres Virgen del Carmen of Lima, Peru and photographs of the women who sew them illustrate the book. Arpilleras are hand sewn, three-dimensional cloth wall hangings that tell stories of day-to-day life. A glossary concludes the book.

Landau, Elaine. *Mardi Gras: Parades, Costumes, and Parties*. Berkeley Heights, N.J.: Enslow, 2002. 48p.
Grades: 2–5. Mardi Gras, one of the most enjoyable holidays of the year, includes music and parades with toys and beads being tossed to the crowds. People are dressed in glamorous and sometimes out-rageous costumes. The book recounts the history of this celebration, details similar festivities held in Galveston, Texas, and suggests a variety of different ways to commemorate Mardi Gras. The book, part of the Finding Out about Holidays series, includes a craft project,

margin notes, pictures, a glossary, a bibliography, Internet addresses, and an index.

MacMillan, Dianne M. *Mardi Gras*. Berkeley Heights, N.J.: Enslow, 1997. 48p.
Grades: 2–5. While Mardi Gras is sometimes thought of as occurring only in New Orleans or other parts of South Louisiana, there are several places in the world that celebrate Fat Tuesday. Rio de Janeiro, Brazil, and Canada celebrate Mardi Gras, as well as several U.S. cities including Galveston, Texas; Mobile, Alabama; and San Luis Obispo, California. A glossary and an index are included. This book is from the Best Holiday Books series.

Ancona, George. *Carnaval*. San Diego: Harcourt Brace, 1999. Unp.
Grades: 3–6. Olinda, a small town in northeastern Brazil, is the setting for this festival of music, dancing, costumes, puppets, singing, and food. Carnaval is celebrated during the five days before Lent, which in Brazil falls in the middle of summer. Colorful photographs of the preparations for Carnaval and the celebration itself fill the pages of the book. An author's note about carnaval, carnival, and Mardi Gras celebrations around the world concludes the book.

Hoyt-Goldsmith, Diane. *Mardi Gras: A Cajun Country Celebration*. Photographs by Lawrence Migdale. New York: Holiday House, 1995. 32p.
Grades: 3–6. In the heart of Cajun country in South Louisiana, Mardi Gras is celebrated on horseback. Riders travel from one house to another collecting food to make gumbo, a characteristically spicy Creole stew. Readers meet Joel and his musical family as they prepare for and join in the Mardi Gras observances. Since music is an important part of the Cajun lifestyle, Mardi Gras features lots of music and dancing. The book begins with a history of the Cajuns and contains color photographs that capture the merriment and festivities of this pre-Lenten jubilee. A glossary and index conclude the book.

Chambers, Catherine. *Carnival*. Austin, Tex.: Steck-Vaughn, 1998. 31p.
Grades: 3–8. Chambers begins by telling the story of Jesus' forty days in the desert as noted today by the solemnity of Lent. Before this time of penance and fasting, people have one last fling with dancing, music, parades, costumes, and food. Readers take a quick trip around the world to learn about carnival celebrations. Readers learn about the drumming in Africa, the elaborate balls and parades

in New Orleans, the dazzling costumes in Trinidad and Tobago, the loud, colorful parades in Brazil, and pancake racing in Europe. At the end of the carnival tour, the rites of Ash Wednesday are described. The book includes a glossary, books for further reading, and an index. This book is from the World of Holidays series.

Vidrine, Beverly B. *A Mardi Gras Dictionary.* Illustrated by Patrick Soper. Lafayette, La.: Sunflower Press, 1994. Unp.
Grades: 3 and up. Words and vivid illustrations capture the excitement and wonder of Mardi Gras celebrations in South Louisiana. This is a brief introduction to the history and the language of Mardi Gras.

Leecan, Bobby. *Mardi Gras in New Orleans.* CD. New Orleans: Mardi Gras Records, 1995, 1987.
Grades: 3 and up. Several different New Orleans musicians perform the twelve songs on this music CD. Mardi Gras celebrations are noted for their lively music and this CD puts everyone in the mood to party.

EXPLORATIONS

1. After students read and discuss some of the books on carnival or Mardi Gras, have them produce a ten-minute "quick write" about what they learned. Later, during writing workshop they may want to expand on and clarify their "quick write" (Tompkins, 1998).

2. *A Mardi Gras Dictionary* (Vidrine, 1994) can serve as a model for students to use when they create their own dictionaries, as they study other holidays. In learning about Mardi Gras, they may want to create another edition of this dictionary supplementing it with additional words.

3. Play *Mardi Gras in New Orleans* and have students draw or practice a creative movement routine based on what comes to mind as they listen to the music. Then, let them share their drawings and routines with each other in small groups.

4. After learning about Mardi Gras, Calle Ocho, and Carnaval have students complete a chart such as the one below to compare the festivals.

Comparison Chart			
Questions	Mardi Gras	Calle Ocho	Carnaval
Who celebrates?			
Why do they celebrate?			
How do they celebrate?			

Figure 9-1. Comparing Mardi Gras, Calle Ocho, and Carnaval provides students with an opportunity to discover similarities and differences between these pre-Lenten celebrations.

LENT

After the raucous celebrations of carnival and Mardi Gras, comes Lent—forty days of prayer, self-denial, and repentance in preparation for Easter. Roman Catholics, Anglicans, Orthodox and other liturgically minded Christians observe the first day of Lent, Ash Wednesday with solemn rituals (Moehn, 2000). On this day, foreheads are marked with ashes applied in the sign of the cross indicating sorrow for sins. The forty days of Lent symbolize the forty days Jesus spent in the desert fasting and praying, which relates to the forty years that the Israelites wandered in the wilderness following their Exodus from Egypt. Fasting is less common today than it was in the past, having been replaced with Christians practicing abstinence by giving up something such as sweets. Holy Week is the last week of Lent, starting with Palm Sunday, when Jesus rode into Jerusalem for the beginning of the Jewish Passover (Thompson, 1997). Later in the week, Maundy Thursday (Holy Thursday) commemorates the Last Supper and Good Friday commemorates the day Jesus died on the cross. Lent culminates with jubilation on Easter Sunday, in remembrance of the resurrection of Jesus from the dead.

EASTER—RELIGIOUS

Easter is the day Christians celebrate Jesus' resurrection; it falls on a Sunday between March twenty-first and April twenty-fifth (Thompson, 1997). Easter services are often held at sunrise to mark the passage from darkness to light. The resurrection of Jesus symbolizes his start of a new life and churches are transformed from the somber self-denial of Lent into glorious celebration with spring flowers and glorious music. Eggs are a symbol of new life and are an important tradition in Easter celebrations around the world (Moehn, 2000). Orthodox Christians celebrate Fassika (Easter) at a later date as their year is based on the ancient Orthodox calendar (Kindersley, 1997).

BOOK AND MEDIA CHOICES

Gibbons, Gail. *Easter*. New York: Holiday House, 1989. Unp.
Grades: P–2. Simple, descriptive text and colorful pictures in spring pastels tell the Easter story. The book includes brief descriptions of the Easter symbols and a description of the Easter Holy Days.

Wildsmith, Brian. *The Easter Story*. Grand Rapids, Mich.: Eerdmans Books for Young Readers, 2000. Unp.
Grades: P–3. This version of the Easter story is told from the perspective of the donkey that carried Jesus into Jerusalem on Palm Sunday. The donkey stayed in Jerusalem with Jesus and carried Jesus' body to the tomb. When Jesus ascended into heaven, the donkey went back to his home. Huge double page spreads in vivid, blues, greens, and purples highlighted with red and gold make the book a sumptuous feast for the eyes.

French, Fiona. *Easter: With Words from the King James Bible*. New York: HarperCollins, 2002. 24p.
Grades: P–4. Illustrated in the form of stained-glass windows, this book begins with the triumphant entrance of Jesus Christ into Jerusalem. The Last Supper is described, as is the betrayal of Jesus in the garden. Next is the appearance of Jesus before Pontius Pilate, his crucifixion, his resurrection, and his ascension. Words from the King James Version of the Bible combined with artwork inspired by England's stained-glass cathedral windows make this a book to share each year at Easter.

Easter. Video. Bala Cynwyd, Penn.: Schlessinger Video Productions-Library Video Company, 1994. 25 min.
Grades: K–4. Viewers hear the Easter story of the Lord's death and resurrection, they attend an Easter egg hunt, watch a lively troupe of Greek dancers, and visit a Polish American family. Along the way, they discover the traditions and religious significance of Easter Sunday. This video is part of the Holidays for Children series.

Thompson, Lauren. *Love One Another: The Last Days of Jesus*. Illustrated by Elizabeth Uyehara. New York: Scholastic, 2000. Unp.
Grades: 1–3. Simple, easy-to-understand text describes Jesus' last days and his resurrection. Bold, vivid illustrations capture the horror and hope of this timeless story.

Chambers, Catherine. *Easter*. Austin, Tex.: Raintree Steck-Vaughn, 1998. 31p.
Grades: 2–5. Jesus' death and resurrection are the focus of the book. Reenactments of these events from around the world are shown in color photographs and described in the text. Russia, Sweden, the Czech Republic, Northern African, Ireland, and Greece are just some of the countries with celebrations featured in the book.

EXPLORATIONS

1. Before reading *The Easter Story* (Wildsmith, 2000), explain to students that the story is told from a donkey's point of view. After reading the story, point out to the students how the donkey's perspective influenced the story. One way to do this is to read Easter: With Words from the *King James Bible* (French, 2002) and compare differences between the stories.

2. After reading *Easter: With Words from the King James Bible* (French, 2002) aloud, place the book in the reading corner and encourage the students to examine the pictures and pick out the details they see tucked into the stained glass.

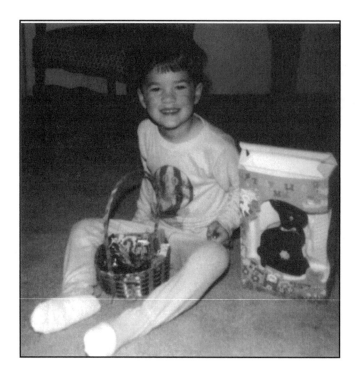

EASTER—SECULAR

Easter morning is the time to awaken to Easter baskets filled with chocolate bunnies, jellybeans, candy eggs, and marshmallow chickens from the Easter Bunny. Dyeing hard-boiled eggs and Easter egg-hunts are two of the traditions associated with this holiday. Traditionally, at the White House on Easter Monday, an egg-rolling contest is held. In Italy, Mexico, Spain, Portugal, Latin America, and Sweden fireworks are part of the Easter celebrations (Barth, 1998). Easter is a time for family gatherings and sumptuous feasts.

BOOK AND MEDIA CHOICES

Henkes, Kevin. *Owen's Marshmallow Chick*. New York: HarperCollins, 2002. Unp.
Grades: P–K. On Easter morning, Owen savors each of the candies in his Easter basket declaring each of them his favorite. However, when he comes across the yellow marshmallow chick, which is the same color as his beloved blanket, he cannot bear to eat it. So, he

plays with it all day, kisses it goodnight, and puts it on his shelf. This is a small board book that children enjoy looking at on their own.

Parker, Toni Tent. *Painted Eggs and Chocolate Bunnies*. Photographs by Earl Anderson. New York: Scholastic, 2002. Unp.
Grades: P–K. Adorable children in their Easter finery, are admiring their clothes and their treats. Simple rhyming text and color photographs highlight what young children consider to be the best parts of Easter.

Wells, Rosemary. *Max's Chocolate Chicken*. New York: Penguin Putnam Books for Young Readers, 1989. Unp.
Grades: P–1. A large chocolate chicken awaits the child who finds the most Easter eggs. Ruby finds a variety of multicolored eggs and keeps reminding Max that he needs to find Easter eggs if he wants to win the chicken. Max finds a spoon and some acorns, but no egg. Desperate, he runs away from Ruby, grabs the chocolate chicken, and hides out to devour the prize.

Wiencirz, Gerlinde. *Teddy's Easter Secret*. Illustrated by Giuliano Lunelli. Translated by J. Alison James. New York: North-South Books, 2001. Unp.
Grades: P–1. A small brown teddy bear left behind in the sandbox one night, sees a rabbit in the hen house taking all the eggs. Teddy sets out following the rabbit and stumbles upon the Easter Bunny and his helpers busy coloring eggs to deliver that night. This is a cute story that small children enjoy. The end pages of the book are filled with brightly colored eggs, sure to give children ideas for decorating eggs.

Berlin, Irving. *Easter Parade*. Illustrated by Lisa McCue. New York: HarperCollins, 2003. Unp.
Grades: P–2. Irving Berlin's words have been transformed into a charming picture book. Warm, inviting illustrations capture the special magic between father bunny and his daughter as they participate in the Easter parade.

Gibbons, Gail. *Easter*. New York: Holiday House, 1989. Unp.
Grades: P–2. This book uses simple language to explain both the religious and secular reasons for the celebration of Easter. The story of the birth, life, death and resurrection of Jesus Christ is told as well as the practice of dying and giving eggs to one another, the practice

of sharing food and spring flowers, and wearing Easter finery. The book also lists Easter holy days.

Kroll, Steven. *The Big Bunny and the Easter Eggs*. Illustrated by Janet Stevens. New York: Scholastic, 1982. Unp.
Grades: P–2. The eggs are dyed and the baskets are filled, but the Easter Bunny ends up sick in bed. When his friends realize he is too sick to deliver eggs, they decide to deliver them for him. That does not work, so they rouse the Easter Bunny from his bed with promises to help him deliver the eggs. It is starting to get light and people are waking up and everybody knows you are not supposed to see the Easter Bunny. His friends spring into action with a variety of diversionary tactics to keep people from seeing the Easter Bunny. Hilarious illustrations show a very sick Easter Bunny and a group of clever, loyal friends willing to help in any way they can.

Zolotow, Charlotte. *The Bunny Who Found Easter*. Illustrated by Helen Craig. Boston: Houghton Mifflin, 1998, 1987, 1959. Unp.
Grades: P–2. A lonely bunny hops through the seasons in search of Easter. When spring arrives, he finds a female bunny and his search for Easter ends. He realizes that Easter is really a time when everything begins again.

Auch, Mary Jane. *The Easter Egg Farm*. New York: Holiday House, 1992. Unp.
Grades: P–3. Pauline is under pressure to lay eggs, but she just cannot lay eggs in the midst of the confusion in the hen house. She concentrates very hard and does begin to lay eggs, but they are not plain eggs. Her eggs reflect whatever she is looking at when she lays the eggs. Mrs. Pennyworth, her owner, begins to take Pauline on field trips so she will lay eggs that are even more glamorous. However, the eggs do not last; they begin to hatch into multicolored chicks. With all the talented egg layers, Mrs. Pennyworth opens an Easter egg farm and Pauline retires.

DJ's Choice: Easter Bunny's Favorite Songs. CD. Kenilworth, N.J.: Turn Up the Music, 2002.
Grades: P–3. The CD contains ten Easter songs including: "Here Comes Peter Cottontail," "Bunny Hop," "The Chicken Dance," and "Easter Parade." This is a lively CD that has children singing along and hopping to the beat.

Friedrich, Priscilla, and Otto Friedrich. *The Easter Bunny That Overslept*. Illustrated by Donald Saaf. New York: HarperCollins, 2002. Unp.
Grades: P–3. One Easter the Easter Bunny overslept and did not deliver his Easter eggs. When he awoke several weeks later and tried to deliver them, no one would take them, scolding him for missing Easter. He tried decorating them for the Fourth of July and delivering them, and he was rejected once again. The same thing happened when he tried to give them away on Halloween. Then, Santa Claus tells him he can help build and deliver Christmas toys and gives him an alarm clock, so he never oversleeps again.

Gibbons, Gail. *Easter*. New York: Holiday House, 1989. Unp.
Grades: P–3. Through descriptive text and colorful illustrations Gibbons explains the signs and symbols of Easter. She tells how eggs came to symbolize Easter, describes foods prepared for Easter meals, and illustrates Easter apparel. The book ends with definitions of the Easter Holy Days.

Kimmel, Eric A. *The Birds' Gift: A Ukrainian Easter Story*. Illustrated by Katya Krenina. New York: Holiday House, 1999. Unp.
Grades: P–3. An early winter storm traps birds in the snow and the ice. Katrusya gathers as many as she can and carries them home. Soon the whole village is collecting the birds and the priest opens the church to them. Even though winter is not over, the birds one day decide it is time to leave. On Easter morning the villagers go outside and discover beautiful, decorated eggs each with a different pattern. Since that Sunday, the Ukrainian women have created elaborate eggs, pysanky. An author's note at the end of the book describes how the eggs are made.

Polacco, Patricia. *Rechenka's Eggs*. New York: Philomel Books, 1988. Unp.
Grades: P–3. Babushka befriends a wounded goose, Rechenka, who keeps Babushka company on long Russian winter days, as she paints magnificent eggs for the Easter Festival. The goose accidentally breaks all of the eggs. However, she lays a beautiful egg each morning to replace the broken eggs. When Babushka goes to the Easter festival in Moskva to display her eggs, the recovered Rechenka flies away with her flock. Left behind in her nest is a special gift for Babushka. This Russian tale introduces children to the Ukrainian art of egg painting. This book is also available on audiocassette and on video.

Weninger, Brigitte. *Happy Easter, Davy!* Illustrated by Eve Tharlet. Trans. by Rosemary Lanning. New York: North-South Books, 2001. Unp.
Grades: P–3. Dan has exciting news to share with the rabbit family. There is an Easter Bunny living in their woods and tomorrow human children will awaken to eggs he leaves them. Dan, Davy, and the other rabbit children search high and low but cannot find the Easter Bunny. So Davy decides he will surprise his brothers and sisters in the morning. The next morning his siblings are surprised, and so is Davy.

Merrick, Patrick. *Easter Bunnies*. Chanhassen, Minn.: The Child's World, 2000. 32p.
Grades: K–3. This is a brief introduction to the history, symbols, and traditions of Easter. Large, clear, color photographs capture the excitement and wonder of the holiday. The book concludes with an index and a glossary.

Milich, Melissa. *Miz Fannie Mae's Fine New Easter Hat*. Illustrated by Yong Chen. Boston: Little, Brown, 1997. Unp.
Grades: K–3. On the Saturday before Easter, Daddy announces he and Tandy are going to town to buy Mama a new hat for Easter. He hitches up the horse and wagon for the trip. They find the perfect flowered hat with a tiny bird's nest and eggs tucked on the brim. In the middle of the church service, the eggs start hatching.

Polacco, Patricia. *Chicken Sunday*. Illustrated by Edward Miller. New York: Putnam, 1998. Unp.
Grades: K–3. Polacco shares her childhood memories of two African American friends who invited her to fried chicken dinners at their grandmother's house on Sundays. The grandmother longs for an Easter bonnet from Mr. Kodinski's shop. Polacco shares her family tradition and teaches her friends to create Ukrainian "Pysanky" eggs. When the shopkeeper sees the remembrances from his homeland he allows the children to sell the eggs in his shop. In exchange for the eggs, the children get to select a hat for grandmother.

Stevenson, James. *The Great Big Especially Beautiful Easter Egg*. New York: Scholastic, 1983. Unp.
Grades: K–3. Grandpa tells a very tall tale about his adventures locating a great big especially beautiful Easter egg for his childhood sweetheart. At the Easter Bunny's suggestion, he, and his faithful canine companion head to the Frammistan Mountains. Getting there

was easy, getting back was an ordeal. Appealing cartoon illustrations tell the story of the outlandish trek.

Hague, Michael, comp. *Michael Hague's Family Easter Treasury*. New York: Henry Holt, 1999. 134p.
Grades: K and up. Bible verses, poems, and stories from noted writers including Emily Dickinson, Lucille Clifton, and Joyce Kilmer are found in this carefully selected anthology. The anthology is divided into four sections: A Time of Faith, A Time of Rebirth, A Time of Celebrations, and A Time of Love. All are tied together with Hague's beautiful illustrations.

Greenfield, Eloise. *Easter Parade*. Illustrated by Jan Spivey Gilchrist. New York: Hyperion Books for Children, 1998. 64p.
Grades: 1–3. In 1943, the world was at war as two young cousins prepare for the Easter parade. Although Leanna is in Chicago and her cousin Elizabeth is in Washington, D.C., they share strong family bonds. Greenfield's lyrical prose contained in brief chapters shows the strength of family ties, a strength reflected in the sepia drawings that look as though they came from a family album.

Griest, Lisa. *Lost at the White House: A 1909 Easter Story*. Illustrated by Andrea Shine. Minneapolis, Minn: Carolrhoda Books, 1994. 48p.
Grades: 1–3. A nine-year old lost at the annual White House Easter egg roll has an opportunity to meet President Taft. The author based the story on her grandmother's experience, which is explained in an author's note is at the beginning of the book.

Barth, Edna. *Lilies, Rabbits, and Painted Eggs: The Story of the Easter Symbols*. Illustrated by Ursula Arndt. New York: Houghton Mifflin, 1998, 1970. 64p.
Grades: 4–8. In America, we do not usually associate fireworks with Easter celebrations, but in Italy, Mexico, Spain, Portugal, Latin America, and Sweden they are a part of the Easter celebration. This is just one example of the interesting details about Easter included in this resource book. Easter traditions from around the world are described in easy-to-understand prose. The book includes craft activities, riddles, a bibliography, and an index.

EXPLORATIONS

1. After reading *Painted Eggs and Chocolate Bunnies* (Parker, 2002), return to the text and write the rhyming words on the board. Then, have the children read the words with you and listen to the rhymes.

2. Before reading *Easter Parade* (Berlin, 2003), play a recording of the song for the students. The song is on *DJ's Choice: Easter Bunny's Favorite Songs*.

3. After reading *The Big Bunny and the Easter Eggs* (Kroll, 1982), ask the students which part of the story they liked best and why. Expect lively discussions as readers young and old can find many parts of the story to be favorites.

4. After reading *The Easter Egg Farm* (Auch, 1992), explain to children how artists get inspiration from things around them just as Pauline does. Then, have the students design Easter Eggs based on things they have seen.

5. After reading *The Easter Egg Farm* (Auch, 1992), ask students why Pauline at first had trouble laying eggs. How did she overcome her problem? What do the students do when they have difficulty completing a task?

6. *The Easter Bunny That Overslept* (Friedrich and Friedrich, 2002) has a cause and effect organization. After reading the story, model for the students how to create a diagram of the cause and effect relationships in the story.

7. After reading *Chicken Sunday* (Polacco, 1998) and *Rechenka's Eggs* (Polacco, 1988) show the students how both stories included the beautiful painted eggs. Relate to students how Polacco's knowledge of the eggs comes from her family background. This is an example of how an author writes about what she knows. Ask students to brainstorm about family traditions about which they might write. Then, have the students put the list in their writing folder.

8. After reading *The Great Big Especially Beautiful Easter Egg* (Stevenson, 1983), have the students decide which parts of the story could have been true and which parts are fiction.

9. After reading *Easter Parade* (Greenfield, 1998), have students compare their lives today with the girls' lives during World War II.

10. Before reading *Lost at the White House: A 1909 Easter Story* (Griest, 1994), ask the students if they have ever been lost. How did they feel? What did they do? How did it feel to be found?

11. Divide the students into groups and randomly assign them to research an Easter symbol. *Lilies, Rabbits, and Painted Eggs: The Story of the Easter* Symbols (Barth, 1998) and the Easter video are possible resources. Then, challenge them to find creative ways to present what they learn to their classmates, such as creating a mural depicting the Easter symbols and their origins.

PURIM

On the fourteenth day of the Hebrew month of Adar— between February 24 and March 25—Jews celebrate the holiday of Purim. This holiday recalls the biblical story of Queen Esther, who saved the Jewish people from destruction by Haman, the Persian king's grand vizier (Scharfstein, 1999). Purim is a joyous celebration of feasting, plays, carnivals, graggers (noisemakers), and hamantaschen (a filled triangular cookie). Friends, the elderly, and shut-ins receive gift baskets of foods, such as candy, nuts, and hamantaschen, and people make monetary donations to charities (Burghardt, 2001).

BOOK AND MEDIA CHOICES

Nerlove, Miriam. *Purim*. Morton Grove, Ill.: Albert Whitman, 1992. Unp.
Grades: P–2. With the arrival of spring comes Purim and as this young boy gets ready to celebrate, the story of Purim unfolds. The rhyming verse and colorful illustrations let children know this is a time for rejoicing.

Fishman, Cathy Goldberg. *On Purim*. Illustrated by Melanie W. Hall. New York: Atheneum Books for Young Readers, 2000. Unp.
Grades: P–3. Through a family's preparations for Purim, readers learn the history and symbolism associated with this holiday celebration. Readers join the family as they make costumes, cook special foods, participate in a carnival, and watch a parade. Warm pastel illustrations depict the history and present-day events. A glossary concludes the book.

Goldin, Barbara Diamond. *Cakes and Miracles: A Purim Tale*. Illustrated by Erika Weihs. New York: Viking, 1991. Unp.
Grades: P–3. Because Hershel is blind, his mother does not think he can be very helpful when she makes hamantashen (cookies) to sell for Purim. An angel comes to him in the night and tells him to make what he sees in his mind. While his mother sleeps, Hershel shapes magnificent cookies from the dough she has in the kitchen. The next day at the market, Hershel and his mother sell all of the cookies.

Wolkstein, Diane. *Esther's Story*. Illustrated by Juan Wijngaard. New York: Morrow Junior Books, 1996. Unp.
Grades: 1–6. Readers learn Esther's story by reading her diary entries. Glorious, full-page bordered illustrations accompany each

diary entry. Together the text and illustrations combine to form a gripping tale of a young woman's courage. At the beginning of the book is a pronunciation guide and an author's note.

EXPLORATIONS

1. After reading *Purim* (Nerlove, 1992), ask students what they liked about the story and what they did not like about the story. Have them imagine the most enjoyable way to celebrate Purim.

2. After reading *On Purim* (Fishman, 2000), have students write and produce their own Purim play. The costumes and props do not have to be elaborate. The focus should be on having the students write their version of the story.

3. Before reading *Cakes and Miracles: A Purim Tale* (Goldin, 1991), tell the students that because the boy in the story is blind, his mother does not think he can help her make cookies; but he knows he can. This story is a good way to begin a discussion of the things that physically challenged individuals can do and the importance of not underestimating them.

4. As students read *Esther's Story* (Wolkstein, 1996), have them examine the illustrations that accompany each diary entry. Ask them to jot down brief notes to answer questions such as: Does the illustration match the diary entry? What else could have been put in the illustration? What if anything could have been left out of the illustration?

PASSOVER

Passover (Pesach) reminds Jewish people of the bondage of slavery and the value of freedom. It is celebrated annually, for eight days between March 27 and April 24 (Moehn, 2000). The Israelites, ancestors of the Jews, were enslaved by the pharaoh (king) of Egypt. When Moses asked Pharaoh to free them, he refused, so God sent plagues to Egypt to persuade him. Still Pharaoh refused. Then, God determined to send the angel of death to kill the firstborn sons of the Egyptians. Before that fateful night, the Israelite sacrificed lambs and smeared the blood on their doorways so the angel of death would know to pass over their houses and not kill their first-born sons. After finding his own son dead, Pharaoh told Moses to take the Israelites and leave Egypt. In their hurry to leave, there was no time for dough to rise, and instead they baked unleavened bread. Soon thereafter, Pharaoh changed his mind and sent his army after the fleeing band of slaves. When the Israelites arrived at the Red Sea, God parted the water for them to pass through; however, when the Egyptians tried to follow, the waters came crashing down, and drowned them. Passover is one of Judaism's most important holidays and it begins with a ritual meal called a seder (Hoyt-Goldsmith, 2000).

BOOK AND MEDIA CHOICES

My First Passover Board Book. New York: DK Publishing, 2002. Unp.
Grades: P–K. This small, chubby book has bright colorful photographs of the Passover symbols. Brief sentences and photographs of children tell the story of Passover and how it is celebrated.

Hildebrandt, Ziporah. *This Is Our Seder*. Illustrated by Robin Roraback. New York: Holiday House, 1999. Unp.
Grades: P–2. This simple poem with its short phrases and pastel illustrations describes the foods and rituals of Seder. Cartoon-like illustrations depict a warm, loving family giving thanks and praise for their freedom. The book concludes with a description of the Seder and the foods used in the celebration.

Zalben, Jane Breskin. *Happy Passover*, Rosie. New York: Henry Holt, 1990. Unp.
Grades: P–2. Since Rosie is the youngest child, this year she gets to ask the four questions at the family's Passover Seder. First, though there is cleaning, cooking and preparing to do. The traditions of this holiday celebration gradually unfold as the evening progresses. Information on the Seder plate and the four questions conclude the book along with a recipe for Mama's Matzah Balls.

Manushkin, Fran. *The Matzah That Papa Brought Home*. Illustrated by Ned Bittinger. New York: Scholastic, 1995. Unp.
Grades: P–3. This lyrical, cumulative tale tells the story of a family's Passover Seder, which all started with the matzah that Papa brought home. The text moves along quickly but the warm, rich illustrations should be slowly and carefully examined. The foods and rituals of Passover are described at the end of the book.

Schotter, Roni. *Passover Magic*. Illustrated by Marylin Hafner. Boston: Little, Brown, 1995. Unp.
Grades: P–3. When your family includes Uncle Harry, a magician, Passover magic is bound to happen. Everyone has a job to do as this large family prepares for the Passover Seder. This year Uncle Harry is given the afikomen to hide and the children are sure they will never be able to find it in his hiding place. Detailed illustrations depict a loving family enjoying each other as they celebrate Passover. The book concludes with the story of Passover and the traditional four questions, which are asked as part of the seder.

Rothenberg, Joan. *Matzah Ball Soup*. New York: Hyperion Books for Children, 1999. Unp.
Grades: P–4. A Passover Seder has certain rituals and traditions, but this family's seder, like those of other families, has something that is special to this family. Each bowl of chicken soup has to have four matzah balls. As Rosie helps her grandmother prepare the matzah balls, she tells Rosie of the year her four aunts each declared their matzah balls were the best. When they continued to argue about whose matzah balls should go in the soup, an uncle declared that each bowl of soup would have four matzah balls so the family could decide whose was the best. In the end, the uncle declared that all of them were the best, and so began the family tradition of having four matzah balls in each bowl of chicken soup. The book ends with a recipe for matzah balls and variations for the aunts' recipes.

Kimmelman, Leslie. *Hooray! It's Passover*. Illustrated by John Himmelman. New York: HarperCollins, 1996. Unp.
Grades: K–2. The relatives come to share the Passover Seder and readers join the family for this special dinner. Brief sentences describe the observance and colorful illustrations depict the celebrations. The family's cats have decided to join the celebration and readers enjoy their lively antics.

Pushker, Gloria Teles. *Toby Belfer's Seder: A Passover Story Retold*. Illustrated by Judith Hierstein. Gretna, La.: Pelican Publishing, 1994. Unp.
Grades: K–3. Toby Belfer invites her non-Jewish friend, Donna, to join her family as they celebrate Passover. As Donna develops an understanding and an appreciation of her friend's religious beliefs, so too do readers. At the end of the book is a listing of the similarities between Passover and Easter, glossary, and a bibliography.

Hanukkah/Passover. Video. Bala Cynwyd, Penn.: Schlessinger Video Productions-Library Video Company, 1996. 25 min.
Grades: K–4. Stories, puppets, games, and songs explain the significance of the Jewish holidays of Hanukkah and Passover. A traditional Seder meal, a visit to a matzo bakery, a presentation by Jewish folk singers, and making a dreidel involve children in exploring and learning about the traditions associated with these holidays. This video is part of the Holidays for Children series.

Manushkin, Fran. *Miriam's Cup: A Passover Story*. Illustrated by Bob Dacey. New York: Scholastic, 1998. Unp.
Grades: K–4. During Seder preparations, a mother tells her children the story of Passover and highlights the role of Moses' sister, Miriam. She helped lead the Israelites to freedom in Egypt. To honor Miriam a cup of water is placed on the table. The illustrator, Bob Dacey, made costumes for his friends and neighbors to wear as they posed for the book's illustrations. An author's note, a bibliography, and an excerpt of Miriam's Song are included.

Simon, Norma. *The Story of Passover*. Illustrated by Erika Weihs. New York: HarperCollins, 1997, 1965. Unp.
Grades: 2–5. The book begins with the story of the first Passover and then describes how families today celebrate Passover. Readers find the information on Passover more detailed than in other books, but they are not overwhelmed by the text. The left side of the two-page spread contains text and the right side contains an illustration. Instructions for making Matzoh balls, Charoseth, and place cards for the table conclude the book.

Hoyt-Goldsmith, Diane. *Celebrating Passover*. Photographs by Lawrence Migdale. New York: Holiday House, 2000. 32p.
Grades: 3–6. Nine-year-old Micah and his family invite readers to share their Passover seder. Photographs of a contemporary family and descriptive narrative help readers understand the significance and rituals of this holiday celebration. The book includes a comparison of the Hebrew lunar calendar to the familiar Gregorian calendar, a summary of the Passover story, a glossary, and an index.

Schecter, Ellen. *The Family Haggadah*. Illustrated by Neil Waldman. New York: Viking, 1999. 66p.
Grades: 4–8. Haggadah, prayer book and Biblical texts, commentaries, stories, activities, and explanations combine to provide information for children and parents as they prepare and celebrate

Passover. The importance of both men and women in the Exodus is portrayed. Instead of the traditional four sons, there are four children in the ritual. Black-and-white illustrations are included.

Goldin, Barbara Diamond. *The Passover Journey: A Seder Companion.* Illustrated by Neil Waldman. New York: Puffin Books, 1994. 55p.
Grades: 4 and up. The story of the Exodus comprises the first part of the book and the second part describes and details the fourteen steps of the seder. The book contains easy to understand explanations for the Passover rituals, with variations from different countries and ideas for making the rituals personally meaningful. Watercolor illustrations in soft pinks, blues, and greens portray the somber bondage and the joyous freedom of the people. Notes on the sources and a glossary conclude the book.

EXPLORATIONS

1. After reading *This Is Our Seder* (Hildebrandt, 1999), go back through the story and explain the symbolism of the items mentioned such as the parsley and the matzah. The explanations can be found at the end of the story.

2. Read *The Matzah That Papa Brought Home* (Manushkin, 1995) more than once and on subsequent readings encourage the children to join in and chant the lines with you. (See *On the Morn of Mayfest* by Erica Silverman for another cumulative tale.)

3. While reading *Matzah Ball Soup* (Rothenberg, 1999), share with students any questions that come to your mind as you are reading the book aloud. Modeling questioning while reading aloud helps children learn to question text as they read.

4. Before reading *Toby Belfer's Seder: A Passover Story Retold* (Pushker, 1994), explain to students that Donna, has been invited to join Toby and her family for their Passover celebration. Use this as a basis for a class discussion on the proper behavior to follow if they are invited to celebrate a holiday with a friend so as not to offend the friend or their parents.

5. Preview the video *Hanukkah/Passover* before showing it to the students. Briefly, describe to the students what they will

see in the video. After watching the video, put the students in small groups to discuss what they learned.

6. Before reading *Celebrating Passover* (Hoyt-Goldsmith, 2000), have students spend time comparing the Hebrew lunar calendar and the Gregorian calendar found at the beginning of the book.

7. After reading *Celebrating Passover* (Hoyt-Goldsmith, 2000), place the students in small groups and have them retell the Passover story.

8. After reading about Passover in *The Passover Journey: A Seder Companion* (Goldin, 1994), ask the students the questions from an ancient Baghdad custom. How would you get ready for the journey? What would you take? How would you feel?

QING MING (CLEAR BRIGHTNESS FESTIVAL)

Qing Ming (Ch'ing Ming) occurs 106 days after the winter solstice on either April 5 or April 6. Clear Brightness Festival and the Feast of the Dead are alternative names for Qing Ming (Winchester, 1996). The occasion's connection to dead relates to the tradition of remembering the dead by cleaning and weeding graves and bringing offerings of food to share with the dead (Stepanchuk and Wong, 1991). Sometimes trees are planted in honor of the dead and to celebrate the coming of spring. After paying respects to the dead, this day is celebrated outdoors with picnics, games, and kite flying. (See Obon Festival, Yom Kippur, All Souls' Day, All Saints' Day, Dia de los Muertos, Id-Al-Fitr, and TET for other holidays that commemorate the dead.)

HOLI (FESTIVAL OF COLOR)

In February or March, the Hindu festival of Holi (Festival of Color) celebrates the coming of spring and the end of the wheat harvest (see Mardi Gras, Carnaval). The celebration relates to the story of Prahlada, whose wisdom and virtue from worshipping Vishnu protected him from his wicked aunt Holika, when she attempted to kill Prahlada by holding him in her lap as she sat in a fire. To ward off evil spirits and to remind themselves that good triumphs over evil,

Hindus light bonfires the night before Holi (Kindersley, 1997). Holi's carnival atmosphere gives people license to engage in wild behavior, singing, dancing, drinking, and partying. Everyone wears old clothes, because they throw gulal, multicolored powders, on one another, and children mix gulal with water and squirt it on each other (Viesti and Hall, 1996). In the evening, the families visit with relatives and friends.

BOOK AND MEDIA CHOICES

Krishnaswami, Uma. *Holi*. New York: Children's Press, 2003. 32p.
Grades: P–2. Colorful photographs and large print text explain this Hindu holiday to young readers. A picture glossary and an index are included. This book is from the Rookie Read-About Holidays series.

Kadodwala, Dilip. *Holi*. Chicago, Ill.: Raintree: 1997. 32p.
Grades: 2–5. Readers learn that this Hindu festival celebrated in the spring focuses not only on the spring planting but also the fall harvest. This is a joyous time when both young and old spray each other with colored dyes made from vegetable powders. Food is offered to the gods, family feasts, and the Holi bonfire are some of the traditions associated with this celebration.

EXPLORATIONS

1. Before reading *Holi* (Krishnaswami, 2003) or *Holi* (Kadodwala, 1997), talk to students about balloon and water fights they have enjoyed. They may be surprised to learn that during Holi water fights involve colored water.

2. After reading *Holi* (Kadodwala, 1997), engage students in a discussion of why Hindus celebrate the fall harvest in the spring.

REFERENCES

Ancona, George. 1999. *Carnaval*. San Diego: Harcourt Brace.
Barth, Edna. 1998. *Lilies, Rabbits, and Painted Eggs: The Story of the Easter Symbols*. New York: Houghton Mifflin.
Burghardt, Linda. 2001. *Jewish Holiday Traditions: Joyful Celebrations from Rosh Hashanah to Shavuot*. New York: Kensington Publishing.

Coil, Suzanne M. 1994. *Mardi Gras!* New York: Macmillan Publishing.

France. 1999. Danbury, Conn.: Grolier Educational.

Hoyt-Goldsmith, Diane. 2000. *Celebrating Passover*. New York: Holiday House.

Kindersley, Anabel. 1997. *Celebrations*. New York: DK Publishing.

Menard, Valerie. 2000. *The Latino Holiday Book: From Cinco de Mayo to Dia de los Muertos — The Celebrations and Traditions of Hispanic Americans*. New York: Marlowe.

Moehn, Heather. 2000. *World Holidays: A Watts Guide for Children*. New York: Franklin Watts.

Scharfstein, Sol. 1999. *Understanding Jewish Holidays and Customs: Historical and Contemporary*. Hoboken, N.J.: KTAV Publishing House.

Silverman, Erica. 1998. *On the Morn of Mayfest*. New York: Simon & Schuster Books for Young Readers.

Stepanchuk, Carol, and Charles Wong. 1991. *Mooncakes and Hungry Ghosts: Festivals of China*. San Francisco: China Books & Periodicals.

Tompkins, Gail E. 1998. *Language Arts: Content and Teaching Strategies*. Upper Saddle River, N.J.: Prentice-Hall.

Thompson, Jan. 1997. *Christian Festivals*. Crystal Lake, Ill.: Heinemann.

Winchester, Faith. 1996. *Asian Holidays*. Mankato, Minn.: Capstone Press.

MARCH HOLIDAYS AND CELEBRATIONS 10

March winds seem to blow away the last remnants of winter, which exits ever-so reluctantly, while spring cannot wait to burst on the scene. March is for celebrating Hina Matsuri, St. Patrick's Day, and St. Joseph's Day. The third of March in Japan is Hina Matsuri (Dolls' Day Festival), a day of purification when, traditionally, people created miniature paper dolls, transferred their human impurities to the dolls, and then sent them off on a river or in the ocean. St. Patrick's Day is celebrated on March 17 in Ireland and the United States. Two days later, on March 19, Catholics celebrate St. Joseph's Day, in honor of the patron saint of carpenters, Christ's father. The Spring or Vernal Equinox occurs on March 20 or 21 and marks the beginning of Spring. The Vernal Equinox also means the start of the Persian New Year, Now Ruz. In Iran this celebration lasts for almost two weeks. On the thirteenth day of the festival a large national picnic takes place as it is considered unlucky to stay at home on this day.

HINA MATSURI (DOLL FESTIVAL)

In Japan, March third is a special day, because on it everyone celebrates Hina Matsuri (Doll Festival). That day people thank the kami (spirits) for life, and pray for the happiness and health of their daughters. Because purity is of utmost importance in traditional Japanese religion and culture, these prayers were accompanied by acts of ritual purification. Originally, this meant transferring bad fortune to a simple paper doll then sending it into the purifying waters, but over time a more elaborate doll replaced the paper cut-out. Now human "dolls"—young women (around twenty-years-old)—dress in kimonos to match their ornately adorned antique doll collections, followed by a traditional tea party (MacMillan, 1997). These doll collections are often passed on from mother to daughter and they are displayed on shelves covered with red cloth. The dolls are dressed as ancient Japanese royalty including an emperor, an empress, court attendants, and servants (MacMillan, 1997). The dolls represent values such as calmness and dignity that parents want their daughters to emulate (Kindersley, 1997). After two or three weeks, the dolls are taken down and stored away until the following year (Krasno, 2000).

BOOK AND MEDIA CHOICES

MacMillan, Dianne M. *Japanese Children's Day and the Obon Festival.* Berkeley Heights, N.J.: Enslow, 1997. 48p.
Grades: 2–5. Brief descriptions and color photographs provide information on Children's Day, the Boys' Festival, and the Dolls' Day Festival. The photographs contain information essential to understanding the traditions and rituals of these Japanese celebrations. The book, part of the Best Holiday Books series, includes a glossary and an index.

EXPLORATIONS

1. Students interested in learning more about Hina Matsuri can find additional information at www.jinjapan.org/kidsweb/calendar/march/hinamatsuri.html. They will also find photographs of doll displays.

2. While students may not have elaborate doll collections such as the ones used for these displays, they may have favorite dolls they would like to share with the class. Some students may have dolls that have been passed down from their mothers or grandmothers that they would like to share with the class.

ST. PATRICK'S DAY

Wearing green clothing and shamrocks are two of the traditions associated with commemorating the life of the patron saint of Ireland, St. Patrick, on March seventeenth, the day on which he died in 461. Born in Britain around 390 C.E., Patrick was kidnapped as a youth and taken north to Ireland as a slave. He spent his days tending sheep and during this time became very religious. He ran away and after some time ended up in France where he studied to become a priest. Later, he returned to Ireland to share the Christian gospel with the Irish people. Throughout his life, his strong faith in God sustained him and led him to do great works. There are many stories and legends about St. Patrick, such as the famous stories of how he drove the snakes from Ireland and that he used the shamrock to teach about the Holy Trinity (Landau, 2002). Many cities in America, populated with cathedrals dedicated to St. Patrick, celebrate this day with parades and festivities, testimony to the large number of Irish immigrants who settled throughout the United States. Dublin has the largest St. Patrick's Day parade in Ireland, but the St. Patrick's Day parade in New York City is bigger.

BOOK AND MEDIA CHOICES

de Paola, Tomie. *Patrick: Patron Saint of Ireland*. New York: Holiday House, 1992. Unp.
Grades: P–2. Brief paragraphs and full-page color illustrations tell the story of Ireland's patron saint and his faith in God that led him to spread Christianity throughout the country. The book includes five short descriptions of legends about St. Patrick.

MacGill-Callahan, Sheila. *The Last Snake in Ireland: A Story about St. Patrick*. Illustrated by Will Hillenbrand. New York: Holiday House, 1999. Unp.
Grades: P–3. This is a fanciful tale about how St. Patrick drove the snakes from Ireland, although getting rid of the last one was quite a challenge. One large red snake decided he was staying and St. Patrick devised a number of tricks to get rid of him. He finally dumped him in the Loch Ness and years later when he went back to check on the snake found out he had become the Loch Ness Monster. Mixed media pastels capture the twists and turns in the story.

Tucker, Kathy. *The Leprechaun in the Basement*. Illustrated by John Sandford. Morton Grove, Ill.: Albert Whitman, 1999. Unp.
Grades: P–3. What do you do if your Dad is out of work and you need new baseball shoes? Well, if you happen to have a leprechaun living in your basement like Michael McKeever, you ask him for the money to buy the shoes. The leprechaun does not want to share any of his gold, but he does manage to surprise Michael with a new pair of lucky, green baseball shoes. Watercolor illustrations fill the pages of this charming story.

Gibbons, Gail. *St. Patrick's Day*. New York: Holiday House, 1994. Unp.
Grades: K–3. The book introduces young readers to St. Patrick with information about his life and why he is honored. Then, readers learn about traditions and customs associated with this green holiday including: shamrocks, leprechauns, shillelaghs, harps, flowers, foods, plays, and parades. The book concludes with very brief descriptions of six of the legends surrounding St. Patrick's life.

St. Patrick's Day. Video. Bala Cynwyd, Penn.: Schlessinger Video Productions-Library Video Company, 1996. 25 min.
Grades: K–4. Viewers are treated to a rich mix of history, biography, music, step-dancing, and puppetry as they learn about the traditions

associated with St. Patrick's Day. Directions are given for creating a leprechaun puppet and a folktale about a leprechaun is included. This video is part of the Holidays for Children series.

Tompert, Ann. *St. Patrick*. Illustrated by Michael Garland. Honesdale, Penn.: Boyds Mill Press, 1998. 156p.
Grades: 1–4. This picture book biography combines engaging text with luminous illustrations to tell the story of the life of Ireland's patron saint. An author's note concludes the book and contains information on two well-known legends about St. Patrick, using the shamrock to teach about the Holy Trinity and driving the snakes from Ireland.

Markham, Marion M. *The St. Patrick's Day Shamrock Mystery*. Illustrated by Karen A. Jerome. Boston: Houghton Mifflin, 1995. 46p.
Grades: 2–4. When a green shamrock is painted on their neighbor's front door, the neighbor's cat is missing, and the sign to their clubhouse is defaced, the Dixon twins, Kate and Mickey, set out to uncover the culprit. The detective team gathers their clues and in the end finds the culprit and makes a new friend.

Freeman, Dorothy Rhodes. *St. Patrick's Day*. Berkeley Heights, N.J.: Enslow, 1992. 48p.
Grades: 2–5. Saint Patrick, the patron saint of Ireland, is the person honored on this special day, which commemorates the anniversary of his death. Patrick was born in and grew up in Britain. When he was sixteen he was kidnapped, taken to what is now Ireland, and was sold as a slave. This book tells of his life from that point on, and includes some of the legends about St. Patrick, as well as a glossary and an index. This book is from the Best Holiday Books series.

Landau, Elaine. *St. Patrick's Day*. Berkeley Heights, N.J.: Enslow, 2002. 48p.
Grades: 2–5. Imagine everyone wearing green clothes, seeing green decorations everywhere, and green food being served everywhere! This is the way it is on St. Patrick's Day. There are parties, parades, and four-leaf clovers galore. Information on the legends, symbols, and traditions associated with the holiday help readers understand why this holiday is associated with green food, shamrocks, leprechauns, and parades. The author provides a detailed account of the life of St. Patrick including his years as a slave and how his strong religious beliefs helped him to overcome adversity. There are margin notes and pictures as well as a craft project, a

glossary, a bibliography, Internet addresses, and an index. This book is from the Finding Out about Holidays series.

Nolan, Janet. *The St. Patrick's Day Shillelagh*. Illustrated by Ben F. Stahl. New York: Albert Whitman, 2002. Unp.
Grades: 2–5. Here is the story of a family of Irish immigrants who came to America during the potato famine. Before he leaves Ireland, Fegus, cuts a branch from a blackthorn tree and as he sails to America, he carves the branch into a shillelagh. Each generation passes the shillelagh on to the next and retells the family story, which keeps the family history alive. Acrylic illustrations realistically portray the story.

Barth, Edna. *Shamrocks, Harps, and Shillelaghs: The Story of St. Patrick's Day Symbols*. Illustrated by Ursula Arndt. New York: Houghton Mifflin, 2001. 96p.
Grades: 5 and up. Lively text enhanced by simple illustrations explains the stories, the legends, and the history of St. Patrick's Day. Readers learn about the origins of the symbols of St. Patrick's Day and how we celebrate this holiday in different countries. Activities and crafts fill the inside of the book's covers. An index is included.

Dunlop, Eileen. *Tales of St. Patrick*. New York: Holiday House, 1997. 125p.
Grades: 6–8. Since little is known about St. Patrick's life, Dunlop describes how his life might have been. The tale is based on her research using his writings and other sources. This is a fictionalized account of his life with a few facts and the author's suppositions. The book reads like a novel and students learn a great deal about the patron saint of Ireland.

Celebrating the Green: The History of St. Patrick's Day. Video. South Burlington, Va.: A & E Television Networks, 1998. 50 min.
Grades: 6 and up. In Ireland, this day is for celebrating the life of St. Patrick who brought Christianity to Ireland. Irish immigrants brought this celebration to America as a way to celebrate their Irish heritage. This lively, festive video features parades from across the country. This video is part of the History of the Holidays series.

EXPLORATIONS

1. Before studying about St. Patrick's Day, introduce words students are not likely to know but will encounter by presenting them as mysteries to be solved. Words might

include shamrock, step-dancing, leprechaun, shillelagh, harp, Emerald Isle, and jig. Provide the students with a list of the words and read them aloud. Divide the students into groups and have them discuss what they think the words mean. Have them write down the group's decision on what the words mean. Then, using the dictionary or books on St. Patrick's Day have them look up the words and write down the definitions of the words. Ask them to compare their guesses of the words' meanings with the definitions they found.

2. On the Kids Domain Web site at www.kidsdomain.com/holiday/patrick, students can learn about St. Patrick, e-mail a St. Patrick's Day card to a friend, read stories, play games, print out recipes, and find party activities.

3. Before reading *The Last Snake in Ireland: A Story about St. Patrick* (MacGill-Callahan, 1999), remind students that authors often use a problem solution structure to tell a

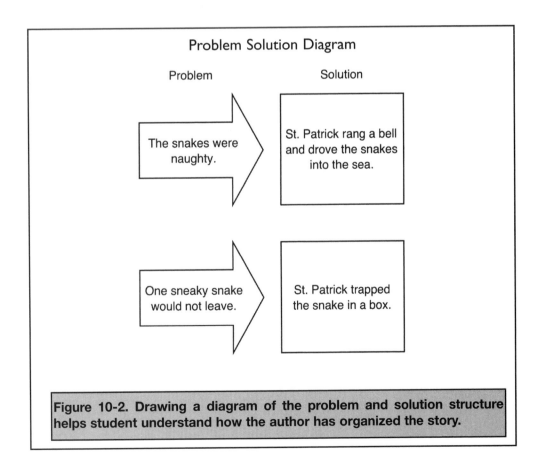

Problem Solution Diagram

Problem

Solution

The snakes were naughty.

St. Patrick rang a bell and drove the snakes into the sea.

One sneaky snake would not leave.

St. Patrick trapped the snake in a box.

Figure 10-2. Drawing a diagram of the problem and solution structure helps student understand how the author has organized the story.

story. Tell them that as you read the story, they are to listen carefully to determine the problems St. Patrick faced. After reading the story have students discuss what they think the problems and solutions were in the story. The example below can be used for younger students and more details can be added for older students.

4. After reading *The Last Snake in Ireland: A Story about St. Patrick* (MacGill-Callahan, 1999) and *St. Patrick* (Tompert, 1998) have students discuss the different methods used for driving snakes out of Ireland, for example, beating a drum and ringing a bell. Then have students brainstorm a list of ways to get rid of snakes. Remind them that they can be as fanciful as they like and should be accepting of each other's ideas. Let the class select one way and model for them how to create a story map to develop their ideas.

5. While reading *The St. Patrick's Day Shamrock Mystery* (Markham, 1995), have the students keep a detective

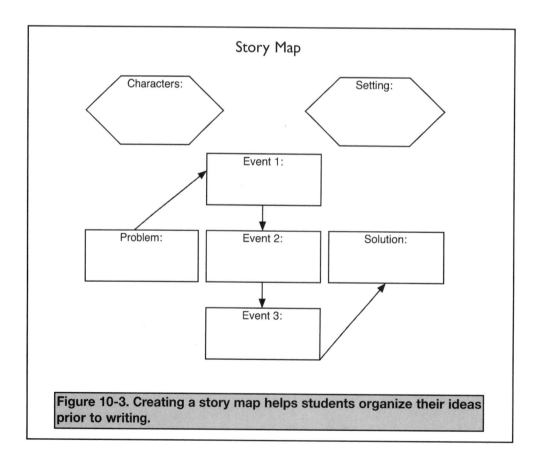

Figure 10-3. Creating a story map helps students organize their ideas prior to writing.

notebook to record their clues. After the students finish reading the book, have them share their notebooks with a partner and discuss how the clues gradually led them to the solution of the mystery.

6. After reading *The St. Patrick's Day Shamrock Mystery* (Markham, 1995) and examining how the author developed the plot, have the students work with a partner to write an outline for a detective story. Remind them to include the characters, setting, mystery to be solved, and sufficient clues to solve the mystery.

7. After reading *The St. Patrick's Day Shillelagh* (Nolan, 2002), ask the students to talk to their family members about family stories, traditions, or heirlooms that have been handed down from one generation to the next. Have students write down their family story or record a description of the tradition or heirloom. These can then be collected into a class book of family memories.

8. While reading *St. Patrick* (Tompert, 1998) or *Tales of St. Patrick* (Dunlop, 1997), have students sketch a flow chart depicting his life and travels.

ST. JOSEPH'S DAY

On the nineteenth day of March, Roman Catholics honor St. Joseph, the father of Christ, and give thanks for favors granted during the past year. This holiday started in Sicily in the Middle Ages, when the people prayed to St. Joseph to deliver them from a drought. Grateful for the rainy weather they received, the people set up banquets and invited everyone to attend. Christians in North America, South America, and Western Europe celebrate this feast day (Moehn, 2000). Santino (1994) refers to it as a festival that is an important part of the ethnic identity of Sicilian Catholics throughout the United States. It is a day of feasting and sharing with the poor (Henderson and Thompson, 2002). Communities prepare elaborate altars filled with food and candles. The food is blessed and distributed to the poor. In New Orleans, St. Joseph's Day is celebrated by visiting these elaborate altars, which are constructed in churches and private homes. More information about this holiday and pictures of St. Joseph's Day altars can be accessed at www.erc.msstate.edu/~achupa/StJo/sj_stand.html.

REFERENCES

Henderson, Helene, and Sue E. Thompson. 2002. *Holidays, Festivals, and Celebrations of the World Dictionary*, 3rd ed. Detroit, Mich.: Omnigraphics.

Kindersley, Anabel. 1997. Celebrations. New York: DK Publishing.

Krasno, Rena. 2000. *Floating Lanterns and Golden Shrines: Celebrating Japanese Festivals*. Berkeley, Calif.: Pacific View Press.

Landau, Elaine. 2002. *St. Patrick's Day*. Berkeley Heights, N.J.: Enslow.

MacMillan, Dianne M. 1997. *Japanese Children's Day and the Obon Festival*. Berkeley Heights, N.J.: Enslow Publishers.

Moehn, Heather. 2000. *World Holidays: A Watts Guide for Children*. New York: Franklin Watts.

Santino, Jack. 1994. *All Around the Year: Holidays and Celebrations in American Life*. Urbana, Ill.: University of Illinois Press.

APRIL HOLIDAYS AND CELEBRATIONS **11**

In April, the earth is once again green, colorful flowers are blooming, the weather is warming, and our thoughts turn to cleaning and gardening. Before we celebrate serious festivals, we start the month with April Fools' Day pranks and practical jokes. After April Fools' Day come International Children's Book Day, Hana Matsuri, Earth Day, and Arbor Day. April 2 is the birthday of Hans Christian Andersen commemorated with International Children's Book Day. Celebrated on April 8 in Japan, Hana Matsuri (Buddha's birthday) is quite distinct from the Hina Matsuri (Dolls Day Festival) one month earlier. On the twenty-second of the month is Earth Day, a day to commit to taking care of the Earth all year long. The founder of Arbor Day, Julius Sterling Morton, was born on April 22, which is when his home state of Nebraska celebrates Arbor Day. Each state sets its own date for Arbor Day. April festivals go from silly, to serious, as the month starts with pranks and ends with a dedicated effort to improve the environment and protect it for future generations.

APRIL FOOLS' DAY

The first of April is the day for harmless pranks, practical jokes, and hoaxes. There are various traditions about the origin of April Fools' Day. Some believe it originated when the Gregorian calendar was adopted and the first day of the year was changed, some say it originated with the Hindu festival of "Holi," and others that it originated in Scotland with the hunting of the gowk, a cuckoo, on April first (Henderson and Thompson, 2002; Zalben, 1999). People who are tricked in Scotland are referred to as a gowk or a cuckoo; and in England, they are called a noodie or gawby (Moehn, 2000). In France, they try to pin paper fish on each other's backs and the person with a fish pinned on their back is called an "April fish" (Moehn,

2000). Literature from around the world contains stories about fools or noodleheads, and one way to commemorate April Fools' Day is to share stories about fools.

BOOK AND MEDIA CHOICES

Minarik, Else Holmelund. *April Fools!* Illustrated by Chris Hahner. New York: HarperCollins, 2002. 24p.
Grades: P–1. Readers join Little Bear and his friends as they play tricks on each other on April Fools' Day. Charming illustrations accompany the story of the gentle bear and his friends.

Ruelle, Karen Gray. *April Fool!* New York: Holiday House, 2002. 32p.
Grades: K–3. Harry and his little sister, Emily, visit the magic store as they prepare for April Fools' Day foolishness. They succeed in tricking their parents and just as Harry decides that Emily is not going to be able to surprise him, she does. In fact, the artwork reveals that Emily has one last surprise planned for her brother when he crawls into bed. Simple watercolor illustrations complement the charming story. This book is from the Holiday House Reader series.

Salley, Coleen. *Epossumondas*. Illustrated by Janet Stevens. San Diego: Harcourt, 2002. Unp.
Grades: P–4. Professional storyteller Coleen Salley brings to life loveable noodlehead Epossumondas, a charming possum, who just cannot seem to figure out how safely to transport things his aunt sends home to his mother. It is not that he cannot follow directions; he just takes them too literally. Young and old delight at his antics and eagerly anticipate each visit to his aunt's house. A storyteller's note at the end of the tale provides information on folktales and noddlehead stories, and it raises the question as to whether or not Epossumondas was just trying to get out of running all those errands.

Stevenson, James. *Mud Flat April Fool*. New York: Greenwillow Books, 1998. 48p.
Grades: K–2. The animals in Mud Flats spend April Fools' Day trying out tricks on one another. Some of them work and some of them fall flat. A water-squirting rose, buckets of water, a dollar bill on a string, a singing tree, and a head put on backwards are just some of the foolish pranks encountered in this book filled with short chapters, just right for readers who are ready to move into chapter books.

Brown, Marc. *Arthur's April Fool*. New York: Scholastic, 1983. Unp.
Grades: K–4. Arthur is worried. Binky Barnes has taken Arthur's pen and threatened to pulverize him. On top of that, he is concerned about doing his magic tricks at the school assembly on April Fools' Day. In typical Arthur fashion he manages to get his pen back, avoid being pulverized, and have his audience, including Mr. Ratburn, laughing at his magic tricks. This book is also available on audiocassette.

Denise, Christopher. *The Fool of the World and the Flying Ship*. New York: Philomel Books, 1994. Unp.
Grades: K–4. When the Tsar proclaims that he will wed his daughter to anyone who can build a flying ship, the Fool sets out to win the hand of the Tsar's daughter. Along the way he meets the Old One and shares his meal with him. Then, the Old One directs him to a flying ship. As he flies, he collects an unlikely band of animals, who join him on his trip. When he reaches his destination the animals he befriended on the way help him overcome the obstacles the Tsar continues to put in his way and in the end he weds the Tsar's daughter. The illustrator depicted all of the characters as animals and dressed them in traditional Russian garb.

Markham, Marion M. *The April Fool's Day Mystery*. Illustrated by Pau Estrada. Boston: Houghton Mifflin, 1991. 42p.
Grades: 2–4. When the Dixon twins arrive at school on April Fool's Day everyone is playing April Fools' pranks such as dangling black rubber spiders, switching desks, and giving fake tests. Suddenly, a terrified scream pierces the air, and students learn that someone put a snake in the flour bin in the school cafeteria. Billy Wades is accused of the prank, and he hires the Dixon detectives to prove he is innocent.

Hamilton, Martha, and Mitch Weiss. *Noodlehead Stories: World Tales Kids Can Read and Tell*. Little Rock, Ark.: August House Publishers, 2000. 96p.
Grades: 3–8. This is a delightful collection of noodlehead stories for sharing. The authors caution that noodle stories are not for making fun of others. Rather they are told because we have all done noodle things ourselves and these stories enable us to laugh at ourselves. A map at the beginning of the book shows the countries of origin for the twenty-three stories in the collection. The book concludes with tips for telling stories, follow-up activities for the stories, and sources for the stories.

Hoaxes and Deceptions. Richmond, Va.: Time-Life Books, 1991. 152p.
Grades: 7 and up. Forgeries, fakes, impostors, frauds, counterfeits, and pranks fill the pages of this book. Photographs, reproductions, and illustrations depict the people responsible and some of their creations. These hoaxes and deceptions span the globe and the years.

EXPLORATIONS

1. After reading *Epossumondas* (Salley, 2002), have children discuss whether Epossumondas was really a noodlehead or was he really quite clever.

2. After reading *Mud Flat April Fool* (Stevenson, 1998), have students discuss which pranks were funny and which ones were not. Then, have them determine why some of the pranks worked and some of them did not.

3. Before reading *The Fool of the World and the Flying Ship* (Denise, 1994) tell the students that the folktale has a cause and effect pattern. As they listen to the story, have them sketch the cause and effect pattern of the story.

4. After reading *The April Fool's Day Mystery* (Markham, 1991), have the students make a two-column chart. In the first column, list harmless April Fools' Day pranks; in the second, list those that could have serious consequences. Remind students of the importance of thinking about the consequences of their actions before attempting a prank.

5. After sharing some of the stories in *Noodlehead Stories: World Tales Kids Can Read and Tell* (Hamilton and Weiss, 2000), go over the storytelling tips in the book. Encourage the students to pick their favorite story and practice telling the story to their classmates. Some students may be interested in telling their stories to younger students in the school.

6. Students may enjoy working together to create other adventures for characters from the stories in *Noodlehead Stories: World Tales Kids Can Read and Tell* (Hamilton and Weiss, 2000). The students can work on their noodlehead tales during writing workshop.

7. On April Fools' Day read aloud selections from *Hoaxes and Deceptions* and provide time for students to discuss them.

Then, place the book in a reading center for students to peruse when they have time.

INTERNATIONAL CHILDREN'S BOOK DAY

Hans Christian Andersen was born on April 2, 1805, in Denmark, the date on which we celebrate International Children's Book Day. Since Andersen could not make a living as an actor, he began writing fairy tales (Barkin and James, 1994). The fairy tales he wrote remain favorites of children of all nationalities (Henderson and Thompson, 2002). The International Board on Books for Young People (IBBY) presents the Hans Christian Andersen Awards to one author and one illustrator who have made significant contributions to children's literature (Barkin and James, 1994). These awards are presented every other year and recipients include Paula Fox, Virginia Hamilton, Katherine Patterson, Maurice Sendak, Mitsumasa Anno, and Anthony Browne. For additional information on these awards, check the IBBY Activities link at www.ibby.org.

BOOK AND MEDIA CHOICES

Andersen, Hans Christian. *Ugly Duckling*. Illustrated by Jerry Pinkney. New York: William Morrow, 1999. Unp.
Grades: P–4. Exceptional watercolor illustrations capture the harsh winter, the warm spring, and the beauty of the ugly duckling that changes into a beautiful swan. This is a timeless tale that reminds readers that unhappiness and loneliness can be overcome.

Andersen, Hans Christian. *The Steadfast Tin Soldier*. Illustrated by Fred Marcellino. Retold by Tor Seidler. New York: HarperCollins, 1992. Unp.
Grades: K–4. A one legged tin soldier standing under the Christmas tree falls in love with a paper ballerina poised on one leg. He survives a series of mishaps only to end up being tossed in a burning fire, when a gust of wind from an opened door sends the ballerina to his side. The next morning all that remains of them is a heart-shaped piece of tin and a blackened spangle from the ballerina's dress. The illustrations beckon readers to explore them.

Andersen, Hans Christian. *The Little Match Girl*. Illustrated by Jerry Pinkney. New York: Phyllis Fogelman Books, 1999. Unp.

Grades: K–8. This adaptation places the little match girl in America on crowded city streets in the early 1920s. On a cold, snowy New Year's Eve, she stands on the street corner trying to sell matches and flowers. To warm herself, she lights her matches and in the brief flames visions of food, warmth, love, and happier times appear. In the morning, she is found frozen in the corner of a building.

EXPLORATIONS

1. After reading *Ugly Duckling* (Andersen, 1999) talk to students about the changes in the illustrations and the changes in the duckling as winter turns to spring. Relate this to the changes they can observe in their own backyards or on the school playground as the seasons change.

2. After reading *The Steadfast Tin Soldier* (Andersen, 1992), have students return to the text and create a flow diagram (Moline, 1995) of the mishaps encountered by the tin soldier. Students can create the diagram on plain paper with a pencil or they can use the drawing tools in a word processing program.

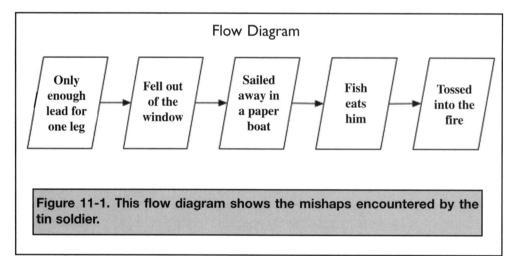

Flow Diagram

Only enough lead for one leg → Fell out of the window → Sailed away in a paper boat → Fish eats him → Tossed into the fire

Figure 11-1. This flow diagram shows the mishaps encountered by the tin soldier.

3. In *The Steadfast Tin Soldier* (Andersen, 1992), the soldier is placed in a folded paper boat for a wild ride through the sewers. Instructions for folding a paper boat can be found on The Upper Mississippi, Yesterday and Today Web site at www.uppermississippi.info. These illustrated step-by-step instructions provide students with an opportunity to work on reading and following directions.

4. In *The Little Match Girl* (Andersen, 1999) the child is unseen by those around her as they hurry to their holiday celebrations. Take this opportunity to talk about looking out for others and helping those less fortunate.

HANA MATSURI (BUDDHA'S BIRTHDAY)

Hana Matsuri (Festival of the Flowers) is the Japanese observance of Buddha's birthday. Although the Chinese celebrate his birth on the last full moon of May, in Japan festivities are held on April 8is (Winchester, 1996). Temple ceremonies include anointing a statue of Buddha with sweet tea made from hydrangea leaves (Henderson and Thompson, 2002). In Japan his birth, enlightenment, and death are celebrated on different dates, whereas other countries combine these major events in one celebration—the Vesak (Wesakfestival—when the moon is full in the constellation of Scorpio and the sun is in Taurus, usually in May (Erricker and Erricker, 1997). The books annotated below contain information on Gautama Buddha, the Buddhist religion, and the Dalai Lama, the leader of the Tibetan Buddhist tradition.

BOOK AND MEDIA CHOICES

Demi. *Buddha*. New York: Henry Holt, 1996. Unp.
Grades: 2–4. This is the story of the young prince, Siddhartha, who gave up his life of privilege to find the truth of life over death. After discovering the truth, he became a Buddha and devoted his life to teaching others how to find inner peace using the Eightfold Path and meditations. Indian, Chinese, Japanese, Burmese, and Indonesian paintings were the inspirations for the illustrations in this book.

Pandell, Karen, with Barry Bryant. *Learning from the Dalai Lama: Secrets of the Wheel of Time*. Photographs by John B. Taylor. New York: Dutton Children's Books, 1995. 40p.
Grades: 4–8. An introduction to Buddhism and the Dalai Lama precedes information on the Dalai Lama's visit to New York City where he was the Vajra Master for a Kalachakra Initiation. A Kalachakra (Wheel of Time mandala) is an elaborate sand painting seven feet in diameter that takes eight days to construct. Some of the images included in the painting are seven hundred twenty-two gods and goddesses, seven hundred twenty-one other deities, flowers, and

animals. On the twelfth day of the ceremony, the sand in the mandala is brushed away and ceremonially placed in a body of water. The book includes instructions for making a mandala, a glossary, and an index.

EXPLORATIONS

1. Before reading *Buddha* (Demi, 1996), show the students the pictures. Based on what they see in the illustrations have them generate a list of questions they would like to have answered. Read the story and see if they can find answers to their questions. Ask if any other questions came to mind as you read the story.

2. After reading Learning from the *Dalai Lama: Secrets of the Wheel of Time* (Pandell and Bryant, 1995), students can visit an online photo gallery of Mandala sand paintings at www.newportnet.com/archives/mandala/nancy/home.htm.

EARTH DAY

The first Earth Day held on April 22, 1970, called attention to the Earth's serious environmental problems. In the 1970s, the governor of Wisconsin, Gaylord Nelson, traveled across America speaking about the hazards of pollution (Landau, 2002). He enlisted the aid of a college student, Dennis Hayes, to plan the first Earth Day. Celebrating Earth Day has made people stop and think about ways to protect the environment. Laws have been enacted to protect the environment and people continue to work to clean up the environment (Spies, 1992). Some changes growing out of this renewed environmental consciousness include the establishment of the Environmental Protection Agency, the Clean Air Act, the Clean Water Act, and the Endangered Species Act (Landau, 2002). Earth Day is not a national holiday, but many states and cities celebrate by promoting recycling, saving energy, and cleaning up beaches and other public land. More work to preserve our natural resources remains to be done and Earth Day encourages people around the globe to be concerned about the environment and take steps to protect it. (See Arbor Day and Tu Bi-Shevat.)

Book and Media Choices

Asch, Frank. *The Earth and I*. San Diego: Harcourt Brace, 1994. Unp.
Grades: P–1. Rainbow illustrations and simple text tell of a young child's connections to the earth. Watercolors, acrylics, and colored pencils were used to create bright, radiant illustrations that portray everything the earth has to offer. Knowing that the earth is sad when used as a dumping ground, the young child cleans up the dumping ground.

Garbage. Video. Bala Cynwyd, Penn.: Schlessinger Video Productions-Library Video Company, 1994. 25 min.
Grades: P–2. This award winning video takes students on a field trip with a sanitation worker, who shows them what happens to their garbage after it is picked up from their houses. Along the way, they learn about landfills and recycling.

Thornhill, Jan. *Before and After: A Book of Nature Timescapes*. Washington, D.C.: National Geographic, 1997. Unp.
Grades: P–2. Nature's changes over time are explored in these bright, colorful illustrations. The first two-page spread features the "before" scene; the second two-page spread depicts the same scene after an hour, a day, or a year. Nature notes at the end of the book tell more about the illustrations. The environments depicted include a tropical coral reef, a savannah, a forest edge, a wetland, a meadow, a rainforest, and a schoolyard.

Gibbons, Gail. *Recycle: A Handbook for Kids*. Boston: Little, Brown, 1992. Unp.
Grades: P–3. In this book, children learn how to recycle and discover what happens to items that are recycled. Colorful pictures and concise text assure that young children grasp the concepts. The book concludes with facts about recycling and garbage in addition to ideas for how children can help clean up the environment.

Environmental Songs for Kids. CD. Washington, D.C.: Smithsonian Folkways Recordings, 1999.
Grades: K–3. Twenty-four songs sung by Coco Kallis tell of the importance of recycling, conserving water, and disposing of trash wisely. Some of the songs included on the CD are: "If We Don't Fix It," "Recycle," and "The Strangest Dream."

McLeod, Elaine. *Lessons from Mother Earth*. Illustrated by Colleen Wood. Toronto, Can.: Groundwood Books, 2002. Unp.
Grades: K–3. Grandma invites Tess to visit her garden. Tess learns that all the land outside of Grandma's house is her garden. Grandma teaches Tess how to care for the land by only taking what you need when it is ready to be picked. Watercolor illustrations show the wonder and bounty of nature that is to be revered.

Wallace, Nancy Elizabeth. *Recycle Every Day!* New York: Marshall Cavendish, 2003. Unp.
Grades: K–3. Wallace's delightful use of origami and paper collage enhance the story of Minna and her family as they decide how to help Minna with her school recycling plans. There is a recycle game, a recycle activity, an author's note and an opportunity for readers to find recycled pages in the book. This is a good introductory book for young children to become aware of recycling.

Crunch, Smash, Trash!: Monster Machines that Recycle. Video. Bala Cynwyd, Penn.: Schlessinger Video Productions-Library Video Company, 1994. 30 min.
Grades: K–4. Students discover what happens to the items they place in recycle bins in this award winning video. In behind the scene footage, loud, massive machinery changes discarded items into reusable raw material.

Maass, Robert. *Garbage*. New York: Henry Holt and Company, 2000. Unp.
Grades: K–4. Household garbage is followed from curbside to a landfill in this photo essay that causes students to stop and think about the garbage generated each day in homes across America. Students also learn about recycling and composting. The book concludes with a glossary.

Van Allsburg, Chris. *Just a Dream*. Boston: Houghton Mifflin, 1990. Unp.
Grades: K–4. Walter scoffs at sorting trash and at his friend getting a tree for a birthday present. Walter dreams of living in the future, in a world of robots and machines. One night as he sleeps he is whisked away to the future where he experiences first-hand the effects of pollution on the earth. He lands on a huge garbage dump, coughs from the tops of belching smokestacks, and meets fishermen elated at catching two very small fish. When he awakens, he runs outside to sort the trash and asks for a tree for his birthday. The

graphic depictions of what the future could hold make readers stop and think about what they can do to make changes.

Spinelli, Eileen. *Song for the Whooping Crane*. Illustrated by Elsa Warnick. Grand Rapids, Mich.: Eerdmans Books for Young Readers, 2000. Unp.
Grades: K and up. Lyrical, graceful, poetic narrative describes the habits and movements of the endangered whooping crane. Soft, flowing paintings depict the birds in flight and at rest. By learning more about these animals, readers develop an appreciation for them and an understanding of why they need to be protected.

Kids & the Environment. Win/Mac CD-ROM. Watertown, Maine: Tom Snyder Productions.
Grades: 2–6. When faced with a litter-strewn playground the soccer team has to decide whether they will pick up the litter or practice during recess. Students use higher order thinking skills as they consider their options and the possible consequences of their decisions. As they participate in the simulation, they learn about taking care of the environment, recycling, and garbage pickup. This software is from the *Choices, Choices 5.0* software series.

Arnosky, Jim. Field Trips: *Bug Hunting, Animal Tracking, Bird-Watching, and Shore Walking with Jim Arnosky*. New York: HarperCollins, 2002. 96p.
Grades: 3 and up. One way to help students develop an appreciation of the earth and its creatures is by having them take field trips to explore and discover. Arnosky's guidebook provides students with ideas for observing wildlife and hints for improving their observational skills. He suggests carrying a pencil and notepad for recording findings and sketching what they see. The book's black-and-white illustrations help students identify the animals and tracks they uncover on their trips. The book concludes with a glossary.

Allen, Judy, ed. *Anthology for the Earth*. Cambridge, Mass.: Candlewick Press, 1998. 96p.
Grades: 4 and up. Inspiring words from authors including an eleven-year-old boy, Willa Cather, and Rudyard Kipling are coupled with stunning artwork from illustrators including Nicola Bayley, Cathie Felstead, and Jean Paul Tibbles. Together the words and the artwork create a masterpiece that reminds readers why the earth and her creatures are to be treasured and protected. The book concludes

with brief biographies of the authors, an index of authors, and an index of illustrators.

Landau, Elaine. *Earth Day: Keeping Our Planet Clean*. Berkeley Heights, N.J.: Enslow, 2002. 48p.
Grades: 2–5. A large body of people worries about the condition of the environment on Earth. With as many people as we have polluting and using up our natural resources, they fear planet Earth will not be fit to live on in a number of years. They started Earth Day in the 1970s on a small scale, but now it is celebrated all over the United States and in some foreign countries. This book is a good introduction to young readers about this important day. Margin notes and pictures add information and appeal to this book. It closes with a craft project, a timeline, a glossary, a bibliography, a list of Internet addresses, and an index. This book is from the Finding Out about Holidays series.

The Environment. Win/Mac CD-ROM. Watertown, Maine: Tom Snyder Productions.
Grades: 2–6. This software program mixes science and social studies as students figure out how to clean the city's polluted pond. Recycling, landfills, the greenhouse effect, and political trade-offs are all encountered as they make decisions about the pond. This software is from the *Decisions, Decisions 5.0* software series.

Chandler, Gary, and Kevin Graham. *Recycling*. New York: Henry Holt, 1996. 64p.
Grades: 5–8. Recycling activists have a story to tell, and this collection shares their stories. By activists, this book means children, adults, companies, and communities that took the initiative and created useful products from recycled materials. For example, plastic bottles are recycled into fences, old maps are recycled into envelopes, and old circuit boards are recycled into clocks. At the end of each story, contact information, gives readers an opportunity to learn more about the product. The book concludes with a list of recycling facts, a glossary, books for further reading, and an index.

Gardner, Robert. *Celebrating Earth Day: A Sourcebook of Activities and Experiments*. Illustrated by Sharon Lane Holm. Brookfield, Conn.: The Millbrook Press, 1992. 96p.
Grades: 6–10. Hands-on learning activities and experiments ensure that students understand the Earth's environmental problems and provide them with ideas for things they can do everyday to improve

their environment. While the book is for older students, teachers of younger students will find ideas for hands-on activities they can share with their students as they teach about the importance of taking care of the Earth. A bibliography and an index conclude the book.

Garbage. Video. The History Channel, A & E Television Networks, 1999. 25 min.
Grades: 7 and up. Rather than dumping garbage in the ocean, burying it, or burning it this video examines modern alternatives. Viewers hear from garbologists, scientists, sanitation workers, and public officials about how they dispose of garbage. In this video from the Modern Marvels Science Series, viewers travel from landfills to recycling centers as they learn about this persistent environmental problem.

EXPLORATIONS

1. Students can learn more about the Earth's environmental problems and what they can do to help on the U.S. Environmental Protection Agency Web site. The Web site for elementary students is located at www.epa.gov/kids. Middle school and high school students can find age-appropriate information at www.epa.gov/students.

2. Before watching *Garbage Day* or *Crunch, Smash, Trash!: Monster Machines that Recycle*, begin a class discussion of what happens to items they throw away or recycle. Then, have them write about their ideas. After watching the videos, engage students in a discussion about what they learned, before having them write about what happens to the items. Finally, have them compare the two pieces of writing and discuss what they learned.

3. After watching *Garbage Day* or *Crunch, Smash, Trash!: Monster Machines that Recycle* or after reading *Recycle: A Handbook for Kids* (Gibbons, 1992) ask the students to brainstorm a list of objects they have in their homes that can be recycled. From the list, select one item such as plastic bottles or newspapers and have the students estimate how many they throw away each week in their homes. Combine their estimates for a total figure. Then, explain that for the next week they are to bring the items to school. At the end of the week, compare the total number of items they brought in with their original estimate. Use

the total number of items the class collected to have them estimate how many would have been thrown away by all the families in their school or town.

4. Before reading *Just a Dream* (Van Allsburg, 1990) have the students raise their hands to indicate if they would like to receive a tree for a birthday present. After reading the book share with them that for Tu Bi-Shevat and for Arbor Day, people often have trees planted in their honor.

5. After reading *Song for the Whooping Crane* (Spinelli, 2000), write one of the descriptive sentences on the board. Then, have students discuss the definitions of any unfamiliar words. Help them see how the author used descriptive words to paint vivid, action pictures in their minds as they read. Show them the illustration for the sentence that was written on the board and have them offer opinions on whether or not the illustrator captured the words in the picture.

6. Using the information in *Field Trips: Bug Hunting, Animal Tracking, Bird-Watching, and Shore Walking with Jim Arnosky* (Arnosky, 2002) have students practice keeping a nature notebook while examining bugs, animals, or birds on the school playground or at a nearby park. Then, arrange a field trip to a nature center for the students to continue their nature observations.

7. Provide students with information about recycling efforts in their neighborhood. Then, have them discuss ways they can help with recycling in their neighborhood.

8. While studying about recycling have the students make one list of things they find in their homes that can be recycled and another list of things in their homes that are made of recycled materials. Look around your own home and bring in items with markings on the bottom that indicate they can be recycled and items made from recycled materials. Show the items to the students to give them ideas for what they might find in their homes.

9. Allow students an opportunity to pick out their favorite words in *Anthology for the Earth* (Allen, 1998) and draw an illustration reflecting their interpretation of the words.

10. After watching the video *Garbage*, ask students if anything in the video surprised them; or, ask them what they learned

that might help them make wise decisions about disposing of garbage.

ARBOR DAY

Arbor Day is designated as a time to plant trees and take care of the Earth. Each state sets its own date for celebrating Arbor Day. In Nebraska, it is celebrated on April 22, Julius Sterling Morton's birthday. After moving from New York to Nebraska in 1854, Morton realized that the settlers needed to plant trees to provide them with shade, protect them during blizzards, and keep the soil from blowing away (Spies, 1992). Johnny Appleseed spent his life growing apple trees and sharing seedlings with settlers who moved west. For this reason his work is often commemorated on Arbor Day. Some people celebrate Johnny Appleseed Day on March 11, which is the day he died (Barkin and James, 1994). To learn when your state celebrates Arbor Day and to obtain additional information, visit the National Arbor Day Foundation Web site at www.arborday.org. (See Earth Day and Tu Bi-Shevat.)

BOOK AND MEDIA CHOICES

Bennet, Kelly. *Arbor Day*. New York: Children's Press, 2003. 32p.
Grades: P–2. The book contains brief background information on the history of Arbor Day and information on activities for marking its observance. Large, easy-to-read text and color photographs encourage beginning readers to read this text on their own. A picture glossary is included. This book is from the Rookie Read-About Holidays series.

Bulla, Clyde Robert. *A Tree Is a Plant*. Illustrated by Stacey Schuett. New York: HarperCollins, 2001. 33p.
Grades: P–2. As an apple seed grows into a tree, readers follow its life cycle. They watch the tree grow as the seasons change and learn how it takes in food and water. The book concludes with an experiment on what happens to water once it travels to the leaves of the tree, instructions for estimating the age of a tree, and resources for learning more. This book is from the Let's-Read-and-Find-Out Science series.

Arbor Day. Video. Bala Cynwyd, Penn.: Schlessinger Video Productions-Library Video Company, 1994. 30 min.
Grades: K–4. Viewers learn about J. Sterling Morton the founder of Arbor Day and how the day was named after his home, Arbor Lodge. The legend of Johnny Appleseed is told in animated pictures. Students learn the importance of respecting nature and the importance of trees in our lives. A teacher's guide is included. This video is from the Holidays for Children series.

Kellogg, Steven. *Johnny Appleseed*. New York: Morrow Junior Books, 1988. Unp.
Grades: 1–4. Fact and fiction are woven together in the legend of Johnny Appleseed, whose real name was John Chapman. He traveled west from Massachusetts clearing land and planting apple orchards for the settlers he knew would follow. Kellogg's lush illustrations are filled with details that draw readers in for closer examinations. Young students return to the book repeatedly because the illustrations alone will tell the story.

Warrick, Karen Clemens. *John Chapman: The Legendary Johnny Appleseed*. Springfield, N.J.: Enslow, 2001. 128p.
Grades: 4–8. Legends abound regarding the life of Johnny Appleseed, and Warrick presents fables as well as the known facts about his life. Two known facts are that he traveled west planting apple trees along the routes he knew settlers would travel and that he was a very religious man. The book includes a map showing where he planted apple trees in Ohio and Indiana and a photograph of the last surviving apple tree known to be planted by Chapman. A chronology, chapter notes, a glossary, resources for learning more, and an index are included.

EXPLORATIONS

1. By joining The National Arbor Day Foundation for a nominal fee, members receive ten small trees that can be planted in the schoolyard. Information on joining The National Arbor Day Foundation can be found on their Web site at www.arborday.org/join/index2.html.

2. If there is no room on the school grounds, for just ten dollars trees can be bought to commemorate a special event or a person. These trees are planted in national forests.

Information on this program can be found at www.arbor-day.org/join/treecelebration.html.

3. Using the instructions in *A Tree Is a Plant* (Bulla, 2001) students can estimate the age of a tree in the schoolyard, a nearby park, or their own backyard.

4. After reading *A Tree Is a Plant* (Bulla, 2001), have students create a simple circle map using words and/or pictures to show the life cycle of the tree. A template for the map might look something like the one below.

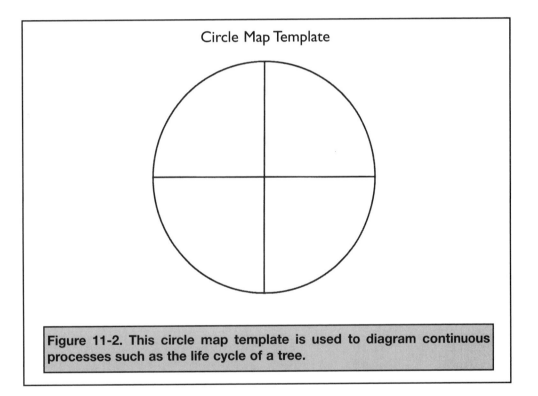

Circle Map Template

Figure 11-2. This circle map template is used to diagram continuous processes such as the life cycle of a tree.

5. After reading *Johnny Appleseed* (Kellogg, 1988) or John Chapman: The Legendary Johnny Appleseed (Warrick, 2001), invite students to an apple tasting with different varieties of apples. At the tasting have students write down descriptions of the different tastes of the apples using words such as tart, sweet, mushy, or crisp. Encourage them to be imaginative in their descriptions, such as relating the taste to a feeling or memory, and perhaps compare the taste of the apples to other foods.

6. After reading *John Chapman: The Legendary Johnny Appleseed* (Warrick, 2001) engage the students in a discussion of the legends surrounding Johnny Appleseed and encourage them to speculate on how they came to be.

REFERENCES

Barkin, Carol, and Elizabeth James. 1994. *The Holiday Handbook.* New York: Clarion Books.

Erricker, Clive, and Jane Erricker. 1997. *Buddhist Festivals.* Crystal Lake, Ill.: Heinemann Library.

Henderson, Helene, and Sue E. Thompson. 2002. *Holidays, Festivals, and Celebrations of the World Dictionary*, 3rd ed. Detroit, Mich.: Omnigraphics.

Landau, Elaine. 2002. *Earth Day: Keeping Our Planet Clean.* Berkeley Heights, N.J.: Enslow.

Moehn, Heather. 2000. *World Holidays: A Watts Guide for Children*. New York: Franklin Watts.

Moline, Steve. 1995. *I See What You Mean: Children at Work with Visual Information*. York, Maine: Stenhouse.

Spies, Karen. 1992. *Our National Holidays.* Brookfield, Conn.: The Millbrook Press.

Winchester, Faith. 1996. *Asian Holidays*. Mankato, Minn.: Capstone Press.

Zalben, Jane Breskin. 1999. *To Every Season: A Family Holiday Cookbook.* New York: Simon & Schuster Books for Young Readers.

MAY HOLIDAYS AND CELEBRATIONS 12

May brings warm sunshine, lengthening days, and birds singing. In this month at the height of spring, we celebrate May Day, Cinco de Mayo, Tango-no-sekku, Kodomono-Hi, Mother's Day, and Memorial Day. The first day of the month is May Day, a celebration of spring. Cinco de Mayo (May fifth) commemorates the Mexican army defeating the French and for Mexican Americans this is a day to celebrate their heritage. To the Japanese, May fifth is Tango-no-sekku (Boys' Day) and Kodomono-Hi (Children's Day). Mother's Day, the second Sunday in May, gives us occasion to pause and remember all that mothers do for us. The last Monday in May is Memorial Day for honoring veterans, who have died in wars. May is a month for celebrating new life, mothers and children, and for remembering battles and those who died fighting for freedom.

MAY DAY

The first day of May was originally considered the first day of spring and observances focused on sprouting plants and hopes for a bountiful harvest. The Celts called this day Beltane and it marked the end of winter and the beginning of spring (Leslie and Gerace, 2000). The May pole dance consists of a tall pole decorated with flowers and long ribbon streamers. As the dancers twirl around the pole holding onto the ribbons, the ribbons become woven around the pole. Christians commemorate this day by placing a crown of flowers on a statue of the Virgin Mary and recognizing her importance in the church. In Hawaii, May first is Lei Day. Everyone is encouraged to wear leis and celebrate the day with dancing, music, lei-making demonstrations, and lei-making contests. For some, May Day is for commemorating workers' rights with parades, speeches, and fireworks (Moehn, 2000). (See Labor Day for books on workers' rights.)

BOOK AND MEDIA CHOICES

Silverman, Erica. *On the Morn of Mayfest*. Illustrated by Marla Frazee. New York: Simon & Schuster Books for Young Readers, 1998. Unp.
Grades: P–3. In this cumulative tale, on the first of May, a sleepwalking lass "with hair like a nest" attracts a string of followers. The result of her stroll is an impromptu May Day parade that involves the entire village. Detailed, colorful illustrations bring this celebration of spring to life.

Kroll, Steven. *Queen of the May*. Illustrated by Patience Brewster. New York: Holiday House, 1993. Unp.
Grades: P–4. Sylvie planned to collect the most beautiful bouquet of flowers to take to the village so she would be chosen Queen of the May. Her stepsister and stepmother had other plans for her and kept her busy with chores. With help from animals that she rescued, she arrives in the village in a beautiful white dress with a bouquet of flowers and is crowned Queen of the May.

EXPLORATIONS

1. Before reading *On the Morn of Mayfest* (Silverman, 1998), explain what a cumulative tale is to the students. Read the story to the students so that they will understand how a cumulative tale is written. Then, divide the children into nine groups for the nine items in the tale: lass, dove, huntsman, mouse, cat, sheepdog, laundress, jugglers, monkey, children, minstrel, and milkmaid. Read the story again having the students chime in when their item is read. (See *The Matzah That Papa Brought Home* under the Passover section of chapter nine for another cumulative tale.)

2. Before reading *Queen of the May* (Kroll, 1993), have a student briefly recall the story of Cinderella. After reading *Queen of the May* (Kroll, 1993) have students determine which story elements are common to both tales. For example, both stories have a stepmother, who tries to prevent the heroine from doing something.

3. Have students visit the Web page "'Round the Maypole: Celebrating May Day" at www.umkc.edu/imc/mayday.htm to discover how May Day is celebrated in different countries around the world.

CINCO DE MAYO

On May 5, 1862, at the Battle of Puebla, the Mexican army defeated the French who were trying to take control of Mexico (Spies, 1992). A small, brave Mexican army was outnumbered two to one, but with resolve and ingenuity, they overcame the French army (Menard, 2000). Although this battle was not the end of the war with France, eventually Mexico won the war (Goring, 1995). Mexican independence did not come until five years after this battle, although Cinco de Mayo is often mistaken as a celebration of Mexico's independence from Spain (Menard, 2000). In Mexico, festivities include parades, battle reenactments, and fiestas. A fiesta is a big party with food, crafts, flowers, musicians, dancers, games, carnival rides, and singing (Gnojewski, 2002). Cinco de Mayo celebrations include music, folklorico dancers, food, carnival rides, and low-rider car shows. Additional information about this holiday and resources for teachers can be found at www.kiddyhouse.com/Holidays/Cinco. (See Mexican Independence Day.)

BOOK AND MEDIA CHOICES

Wade, Mary Dodson. *Cinco de Mayo*. New York: Children's Press, 2003. 32p.
Grades: P–2. This is a brief introduction to Cinco de Mayo for young students. Beginning readers can read the book on their own. Colorful photographs are included in the text and in the accompanying picture glossary. This book is from the Rookie Read-About Holidays series.

Christina, Maria Urrutia. *Cinco de Mayo: Yesterday and Today.* Toronto, Ont.: Groundwood Books, 2002. Unp.
Grades: K–3. In San Miguel Tlaxipan, Mexico, the town reenacts the Battle of Puebla on May fifth. In this book photographs of the reenactment are juxtaposed with French and Mexican engravings of the battle. The simple text is easy for young readers to understand and includes information about the battle and the reenactment.

Cinco de Mayo. Video. Bala Cynwyd, Penn.: Schlessinger Video Productions-Library Video Company, 1994. 25 min.
Grades: K–4. Puppets, animation, and live action video teach students about the significance of Cinco de Mayo and the traditions surrounding this lively celebration. Students listen to a mariachi band and learn to make maracas as they participate in a lively fiesta. This video is part of the Holidays for Children series.

Riehecky, Janet. *Cinco de Mayo*. Illustrated by Krystyna Stasiak. New York: Children's Press, 1993. Unp.
Grades: K–4. Maria wakes up excited about celebrating Cinco de Mayo. Her enthusiastic attempts to help prepare for the celebration cause problems as she spills the grated cheese and smashes a hammer on her dad's thumb. Children relate to Maria's excitement about the holiday and her enthusiastic attempts to help with the preparations. The book includes instructions for making paper flowers, paper lanterns, and tacos. At the end of the book is a brief, historical description of the holiday.

Gnojewski, Carol. *Cinco de Mayo: Celebrating Hispanic Pride*. Berkeley Heights, N.J.: Enslow, 2002. 48p.
Grades: 2–5. This holiday, celebrated on May fifth each year, includes games, carnival rides, musicians playing and walking through the streets, and dancers in traditional costumes. The holiday commemorates the victory of the Mexicans over the French on May 5, 1862. The book includes margin notes and pictures, a craft project, a glossary, a bibliography, Internet addresses, and an index. This book is from the Finding Out about Holidays series.

Palacios, Argentina. *Viva Mexico! The Story of Benito Juarez and Cinco de Mayo*. Illustrated by Howard Berelson. Austin, Texas: Raintree, 1992. 32p.
Grades: 2–8. Benito Juarez was a Zapotec Indian from a poor family who studied law and became a politician in order to help the poor. He became president of Mexico in 1861 and it was during his presidency that the Mexicans overcame the French in the Battle of Puebla on May 6, 1862. He is known as the architect of modern Mexico.

EXPLORATIONS

1. Before viewing the video *Cinco de Mayo*, read either *Cinco de Mayo* (Wade, 2003) or *Cinco de Mayo: Celebrating*

Hispanic Pride (Gnojewski, 2002) to the students to provide them with background information to help them understand the video.

2. After reading *Cinco de Mayo: Yesterday and Today* (Cristina, 2002) or after viewing Cinco de Mayo on video, have students work in groups to create a mural depicting the Battle of Puebla.

3. After reading *Viva Mexico! The Story of Benito Juarez and Cinco de Mayo* (Palacios, 1992) have students discuss characteristics of Benito Juarez that enabled him to overcome his impoverished background and lead his country. How did his background help him? How did his background hinder him?

TANGO-NO-SEKKU (BOYS' DAY)

Traditionally, Tango-no-sekku (Boys' Day) is celebrated on May 5. On this day, a tall bamboo pole is placed in the garden with a pinwheel at the top. Carp windsocks are attached to the pole, one for each boy in the family (MacMillan, 1997). Carp are fish noted for their strength, courage, and determination—the same characteristics parents hope that their sons will develop. Iris leaves are thought to protect boys from illnesses and make them strong, so on this days boys bathe with iris leaves (Kindersley, 1997). Boys' Samurai warrior dolls representing strength and fearlessness are displayed (Kindersley, 1997). The books below contain information on this festival and information on the Samurai. Some families celebrate Kodomono-Hi (Children's Day) on this date and that holiday is discussed below (see the parallel Japanese festival for girls under Hina Matsuri).

BOOK AND MEDIA CHOICES

Riehecky, Janet. *Japanese Boys' Festival*. Illustrated by Krystyna Stasiak. Chicago: Children's Press, 1994. 32p.
Grades: K–4. Hiroshi and Kenji's parents have placed two carp on bamboo poles in their front yard to honor their sons. Inside the house is a display of swords, spears, and warriors to remind them to be courageous and strong. They spend the day with their friends at the community center festival playing games and watching a kite-flying contest. The book concludes with Japanese Boys' Festival activities

and information on Japanese Girls' Festival (Dolls' Day), which is celebrated in March.

Macdonald, Fiona. *A Samurai Castle*. Illustrated by John James and David Antram. New York: McGraw-Hill, 1995. 48p.
Grades: 5–8. Explore the sixteenth- and seventeenth-century castles of Japan's Samurai warriors in the pages of this book. Detailed, color illustrations enhance the clear, succinct text and contain additional information about these noted warriors. While the book focuses on the castles, it also contains information on the lives of the Samurai including brief biographies of some of them.

Schomp, Virginia. *Japan in the Days of the Samurai*. Tarrytown, N.Y.: Marshall Cavendish, 1998. 80p.
Grades: 6–10. The history, culture, and belief systems of seventeenth century Japan are explored in this informative look at the past. Readers develop an understanding of the role of Samurai warriors in medieval Japan. While Samurai were noted warriors, they were also trained in literature and the arts. A timeline, a three page glossary, a bibliography, and an index are included. This book is from the Cultures of the Past series.

EXPLORATIONS

1. Before reading *Japanese Boys' Festival* (Riehecky, 1994), ask the students what animals come to mind when they think of animals that are courageous and strong. Then, explain that in this book they will learn about a fish that is courageous and strong.

2. In *Japanese Boys' Festival* (Riehecky, 1994), the mother puts "long, sword-like leaves" from an iris plant in the boys' bath water to make them strong. This is something that their mother does to show that she loves them and cares for them. Ask the students to think for a few minutes about special things their parents do for them that lets them know they love and care for them.

3. After reading *Japan in the Days of the Samurai* (Schomp, 1998), engage students in a discussion of why the Samurai were trained in literature and the arts, as well as martial skills. Then, have students write about either the pros or cons of studying literature and the arts.

KODOMONO-HI (CHILDREN'S DAY)

Rather than have separate days for girls (Hina Masuri on March 3) and boys (Tango-no-sekku on May fifth) some families celebrate Kodomono-Hi (Children's Day) on May 5. Japanese Americans may fly carp streamers for both boys and girls and hold festivals where children can learn about their Japanese heritage. In Japan, families enjoy picnic lunches in the park and then watch sumo wrestlers and kendo fighters in sports stadiums (Krasno, 2000).

BOOK AND MEDIA CHOICES

Kroll, Virginia. *A Carp for Kimiko.* Illustrated by Katherine Roundtree. Watertown, Mass.: Charlesbrigdge Publishing, 1993. Unp.
Grades: P–3. As her family prepares for Children's Day, Kimiko wants a carp like the ones her parents will fly for her three brothers. She is gently reminded that the carp are only for the boys in the family and that her dolls were displayed on March 3 for the Doll Festival. Kimiko persists in asking for a carp kite like her brothers. Her parents insist that they cannot change the tradition, but when Kimiko awakens on Children's Day there is a real carp swimming in a fishbowl just for her.

MacMillan, Dianne M. *Japanese Children's Day and the Obon Festival.* Berkeley Heights, N.J.: Enslow, 1997. 48p.
Grades: 2–5. Brief descriptions and color photographs provide information on Children's Day, the Boys' Day Festival, and the Dolls' Day Festival. The photographs supply information essential to understanding the traditions and rituals of these Japanese celebrations. The book, from the Best Holiday Books series, includes a glossary and an index. .

EXPLORATIONS

1. After reading *A Carp for Kimiko* (Kroll, 1993), ask students about things they are prevented from doing or not allowed to do because of their age or gender.

2. After reading *A Carp for Kimiko* (Kroll, 1993), engage students in a discussion of the book by asking them questions about the book and encouraging them to develop their own questions about the book. What did you think of the book? What would you do if you were Kimiko? How would you

feel if you were Kimiko? What else could Kimiko's parents have done? What would your parents have done in a similar situation?

MOTHER'S DAY

Anna Jarvis was not the first person to try to start a holiday honoring mothers, but from two memorial services to honor her own mother on May 10, 1908 one in Pennsylvania and one in West Virginia came our national holiday (West, 2002). She asked people attending the services to wear a white carnation, her mother's favorite flower (Moehn, 2000). Today, people wear white carnations to symbolize mothers who have died and either red or pink carnations to symbolize mothers who are living (Henderson and Thompson, 2002). In 1914, President Woodrow Wilson declared Mother's Day, the second Sunday in May, a national holiday. Mother's Day is also celebrated in England, Denmark, Finland, Italy, Mexico, France, Turkey, Australia, and Belgium (Barkin and James, 1994). Mother's Day is a time for thanking mothers for all they do. Some families celebrate this day by serving mother breakfast in bed, and giving her cards, flowers, or presents. In discussing this holiday with children, it is important to be sensitive to those children in the classroom who may not live with their mothers or whose mothers have died.

BOOK AND MEDIA CHOICES

Bauer, Marion Dane. *My Mother is Mine*. Illustrated by Peter Elwell. New York: Simon & Schuster Books for Young Readers, 2001. Unp. Grades: P–1. Gentle, simple, repetitive verse describes how mothers take care of their children. The mothers in the muted pastel illustrations are a variety of wild animals. The verse and the illustrations portray the loving relationships between mother and child.

Baker, Liza. *I Love You Because You're You*. Illustrated by David McPhail. New York: Scholastic, 2001. Unp.
Grades: P–2. Lyrical rhyming text and soft illustrations tell of a mother's unconditional love for her child. This is a loving tribute to mothers who are there when you need them and who understand your needs.

French, Vivian. *A Present for Mom*. Illustrated by Dana Kubick. Camridge, Mass.: Candlewick Press, 2002. Unp.

Grades: P–2. The day before Mother's Day, Stanley is frantically searching for just the right present for his mother. His brother and sisters all have their presents ready for the big day. Stanley spends a sleepless night, but in the morning wakes up and prepares the perfect Mother's Day gift. This is a charming story of a loveable cat family. Family snapshots fill the end pages of the book.

Smalls-Hector, Irene. *Jonathan and His Mommy*. Illustrated by Michael Hays. Boston: Little, Brown, 1992. Unp.
Grades: P–2. As Jonathan and his Mommy travel through their neighborhood, they zigzag, take giant steps, take baby steps, bunny hop, and run like the wind. Readers thoroughly enjoy this delightful excursion depicting a warm, loving relationship between a mother and a son.

Wood, Douglas. *What Moms Can't Do*. Illustrated by Doug Cushman. New York: Simon & Schuster Books for Young Readers, 2001. Unp.
Grades: P–2. The youngster in this book lists many of the things moms can't do, such as picking out clothes for school and picking up after he scatters them, saying goodbye quickly at school, putting popsicles in his lunch box, or watching movies on television without him. But the best thing of all that moms can do is love their children very much.

Glassman, Peter. *My Working Mom*. Illustrated by Tedd Arnold. New York: HarperCollins, 1994. Unp.
Grades: P–3. This working mother is like other mothers, who enjoy their work, run off to meetings, have bad days at work, and sometimes cook weird meals. She throws great birthday parties, shows up for the school play, and on career day flies the entire class off on her broom, because this mom is a witch. Hilarious watercolor illustrations of lizards, mice, and monsters have children giggling throughout the story.

Leuck, Laura. *My Monster Mama Loves Me So*. Illustrated by Mark Buehner. New York: HarperCollins, 1999. Unp.
Grades: P–3. This charming bedtime story depicts the warm, loving relationship between a mother and a child who just happen to be green, three-eyed monsters. Little monster recounts all the things his mother does that show she loves him, such as giving him lizard juice with ice when he is sick and taking him swimming in the swamp. The

bright, colorful illustrations filled with charming, spooky creatures amuse rather than scare youngsters.

Ziefert, Harriet. *31 Uses for a Mother*. Illustrated by Rebecca Doughty. New York: Penguin Putnam Books for Young Readers, 2003. Unp.
Grades: P–3. Moms seen from a child's point of view fulfill a variety of roles, from chauffer, to answering service, to encyclopedia. One- or two-word descriptors accompany the child-like drawing of these thirty-one things mothers do for their children.

Mora, Pat, editor. *Love to Moma: A Tribute to Mothers*. Illustrated by Paula S. Barragan M. New York: Lee & Low Books, 2001. Unp.
Grades: P–4. From Puerto Rican, Cuban, Venezuelan, and Mexican American heritage these poets wrote loving tributes to their mothers and grandmothers. The poems tell of the special bonds between grandmothers and their grandchildren and between mothers and their children. The poetry reveals the universality of motherhood and each reader is sure to recognize a mother or a grandmother in the poems. Exuberant paintings accompany the poems.

Cleary, Beverly. *Ramona and Her Mother*. Illustrated by Alan Tiegreen. New York: William Morrow, 1990. 208p.
Grades: K–4. As Ramona tries to understand her family, she at times makes erroneous assumptions that lead to amusing situations. Always ready to help, she tackles cheering up her father after he loses his job and at the same time tries to help him quit smoking. When her efforts go awry she makes up her mind that no one loves her and decides to leave home. To her surprise, her mother volunteers to help her pack.

Myers, Walter Dean. *Angel to Angel*: A Mother's Gift of Love. New York: HarperCollins, 1999. 40p.
Grades: 4 and up. Vintage photographs of African American women and children tell stories all their own. Myers tells their stories in poems that become more meaningful after carefully examining the photographs. The love and relationships between the mothers and their children provide a fitting tribute to the special bonds of mothers and children everywhere.

Patterson, Katherine. *The Great Gilly Hopkins*. New York: HarperCollins Children's Book, 1988. 160p.

Grades: 5–8. Gilly has been bounced from one foster home to another. She longs for the day she will be able to live with her flower-child mother. When she reaches the home of Marnie Trotter, she finds a mother who is unwavering in her belief in Gilly and her abilities. While the story is about Gilly and the changes she undergoes, soft-spoken Marnie Trotter is a catalyzing force in Gilly's life. This book is also available on audiocassette.

Explorations

1. After reading *My Mother is Mine* (Bauer, 2001), have students draw a picture of themselves and their mothers. When they finish, ask them about the pictures, and write a one sentence description beneath their pictures.

2. After reading *I Love You Because You're You* (Baker, 2001), go back through the illustrations and have children point out the pictures that remind them of things they have done.

3. After reading *A Present for Mom* (French, 2002), remind students that sometimes the best present for someone you love is a simple card telling them how you feel such as the one below.

Figure 12-1. Moms treasure handmade cards such as this one.

4. After reading *Jonathan and His Mommy* (Smalls-Hector, 1992), take students outdoors to try out all the different steps Jonathan and his mommy take as they explore their neighborhood.

5. After reading *What Moms Can't Do* (Wood, 2001), have students brainstorm a list of things they help their mothers do. Then, have the students draw pictures to illustrate these things or have them write about them.

6. At the end of *My Working Mom* (Glassman, 1994), the character states that she cannot picture her mother any other way. Provide students with drawing paper and have them draw what life with their mother is like. Older students can write descriptions to accompany their pictures.

7. While *31 Uses for a Mother* (Ziefert, 2003) is a book for younger students, students of all ages can relate to these inventive uses for mothers and add more uses when they think of their own mothers or primary caregivers. Challenge students to think up even more uses for a mother or create their own uses for a father. Remind students that there are only a few words on the pages and that their illustrations should tell the story.

8. Read one of the poems in *Love to Moma: A Tribute to Mothers* (Mora, 2001) and have students create their own illustration for the poem before sharing the illustration in the book with them. Remind them that the poem is open to their personal interpretation and that the poem means different things to different people.

9. Before reading *Ramona and Her Mother* (Cleary, 1990) ask students if they have ever thought about running away from home. Why did they decide to leave? Did they actually leave? Where did they go? What was their mother's reaction?

10. After reading *Angel to Angel: A Mother's Gift of Love* (Myers, 1999) have students pick their favorite picture and write about the story they see in the picture. Give students the opportunity to first talk about the pictures in small groups. Then let them choose whether they will write a poem or a narrative.

MEMORIAL DAY

Memorial day is celebrated on the last Monday in May to remember those who died in wars. It began as a day to honor soldiers who died in the Civil War (Penner, 1993). After the Civil War, on April 26, 1866, the women of Columbus, Mississippi decorated the graves of both the Union and Confederate soldiers (Spies, 1992). This gracious act of kindness received national attention. Others believe Memorial Day started in 1864 in Boalsburg, Pennsylvania when two women met in a cemetery as they put flowers on the graves of their family members, who died in the Civil War, and they agreed to return each year to decorate the graves (Spies, 1992). Memorial Day is celebrated with parades and programs that honor veterans, and families in many places decorate the graves of fallen loved ones. To understand why we celebrate Memorial Day it is important to know about the wars that we fought, to recognize the roles played by women in the war, and to think about the impact of war on families and communities. The books and video annotated below provide students with the information they need to appreciate veteran's sacrifices. Additional information on Memorial Day can be found on this Web site www.usmemorialday.org. (See Veterans Day.)

BOOK AND MEDIA CHOICES

Memorial Day/Veterans Day. Video. Bala Cynwyd, Penn.: Schlessinger Video Productions-Library Video Company, 2003. 23 min.
Grades: K–4. Songs, stories, and interviews with veterans help students understand why we honor veterans on these very special days. Visiting Arlington National Cemetery with its rows of white headstones is a dramatic sight that stays with viewers. A teacher's guide is available. This video is part of the Holidays for Children series.

Ransom, Candice F. *The Promise Quilt.* Illustrated by Ellen Beier. New York: Walker, 1999. Unp.
Grades: K–4. Before Addie's father leaves to join Gen. Lee, he promises that when she is bigger he will take her over the mountain to go to school. Her father does not return from the war and the school has burned down. A farmer offers the use of his shed for the school and Addie's mother makes a quilt to auction to raise money for books for the school. When she runs out of material for the border, Addie gives her the only thing she has of her father's, his red shirt, to finish the quilt. Addie figures it was her father's way of keeping his promise

Ray, Deborah Kogan. *My Daddy Was a Soldier: A World War II Story.* New York: Holiday House, 1990. Unp.
Grades: 2–4. When parents are fighting wars, children are left behind missing them and adjusting to changes in their lives. This story is based on stories of children who grew up during World War II. Children with parents in the armed forces make connections to the child in the story who anxiously awaits the return of her father. The loneliness and sadness of the child are aptly portrayed in the charcoal illustrations.

Polacco, Patricia. *Pink and Say.* New York: Putnam, 1994. Unp.
Grades: 3 and up. Based on a story handed down in her family, Polacco tells of the friendship between two fifteen-year old Union soldiers during the Civil War. Pink carries the wounded Say back to his mother's slave quarters in Georgia. She nurses Pink back to health and Pink teaches Say to read. Confederate soldiers kill Pink's mother and drag the two young soldiers to Andersonville Prison where Pink is hanged.

Sandler, Martin W. *Civil War.* New York: HarperCollins, 1996. 91p.

Grades: 3 and up. Posters, paintings, photographs, and quotes from the soldiers provide a gripping account of this war that tore apart a nation. The illustrations and the quotes are allowed to tell the story with just enough text to tie them all together. Information on the Library of Congress and an index are included. This is A Library of Congress Book.

Haskins, Jim. Black, *Blue & Gray: African Americans in the Civil War.* New York: Simon & Schuster Books for Young Readers, 1998. 154p. Grades: 5 and up. At the urging of Frederick Douglass, African Americans enlisted and fought in the Civil War. Their contributions went unrecognized, although some veterans did receive military pensions. Letters, documents, government transcripts, photographs, and reproductions help to tell the story of these brave soldiers. The size of the book and the spacing of the text on the pages make this book accessible to students on a variety of reading levels. Included in the book are a chronology, a list of the African-American Medal of Honor Recipients in the Civil War, a bibliography, and an index.

Kuhn, Betsy. *Angels of Mercy: The Army Nurses of World War II.* New York: Atheneum Books for Young Readers, 1999. 114p. Grades: 5 and up. During World War II, approximately four hundred thousand women served and over fifty-nine thousand of them were Army nurses. Nurses were wounded, held prisoner, and killed serving their country, yet their contributions are often overlooked. They received less pay and had fewer privileges than their male counterparts. This book is a glowing tribute to these dedicated, selfless women. Quotes from the women provide personal glimpses into their lives that help readers understand the hardships they endured and the valuable contributions they made. A bibliography and an index are included.

Gaeddert, Louann. *Friends and Enemies.* New York: Atheneum Books for Young Readers, 2000. 177p. Grades: 6–10. The friendship between a Methodist minister's son, Will, and a Mennonite, Jim, is shattered when the impact of World War II is felt in Kansas. Will and most of the town folks do not understand the pacifist stance of the Mennonites. How can they not fight when their friends and neighbors are being killed and injured? How can they enjoy the freedom America provides and not be willing to fight to protect that freedom? What does it mean to be courageous? This is a powerful story that raises questions for which there are no easy answers.

Explorations

1. After viewing the video *Memorial Day/Veterans Day* have students examine some of the images on the Memorial Day Web site at www.usmemorialday.org/gallery.html. As they view the images, have them write down their feelings. Ask them which photograph was the most striking or had the greatest impact on them. Then, help the students realize that every white headstone represents a person who died and left behind family members.

2. After reading *Pink and Say* (Polacco, 1994), return to the evocative illustrations and have students examine the placement and gestures of the characters' hands as they tie into the statement at the end of the book about "hands that have touched the hand."

3. After reading *Angels of Mercy: The Army Nurses of World War II* (Kuhn, 1999) students wishing to learn more about these women can visit the "Angels of Mercy: Nurses' Tales" Web page at www.pbs.org/wgbh/amex/guts/sfeature/nurses.html.

4. Before reading *Angels of Mercy: The Army Nurses of World War II* (Kuhn, 1999) or Black, Blue & Gray: African Americans in the Civil War (Haskins, 1998) have students examine the photographs in the books. What stories do the photographs tell? Ask them to write down their thoughts about the pictures in the book and share their written responses with other students in small groups. Often the photographs convey meanings that the text does not. This activity calls students attention to the information that can be gained from the photographs and illustrations in nonfiction books.

5. On page seventy of *Black, Blue & Gray: African Americans in the Civil War* (Haskins, 1998) is an excerpt from Lincoln's "Gettysburg Address," where he pays tribute to the veterans of the Civil War. Ask students what they think he meant when he said, "The brave men, living and dead, who struggled here have consecrated it far above our poor power to add or detract."

6. To learn more about the veterans described in *Black, Blue & Gray: African Americans in the Civil War* (Haskins, 1998)

students can visit the National Park Service Web site at www.itd.nps.gov/cwss/history/aa_history.htm.

7. Before reading *Friends and Enemies* (Gaeddert, 2000) briefly introduce the main characters to the students. Then have the students select one character they will focus on as they read. While reading have them take brief notes on how the author develops the character and whether or not the character changes during the story.

8. After reading *Friends and Enemies* (Gaeddert, 2000), provide students with opportunities to discuss the issues raised by this book regarding the characters' acceptance and tolerance for the beliefs of others, or lack of acceptance and tolerance. Challenge the students to think up ways to develop acceptance and tolerance for the beliefs that differ from theirs.

REFERENCES

Barkin, Carol, and Elizabeth James. 1994. *The Holiday Handbook*. New York: Clarion Books.

Gnojewski, Carol. 2002. *Cinco de Mayo: Celebrating Hispanic Pride*. Berkeley Heights, N.J.: Enslow Publishers.

Goring, Ruth. 1995. *Holidays and Celebrations*. Vero Beach, Fla.: Rourke Publications.

Henderson, Helene, and Sue E. Thompson. 2002. *Holidays, Festivals, and Celebrations of the World Dictionary*, 3rd ed. Detroit, Mich.: Omnigraphics.

Kindersley, Anabel. 1997. Celebrations. New York: DK Publishing.

Krasno, Rena. 2000. *Floating Lanterns and Golden Shrines: Celebrating Japanese Festivals*. Berkeley, Calif.: Pacific View Press.

Leslie, Clare Walker, and Frank E. Gerace. 2000. *The Ancient Celtic Festivals and How We Celebrate Them Today*. Rochester, Vt.: Inner Traditions.

MacMillan, Dianne M. 1997. *Japanese Children's Day and the Obon Festival*. Berkeley Heights, N.J.: Enslow Publishers.

Manushkin, Fran. 1995. *The Matzah That Papa Brought Home*. New York: Scholastic.

Menard, Valerie. 2000. *The Latino Holiday Book: From Cinco de Mayo to Dia de los Muertos—The Celebrations and Traditions of Hispanic Americans*. New York: Marlowe.

Moehn, Heather. 2000. *World Holidays: A Watts Guide for Children.* New York: Franklin Watts.

Penner, Lucille Recht. 1993. *Celebration: The Story of American Holidays*. New York: Macmillan Publishing.

Spies, Karen. 1992. *Our National Holidays*. Brookfield, Conn.: The Millbrook Press.

West, Robin. 2002. *My Very Own Mother's Day: A Book of Cooking and Crafts*. New York: Paperback Books.

PART V. SUMMER

Summer Celebrations and Holidays with Moveable Dates

13

With summer comes freedom from school, time for vacations, heat, and unrelenting sunshine necessitating searches for shade, cool breezes, and ice-cold beverages. Summer is traditionally the time for extended family vacations and trips to summer camps that build memories to last a lifetime. Summer is also the time for weekend trips to the seashore, fishing on a favorite lake, camping in the woods, and picnics in the park. Lacking the number of formal holidays as the other seasons of the year, the summer months focus on celebrating the simple pleasures of life. Summer includes the religious and cultural celebrations of Shavuot, Obon, and Duanwu Jie (Dragon Boat Festival), as well as family excursions. Shavuot is a Jewish celebration that takes place seven weeks after Passover, which means it is celebrated in late May or early June (Burghardt, 2001). Japanese Buddhists remember their ancestors with the Obon Festival held in either July or August. Obon is celebrated not only in Japan but also in Hawaii and California. Duanwu Jie is celebrated on the fifth day of the fifth month of the Chinese lunar calendar (near the summer solstice) and commemorates the Chinese poet, Chu'ü Yüan, of the Chou Dynasty (Moehn, 2000).

SHAVUOT

Seven weeks after the second day of Passover, Jews celebrate the agricultural holiday of Shavuot; hence its name the Festival of Weeks. Also called the Feast of the Harvest, this holiday signifies the beginning of the wheat or barley harvest (Henderson and Thompson, 2002). On Shavuot, tradition holds that God gave the children of Israel the Ten Commandments (Scharfstein, 1999). The eve of Shavuot is a time for studying the Torah given to Moses on

Mount Sinai and for some Jews this studying lasts until the next morning (Burghardt, 2001). Traditional foods prepared for this celebration include dairy products, such as cheese blintzes. In the Christian tradition, this festival corresponds with Pentecost.

Book and Media Choices

Goldin, Barbara Diamond. *A Mountain of Blintzes*. Illustrated by Anik McGrory. San Diego: Gulliver Books, 2001.
Grades: P–2. With Shavuot approaching, Sara and Max worry about how to provide a mountain of blintzes so their large family can celebrate properly. They decide both of them should find additional work to earn money to save for the celebration. However, Sarah assumes Max is saving his coins and that there will be plenty; and Max makes the same misguided assumption. Consequently, Sarah spends her coins on candles and material to make new clothes for the children, while Max uses his money to buy wine for the celebration and new shoes for the children. When they discover the coin box is empty, the children come to the rescue. Each has been bartering their services to the neighbors in exchange for the ingredients for the blintzes. Watercolor illustrations depict a cheery, loving mountain family. An author's note explains the origin of the story and why dairy foods are eaten at Shavuot.

Explorations

1. After reading *A Mountain of Blintzes* (Goldin, 2001) help the children make connections between the family in the story and their own families. Ask the children to recall Max, Sarah, and the children's holiday preparations. Then, ask the children about their own families' preparations for holidays. Buying new clothes, fixing special foods, and cleaning house are holiday preparations that are common in many cultures.

2. *A Mountain of Blintzes* (Goldin, 2001) has a cause and effect organizational pattern that can be used to introduce children to the topic. After reading the story, have the children work together to complete a diagram such as the one below.

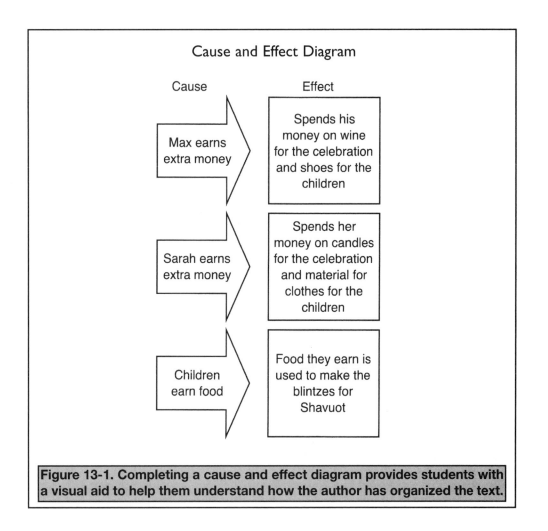

Figure 13-1. Completing a cause and effect diagram provides students with a visual aid to help them understand how the author has organized the text.

OBON FESTIVAL

The Japanese Obon Festival is known variously as the Festival of the Dead, All Souls' Day, Lantern Festival, or simply the Bon Festival. It is celebrated from July 13 to the 15 or August 13 to the 15 by Japanese Buddhists (Henderson and Thompson, 2002). Because of their reverence for the dead, entire families devote themselves to remembering and honoring their ancestors, by cleaning and adorning their graves with flowers and incense (Japan, 2001). Small bonfires and a special meal on the first night of the three-day festival welcome the spirits of dead ancestors. On the third night, Bon Odori, traditional folk dances bid the spirits farewell. In addition, on this night some families gather left over festival food and place it in small boats with paper lanterns and set them adrift to carry the spirits home (Henderson and Thompson, 2002). Japanese Americans celebrate this festival, as well. (See All Saints' Day, All Souls' Day, Dia de los Muertos, Yom Kippur, Qing Ming, Id-Ul-Fitr, and TET for other holidays that commemorate the dead.)

BOOK AND MEDIA CHOICES

McCoy, Karen Kawamoto. *Bon Odori Dancer*. Illustrated by Carolina Yao. Chicago, Ill.: Polychrome Publishing, 1998. Unp.
Grades: 1–3. Readers who have found it difficult to learn to dance empathize with Keiko as she struggles to learn the Obon Festival dances. When the other dancers, decide to help her rather than laugh at her, she succeeds. With patience and teamwork, the dancers all succeed. Colorful illustrations and a diagram of the dance steps are included.

MacMillan, Dianne M. *Japanese Children's Day and the Obon Festival*. Berkeley Heights, N.J.: Enslow, 1997. 48p.
Grades: 2–5. Fourteen hundred years ago, Buddhism was brought to Japan from Korea. Obon is a national holiday in Japan. Incense is burned and small offerings of food are made to the spirits of the dead. Joyful dances and lots of music accompany this festival. The book includes a glossary and an index. This book is from the Best Holiday Books series.

Come Celebrate with Me: Obon—Japanese Festival of Spirits. Video. Morris Plains, N.J.: Lucerne Media, 2001. 10 min.
Grades: 3–6. Viewers learn about the traditions and customs associated with the Obon Festival. A teacher's guide is included.

EXPLORATIONS

1. Prior to reading *Bon Odori Dancer* (McCoy, 1998), have students share their experiences with learning a new skill such as dancing, riding a bike, or skating to enable them to make connections between their experiences and Keiko's experiences.

2. After reading *Bon Odori Dancer* (McCoy, 1998), ask students to return to the text to make a list of the ways Keiko's friends helped her learn the dances. Ask them for suggestions about how they can help others learn new skills.

3. After reading about the *Obon Festival in Japanese Children's Day and the Obon Festival* (MacMillan, 1997) read *Day of the Dead* (Hoyt-Goldsmith, 1994). Then have students work in small groups or as a large group to complete a Venn diagram comparing the two holidays. Students put similarities between the holidays in the overlapping space formed by the two circles and the differences between the holidays are written in the main portion of the circles.

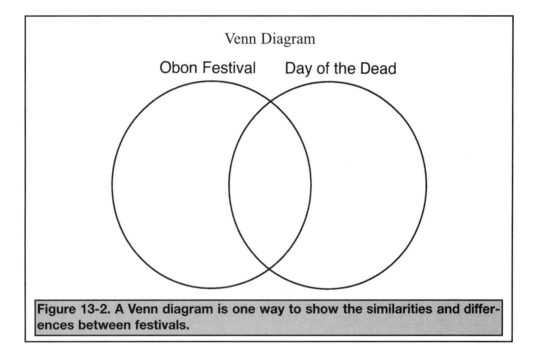

Venn Diagram

Obon Festival   Day of the Dead

Figure 13-2. A Venn diagram is one way to show the similarities and differences between festivals.

DUANWU JIE (DRAGON BOAT FESTIVAL)

Duanwu Jie (Dragon Boat Festival) is celebrated on the fifth day of the fifth month of the Chinese lunar calendar in China and in Chinese communities around the world (Moehn, 2000). This festival commemorates the Chinese poet, Chu'ü Yüan, of the Chou Dynasty who drowned himself in 277 B.C. The Dragon Boat Festival is a reenactment of the search for his body. Rice dumplings eaten at this festival signify the rice that was thrown in the water to keep the fish away from Chu'ü Yüan's body. This festival is celebrated with Dragon Boat

International Races held in Hong Kong, and elsewhere around the world. Dragon boats are long and narrow distinguished by a dragon's head on the prow, and a drummer on board beats out a rhythm for the rowers (Henderson and Thompson, 2002). Additional information about this festival can be found at www.sandiego-online.com/forums/Chinese/htmls/dragboat.htm. (See Asian holidays.)

SUMMER EXCURSIONS

Camping trips, picnics, swimming, vacations, and reading are activities that fill the long hot days of summer. These less formal types of celebrations emphasize spending time with friends and family, as well as relaxing and enjoying one another's company. Sometimes these simple pleasures can become complicated and prove frustrating, but they always provide unforgettable memories. The books that follow describe summer outings that hold fond memories for readers of all ages.

BOOK AND MEDIA CHOICES

Aliki. *Those Summers*. New York: HarperCollins, 1996. Unp.
Grades: P–2. Remembrances of summers spent in a house by the seashore with aunts, uncles, cousins, and friends form the basis for this loving recollection. Days of swimming, collecting sea shells, building sandcastles, following bird tracks along the shore, and strolling the boardwalk are lovingly described in words and warm, realistic illustrations.

Gliori, Debi. *Mr. Bear's Vacation*. New York: Orchard Books, 2000. Unp.
Grades: P–2. A peaceful, relaxing camping trip is what the bear family has in mind as they set out on a family vacation. The tent has holes, dinner is slightly burnt, the sleeping bags were left at home, and a curious cow collapses their tent in the middle of the night. All of this leads Mr. Bear to conclude laughingly that they need a vacation to recover from their vacation. Readers young and old can relate to a family outing that does not go according to plan, but provides amusing memories to remember fondly from the comfort of home.

Hutchins, Pat. *We're Going on a Picnic*. New York: Greenwillow Books, 2002. Unp.

Grades: P–2. A hen, a duck, and a goose decide one fine day to go on a picnic. Each contributes a favorite fresh fruit to the picnic basket. They take turns carrying the basket while searching for the perfect location for their picnic. Eventually, they end up back at the house, still not having found the perfect location and carrying an empty picnic basket. Observant youngsters notice that as the hen, the duck, and the goose searched for just the right picnic spot a mouse, a rabbit, and a squirrel helped themselves to the delicious fruit tucked away in the picnic basket.

Walton, Rick. *Bunnies on the Go: Getting from Place to Place*. Illustrated by Paige Miglio. New York: HarperCollins, 2003. Unp.
Grades: P–2. The bunny family embarks on a family vacation across the country using a variety of modes of transportation including, a tractor, a train, and a hot air balloon. This rollicking trip written in rhyming prose invites readers to guess what the bunnies' next mode of transportation will be. Lush, realistic images entice readers to explore the illustrations looking for additional details about the bunnies' trip.

Bauer, Marion Dane. *When I Go Camping with Grandma*. Illustrated by Allen Garns. Memphis, Tenn.: Troll Associates, 1995. Unp.
Grades: P–3. In this family-oriented story, a grandmother and her granddaughter spend precious time together on an overnight camping trip. Told from the granddaughter's perspective, she realizes that one day in the future when they go camping, she will be the one rowing the boat, building the fire, and taking fish off the line. The sparse text and shadowy, realistic illustrations reflect the loving relationship between a grandmother and her granddaughter as well as capture the calm, peacefulness of the woods and lake.

Krensky, Stephen. *Lionel in the Summer*. Illustrated by Susanna Natti. New York: Dial Books for Young Readers, 1998. 48p.
Grades: K–2. Summer excitement and adventures are packed into four short chapters for beginning readers. On the first day of summer, Lionel wakes up early with a list of things he cannot wait to do. At the Fourth of July carnival, he has a unique way to be sure he stays awake for the fireworks. His lemonade stand and the car trip with his family are other familiar summer time activities students can relate to as they read about Lionel's summer. This is an Easy-to-Read Book.

Bunting, Eve. *I Don't Want to Go to Camp*. Illustrated by Maryann Cocca-Leffler. Honesdale, Penn.: Boyds Mills Press, 1996. Unp.
Grades: K–4. When Lin's mother announces she is going away to a camp for mothers, Lin decides she is not going to camp even when she is old enough. On visiting day, she learns that her mother has been enjoying midnight feasts, sharing passwords, creating secret codes, racing, swimming, and playing games. During the ride home, she confides to her dad that when she is old enough, she wants to go away to camp.

Hopkinson, Deborah. *Bluebird Summer*. Illustrated by Bethanne Andersen. New York: Greenwillow Books, 2001. Unp.
Grades: K–4. For Mags and Cody summer means spending time on Grandma and Gramp's farm gardening with Grandma, spitting watermelon seeds with Gramps, and watching bluebirds. It is different this summer since Grandma died. Her garden is overgrown and the bluebirds are gone. Mags and Cody set out to restore the garden and put up birdhouses to encourage the bluebirds to return. This engaging story of renewal is captured in sensitive, evocative illustrations. The book concludes with information on efforts to restore the bluebird population.

Hurwitz, Johanna. *Summer with Elisa*. Illustrated by Heather Harms Maione. New York: HarperCollins, 2000. 89p.
Grades: 1–3. With her older brother away at summer camp, Elisa enjoys a vacation from her brother's teasing and has a chance to be the oldest in the family. When her brother returns, the whole family leaves behind their apartment in the city for a vacation house in the country. Young readers relate to Elisa's summer escapades as she makes a bet with her brother about eating a whole jar of mustard, gets stuck in a tree, rescues a seagull, and picks the neighbor's flowers. She recounts her adventures in letters to her grandparents and her friends back home.

Hoffman, Mary. *Starring Grace*. Illustrated by Caroline Binch. New York: Phyllis Fogelman Books, 2000. 95p.
Grades: 2–6. Grace and her friends, who are spending the summer at home, use their imaginations to create their own summer adventures. Without ever leaving their neighborhood they join a circus troop, hunt for ghosts, venture out on a safari, blast off in a space shuttle, build a time traveling machine, and participate in a local theater musical. Along the way, they learn about helping others and the importance of family and friends. Grace's enthusiasm and adventur-

ous, irrepressible spirit show readers that imagination and family support are all that is needed for a wonderful summer.

Scieszka, Jon. *Summer Reading is Killing Me*. Illustrated by Lane Smith. New York: Viking, 1998. 73p.
Grades: 2–6. Anyone who has ever been handed the dreaded summer reading list can relate to this adventuresome trio trapped inside their summer reading list. When Fred puts the trio's summer reading list in The Book, the time traveling trio find themselves in a fantasy world where the evil characters from the books on the list are attempting to do away with the good characters and take over the stories. This action-packed adventure contains a variety of storybook characters that students may have encountered in their summer reading. This book is from the Time Warp Trio series. (See *Thanksgiving on Thursday*, by Mary Pope Osborne, for another book involving time travel.)

EXPLORATIONS

1. Before reading *Those Summers* (Aliki, 1996), have students brainstorm together to create a list of things they do at the seashore. Place their responses in a chart on the board. After reading the story, revisit the chart and place a check next to those activities that they read about in the story. Leave space at the bottom of the chart to put in activities from the story that they did not mention.

2. After reading *Mr. Bear's Vacation* (Gliori, 2000) work with students to create a list of all the things that went wrong on the bears' vacation. Then, have them offer suggestions of things the family could have done to prevent the disasters.

3. Prior to reading *We're Going on a Picnic* (Hutchins, 2002), have the students predict what foods they think the animals will take on their picnic.

4. After reading *When I Go Camping with Grandma* (Bauer, 1995), have the students talk about special times they have spent with a grandparent.

5. Combine *When I Go Camping with Grandma* (Bauer, 1995) with *Thank You, Grandpa* (Plourde, 2003), since both books have a similar theme. (See Grandparents Day.)

6. Before reading *I Don't Want to Go to Camp* (Bunting, 1996), have students share their feelings about summer

camp. Whereas younger students may not have gone to camp, they may be able to share stories about older siblings who have been to camp.

7. After reading *I Don't Want to Go to Camp* (Bunting, 1996), introduce students to *The Viper* (Thiesing, 2002). This book is based on a tale the author remembers hearing at summer camp.

8. After reading *Bluebird Summer* (Hopkinson, 2001), have students visit the North American Bluebird Society Web site at www.nabluebirdsociety.org, to learn about what they can do to help restore the bluebird population. Bluebirds range over the continental United States and part of Alaska.

9. After reading *Bluebird Summer* (Hopkinson, 2001), share *The Christmas Thingamajig* (Manuel, 2002) or *Ghost Wings* (Joosse, 2001) with the students. These books are about children celebrating a holiday after the death of a grandmother. Then, have students discuss how the children in the books began to accept the death of their grandmothers.

10. While reading *Summer with Elisa* (Hurwitz, 2000), have students make a list of things Elisa does, which cause her to get in trouble. After reading the book, have them work with a partner to brainstorm ideas for things Elisa could have done to avoid getting in trouble.

11. Before reading *Summer Reading is Killing Me* (Scieszka, 1998), have the students go over the summer reading lists at the back of this book and identify the books they have read. Then, have them work together to create a list of characters they remember from these books.

12. After reading *Summer Reading is Killing Me* (Scieszka, 1998), encourage students to check out one of the books they have not read on their summer reading lists, the next time they visit the library.

REFERENCES

Burghardt, Linda. 2001. *Jewish Holiday Traditions: Joyful Celebrations from Rosh Hashanah to Shavuot*. New York: Kensington Publishing.

Hoyt-Goldsmith, Diane. 1998. *Day of the Dead: A Mexican-American Celebration*. New York: Holiday House.

Henderson, Helene, and Sue E. Thompson. 2002. *Holidays, Festivals, and Celebrations of the World Dictionary*, 3rd ed. Detroit, Mich.: Omnigraphics.

Japan. 2001. Danbury, Conn.: Grolier Educational.

Joosse, Barbara M. 2001. *Ghost Wings*. San Francisco: Chronicle Books.

Manuel, Lynn. 2002. *The Christmas Thingamajig*. New York: Dutton Children's Books.

Moehn, Heather. 2000. *World Holidays: A Watts Guide for Children*. New York: Franklin Watts.

Plourde, Lynn. 2003. *Thank You, Grandpa*. New York: Penguin Putnam.

Scharfstein, Sol. 1999. *Understanding Jewish Holidays and Customs: Historical and Contemporary*. Hoboken, N.J.: KTAV Publishing House.

Thiesing, Lisa. *The Viper*. New York: Dutton Children's Books, 2002.

JUNE HOLIDAYS AND CELEBRATIONS 14

June's arrival brings the first days of summer freedom for many students as schools close and swimming pools open. Father's Day on the third Sunday, Flag Day on the fourteenth, Juneteenth on the nineteenth, and the Stonewall Rebellion on the twenty-seventh provide opportunities for pausing, reflecting, and rejoicing. Father's Day is set aside to honor fathers and their devotion to their families. Flag Day is to remember why the American flag is an important symbol worthy of honor and respect. Juneteenth celebrates the delayed independence of slaves in Texas. Juneteenth, as with many American holidays, was once a local celebration that has gradually spread across the nation. June 20, 21, or 22 mark the summer solstice in the northern hemisphere, when the sun is farthest away from the equator. As the longest day of the year, the summer solstice heralds the gradual shortening of daylight hours, and darkness overcoming light (Leslie and Gerace, 2000). June 27 commemorates the Stonewall Rebellion, which eventually led to lesbian, gay, bisexual, and transgender pride events held throughout the year and around the world.

FATHER'S DAY

Sonora Louise Smart Dodd of Spokane, Washington, proposed a day to honor her father, William Jackson Smart, who upon the death of his wife raised six children. The idea for Father's Day came to Mrs. Dodd after hearing a Mother's Day sermon (Moehn, 2000). She originally proposed the idea to her pastor and suggested the celebration be June 5, her father's birthday. Since the minister did not have enough time to prepare a sermon, he suggested June 19, which was the third Sunday in June. With the help of the Spokane Young Men's Christian Association (YMCA), who agreed to publicize the holiday for Mrs. Dodd, Father's Day was first celebrated in 1910. Eventually by presidential proclamation, the day now is celebrated annually in the United States on the third Sunday in June. The official flower for Father's Day is a rose, white in remembrance of deceased fathers and red for living fathers (Zalben, 1999).

In discussing this holiday with children it is important to be sensitive to those in the classroom who may not live with their fathers for one reason or another. One of the books annotated below is about a child trying to complete a school assignment about fathers when she does not have a father.

BOOK AND MEDIA CHOICES

Clements, Andrew. *Secret Father's Day Present: A Lift-the-Flap Story.* Illustrated by Varda Livney. New York: Simon & Schuster, 2000. 16p.
Grades: P–1. James and Sarah locate the tools they need to prepare a special Father's Day gift. Unfortunately, when Dad looks for his tools to do his Saturday chores he cannot find them. On Father's Day, Dad has a large present to open. It is James and Sara wrapped in a big box filled with his missing tools. Each tool has a note telling him how the children will use the tool to complete his chores.

Alden, Laura. *Father's Day*. Illustrated by Linda Hohag. Chicago: Children's Press, 1994. 31p.
Grades: P–2. Two siblings plan a fishing trip and a picnic to celebrate Father's Day. The night before, they learn that it will rain on Father's Day. Therefore, they alter their plans to be an indoor fishing trip, and fill a make-believe pond with paper fish inscribed with promises such as a pledge to weed the garden. The book suggests that since Father's Day is in the summer, the teachers and students could pick a day during the school year to celebrate. The book ends with activities for celebrating Father's Day, songs, and finger plays. This book is one of the Circle the Year with Holidays series.

Smalls, Irene. *Kevin and His Daddy*. Illustrated by Michael Hays. Boston: Little, Brown, 1999. Unp.
Grades: P–2. A Saturday with Dad includes chores, playing baseball, a movie, and a quiet talk. This touching recollection of a special day is told in short sentences with warm, textured, acrylic illustrations.

Spinelli, Eileen. *Night Shift Daddy*. Illustrated by Melissa Iwai. New York: Hyperion Books for Children, 2000. Unp.

Grades: P–2. Daddy tucks his little girl into bed before he leaves for the night shift. In the morning when the sun comes up Daddy is there to share breakfast with her. She then tucks him into bed before she goes out to play. Rhyming text and colorful illustrations tell of a very special bond between a girl and her father.

Bunting, Eve. *A Perfect Father's Day*. Illustrated by Susan Meddaugh. New York: Houghton Mifflin, 1993. 32p.
Grades: P–3. Susie's idea of a perfect Father's Day is to do all of the things she likes to do, such as eat at a fast food restaurant, feed the ducks, and play at the playground. Father cheerfully participates in the activities, happy to be spending time with his daughter doing things she wants to do. This book is also available on audiocassette.

Wood, Douglas. *What Dads Can't Do*. Illustrated by Doug Cushman. New York: Simon and Schuster Books for Young Readers, 2000. Unp.
Grades: P–3. A dinosaur son and his dad spend memorable times together, as the son explains there are many things a dad cannot do. For example, dads need extra practice putting worms on hooks, so the son consents to let his dad get a great deal of practice. Young and old readers can see themselves in this story and make personal connections between the characters' lives and their own. A mother does not appear in this book and children who live with their fathers like to see single-parent families like theirs.

Yolen, Jane. *Owl Moon*. Illustrated by John Schoenherr. New York: Putnam, 1987. Unp.
Grades: P–4. On a magical, frosty winter night a young girl and her father make their way through the snowy woods in search of owls. The father patiently imitates the call of the Great Horned Owl, until finally one answers. The watercolor washes complement the gentle, quiet tone of the text and beautifully portray winter in New England.

Smalls, Irene. *Father's Day Blues: What Do You Do about Father's Day When All You Have are Mothers?* Illustrated by Kevin McGovern. Stamford, Conn.: Longmeadow Press, 1995. Unp.
Grades: K–3. When faced with writing a Father's Day composition, Cheryl is perplexed about what to write. Her father does not live with her and she is not sure what fathers do. She is surrounded by love from her mother, her grandmother, and her aunt and she realizes that love is what makes a family. Most importantly, she learns that she is special and unique no matter what her family is like.

Steptoe, Javaka. *In Daddy's Arms I Am Tall: African Americans Celebrating Fathers*. New York: Lee & Low Books, 2000. Unp.
Grades: 3 and up. Mixed media collages and eloquent, short poems offer loving tributes to fathers. These are poems for reading aloud and savoring. The illustrations beckon the reader to examine them carefully both for their message and their composition. The book concludes with information on the poets and a note about the illustrations. This book won a Coretta Scott King picture book award.

Clements, Andrew. *The Janitor's Boy*. Illustrated by Brian Selznick. New York: Aladdin Paperbacks, 2001. 160p.
Grades: 4–6. According to Jack, nothing could be worse than being in fifth grade and having your classmates learn that your dad is the school janitor. As revenge for calling him "son" in front of his friends, Jack sticks a very, large wad of bubble gum on a desk. When he is caught, he is assigned to spend three weeks working with his dad after school. While he works with his father, he gets to know him and becomes proud of his father and his work.

EXPLORATIONS

1. After reading *Secret Father's Day Present: A Lift-the-Flap Story* (Clements, 2000), have students talk about the different things that adults do around the house. Collect their comments into a class book for them to take home.

2. After reading *Father's Day* (Alden, 1994), have students share their experiences with changing their plans because of rain. Have them brainstorm creative ideas for how to move outdoor activities indoors. Then, have them write a plan for moving an outdoor activity indoors.

3. Before reading *A Perfect Father's Day* (Bunting, 1993), have students work with a partner to plan a perfect Father's Day or a perfect Saturday for their family. Then, have them review their plans with another pair of students to determine if their plans are things they would like to do or things their families would like to do.

4. Before reading *What Dads Can't Do* (Wood, 2000), ask students what sorts of things their fathers do for them. Write their comments on chart paper. After reading the book, compare their list with the things the Dad in the story does for his child.

5. After reading *The Janitor's Boy* (Clements, 2001), lead students in a discussion of social status assigned to people based on their jobs and possessions.

FLAG DAY

On June 14, 1777, the Marine Committee of the Second Continental Congress adopted a resolution describing the nation's flag. The resolution was introduced by John Adams and stated: "Resolved, that the Flag of the United States be thirteen stripes, alternate red and white, that the Union be thirteen stars white in a blue field representing a new constellation." As new states were added to the Union the number of stars on the American flag changed to reflect the additions. Over a century later, on June 14, 1899, a kindergarten teacher named George Balch had his students perform a school program in honor of the American Flag. On May 30, 1916, President Woodrow Wilson established Flag Day, but it was not until August 3, 1949 that President Truman signed an Act of Congress making June 14, National Flag Day (Moehn, 2000). Additional information on Flag Day can be found at The National Flag Day Foundation Web site at www.usflag.org/toc.

BOOK AND MEDIA CHOICES

The Pledge of Allegiance. New York: Scholastic, 2000. Unp.
Grades: P–2. Spectacular color photographs of America fill the pages of the book with phrases of the Pledge of Allegiance scrolling across the bottom. At the end of the book, readers find information about some of the photographs and explanations of the meanings of the words in the pledge. Facts about the flag conclude the book. This book helps young students understand and appreciate the pledge that they memorize and recite.

Kroll, Steven. *By the Dawn's Early Light: The Story of the Star-Spangled Banner*. Illustrated by Dan Andreasen. New York: Scholastic, 1994. Unp.
Grades: P–3. Francis Scott Key helplessly watched from a British ship as they shelled Fort McHenry. When morning came, the flag still waved above the fort and the Americans retained control of the fort. The book begins with background information on the War of 1812 and an author's note with additional details concludes the book.

Warm, luminous paintings accompany the well-researched text, which includes a photograph of the original manuscript of the Star-Spangled Banner. The book concludes with a bibliography and an index.

Herman, John. *Red, White and Blue: The Story of the American Flag*. Illustrated by Robin Roraback. East Rutherford, N. J.: Putnam Publishing Group, 1998. 48p.
Grades: K–3. This book for young readers shows how the American flag evolved over the years. Cartoon-like illustrations accompany the factual, easy-to-read text. The book helps young students understand the importance of the flag as a symbol of our country. This book is from the All Aboard Reading, Level 2 series.

America! A Celebration of Freedom from Our Nation's Finest. CD. Nashville, Tenn.: Coker & McCree, 1999.
Grades: K and up. The U.S. Air Force Band and the Singing Sergeants perform a collection of patriotic songs. Some of the songs included on this CD are: "This Land is Your Land," "The Stars and Stripes Forever," "Star Spangled Banner," "American the Beautiful," and "This Is My Country."

Wallner, Alexandra. *Betsy Ross*. New York: Holiday House, 1994. Unp.
Grades: 1–4. The legend of Betsy Ross suggests that she designed the first American flag; however, there is no proof that she sewed the first American flag. As an accomplished seamstress and upholsterer, she did sew American flags. This is the story of an American patriot whose first two husbands died fighting for America's freedom. Her sewing business enabled her to support herself and her children at a time when few women owned their own businesses.

Old Glory. Video. Raleigh, N.C.: Rainbow Educational Media, 1994. 10 min.
Grades: 2–5. This short video shows students the evolution of the flag, describes the symbolism behind the flag, and how to properly fold, fly, and display the flag. A teacher's guide is included.

Ryan, Pam Muñoz. *The Flag We Love*. Illustrated by Ralph Masiello. Watertown, Mass.: Charlesbridge, 1996. Unp.
Grades: 2 and up. The author's fruitless search for a picture book for her own children to help them understand the importance of the American flag led her to write this patriotic book celebrating the flag.

Short four-line verses accompanied by text boxes of information about the flag are on the left side of the double-page spread. On the right side is a glorious, full-page painting celebrating the American flag.

St. Pierre, Stephanie. *Our National Anthem*. Brookfield, Conn.: The Millbrook Press, 1992. 47p.
Grades: 3–6. Sidebars, document reproductions, photographs, maps, and illustrations all help to tell the history of the "Star-Spangled Banner." A glossary of words and phrases from the anthem is included, as is a presentation of the four verses. The book provides information on other patriotic songs, as well, including: "America the Beautiful," "The Battle Hymn of the Republic," and "Yankee Doodle Dandy." A chronology, a list of books for further reading, and an index, round out the book. This is from the I Know America series.

Ferry, Joseph. *The American Flag*. Philadelphia, Penn.: Mason Crest Publishers, 2003. 46p.
Grades: 4–8. In addition to discussing the history and evolution of the flag, this book explains the Betsy Ross controversy, describes the origin of the "Star Spangled Banner," and tells how to show respect for the flag. Photographs, illustrations, and sidebars help convey the history of the flag. A chronology, books for further reading, Web sites, and an index are included for further reference. From the American Symbols and their Meanings series.

Kreitler, Peter Gwilliam. *United We Stand: Flying the American Flag*. San Francisco, Calif.: Chronicle Books, 2001. 120p.
Grades: 6 and up. Stirring images of the American flag fill the pages of this book. The summer after Pearl Harbor major United States magazines featured the American flag on their covers to celebrate Independence Day. These original images are collected and published in this unique, visual tribute to the American flag.

EXPLORATIONS

1. At the end of *The Pledge of Allegiance*, readers learn that the colors of the flag symbolize important American ideals. Red is for bravery, white for liberty, and blue for justice. These words are often difficult for students to understand. Begin by asking students what they think they mean and then help them develop an understanding of the words.

2. In *By the Dawn's Early Light: The Story of the Star-Spangled Banner* (Kroll, 1994) students discover that Francis Scott Key wrote poetry all of his life and that our national anthem was originally written as a poem. Provide the students an opportunity to talk about important events in their lives and write brief poems about them. They can also create illustrations to go with their poems.

3. After reading *Betsy Ross* (Wallner, 1994) help students learn how unusual it was for a woman to own her own business, whereas in today's society many women own their own business, in Betsy Ross's day few women did.

4. After watching *Old Glory*, have the students practice folding an American flag. Sometimes schools have old flags that can be borrowed for this purpose, or perhaps the class can be put in charge of raising and lowering the school flag daily.

5. Prior to reading, *The Flag We Love* (Ryan, 1996) share with students that the author wrote the book to help her own children understand the importance of respecting the flag (James, 1999). While grocery shopping she saw a large flag draped over a display of cases of beer and she complained to the assistant manager and wrote a letter of complaint to the president of the company. Her children did not understand why she was upset. She searched to find such a book to help explain to them the proper uses of the flag and its importance to Americans. When she could not find a book that met her need, she wrote this book for them.

6. After reading *Our National Anthem* (St. Pierre, 1992), provide students an opportunity to listen to the "Star-Spangled Banner" and other patriotic songs mentioned in the text. The music CD America! A Celebration of Freedom from Our Nation's Finest contains a collection of patriotic songs.

7. After reading *The American Flag* (Ferry, 2003), have students visit the Web site A Guide to American flags at www.law.ou.edu/hist/flags. On the Web site are graphics depicting the flags described in the chapter on the evolution of the flag, such as the one with the motto "Don't Tread on Me." Then, have the students create a pictorial timeline showing the evolution of the flag.

8. Before reading *United We Stand: Flying the American Flag* (Kreitler, 2001), share with students the history behind the collection of images in the book.

9. After reading *United We Stand: Flying the American Flag* (Kreitler, 2001), have students carefully examine the images and focus on the lines, colors, and shapes of the flags. *Hiller* (1997) helps his art students realize that by changing some of these characteristics they can redraw the flag while retaining its essence. Then, provide students time to create their own redesigned flag images.

JUNETEENTH

Juneteenth is celebrated in the United States on June 19, because on that date in 1865 news reached Galveston, Texas that Abraham Lincoln had signed the Emancipation Proclamation giving slaves their freedom. News of the Emancipation Proclamation signed in Washington, D.C. on January 1, 1863, took two and one-half years to reach Galveston, Texas. For African Americans this date became the equivalent of the Fourth of July. As Texans moved to other states they began their own Juneteenth celebrations. African Americans celebrate this holiday with parades, barbeques, games, songs, speeches, and parties. Celebrations of Juneteenth may last for several days culminating on June nineteenth.

BOOK AND MEDIA CHOICES

Welsey, Valerie Wilson. *Freedom's Gifts: A Juneteenth Story*. Illustrated by Sharon Wilson. New York: Simon & Schuster, 1997. 32p.
Grades: K–3. Lillie arrives from New York to visit her family in Texas during the Juneteenth holiday. She is bored with the "dumb, old, slave holiday," until her great, great aunt tells about being born a slave and how joyous she was to be set free. Lillie comes to realize the importance of the holiday to her family and begins to understand why it is celebrated.

Branch, Muriel Miller. *Juneteenth: Freedom Day*. Photographs by Willis Branch. New York: Cobblehill/Dutton, 1998. 54p.
Grades: 2–8. In 1998, Muriel and Willis Branch traveled to Houston to learn about Juneteenth. A local waiter directed them to Galveston,

Texas and suggested that they participate in the Juneteenth celebrations held there. Then, they traveled all over the country to chronicle the Juneteenth celebrations included in this book. Cities, towns, and communities all over the United States now celebrate with either formal ceremonies or simple family picnics. The well-researched text and detailed black-and-white photographs provide readers with a great deal of historical and current information about the special significance of this holiday to African Americans throughout the United States.

Barrett, Anna Pearl. *Juneteenth: Celebrating Freedom in Texas.* Austin, Texas: Eakin Press, 1999. 88p.
Grades: 3–6. This is an account of how the author's family celebrated Juneteenth in 1945 in Barrett, Texas, a town founded by her grandfather. The author uses dialogue, songs from the past, and rich details to explain the weeks of preparations involved in her family's celebration of Juneteenth. There were new clothes to sew, food to cook, and a fence to whitewash in preparation for the arrival of the relatives. An addendum provides information on the struggles of the author's grandfather as he worked to acquire land and how it was taken from him.

Weatherford, Carole Boston. *Juneteenth Jamboree.* Illustrated by Yvonne Buchanan. New York: Lee & Low Books, 1995. 32p.
Grades: 3–6. Cassie and her family celebrate Juneteenth with a parade, a feast, and a balloon release. Cassie learns that it took more than two years for the news of Emancipation to reach the Texas slaves and wonders why.

McKissack, Patricia C., and Frederick L. McKissack. *Days of Jubilee: The End of Slavery in the United States.* Illustrated by Diane Dillon and Leo Dillon. New York: Scholastic, 2003. 144p.
Grades: 4 and up. This superb book by the incomparable McKissacks studies slavery from its early days in the United States to the Emancipation. Freedom from slavery came in stages rather than all at once. This book chronicles the emancipation of the slaves from the Revolutionary War to the signing of the thirteenth amendment to the Constitution. Slave narratives, diaries, military orders, and other primary source documents were used in researching this book. Told in the actual words of slaves from their narratives, the book speaks to the readers in an emotional voice. Sepia photographs and drawings accompany the text and help clarify the material in the reader's eye.

Taylor, Charles. *Juneteenth: A Celebration of Freedom*. Greensboro, N.C.: Open Hand Publishing, 2002. Unp.
Grades: 5–8. Photographs, reproductions, and enthusiastic narrative tell the story of the slaves in Texas learning they were free. Primary source documents containing quotes from slaves and the text of the Emancipation Proclamation are included. Readers learn about the different ways that Juneteenth has been celebrated over the years.

Explorations

1. Before reading, *Freedom's Gifts: A Juneteenth Story* (Welsey, 1997), have students talk to their parents and relatives about a holiday that is significant to the family. Have them find out why the holiday is significant to the family. Then, have students share with their classmates why the holiday is significant and how they celebrate the holiday.

2. After reading *Juneteenth: Freedom Day* (Branch, 1998), students may want to create their own Juneteenth celebration. This book includes information on organizing a Juneteenth celebration.

3. While reading *Juneteenth Jamboree* (Weatherford, 1995), have students work with a partner to list all of the different events associated with the Juneteenth celebration recalled in the book, such as the parade, the feast, and the balloon release. After reading the book, students who have celebrated Juneteenth can compare their celebrations of this holiday with the one in the book. Students who have not celebrated Juneteenth can compare the celebration in the book with another celebration such as Independence Day—the Fourth of July.

4. The primary source documents included in *Days of Jubilee: The End of Slavery in the United States* (McKissack and McKissack, 2003) lend themselves to dramatic readings. The students can select their favorite one and prepare a dramatic reading to share with their classmates.

5. Before students read *Juneteenth: A Celebration of Freedom* (Taylor, 2002), explain how the layout of nonfiction books differs from the layout of fiction books. Ask the students what differences they see in the layouts. In this book, there is a table of contents in the front of the book

set off in a yellow box. The headings are set off in bold font in green boxes. The captions to the pictures are set off in yellow or blue boxes. There are sidebars in the book and some pages are yellow rather than white. At the end of the book we find a glossary, a list of references, photo credits, two resource organizations are listed, and information about the author.

STONEWALL REBELLION

On June 27, 1969, New York police raided Stonewall Inn, a Greenwich Village gay bar. Raids on the bar were not unusual but on this night, the patrons decided to fight back and several nights of protest followed (Harlin, 2002). Lesbian, gay, bisexual, and transgender pride events began to be held on June 27 in cities around the United States to commemorate the Stonewall Rebellion. Now, pride events are held around the world and throughout the year. Like Father's Day, this is an example of a celebration that had local beginnings and eventually spread far and wide. While not everyone may be familiar with the Stonewall Rebellion, it is a celebration that some students, their parents, and friends commemorate. Anderson (1997) reminds us that children need to see books that contain positive portrayals of all segments of our population and children need to see their lives reflected in the books they read.

BOOK AND MEDIA CHOICES

Willhoite, Michael. *Daddy's Roommate*. Los Angeles, Calif.: Alyson Publications, 2000, 1990. Unp.
Grades: P–2. After his parents divorce, a young boy spends weekends with his gay father and his father's roommate, Frank. Brief sentences tell how Daddy and Frank live together and share their lives. On weekends the boy, Daddy, and Frank go to the zoo, go shopping, and spend time together. When the boy asks his mother what "gay" means, she tells him it "is just one more kind of love." Bright, colorful illustrations depict a child and his two families.

Newman, Lesléa. *Heather Has Two Mommies*. Illustrated by Diana Souza. Los Angeles, Calif.: Alyson Publications, 2000, 1990. Unp.
Grades: P–3. When Heather joins a playgroup, she discovers that the other children have daddies and wonders if she is the only one

without a daddy. When the children in the playgroup draw pictures of their families, Heather discovers that families come in a variety of combinations. Stacy has two daddies; Joshua has a mother and two daddies, a father and a stepfather; Carlos has a mother, a daddy and a brother; Miriam has a mommy and a sister; and David's mommy and daddy adopted him, his two brothers, and his sister. As they hang up their pictures the caregiver, Molly, tells the children that the important thing is that the people in the family love one another. An author's note at the end of this tenth anniversary edition explains that the text has been shortened and the details on Heather's conception omitted.

Withrow, Sarah. *Box Girl*. City: Douglas & McIntyre Publishing, 2002. 181p.
Grades: 6–10. As eighth grade starts, Gwen is determined to be a loner and make no attachments. After all she will be leaving for Paris shortly, postcards from her mother in Paris indicate she will be sending for her. Each night she stacks the postcards in the shape of a box following a ritual that she knows will bring more postcards and a reunion with her mother. However, there is a new girl, Clara, at school, who persists in being her friend. Gwen does not want a friend, because a friend will want to come over and will learn that her mother left five years ago and that Gwen lives with her father and his boyfriend. As Gwen discovers, Clara has problems of her own, and Clara likes her just as she is, regardless of her family situation.

EXPLORATIONS

1. After reading *Daddy's Roommate* (Willhoite, 2000), ask the children about how they spent their weekend. Children are usually eager to talk about the things they did on the weekend, particularly if they went somewhere special. Children who spend weekends with noncustodial parents enjoy being able to talk about the special times they had with the parent.

2. After reading *Heather Has Two Mommies* (Newman, 2000), have the children talk about their families. Ask if any of them have grandparents living with them, cousins or other extended family members. Let them draw pictures of their families and write the names of the family members on the their pictures. Let them share the pictures with their classmates and then hang them on the bulletin board.

Older students can write descriptions of their families to go with their pictures.

3. The characters Gwen and Carla in *Box Girl* (Withrow, 2002) are believable, likeable, and struggling to come to terms with difficult issues in their lives. In the course of the story, they develop a genuine friendship. How do the problems in their lives at first hinder them from becoming friends? How do the problems in their lives strengthen their friendship?

REFERENCES

Anderson, Douglas Eric. 1997. "Gay Information: Out of the Closet." In *School Library Journal's Best: A Reader for Children's, Young Adult & School Librarians*, ed. Lillian N. Gerhardt.

Harlin, Ken. "The Stonewall Riot and Its Aftermath." New York: Columbia Universities Libraries, May 2002. www.columbia.edu/cu/lweb/eresources/exhibitions/sw25/case1.html.

Hiller, Peter. 1997. "Flags for America." *Arts and Activities* 121 (June): 29.

James, Helen Foster. 1999. "Talking with Pam Muñoz Ryan." *Book Links 8,* no. 3 (January): 40–43.

Leslie, Clare Walker, and Frank E. Gerace. 2000. *The Ancient Celtic Festivals and How We Celebrate Them Today*. Illustrated by Clare Walker Leslie. Rochester, Vt.: Inner Traditions.

Moehn, Heather. 2000. *World Holidays: A Watts Guide for Children.* New York: Franklin Watts.

Zalben, Jane Breskin. 1999. *To Every Season: A Family Holiday Cookbook*. New York: Simon & Schuster Books for Young Readers.

Ｊｕｌｙ Ｈｏｌｉｄａｙｓ ａｎｄ Ｃｅｌｅｂｒａｔｉｏｎｓ 15

July begins with a bang as fireworks light the skies on July 4 to celebrate America's Independence Day. July's other celebrations include Tanabata, Bastille Day, and Mormon Pioneer Day. On July 7, Japanese celebrate Tanabata—the Star Festival—originally borrowed from the Chinese, who call it Chi His. This festival honors a Chinese legend about parted lovers, who are represented by two stars (Altair and Vega) seen in the summer sky (Henderson and Thompson, 2002). France celebrates its independence, Bastille Day, on July 14. The Mormon's search for religious freedom is commemorated on July 24, Mormon Pioneer Day. July is the month for looking to the skies for fireworks and stars.

FOURTH OF JULY

On July 4, 1776, the American colonists declared their independence from England with the signing of the Declaration of Independence. Fireworks, picnics, and parades commemorate this important occasion. Hot dogs and apple pie are traditional American foods, perfect for celebrating July 4, but as noted in one of the books described below, international foods also have become part of the traditional fare. With nightfall come loud bangs and noisy pops, as the sky explodes in riotous colors from fireworks displays. Over time the new nation developed its own national symbols and patriotic songs, as explained in some of the books annotated below. (See Bastille Day and Mexican Independence Day.)

Book and Media Choices

Ziefert, Harriet. *Hats Off for the Fourth of July!* Illustrated by Gustaf Miller. New York: Puffin Books, 2000. Unp.

Grades: P–2. What better way to celebrate the Fourth of July than with a parade! Bright rollicking illustrations portray the excitement and wonder of a parade as the bands, twirlers, marchers, horses, and floats come into view. Just as the parade ends the sky comes to life with skywriting followed by fireworks.

Berlin, Irving. *God Bless America*. Illustrated by Lynn Munsinger. New York: Harper Collins, 2002. Unp.
Grades: P–3. Pappa Bear and his two young children experience first hand the wonders of America recorded in this patriotic tune. They travel from cities to mountains to prairies to oceans and back home to Momma Bear. The pages are filled with rich color illustrations of America's countless splendors from sea to shining sea, as witnessed by the awestruck loving trio. A brief phrase of the song is found on each page, and a CD containing Barbara Streisand's rendition of "God Bless America" is included. The book concludes with a note that the proceeds from the song go to the God Bless America Fund for American youth.

Wong, Janet S. *Apple Pie 4th of July*. Illustrated by Margaret Chodos-Irvine. San Diego, Calif.: Harcourt, 2002. Unp.
Grades: P–3. A young child is distressed because her parents are in their Chinese store cooking Chinese food on the Fourth of July. She is concerned that her parents just do not understand American ways and that no one will eat Chinese food on the Fourth, when apple pie is the food of choice. Later in the day, though, the store fills with people buying Chinese food. The family ends their day by eating apple pie as they watch the fireworks from their rooftop. Bright, colorful illustrations fill the pages.

Independence Day. Video. Bala Cynwyd, Penn.: Schlessinger Video Productions-Library Video Company, 1994. 25 min.
Grades: K–4. As students learn about Paul Revere's ride and the signing of the Declaration of Independence, they develop an understanding of the spirit of 1776 that propelled the colonists to revolt against England. They also develop an understanding of the ideals of liberty and freedom that we celebrate on the Fourth of July. A teacher's guide is included. This video is from the Holidays for Children series.

Merrick, Patrick. *Fourth of July Fireworks*. Chanhassen, Minn.: The Child's World, 2000. 32p.

Grades: 1–4. A description of Independence Day and a brief history of the origin of the country, provide the background students need to understand why Americans take time to celebrate this holiday. The text explains the tradition of fireworks, how they are made, and raises cautions about lighting fireworks. Throughout, photographs and illustrations explode with color and the excitement of this holiday celebration. The book concludes with an index and a glossary.

Catrow, David. *We the Kids: The Preamble to the Constitution of the United States*. New York: Dial Books for Young Readers, 2002. Unp.
Grades: 1–5. An author's note opens the book, sharing with readers how as a child the Preamble to the U.S. Constitution was a confusing jumble of words to him. As he grew older, he came to understand the words and their importance to American life. He then explains in simple terms what the words to the Preamble mean. He urges readers to pay attention to the dog in the illustrations that follow. The humorous pencil and watercolor illustrations graphically depict the words to the Preamble to help readers fully grasp their meaning.

Gore, Willma Willis. *Independence Day*. Berkeley Heights, N.J.: Enslow, 1993. 48p.
Grades: 2–5. Chapters explain the history of this day, a description of the first Independence Day and ways the day is celebrated across the nation. The book includes a description of famous symbols of independence, and shows the pride felt by Americans for their country. A glossary and an index are incorporated. This book is from the One of the Best Holiday Books series.

Landau, Elaine. *Independence Day—Birthday of the United States*. Berkeley Heights, N.J.: Enslow Publishers, 2001. 48p.
Grades: 2–5. Fireworks, parades, and food are not the only ways Independence Day is celebrated. The author's research has uncovered a variety of ways American's celebrate, such as in the town of Seward, Nebraska where the sheriff stops an out of state family traveling on Interstate 80 and invites them to be the town's guests and participate in the Fourth of July parade. Illustrations, photographs, and sidebars all help tell the story of American Independence Day celebrations. A sparkler craft project, a recipe for an ice cream sundae, a glossary, resources for learning more, and an index fill out this incredibly useful title. This book is from the Finding Out about Holidays series.

West, Delno C., and Jean M. West. *Uncle Sam and Old Glory: Symbols of America*. Illustrated by Christopher Manson. New York: Atheneum Books for Young Readers, 2000. 40p.
Grades: 2 and up. These symbols help to portray Americans' beliefs in liberty and democracy. Readers may be familiar with the Liberty Bell as a symbol of independence, but they may not realize that the abolitionists also adopted it as a symbol of freedom. Although the phrase "Let Freedom Ring" is associated with the bell, it has not been rung since 1846 because of a large crack. Each two-page spread includes a full-page woodcut and a page of text with information about the symbol. In the back of the book we find a list of books for further reading.

Dalgliesh, Alice. *The Fourth of July Story*. Illustrated by Marie Nonnast. New York: Aladdin Paperbacks, 1995. Unp.
Grades: 3–6. Simple, informative text describes the writing of the Declaration of Independence and its distribution throughout the colonies by riders on horseback. Two months later when a copy reached a small southern town, nine-year-old Andrew Jackson read it aloud to the townspeople. Details such as this one set the book apart from many others written for this age group. This book was originally published in 1956.

Bateman, Teresa. *Red, White, Blue and Uncle Who?: The Stories behind Some of America's Patriotic Symbols*. Illustrated by John O'Brien. New York: Holiday House, 2001. 64p.
Grades: 4 and up. Lively, entertaining stories replete with interesting details and amusing cartoon drawings make this a book that students return to repeatedly. The White House has an oval office because the architect found that people frequently gathered around George Washington in an oval. The designer of the Vietnam Veterans Memorial originally submitted the design as an assignment while a student at Yale. The design was awarded a "B" by her professor. These are just two of the fascinating facts to be learned about our patriotic symbols. The book concludes with an index.

Giblin, James Cross. *Fireworks, Picnics, and Flags: The Story of the Fourth of July Symbols*. Illustrated by Ursula Arndt. New York: Clarion Books, 1983. 90p.
Grades: 4 and up. Readers step back in time as they learn about the birth of our nation and the traditional Fourth of July symbols including: Uncle Sam, the eagle, the Liberty Bell, and patriotic songs. The centennial celebration of 1876 and the bicentennial celebration of

1976 are briefly described. Informative text highlighted with black-and-white line drawings holds readers' attention. The book concludes with a chronology and an index.

Statue of Liberty. DVD and video. Alexandria, Va.: Public Broadcasting Service, 2002. 60 min.
Grades: 4 and up. Ken Burns explores the history of the Statue of Liberty and the meaning of liberty. Photographs, paintings, drawings, diaries, letters, and newspapers are the types of varied resources used to gather information for this film. Interviews with Barbara Jordan, Mario Cuomo, and others bring the narrative to life. Additional information and teacher resources can be found at www.pbs.org/kenburns/statueofliberty.

Independence Day: As American as Apple Pie. Video. Bala Cynwyd, Penn.: Schlessinger Video Productions-Library Video Company, 1999. 44 min.
Grades: 6 and up. Students experience the American Fourth of July spirit in this fact-filled video. From the first family of country music, the Carters, to Thomas Jefferson's Monticello, America is a land of diversity filled with interesting people and things. This video is from the Picture This America series.

Independence Day: History of July 4th. Video. South Burlington, Va.: A & E Television Networks, 1998. 50 min.
Grades: 6 and up. Travel back to Independence Hall in Philadelphia in July 1776 and listen to the Declaration of Independence being read aloud to the eager crowd. The origins and history of the Fourth of July unfold through artwork, interviews with historians, parades from around the nation, and glorious fireworks displays. This video is part of the History of the Holidays series.

EXPLORATIONS

1. While reading *Hats Off for the Fourth of July!* (Ziefert, 2000), pause and have students predict what will come next in the parade.

2. After reading *Hats Off for the Fourth of July!* (Ziefert, 2000), discuss how authors use a sequence of events to organize their stories. Then, have the students collaborate with a partner to create a sequence-of-events chart depicting the parade.

3. Before reading *God Bless America* (Berlin, 2002), have the students listen to the song on the CD included with the book. Then, show students that the words in the song are the same as the words in the book.

4. Before reading *Apple Pie 4th of July* (Wong, 2002), have students brainstorm a list of foods and activities that they include in their Fourth of July celebrations.

5. Before reading the book *We the Kids: The Preamble to the Constitution of the United States* (Catrow, 2002), read the Preamble to the students and have them discuss what it means to them. Record their ideas on the board. After reading the book, have them return to the ideas recorded on the board and add to them.

6. After reading *Red, White, Blue and Uncle Who?: The Stories behind Some of America's Patriotic Symbols* (Bateman, 2001), have students work with a partner and select one of the symbols to research. Then, have the students prepare a presentation to share their research with their classmates.

Independence Day Celebrations around the World			
Country	Date They Celebrate	Why They Celebrate	How They Celebrate
United States	July 4th	Freedom from English rule	Fireworks, picnics, parades, baseball games, waving flags
France	July 14	Freedom from a monarchy	Fireworks, parades, dances
Mexico	September 16	Freedom from Spanish rule	Parades, dances, singing

Figure 15-1. Many countries celebrate an independence day. Putting the information about the celebrations in a chart helps students note similarities and differences.

7. America is not the only country to celebrate an Independence Day. Students can research other countries to learn about why and how they celebrate Independence Day. Place the students in groups and have each group research a different country. Create a large chart (similar to the one on the previous page) on bulletin board paper and have each group fill in the information they learn about a country.

TANABATA

Tanabata (Star Festival) is celebrated in Japan on the night of the seventh day of the seventh month when two star lovers are reunited. In China, this celebration is called Chi His (Festival of the Milky Way). In the legend the star Vega represents the Weaving Girl and the star Altair represents the Herd Boy. When these two lovers became engaged, they neglected their responsibilities and her father the Celestial Emperor (the Jade Emperor) decreed that they would live forever separated on opposite sides of the Milky Way. On the night of July seventh, magpies form a bridge over the river and the lovers meet for one night each year. Along with the star Deneb, Vega and Altair form the Summer Triangle visible in the night sky (Dickinson, 1996). The books and media below contain variations of this Chinese legend and information on locating the stars.

BOOK AND MEDIA CHOICES

Kitada, Shin. *The Story of Tanabata*. Oaktag Cards. Illustrated by Yukihiko Mitani. New York: Kamishibai for Kids, 1995.
Grades: P–4. This legend of the weaving girl and the herd boy unfolds on fifteen-inch by eleven-inch cards in the tradition of Kamishibai, Asian picture storytelling. Beautiful, detailed illustrations are on the front of the cards and the Japanese text and English translation are on the back of the cards. The text is composed of dialogue, which enables the storyteller easily to recount this dramatic legend. A teacher's guide is included. Information on Kamishibai and additional stories can be found at www.kamishibai.com.

Birdseye, Tom. *A Song of Stars*. Illustrated by Ju-Hong Chen. New York: Holiday House, 1990. Unp.

Grades: K–3. This book is an adaptation of the Asian legend of the princess weaver and the herdsman separated by the Emperor of the Heavens when they begin to neglect their duties. The lyrical verse is accompanied by colorful, mosaic illustrations. An author's note explains that in Japan love poems written on colored paper are hung on long bamboo poles. In China, incense is offered and women and girls pray for skill in their handiwork. In both countries fruit, sweets and cakes are offered to the stars in hopes of fair weather.

Dickinson, Terence. *Summer Stargazing*. Willowdale, Ont.: Firefly Books, 1996. 64p.
Grades: 6 and up. Grab a pair of binoculars, a reclining lawn chair, and head to the backyard to gaze at the night sky and locate the Summer Triangle. Color photographs and clear, concise descriptions assure that readers are able to find the Milky Way's constellations. This book is just the one to get young stargazers involved in a lifetime hobby. The book includes star charts, planet visibility tables, resources for learning more, and an index.

EXPLORATIONS

1. After reading *The Story of Tanabata* (Kitada, 1995), provide older students with oak tag rectangles for creating their own storytelling cards to retell a favorite story.

2. After reading *Summer Stargazing* (Dickinson, 1996), review the Handy Sky Measures to help students use their hands to measure distances for locating stars in the summer sky.

3. To learn more about the Summer Triangle have the students visit Web sites such as Astronomy: What's Up in the July Skies at www.treehousefun.com/read_and _learn/july.html, or the Skywatchers' Guide at www.flandrau.org/astronomy/skywatchers.

BASTILLE DAY

On July 14, 1789, the people of France stormed the Bastille, a French prison. This notorious fortress held people opposed to King Louis XVI and Queen Marie Antoinette (Moehn, 2000). Just as in America, the ideas of freedom, liberty, and justice were being championed as rights of the French people. As food grew scarce and their living conditions grew worse, the people revolted against the taxes imposed on them to support the excesses of the nobility. Bastille Day is celebrated with street parties, displays of military power, and recognition of veterans (France, 1999). The United States and France both celebrate their independence from a monarchy in July. They also have in common the writings of Thomas Paine, who encouraged overthrowing the monarchy. Thomas Paine wrote, "Common Sense," in support of the American Revolution and he wrote, "The Age of Reason," in support of the French Revolution. The books annotated below provide information on the country of France and the French Revolution. (See Fourth of July and Mexican Independence Day.)

BOOK AND MEDIA CHOICES

Streissguth, Tom. *France*. Minneapolis, Minn.: Carolrhoda Books, 1997. 48p.
Grades: K–2. This is a brief introduction to the land, people, and food of France. Young readers are not overwhelmed by information and the layout of the book encourages them to read and learn. Large font with a handwritten look, color photographs, and fact filled sidebars contain additional information and activities for learning more about France. Words in the glossary appear in bold text. A glossary, more books to read, and an index are included. From the A Ticket To series.

Stevens, Kathryn. *France*. Chanhassen, Minn.: The Child's World, 2001. 32p.
Grades: 2–5. Readers learn about France, its people, and its customs. Large, color and black-and-white photographs show the captivating countryside and the fascinating people of France. Country facts, trivia, a glossary, an index, and Web site URLs are included.

Ngcheong-Lum, Roseline. *France*. Milwaukee, Wis.: Gareth Stevens Publishing, 1999. 96p.
Grades: 5–7. The book begins with an overview of France including information on the geography, history, government, language, arts, festivals, and food. Interesting details about France include information about the people, places, ideas, and festivals of France. In this section, readers learn about the perfume and wine industries, the French Impressionists, famous French people, and the Tour de France among other topics. The concluding section of the book

describes the connections between France, Canada, and the United States. A glossary, resources for learning more, and an index are included. This book is from the Countries of the World series.

Plain, Nancy. *Louis XVI, Marie-Antoinette and the French Revolution*. New York: Marshall Cavendish, 2002. 88p.
Grades: 6 and Up. Descriptions and comparisons of lives of the nobility, clergy, and commoners provide the background readers need to understand the French Revolution. Well-written text filled with illustrations and quotes from primary sources make this an excellent resource for leaning about France and the French Revolution. The book ends with a glossary, books for further reading, a bibliography, notes, and an index. This book is from the Rulers and Their Times series.

EXPLORATIONS

1. Before reading about Bastille Day, have students discuss the reasons why Americans celebrate the Fourth of July. After reading about Bastille Day, help students make connections between France and America's struggles for independence.

2. While reading *France* (Streissguth, 1997), help students make connections between America and France by noting similarities and differences depicted in the pictures.

3. After reading *France* (Streissguth, 1997) or *France* (Stevens, 2001), have students make a chart with two columns. List foods that they eat on the Fourth of July in the first column and then return to the book and list foods that they think the French would eat and drink on Bastille Day in the second column.

4. After reading *France* (Ngcheong-Lum, 1999) have students make a list of festivals celebrated in France, such as Carnival, Bastille Day, Harvest Festivals, and Avignon Festival. Then, have them try to find corresponding festivals celebrated in America. This activity can also be used to make connections with leisure activities in France and America.

MORMON PIONEER DAY

As with other religious groups in America, the members of The Church of Jesus Christ of Latter-day Saints, known as the Mormons, moved frequently in search of religious freedom and to avoid persecution. Mormon Pioneer Day celebrates the end of their quest. After their leader Joseph Smith was murdered in Nauvoo, Illinois, the Mormons traveled westward in search of a new place to settle. On July 24, 1847, their new leader, Brigham Young, decided that the Salt Lake Valley would be the Mormons' home (Henderson and Thompson, 2002). These pioneers worked hard to settle the land and prosper. Church services, parades, and feasting mark this celebration in Salt Lake City and other Mormon communities throughout the United States. The books annotated below focus on the life of Brigham Young and the Mormon religion.

BOOK AND MEDIA CHOICES

Simon, Charnan. *Brigham Young: Mormon and Pioneer*. New York: Children's Press, 1998. 48p.
Grades: 3–5. The story of the Mormon's struggles in America is told through the life of their leader Brigham Young. The Mormon's way of life included shopping only at Mormon owned businesses, attending Mormon run schools, casting votes for the favored candidate, and plural marriages. These activities and beliefs resulted in their being driven from one settlement to another. As they traveled west in search of religious freedom, they followed what eventually became known as the Mormon Trail. Colorful maps, reproductions, and sidebars provide an open format that appeals to young readers. A timeline, resources for learning more, and an index conclude the book. This book is from the Community Builders series.

Sanford, William R., and Carl R. Green. *Brigham Young: Pioneer and Mormon Leader*. Berkeley Heights, N.J.: Enslow Publishers, 1996. 47p.
Grades: 4–7. An author's note at the beginning of the book tells readers that as a Wild West hero many stories about Brigham Young are exaggerated. The book presents only those stories that can be substantiated and chapter notes detail the extensive research used to gather material for the book. The book presents a factual account of Young's life as leader of the Mormon pioneers including information on Mormons' practices, beliefs, and actions that caused discord

between them and their American neighbors. A glossary, a list of books for learning more, and an index are included. This book is from the series Legendary Heroes of the Wild West.

Knight, Hal, and Dr. Stanley B. Kimball. *111 Days to Zion: The Day-by-Day Trek of the Mormon Pioneers*. Illustrated by Robert R. Noyce. Salt Lake City, Utah: Deseret Press, 1978. 263p.
Grades: 6 and up. In April 1978, the Deseret News began publishing a day-by-day account of Brigham Young and his followers' journey along the Mormon Trail from their Winter Quarters on the banks of the Missouri River to their arrival in Salt Lake City. The publication dates matched the dates of the Mormon's one hundred eleven day journey from April through July 1847. These accounts included excerpts from the pioneers' diaries and line drawings, which were later compiled for this book. An epilogue and an index conclude the book.

American Prophet. Video. Alexandria, Va.: Public Broadcasting Service, 1999. 120 min.
Grades: 6 and up. Narrated by Gregory Peck, this video tells the life story of Joseph Smith, the controversial founder of the Mormon church. Additional information on this video, John Smith, and the Mormon church can be found at www.pbs.org/americanprophet.

Williams, Jean Kinney. *The Mormons*. New York: Franklin Watts, 1996. 111p.
Grades: 7–10. Information on the Mormon history, culture, and conflicts with American society is provided in this in-depth account, which includes photographs, reproductions, and maps. Students conducting research on the Mormons will find this an excellent resource. Source notes, books for further reading, Internet sites, and an index are included. This book is form the American Religious Experience series.

EXPLORATIONS

1. Prior to reading about Brigham Young and the Mormons, have the students create a concept map depicting what they know about pioneers who settled the American west.

2. After reading *Brigham Young: Mormon and Pioneer* (Simon, 1998) have students return to the text and examine the pictures of the pioneer families moving west using

covered wagons and handcarts. Have the students brainstorm a list of reasons why the pioneers used handcarts rather than covered wagons as they moved westward. What are the advantages and disadvantages of each? In *Brigham Young: Pioneer and Mormon Leader* (Sanford and Green,1996) the authors state that the number of converts coming from Europe, Asia, and South Africa overwhelmed the wagon trains and handcarts were used to move them.

3. After reading *Brigham Young: Pioneer and Mormon Leader* (Sanford and Green, 1996), have students create a timeline depicting events in the history of the Mormons. Then, have them add in events happening in America such as the Civil War and the California Gold Rush. This activity helps students make connections between what they know about American History and the history of the Mormons.

4. Mormon Pioneer Day commemorates the settlement of Utah by the Mormons. Have students make connections between the groups who settled their state and the Mormon's settlement of Utah.

REFERENCES

Dickinson, Terence. 1996. *Summer Stargazing*. Willowdale, Ont.: Firefly Books.

France. 1999. Danbury, Conn.: Grolier Educational.

Henderson, Helene, and Sue E. Thompson. 2002. *Holidays, Festivals, and Celebrations of the World Dictionary*, 3rd ed. Detroit, Mich.: Omnigraphics.

Moehn, Heather. 2000. *World Holidays: A Watts Guide for Children*. New York: Franklin Watts.

AUGUST HOLIDAYS AND CELEBRATIONS 16

As the long hot days of summer come to an end, some students are preparing to return to school and in some parts of the country, students have already begun a new school year. In August major days to remember include Hiroshima Day, Assumption Day, and Women's Equality Day. This is the month for recalling victims of the atomic bomb on August sixth, Hiroshima Day. On the fifteenth, Christians celebrate the Assumption of Mary into heaven. Women's Equality Day on August twenty-sixth commemorates the ratification of the Nineteenth Amendment giving women the right to vote.

HIROSHIMA DAY

On August 6, 1945, the United States dropped an atomic bomb on the Japanese city of Hiroshima. Three days later another bomb was dropped on Nagasaki to precipitate an end to the war with Japan. Hiroshima Day is a time for reflecting and remembering. It is a day for working toward peace between all nations, to avoid the devastating, long-range effects of war. At the Peace Memorial Park in Hiroshima, people gather in the evening and set lighted lanterns inscribed with the names of victims adrift on the Ota River (Feinberg, 1995). The Children's Memorial in Peace Park contains a granite pedestal with a statute of Sadako, who died of leukemia ten years after the bombing. Sadako holds aloft a giant golden crane. Each year children from all over the world send origami cranes that are strung at the base of the statue. The books and video annotated below tell the story of the development of the atomic bomb, the stories of victims, and the world's hope for peace.

BOOK AND MEDIA CHOICES

Coerr, Eleanor. *Sadako*. Illustrated by Ed Young. New York: G.P. Putnam's Sons, 1993. Unp.
Grades: 1–4. Coerr has rewritten her book *Sadako and the Thousand Paper Cranes* for younger students. The story begins with Sadako going to Peace Memorial Park to honor her grandmother who died when the atom bomb was dropped ten years before. This healthy, young girl falls victim to leukemia, because of her exposure to radiation from the bombing. Her friend visits her in the hospital and recounts the legend of the crane, which says that if a sick person folds one thousand paper cranes the gods will make her well. Sadako dies before she folds one thousand cranes. Her classmates and friends continue folding cranes and 1,000 origami cranes were tucked into her coffin. The illustrations accompanying the text were created for the video version of the novel. (See annotation below.) A careful examination of the illustrations reveals interwoven dual images. For example, on the cover is a close up of Sadako's eyes, which also contains a crane in flight.

Sadako and the Thousand Paper Cranes. Video. Santa Cruz, Calif.: Informed Democracy, 1991. 30 min.
Grades: 4–7. The video is based on the book by Eleanor Coerr, illustrated by Ed Young, and narrated by Liv Ullmann. Ed Young and George Levenson, producer and director, traveled to Hiroshima to research the story presented in this award-winning video.

Coerr, Eleanor. *Sadako and the Thousand Paper Cranes*. New York: Penguin, 2002. 80p.
Grades: 4–7. Originally published in 1977, this is the poignant story of the impact on one young girl of the atom bomb dropped on the city of Hiroshima in the closing days of World War II. This twenty-fifth anniversary edition of the book includes a biography of Eleanor Coerr and instructions for folding paper cranes.

Feinberg, Barbara Silberdick. *Hiroshima and Nagasaki*. Chicago: Children's Press, 1995. 31p.
Grades: 4–7. Readers become eyewitnesses to the events leading up to the dropping of the atomic bombs and their destructive aftermath. At the end of the book are color photographs of lighted lanterns floating on the dark Ota River in remembrance of the victims. Maps and photographs are on almost every two-page spread.

A glossary, a timeline, and an index are included. This book is from the Cornerstones of Freedom series.

Maruki, Toshi. *Hiroshima No Pika*. New York: Lothrop, Lee & Shepard, 1980. Unp.
Grades: 4 and up. Mii was seven when the atomic bomb was dropped on Hiroshima. Mii's mother carried her injured husband as she held her daughter's hand and ran to the safety of a river. Mii's father did not survive and Mii never grew any bigger. An author's note at the end of the book recounts how she first heard this story at an exhibition of her paintings about the atomic bomb. This book was translated from Japanese.

Grant, R. G. *Hiroshima and Nagasaki*. Austin, Tex.: Steck-Vaughn, 1998. 64p.
Grades: 6–9. Readers opening the book immediately notice the color photograph just under the table of contents. It shows lighted lanterns floating on a river past a bombed out structure. Readers learn the reasons for dropping the atomic bombs and the arguments for and against the bombing. The book ends with a somber chapter on nations trying to live in peace and trying to prevent a nuclear war. Maps, photographs, and sidebars filled with quotes from primary sources provide additional information, but also overwhelm the text. The book includes a chronology of World War II, resources for learning more, a glossary, and an index. This book is from the New Perspectives series.

Hamanaka, Sheila, compiler. *On the Wings of Peace: In Memory of Hiroshima and Nagasaki*. New York: Houghton Mifflin, 1995. 144p.
Grades: 6 and up. Sixty authors and illustrators have contributed to this book to support peace throughout the world. Poems, stories, illustrations, letters, and recollections of peace and war and hope and death fill the pages of this collection that reminds readers of the need to work for world peace. The book concludes with instructions for folding a paper crane, information about the contributors, a bibliography of resource materials, and information on the peace organizations who benefit from the book royalties.

Yep, Laurence. *Hiroshima*. New York: Scholastic, 1995. 56p.
Grades: 6 and up. Interspersed with details about the bombing of Hiroshima is the story of twelve-year-old Sachi who was working with her classmates as part of a wrecking crew when the atomic bomb exploded. Based on the written accounts of survivors, this

haunting narrative compels readers to finish the book in one sitting. An afterword and a bibliography conclude the book.

EXPLORATIONS

1. After reading about Sadako, have the students visit the Web site maintained by the video production company, Informed Democracy. The site contains instructions for folding paper cranes, directions for sending cranes to Hiroshima, links to Web sites for learning more, and information on real cranes. A teacher's resource link is also included. The Web site is located at www.sadako.com/informed-dem.html.

2. After reading about Sadako, have students create a wall mural on bulletin board paper depicting the events of her life.

3. After reading *Hiroshima and Nagasaki* (Grant, 1998), have the students return to the text and write down the arguments for and against dropping the atomic bomb. Provide them with opportunities to discuss their findings. Explain that this is a complex issue and one that has been debated for many years.

4. Place the students in small groups and ask them to prepare a choral reading of one of the poems contained in *On the Wings of Peace: In Memory of Hiroshima and Nagasaki* (Hamanaka, 1995) to present to their classmates.

5. Ask the students to select one of the illustrations in *On the Wings of Peace: In Memory of Hiroshima and Nagasaki* (Hamanaka, 1995) to study carefully and discuss with a partner. Then, have the students write about what the illustration means to them. Their writing can be posted on a bulletin board to be shared with their classmates.

ASSUMPTION DAY

Assumption Day on August 15 celebrates the Christian belief that the body of the Virgin Mary was assumed into heaven rather than just her soul (Henderson and Thompson, 2002). Europeans celebrate this day as the Feast of Our Lady of the Harvest and Polish Americans celebrate the day as the Harvest Festival for Our Lady of the Flowers (Cohen and Coffin, 1987). On this day in France banners and flags hang in the trees and people eat outdoors (France, 1999). In the books annotated below short illustrated stories tell about the main events in Mary's life.

BOOK AND MEDIA CHOICES

de Paola, Tomie. Mary: *The Mother of Jesus*. New York: Holiday House, 1995. Unp.
Grades: K–4. An author's note explains that scripture, legend, and tradition were the resources used to gather information on Mary's life. This note also briefly describes visions of Mary seen on Earth after her assumption. Each short story begins with a biblical quotation. The stories are simply told and poignant pastel illustrations help young readers comprehend the text.

Wildsmith, Brian. *Mary*. Grand Rapids, Mich.: Eerdmans Books for Young Readers, 2002. Unp.
Grades: K–4. Beautiful, lavish, detailed illustrations framed in gold depict the story of Mary's life. The stories accompanying the illustrations tell about the main events in her life. The book ends with her assumption into heaven and the Hail Mary prayer.

EXPLORATIONS

1. Before reading *Mary: The Mother of Jesus* (de Paola, 1995) and *Mary* (Wildsmith, 2002), ask the students to describe ways that their mothers take care of them and show their love for them.

2. The large colorful illustrations in *Mary: The Mother of Jesus* (de Paola, 1995) and *Mary* (Wildsmith, 2002) easily lend themselves to further explorations of what students see in the pictures and how the pictures relate to the stories.

3. After reading *Mary: The Mother of Jesus* (de Paola, 1995), provide students with opportunities to examine the illustrations and to create their own pictures modeling his artistic style.

WOMEN'S EQUALITY DAY

On August 26, 1920, the Nineteenth Amendment to the Constitution was ratified and women were given the right to vote. Although Susan B. Anthony died fourteen years before the amendment was ratified, in recognition of her years of crusading for women's rights it is called the Susan B. Anthony Amendment (Sigerman, 2001). Seventy-two years earlier Anthony's friend and coworker Elizabeth Cady Stanton had addressed the audience of the first Women's Rights Convention in Seneca Falls, New York and demanded that women be given the right to vote. Students may find it hard to realize that women were not given the right to vote in the United States Constitution. The first two books annotated below while for younger students may help older students gain an understanding of women's lives in the United States during the nineteen-century. The National Women's History Project Web site at www.nwhp.org contains links for learning more about Women's Equality Day. (See Election Day.)

BOOK AND MEDIA CHOICES

Corey, Shana. *You Forgot Your Skirt, Amelia Bloomer*. Illustrated by Chesley McLaren. New York: Scholastic Press, 2000. Unp.
Grades: K–4. Young girls who have been accused of not being proper young ladies will immediately respond to this story of a woman who dared to be different and challenged the society's beliefs about what was proper. Although not the creator of bloomers nor the first woman to wear them in America, her tireless efforts in getting them accepted resulted in them being named after her. Lively colorful pictures and text introduce students to women's fight for equality.

Equality: A History of the Women's Movement in America. Video. Bala Cynwyd, Penn.: Schlessinger Video Productions-Library Video Company, 1996. 30 min.
Grades: K–4. This is the story of how over the years, women fought for their rights and moved from working in the home to becoming a vital part of the American workforce. The story begins with Abigail Adams and her letters to her husband John Adams as he was helping to establish a government for the new nation. Viewers meet scholars and activists including: Gloria Steinem, Anna Quindlen, Ellen Goodman, Abigail Adams, Susan B. Anthony, and Eleanor Roosevelt.

Blumberg, Rhoda. *Bloomers!* Illustrated by Mary Morgan. New York: Bradbury Press, 1993. Unp.
Grades: 1–4. When Libby Miller traveled to Europe, she discovered an outfit that allowed her the freedom she needed to hike in the Swiss mountains. Instead of corsets, petticoats, and long, sweeping skirts this outfit consisted of baggy pants and a short dress. When she wore the outfit to Seneca Falls to visit her cousin, Elizabeth Stanton, it created a sensation and became the symbol for the fight for women's rights. This is a well-written introduction to the women's struggles for equality. The amusing watercolor illustrations are just right for the engaging text.

Fritz, Jean. *You Want Women to Vote, Lizzie Stanton?* Illustrated by DyAnne DiSalvo-Ryan. New York: G.P. Putnam's Sons, 1995. 88p.
Grades: 3–6. Elizabeth Stanton's father was a judge, and from spending time in his law office she learned firsthand that women had few legal rights. This stayed with her as she grew up, married, and had seven children. In July 1848, she helped stage the first Women's Rights Convention in Seneca Falls, New York. This refreshing, engaging biography accompanied by black-and-white illustrations tells the story of a strong woman who worked throughout her life for women's rights. Notes, a bibliography, and an index are included.

Not For Ourselves Alone: The Story of Elizabeth Cady Stanton and Susan B. Anthony. Video. Alexandria, Va.: Public Broadcasting Service. 180 min.
Grades: 3–6. Together these women fought to provide women equal rights including the right to vote. Neither of them lived to see the Nineteenth Amendment ratified. Interviews and photographs help tell the story of this remarkable alliance that had a profound impact on American society. Additional resources for extending this video can be found at www.pbs.org/stantonanthony.

Levin, Pamela. *Susan B. Anthony: Fighter for Women's Rights.* Philadelphia: Chelsea House, 1993. 79p.
Grades: 5–9. Imagine being tried in a court of law and found guilty of voting in an election. This is what happened to Susan B. Anthony in 1873. She spent her life protesting society's injustices including laws that prevented women from voting. She died in 1906 and it was not until fourteen years later that the Nineteenth Amendment was ratified giving women the right to vote. This informative biography includes black-and-white photographs and reproductions that give readers visual reference points to aid in understanding the text.

Books for further reading, a chronology, a glossary, and an index are included. This book is from the Junior World Biographies series.

Salisbury, Cynthia. *Elizabeth Cady Stanton: Leader of the Fight for Women's Rights*. Berkeley Heights, N.J.: Enslow, 2002. 128p.
Grades: 5–9. Elizabeth Cady Stanton forged a formidable alliance with Susan B. Anthony and Lucretia Mott. Together they worked to promote women's rights in America including the rights to vote and to divorce. Sidebars placed throughout the text contain background information to help readers understand the text. Black-and-white photographs and illustrations, a chronology, chapter notes, a glossary, books for further reading, Internet addresses, and an index are included. This book is from the Historical American Biographies series.

Bohannon, Lisa Frederiksen. *Failure is Impossible: The Story of Susan B. Anthony*. Greensboro, N.C.: Morgan Reynolds, 2002. 112p.
Grades: 6–9. Susan B. Anthony's beliefs in the equality of women were supported by her father's similar strong beliefs and her Quaker religion. She worked diligently for the temperance movement, the abolition of slavery, and for women's rights. She became friends with Elizabeth Cady Stanton as the two fought against society's injustices. Excerpts from her diaries, speeches, and letters provide readers with personal glimpses of this remarkable woman. Notes, a bibliography, Web sites, and an index conclude the book.

One Woman, One Vote. Video. Alexandria, Va.: Public Broadcasting Service, 1995. 120 min.
Grades: 6 and up. Highlights of seventy-two years of women's struggles throughout the United States to have the right to vote are included in this video. The story begins with the first women's rights convention in 1848 and ends with the ratification of the Nineteenth Amendment in 1920.

EXPLORATIONS

1. Before reading *You Forgot Your Skirt, Amelia Bloomer* (Corey, 2000) or *Bloomers!* (Blumberg, 1993), write the word "bloomers" on the board and ask students what they think the word means.

2. After reading *You Forgot Your Skirt, Amelia Bloomer* (Corey, 2000) or *Bloomers!* (Blumberg, 1993), ask the students questions to start a discussion of the book. Why did

many women like bloomers? Why did some women not like bloomers? What did their husbands think of bloomers? Would you have worn bloomers?

3. Have students visit the Susan B. Anthony House Web site at www.susanbanthonyhouse.org/ to take an online tour of her house in Rochester, New York. After students visit the Web site have them share their comments about the house. Students will notice a washstand and washbowl in her bedroom and a long sleeve full-length black dress that she wore. These can be used as starting points for discussions about life in the nineteenth century.

4. After learning about Women's Equality Day provide students with copies of the address Stanton delivered at the Seneca Falls Convention, which can be found at www.nps.gov/wori/address.htm. After reading the address, provide students opportunities to discuss the key points of the speech. What examples did she use to make her case for women's right to vote?

5. The address Stanton delivered at the Seneca Falls Convention provides a natural context for building students' vocabularies by having them discuss the definitions of words found in the address such as abominations, indomitable, franchise, and degradation.

6. Before watching *One Woman, One Vote*, have students visit the One Woman, One Vote, A Short History and Guide Web site at www.pbs.org/onewoman/one_woman.html. Ask the students to review the timeline to help activate their prior knowledge on the topic.

7. After watching *One Woman, One Vote*, have the students meet in small groups to talk about some of the discussion questions posted on the One Woman, One Vote, A Short History and Guide Web site at www.pbs.org/onewoman/one_woman.html. To assist them as they answer the questions, students can find additional information on the History of the Suffrage Movement Web site located at www.pbs.org/onewoman/suffrage.html.

REFERENCES

Cohen, Hennig, and Tristram *Potter Coffin*, eds. 1987. The Folklore of American Holidays. Detroit, Mich.: Gale Research Company.

Feinberg, Barbara Silberdick. 1995. *Hiroshima and Nagasaki*. Chicago: Children's Press.

France. 1999. Danbury, Conn.: Grolier Educational.

Henderson, Helene, and Sue. E Thompson. 2002. *Holidays, Festivals, and Celebrations of the World* Dictionary, 3rd ed. Detroit, Mich.: Omnigraphics.

Sigerman, Harriet. 2001. *Elizabeth Cady Stanton: The Right is Ours*. New York: Oxford University Press.

PART VI: WORLD CULTURES, UNUSUAL EVENTS, AND SPECIAL DAYS

CELEBRATIONS AND HOLIDAYS COLLECTIONS 17

This chapter contains annotations for books and media that include information about more than one holiday including holidays around the world, American holidays, Asian holidays, Central American and Hispanic holidays, Jewish holidays, and books for teachers. Books and media in this chapter also contain information focusing on how one particular holiday is celebrated around the world. As students learn about the holidays and celebrations of different cultures, the goal is for them to develop an appreciation and deeper understanding of the cultures and discover global patterns. For example, students learn the universality of lights in celebrations around the globe and throughout the year. They also discover that local variations exist in how the same celebrations are observed in the same country. Studying holidays and celebrations helps students develop an appreciation and understanding of the culturally diverse world in which they live.

CELEBRATIONS AND HOLIDAYS AROUND THE WORLD

Books and media in this section include information on multicultural festivals, Christmas celebrations around the world, New Year's celebrations around the world, children celebrating a variety of holidays around the world, and information on ancient Celtic festivals that form the basis of many holidays celebrated in the western world today. The books and media encompass different grade levels and use a variety of formats to present the information including photographs of students celebrating favorite holidays from their cultures. These materials provide a wonderful starting place for learning about holidays and celebrations.

BOOK AND MEDIA CHOICES

Christmas Around the World. Video. Bala Cynwyd, Penn.: Schlessinger Video Productions-Library Video Company, 2002. 23 min.
Grades: K–4. Students travel around the globe to discover Christmas traditions and celebrations in several countries around the world. Songs, stories, rituals, and special foods are used to celebrate the birth of Jesus. A teacher's guide is included. This video is part of the Holidays for Children series.

Gilchrist, Cherry. *A Calendar of Festivals*. Illustrated by Helen Cann. Bristol, United Kingdom: Barefoot Books, 1998. 80p.
Grades: K–8. This is a wonderful collection of stories for reading aloud as students learn about a variety of multicultural festivals. Each story is introduced with information about its related festival. The festivals included in the book are: Purim, Holi, Vesak, Tanabata, Halloween, Christmas, Kwanzaa, and New Year's.

Yolen, Jane. *O Jerusalem*. Illustrated by John Thompson. New York: Scholastic, 1996. 30p.
Grades: K–8. Judaism, Christianity, and Islam are three of the largest religions of the world and they all have a deep-rooted connection to Jerusalem, one of the greatest cities of the world. This book of thoughtful poems, each of which is followed by an exposition of the meaning of the poem, is accompanied by beautiful artwork that expands on the text. The author closes with the hope that Jerusalem will one day be the City of Peace.

Bernhard, Emery. *Happy New Year!* Illustrated by Durga Bernhard. New York: Lodestar Books, 1996. Unp.
Grades: 1–4. Around the world the New Year is welcomed with fireworks, bonfires, lights, noisemakers, presents, and house cleaning. Readers travel across the globe and find that there are similarities between the celebrations of diverse cultures. The book concludes with a glossary.

Erlbach, Arlene. *Happy New Year, Everywhere!* Illustrated by Sharon Lane Holm. Brookfield, Conn.: The Millbrook Press, 2000. 48p.
Grades: 1–4. This book contains informative profiles of New Year's celebrations in Belgium, Brazil, Canada, Chile, China, Colombia, Ethiopia, Germany, Ghana, Greece, Haiti, India, Iran, Israel, Japan, Mexico, Nigeria, Scotland, Trinidad, Tobago, and Vietnam. Readers

learn that the New Year starts in spring, summer, or fall depending on the culture. Each country is featured in a two-page spread that includes, the date of the celebration, the name, the greeting, and a brief description of the celebration. The author also includes a craft project, a recipe, a game, or other activity to get students actively involved in learning about these diverse cultural celebrations. A bibliography provides leads to further information on these celebrations.

Erlbach, Arlene, with Herb Erlbach. *Merry Christmas, Everywhere!* Illustrated by Sharon Lane Holm. Brookfield, Conn.: The Millbrook Press, 2002. 48p.
Grades: 1–4. Christmas celebrations in Australia, Bolivia, Canada, Ethiopia, France, Germany, Ghana, Great Britain, Greece, Iceland, India, Jamaica, Japan, Lebanon, Mexico, Nigeria, The Philippines, Poland, Puerto Rico, and Serbia are described. The country's celebrations are on two-page spreads that include a map showing the location of the country, the holiday greeting, a brief description of the holiday, and a craft activity or a recipe. The book concludes with a bibliography.

Chandler, Clare. *Harvest Celebrations*. Brookfield, Conn.: The Millbrook Press, 1997. 32p.
Grades: 2–6. Included in this book are a history of harvest festivals and information on religious and nonreligious harvest festivals. Included are American, Jewish, Hindu, Sikh, Zoroastrian, Japanese, Chinese, and African harvest festivals. Colorful photographs and illustrations, informative sidebars, and instructive text provide readers a brief look at the importance of harvest festivals to different cultures. The book concludes with a calendar of harvest festivals, a glossary, books for further reading, and an index.

Corwin, Judith Hoffman. *Harvest Festivals Around the World*. Parsippany, N.J.: Silver Burdett Press, 1995. 48p.
Grades: 2–6. Around the world throughout the year, people rejoice at harvest time. In May, the ancient Incas celebrated with the Song of Harvest festival, in spring, summer, and early fall, Hopi people celebrated planting and harvesting, and in October, Canadians celebrate Thanksgiving Day. A familiar harvest symbol, the Horn of Plenty or Cornucopia, comes to us from the ancient Greeks who decorated goats' horns. Brief summaries on the different harvest festivals are accompanied by recipes, crafts, and activities to help readers understand the different celebrations.

Luenn, Nancy. *Celebrations of Light: A Year of Holidays around the World*. Illustrated by Mark Bender. New York: Atheneum Books for Young Readers, 1998. 32p.
Grades: 2–6. Throughout the ages and around the world candles, lanterns, torches, and people have used lights to drive away the darkness and ward off danger. Celebrations and religious ceremonies often include warm, glowing, dancing lights. Concise text and luminous illustrations describe twelve celebrations of light from around the world. The celebrations include New Year's Eve, New Year's Day, Lanterns, Lichtmesdag, Buddha's Birthday, Bon Matsuri, Diwali, Loy Krathong, Hanukkah, Luciadagen, Christmas/Las Posadas, and Kwanzaa.

Kindersley, Barnabas, and Anabel Kindersley. *Children Just Like Me—Celebrations*. New York: DK Publishing, 1997. 64p.
Grades: 2–8. This is a large book with colorful photographs of children participating in festivals in eighteen different countries. Brief, highly specific text accompanies photographs depicting rituals, festival dress, foods, and activities specific to each holiday. UNICEF helped sponsor the author and the photographer on their year-long trip traveling the globe to capture children celebrating native holidays in their countries. The celebrations are grouped by the seasons of the year with floating holidays, such as Ramadan, interspersed through out the seasons. The book concludes with a celebration calendar and an index.

Jones, Lynda. *Kids around the World Celebrate*. Illustrations by Michele Nidenoff. New York: John Wiley & Sons, 1999. 128p.
Grades: 3–8. Sixteen celebrations from around the world are introduced and a recipe or activity appropriate for each one is included. The celebrations are: Chinese New Year, China; Hogmanay, Scotland; Año Viejo, Ecuador; New Year's Eve, United States; Carnaval, Brazil; Eid ul-Fitr, Saudi Arabia; Carnevale, Venice; Mardi Gras, New Orleans; Pongal, India; Iriji, Nigeria; Crop-Over, Barbados; Thanksgiving, United States; El Dia de los Reyes, Mexico; Obon, Japan; Hanukkah, Israel; and Kwanzaa, United States. Black-and-white illustrations enhance the text and provide guidance for completing the recipes and activities. The book concludes with an index.

Lankford, Mary D. *Christmas around the World*. Illustrated by Karen Dugan. New York: William Morrow, 1995. 47p.

Grades: 4–8. Christmas traditions, foods, symbols, and celebrations from twelve countries are described in narrative and colorful illustrations. The twelve countries whose celebrations are described include Australia, Canada, Ethiopia, Germany, Great Britain, Greece, Guatemala, Italy, Mexico, the Philippines, Sweden, and in the United States, Alaska. The author includes craft ideas, Christmas fact and fiction, a pronunciation guide, Christmas sayings, a bibliography, and an index.

Leslie, Clare Walker, and Frank E. Gerace. *The Ancient Celtic Festivals and How We Celebrate Them Today*. Illustrated by Clare Walker Leslie. Rochester, Vt.: Inner Traditions, 2000. 58p.
Grades: 4–8. Readers discover that many of our holidays and traditions can be traced back to the Celts. For example, mistletoe was hung on doorways during the winter solstice to bring good luck. The present-day tradition of costumes at Mardi Gras can be traced to the wearing of masks during spring celebrations to frighten away winter demons. The text is filled with interesting details and simple, child-like illustrations containing additional information. A glossary, bibliography, and an index are included.

Moehn, Heather. *World Holidays: A Watts Guide for Children*. New York: Franklin Watts, 2000. 123p.
Grades: 4–8. Brief illustrated introductions to over one hundred celebrations and holidays from around the world are included in this useful guide. Entries are cross-referenced to help students make connections between similar observances. The book concludes with information about calendars from around the world, holiday calendars for 2001 through 2005, a glossary, a bibliography, and an index.

Explorations

1. Before watching *Christmas around the World*, have students make a list of traditions and symbols associated with Christmas from as many countries as possible. While watching the video, have them add to their lists. After watching the video, have them discuss their lists in small groups.

2. After reading *Happy New Year, Everywhere!* (Erlbach, 2000), have students complete a chart, such as the one below, to make comparisons between celebrations in the different countries. The students put a plus sign (+) in the

column if the country includes the ritual in their celebration and a minus sign (—) in the column if the country does not include the ritual.

3. As children read *Happy New Year, Everywhere!* (Erlbach, 2000), have them take notes on similarities and differences between the celebrations in the countries and their own celebrations. Alternately, have them select one thing to focus on such as parades or fireworks to determine which countries include these items in their celebrations.

New Year's Rituals							
Country	Fire-works	Lights	Evil Spirits	Noise	Good Luck Rituals	Presents	House Cleaning
America							
Japan							
India							
China							
West Africa							
Mexico							

Figure 17-1. New Year's celebrations include a variety of rituals. This chart helps students see which countries share common rituals.

Christmas Symbols					
Country	Christmas Tree	Lights	Procession	Songs	Nativity
Australia					
Canada					
Ethiopia					
Germany					
Great Britain					
Greece					
Italy					
Mexico					
Philippines					
Sweden					
United States					

Figure 17-2. Christmas celebrations around the world include a variety of symbols. Comparing symbols used in different countries on a chart such as this one helps students find commonalities among celebrations.

4. After reading *Happy New Year, Everywhere!* (Erlbach, 2000), have students discuss the celebrations in the different countries. Ask them if they learned about a game, activity, or food they might incorporate into their own family's New Year's Day celebration.

5. While reading *Christmas around the World* (Lankford, 1995), have the students complete a chart, such as the one in Figure 17-2, to help them make comparisons between the celebrations in the different countries. They put a plus sign (+) in the column if the country includes the symbol in their celebration and a minus sign (–) in the column if the country does not include the symbol.

6. In *Christmas around the World* (Lankford, 1995), each two-page description about the country's Christmas celebration includes information on the weather in that country on Christmas day. This information can lead to discussions of seasonal weather differences in the northern and southern hemispheres. Students can also visit an online weather site such as weather.com to find out about the current weather in each of the countries.

7. An author's note at the beginning of *Celebrations of Light: A Year of Holidays around the World* (Luenn, 1998) informs the reader that the book describes only twelve celebrations of light. It then lists other festivals of light that are not included in the book. Students can create the second volume of this book by writing about other celebrations of light and drawing illustrations to accompany their descriptions.

AMERICAN CELEBRATIONS AND HOLIDAYS

Books and media in this section focus on collections of holiday celebrations in America. The books contain poems, recipes, descriptions, and color photographs. Some of the books provide information on our national holidays, others focus on celebrations on a month-by-month basis and others are organized seasonally. These books are useful resources for gaining an overview of several holidays.

Book and Media Choices

Murphy, Patricia J. *Our National Holidays*. Minneapolis, Minn.: Compass Point Books, 2002. 24p.
Grades: P–2. The eight holidays in this book are depicted on two-page spreads. On the left side is an illustration and on the right side is large, easy-to-read text, telling the origins of the holiday and when it is celebrated. The small trim size and the large text make this book one that young readers will want to read on their own. Holidays surveyed in the book include: Independence Day, Martin Luther King, Jr. Day, Presidents' Day, Memorial Day, Labor Day, Columbus Day, Veterans Day, and Thanksgiving. A glossary, sources for additional information, and an index complete the book. This is one of the Let's See series.

Livingston, Myra Cohn. *Celebrations*. Illustrated by Leonard Everett Fisher. New York: Holiday House, 1985. 32p.
Grades: P–4. Lyrical poems and vibrant, striking illustrations capture the excitement, solemnity, and wonder of these familiar celebrations. The poems in the book express the solemnity and the jubilation of the following celebrations: New Year's Eve, Martin Luther King, Jr. Day, Presidents' Day, Valentine's Day, St. Patrick's Day, April Fools' Day, Passover, Easter, Memorial Day, Fourth of July, Labor Day, Columbus Day, Halloween, Thanksgiving, Christmas Eve, and birthdays.

Updike, John. *A Child's Calendar*. Illustrations by Trina Schart Hyman. New York: Scholastic, 1999. Unp.
Grades: P–2. Unique events and celebrations for each month of the year are depicted in these rhyming, four- to six-stanza poems. Rich, detailed illustrations show a family and their friends celebrating together. The wonders of nature, the sights, sounds, and smells of the seasons, and the love of family and friends are celebrated all through the year.

Barner, Bob. *Parade Day: Marching through the Calendar Year*. New York: Holiday House, 2003. Unp.
Grades: P–3. Each month of the year has its own special holiday parade in this rollicking introduction to the calendar. Two short lines of lyrical poetry meander across the top of the two-page spreads, describing each month's holiday parade. Bright primary colors fill the joyous illustrations of parades rolling across the pages. At the end of the book, the months of the year are presented along with the holi-

days celebrated in each month. There are simple instructions for making a calendar, information on calendars, and a familiar rhyme for learning the number of days in the months.

Hubbell, Patricia. *Rabbit Moon: A Book of Holidays and Celebrations*. Illustrated by Wendy Watson. New York: Marshall Cavendish, 2002. Unp.
Grades: P–3. Delightful poems for each month of the year give reasons to celebrate. The names of specific religious holidays are not mentioned. For example, the December poem mentions neither Christmas nor Hanukkah, but rather describes glowing candles, special foods, and presents. Each poem is illustrated with a lively group of rabbits enjoying the special gifts each month has to offer.

Moorman, Margaret. *Light the Lights: A Story About Celebrating Hanukkah and Christmas*. New York: Scholastic, 1994. Unp.
Grades: K–1. Emma's family celebrates two festivals of light. With her father, she polishes the menorah, and then her mother steadies her hand as she lights the candles. With her mother she unpacks the Christmas ornaments, and the whole family joins in as they pick the perfect tree and decorate it with friends. This is a simple story of a family that recognizes and appreciates both the Jewish and Christian holiday celebrations.

Celebrate 2. Video. St. Louis, Mo.: Coronet, 1994. 23 min.
Grades: K–6. Viewers learn about celebrations of Americans from different ethnic backgrounds. Celebrations included on the video are: Dr. Martin Luther King, Jr.'s birthday, Diwali, Obon, and Mother's Day.

Owens, Mary Beth. *Be Blest: A Celebration of Seasons*. New York: Simon and Schuster, 1999. Unp.
Grades: 1–3. These poems celebrate the natural world and human's connections to that world. They were inspired by Canticle of Brother Sun by Saint Francis of Assisi, which recognizes the relationships between people and animals in addition to God's presence in nature. These poems remind us to give praise and rejoice each month of the year as the world around us unfolds with new and wondrous sights. The short verses are surrounded by wreaths containing nature's bounty, and on the opposite page is a full-color illustration of the month of the year. It concludes with the musical arrangement to the poem, "Be Blest."

de Paola, Tomie. *What a Year*. New York: G.P. Putnam's Sons, 2002. 75p.
Grades: 1–4. From his birthday in September to New Year's Eve Tomie de Paola remembers first grade by the holidays he celebrated each month. This autobiography presents a unique look at favorite holidays through the eyes of a six-year-old. Readers, young and old, enjoy reading and hearing about his recollections. Older readers smile knowingly as they read about how he and his mother soaked the paper holding the candy decorations for his birthday cake, carefully peeled the decorations off, and put them on his cake. Large shredded wheat biscuits pulled from a box with Niagara Falls on the front and topped with sugar and hot milk, also bring back warm memories.

Tudor, Tasha. *A Time to Keep: The Tasha Tudor Book of Holidays*. New York: Checkerboard Press, 1977. Unp.
Grades: 1–4. A young child sits at her grandmother's knee and asks what it was like when her mother was young. The grandmother describes celebrations for each month of the year. The description for each month begins with a quote appropriate to the season. Detailed, lavish borders frame each page.

Winchester, Faith. *African-American Holidays*. Mankato, Minn.: Bridgestone Books, 1996. 24p.
Grades: 1–4. Beginning with a collection of "Fast Facts" about African-Americans, this is a brief introduction to a variety of African-American holidays. The holidays included are: Martin Luther King, Jr.'s birthday, Black History Month, Malcolm X's birthday, Harambee, Junkanoo, and Kwanzaa. The concise text is accompanied by black-and-white and color photographs. A glossary, resources for learning more, and an index conclude the book.

Spies, Karen. *Our National Holidays*. Brookfield, Conn.: The Millbrook Press, 1992. 47p.
Grades: 3–6. America's national holidays celebrating her past, present and future are briefly introduced. The holidays are grouped by themes including: our nation's roots, famous people, our armed forces, our heritage, and our earth. The concise, fact-filled text is coupled with colorful photographs, illustrations, and sidebars. The book concludes with a chronology, books for further reading, and an index. This book is from the I Know America series.

Zalben, Jane Breskin. *To Every Season: A Family Holiday Cookbook*. New York: Simon & Schuster Books for Young Readers, 1999. 112p. Grades: 3 and up. Celebrations always include food and this book includes recipes for foods to celebrate sixteen American holidays. Following a brief introduction to the holiday are several recipes for food to share with family and friends. Tucked into and around the recipes are wonderful, colorful illustrations.

Penner, Lucille Recht. *Celebration: The Story of American Holidays*. Illustrated by Ib Ohlsson. New York: Macmillan Publishing, 1993. 79p.
Grades: 4–8. In this book songs, poems, crafts, games, and recipes accompany information about traditional holidays. The detailed illustrations provide additional information about the holidays and oftentimes a glimpse into America's past.

Skrepcinski, Denice, Melissa Stock, and Lois Lyles. *Silly Celebrations! Activities for the Strangest Holidays You've Never Heard Of*. Illustrated by Yayo. New York: Aladdin Paperbacks, 1998. 94p.
Grades: 2–8. Open this book and discover celebrations for each month of the year, beginning in January with National Kazzo Day and ending in December with Feast of the Radishes. We are acquainted with each holiday through a description of the celebration, craft ideas, recipes, jokes, experiments, and books related to these not-so-ordinary celebrations. The book contains ideas for adding excitement and fun to the classroom and in the process, students learn using a variety of modalities.

EXPLORATIONS

1. After reading about the national holidays in *Our National Holidays* (Murphy, 2002), *African-American Holidays* (Winchester, 1996), *Our National Holidays* (Spies, 1992), or *Celebration: The Story of American Holidays* (Penner, 1993), have students select a holiday and interview other children in the school about their recollections of the holiday. Provide the students with possible questions to ask in the interview, and have them come up with questions tied to the book they read. What is your favorite memory of this holiday? How do you celebrate the holiday? What do you eat on this holiday? Suggest that the students take notes

during their interviews, as a basis for writing up a summary of the interview.

2. Select one of the poems from *A Child's Calendar* (Updike, 1999) and have the students close their eyes as you read the poem to them twice. Tell them to listen carefully to the poem and draw pictures in their minds as you read. After reading the poem, have students draw pictures about the poem on paper. Display the poem and their illustrations on the bulletin board.

3. After reading *Parade Day: Marching through the Calendar Year* (Barner, 2003), help the students create their own personal calendar for the month using the directions at the end of the book. Students need blank paper, a ruler, and crayons to complete their calendar.

4. Read *What a Year* (de Paola, 2002) to the students during September. Inform them that throughout the school year they are going to write a book about how they celebrated one holiday each month. Collect their writings and bind them together for the students at the end of the year.

5. *African-American Holidays* (Winchester, 1996) contains brief introductions to a variety of African-American holidays. Students interested in learning more about these celebrations can research them and create presentations about them to share with their classmates.

6. *Silly Celebrations! Activities for the Strangest Holidays You've Never Heard Of* (Skrepcinski, Stock, and Lyles, 1998) contains a silly celebration for every month of the year. Divide the students in groups representing each month of the year, and ask each group to plan a class celebration recognizing the holiday for their month.

ASIAN CELEBRATIONS AND HOLIDAYS

The books in this section contain holidays celebrated in Asia, south Asia, Southeast Asia, and China. One of the books contains poems celebrating a year in Chinatown. Another book has legends related to ten Chinese festivals. These books can be used to introduce Asian holidays to students. Throughout this book, readers find references to information and annotations related to specific Asian holidays and these entries contain more details on the holidays.

BOOK AND MEDIA CHOICES

Mak, Kam. My *Chinatown: One Year in Poems*. New York: HarperCollins, 2002. Unp.
Grades: 1–4. From winter, to spring, to summer, to fall, and back to winter again, readers are treated to the changing seasons in Chinatown and the special celebrations. Using free verse, the author wistfully recounts his childhood in Chinatown and living in two cultures. Soft, oil paintings bring the simple words of the poems into sharp focus. This book is both an introduction to Chinese culture and an introduction to Chinese celebrations.

Winchester, Faith. *Asian Holidays*. Mankato, Minn.: Capstone Press, 1996. 24p.
Grades: 1–4. An introduction to Asians begins the book and includes the fact that the Chinese invented fireworks, which are now a part of celebrations around the world. Brief, one-page introductions to the holidays are accompanied by full-page color photographs. New Year's, Buddha's Birthday, Doll Festival, Boys' Festival, and the Harvest Moon Festival are included. A pronunciation guide, a glossary, resources for learning more, and an index conclude the book, which is from the Read-and-Discover Ethnic Holidays series.

Legends of Ten Chinese Traditional Festivals. Illustrated by Zhan Tong. China: Dolphin Books, 2002. 54p.
Grades: 2–5. This book tells about ten Chinese festivals that have been celebrated for many generations. They are the Spring Festival, the Lantern Festival, the Dragon Head Festival, the Clear and Bright Festival, the Double Ninth Day, the Laba Festival, and the Kitchen God Day. There is a story accompanying each festival and colorful illustrations. Each story is written in English and in Chinese.

Viesti, Joe, and Diane Hall. *Celebrate! In South Asia*. Photographs by Joe Viesti. New York: Lothrop, Lee and Shepard Books, 1996. 32p.
Grades: 2–5. Included in this colorful picture book are the following celebrations: Holi, Pushkar Camel Fair, Esala Perahera, Wesak, Baishakhi, Eid-Ul-Fitr, Paro Tsechu, Shwedagon Pagoda Festival, and Tihar. Each one-page description of the festival is accompanied by several full-page color photographs that provide helpful information about these holidays. This book is a wonderful introduction to a variety of South Asian holidays. A map of South Asia concludes the book.

Viesti, Joe, and Diane Hall. *Celebrate! In Southeast Asia*. Photographs by Joe Viesti. New York: Lothrop, Lee and Shepard Books, 1996. 32p.
Grades: 2–5. Descriptions of celebrations of Southeast Asia are contained in this book including: Songkran, Surin Elephant Round-Up, Thaipusam, Moon Cake Festival, Kesada Offering, Cremation Ceremony, Ati-Atihan, Apalit River Festival, Tet, That Luang Festival, and Chaul Chhnaim. Color photographs enhance the text and provide additional information. A map of Southeast Asia concludes the book.

Simonds, Nina, Leslie Swartz, and The Children's Museum, Boston. *Moombeams, Dumplings, and Dragon Boats: A Treasury of Chinese Holiday Tales, Activities, and Recipes*. Illustrated by Meilo So. San Diego: Harcourt, 2002. 74p.
Grades: 3–7. Brief descriptions of Chinese New Year, the Lantern Festival, Qing Ming, the Dragon Boat Festival, and the Mid-Autumn Moon Festival each are followed by stories, recipes, crafts, and games. Gorgeous watercolor illustrations spilling across two-page spreads are tucked into the text, which highlights the recipes and instructions for crafts and games. The book concludes with resources for learning more and a Chinese pronunciation guide.

Erricker, Clive, and Jane Erricker. *Buddhist Festivals*. Crystal Lake, Ill.: Heinemann Library, 1997. 48p.
Grades: 4–8. An introduction to Buddha and Buddhists provides students with the background information needed to develop an understanding and appreciation of Buddhist festivals. Color photographs and quotes from young people complement the descriptions of the festivals. The book concludes with an extensive glossary, a list of more books to read, and an index. This book is from the Celebrate series.

Krasno, Rena. *Floating Lanterns and Golden Shrines: Celebrating Japanese Festivals*. Illustrated by Toru Sugita. Berkeley, Calif.: Pacific View Press, 2000. 49p.
Grades: 4–8. Readers learn about the festivals of Setsubun, Obon, Kodomo no Hi, Hina Matsuri, Oshogatsu, Yuki Matsuri, and Sakura Matsuri. In addition to information on the festivals, there are recipes, crafts, and legends. The book concludes with information on the traditional tea ceremony and an index.

Stepanchuk, Carol. *Red Eggs & Dragon Boats: Celebrating Chinese Festivals*. Berkeley, Calif.: Pacific View Press, 1994. 48p.
Grades: 4–8. Chinese New Year, Clear Brightness Festival, Full-Month Red Egg and Ginger Party, Dragon Boat Festival, and Moon Festival are the five festivals described in this informative book. The author describes the origin of the festival, shares stories, and offers recipes, all accompanied by bright colorful paintings. The book concludes with information on the paintings and the artists.

EXPLORATIONS

1. After reading *My Chinatown: One Year in Poems* (Mak, 2002), have students return to the poems and find examples of simile, such as "where it sounds like the woods in spring" and "where the English words taste like metal in my mouth." Ask them why they think the author used these comparisons. Then, have the students work together to use simile to describe their holiday experiences.

2. After reading about the Lantern Festival in *Moombeams, Dumplings, and Dragon Boats: A Treasury of Chinese Holiday Tales, Activities, and Recipes* (Simonds, Nina, Leslie Swartz, and The Children's Museum, Boston, 2002), have the students make lantern riddles. They can examine the riddles in the book to help them understand how riddles are written. Encourage them to work with a partner to make up their own riddles for their lanterns.

3. An interactive, Japanese calendar, located at www.jinjapan.org/kidsweb/calendar/calendar.htm, contains information and photographs of holidays, annual events, and school activities.

4. Before studying Asian holidays, have students complete this sentence with five things they want to know: "What I want to know about Asian holidays is _____, _____, _____, _____, and _____."

CENTRAL AMERICAN AND HISPANIC CELEBRATIONS AND HOLIDAYS

Holidays in Mexico, the Hispanic Caribbean, Latin America, and Central America are described in the books annotated below. These are colorful, lively fiestas and celebrations. One of the books is filled with songs for celebrations throughout the year and one book focuses only on Christmas celebrations. Information on specific holidays can be found in other chapters in the book.

BOOK AND MEDIA CHOICES

Winchester, Faith. *Hispanic Holidays*. Mankato, Minn.: Capstone Press, 1996. 24p.
Grades: K–3. Beginning with an introduction to Hispanic people, this book presents a brief introduction to Hispanic holidays with succinct text and color photographs. The book includes instructions for making confetti eggs, a pronunciation guide, a glossary, resources for learning more, and an index. From the Read-And-Discover Ethnic Holidays series.

Orozco, José-Luis. *Fiestas: A Year of Latin American Songs of Celebration*. Illustrated by Eliza Kleven. New York: Dutton Children's Books, 2002. 48p.
Grades: K–4. This collection of songs is a musical tribute to Latin American culture and its holidays and festivals from the Los tres Reyes Magos in January to Las Posadas in December. The two-page table of contents is easy to read, allowing the reader to quickly locate songs for holidays or festivals. English and Spanish lyrics are given for each song. Colorful, festive illustrations and bordered pages immediately let readers know that these are joyous songs for celebrating. An index concludes the book.

Viesti, Joe, and Diane Hall. *Celebrate! In Central America*. Photographs by Joe Viesti. New York: Lothrop, Lee and Shepard Books, 1996. 32p.
Grades: 2–5. Celebrations in Central America blend the Catholic religion and the Spanish and Indian traditions of the people. Celebrations in this book include El Dia de los Muertos, El Baile de la Conquista, Carnival, Semana Santa, San José Fair, Virgin of Masaya Celebration, Columbus Day, and Carnival. Brief descriptions

accompanied by bright, lively color photographs introduce these celebrations. A map of Central America is included.

Harris, Zoe, and Suzanne Williams. *Piñatas & Smiling Skeletons: Celebrating Mexican Festivals*. Illustrated by Yolanda Garfias Woo. Berkeley, Calif.: Pacific View Press, 1998. 48p.
Grades: 4–6. Readers are treated to a year of familiar and not-so-familiar Mexican celebrations. Legends, songs, recipes, crafts, and colorful illustrations highlight the descriptions of the festivals. Readers learn a great deal about the history and culture of Mexico as they read about these festivals. Based on the extent of overlap, they recognize that some of Mexican culture has been assimilated into American culture. The book concludes with a glossary.

Ancona, George. *The Fiestas*. Tarrytown, N.Y. Marshall Cavendish, 2002. 48p.
Grades: 4–8. Fiestas fill the Mexican calendar; these celebrations include fireworks, music, dancing, processions, costumes, feasting, and piñatas. The book briefly describes the basic elements of fiestas, and then goes into more detail about Dia de la Bandera (Flag Day), Cinco de Mayo, El Dia del Charro (Day of the Horseman), and Dia de los Muertos (Day of the Dead). Ancona's trademark clear, bright, colorful photographs are filled with additional details. A calendar, glossary, a bibliography, and an index conclude the book. This book is from the Viva Mexico! series.

Presilla, Maricel E. Feliz Nochebuena, *Feliz Navidad: Christmas Feasts of the Hispanic Caribbean*. Illustrated by Ismael Espinosa Ferrer. New York: Henry Holt, 1994. Unp.
Grades: 4–8. History, traditions, foods, cultures, and recipes complemented by watercolor and ink illustrations describe Christmas season celebrations in Cuba and Puerto Rico that have migrated to the United States. Presilla traces the foods included in the celebrations back to their country of origin and tells readers how they became part of the celebrations. For example, Muslims brought marzipan treats to Spain and from Spain marzipan traveled to Cuba. Unfamiliar words are defined in the text and a glossary includes additional information about some of the words.

Menard, Valerie. *The Latino Holiday Book: From Cinco de Mayo to Dia de los Muertos—The Celebrations and Traditions of Hispanic Americans*. New York: Marlowe, 2000. 174p.

Grades: 7 and up. These Latino celebrations are categorized by seasons of the year. Menard describes the social or religious history of each celebration, in addition to telling about the customs and foods. Ideas for crafts and activities to help celebrate the holiday engage readers in active learning about Latino celebrations. Because of her clear writing style, readers unfamiliar with the holidays can easily understand what she is describing. Consequently, readers gain a deeper respect and appreciation for the Latino culture.

EXPLORATIONS

1. As students are reading the songs in *Fiestas: A Year of Latin American Songs of Celebration* (Orozco, 2002), have them jot down notes about what they can learn about the holidays from the songs.

2. After reading *Feliz Nochebuena, Feliz Navidad: Christmas Feasts of the Hispanic Caribbean* (Presilla, 1994), have students return to the text and find all of the words written in italics to create their own dictionary. The students can copy the words and their pronunciations into their dictionary. Then, they can write a definition in their own words and illustrate the entries.

3. As students are learning about Hispanic holidays, have them create an alphabet book using the new words they are learning. *A Mardi Gras Dictionary* (Vidrine, 1994) annotated in Chapter 9 can serve as a model for their work.

4. As students are reading the books annotated above, remind them to read critically to determine if any of the books contain contradictory information.

JEWISH CELEBRATIONS AND HOLIDAYS

This section contains books and media with information about Jewish holidays written for children at a variety of grade levels. Two of the books have stories to share with children about the holidays. One book contains songs for joyous celebrations. A video of a family enjoying Jewish celebrations throughout the year is also annotated below. For additional information about individual holidays, see specific occasions introduced in the various chapters of this book.

Book and Media Choices

Blue, Rose. Good *Yontif: A Picture Book of the Jewish Year*. Illustrated by Lynne Feldman. Brookfield, Conn.: The Millbrook Press, 1997. Unp.
Grades: P–2. In this picture book (no words accompany the pictures themeselves) readers join a family as they celebrate the yearly cycle of festivals and holidays. Letting children talk about the pictures is one way to determine what they know about the celebrations and allows them to respond personally to the book. Two pages of notes at the end of the book describe the festivals and holidays depicted in the pictures.

Gross, Judith. *Celebrate: A Book of Jewish Holidays*. Illustrated by Bari Weissman. New York: Grosset & Dunlap, 1992. Unp.
Grades: P–2. Brief introductions to the Jewish holidays accompanied by appealing, colorful, illustrations help young readers understand the reasons for these observances. The simple text is easy for young children to comprehend.

Kimmelman, Leslie. *Dance, Sing, Remember: A Celebration of Jewish Holidays*. Illustrated by Ora Eitan. New York: HarperCollins, 2000. 35p.
Grades: P–3. Simple descriptions tell the meanings behind these Jewish holidays. Songs, activities, stories, and recipes are included to help celebrate these special occasions. Simple illustrations on patterned pages provide a rich background for the concise text.

Musleah, Rahel, and Michael Klayman. *Sharing Blessings: Children's Stories for Exploring the Spirit of the Jewish Holidays*. Illustrated by May O'Keefe Young. Woodstock, Vt.: Jewish Lights Publishing, 1997. 64p.
Grades: 3–6. Thirteen Jewish holidays each have their own chapter and in each chapter readers are invited to join a family celebration to learn about the meaning of the holiday and the traditions associated with the holiday. A brief paragraph or two introduces each holiday story. Realistic watercolor illustrations help readers understand the holiday celebrations.

Berger, Gilda. *Celebrate! Stories of the Jewish Holidays*. Paintings by Peter Catalanotto. New York: Scholastic, 1998. 114p.
Grades: 4–8. Each story is accompanied by information on why and how the holiday is celebrated along with crafts and recipes. The

book touches on the following holidays: Shabbat, Rosh Hashanah, Yom Kippur, Sukkot, Hanukkah, Purim, Pesach, and Shavuot. An index concludes the book.

Cooper, Ilene. *Jewish Holidays All Year Round: A Family Treasury*. Illustrated by Elivia Savadier. New York: Harry N. Abrams, 2002. 80p.
Grades: 4–8. Clear, concise descriptions of the history and meaning of the holidays are accompanied by activities and recipes to help celebrate the holiday. The preface contains a detailed description of the Jewish lunar calendar. Illustrations in the book are a combination of colorful line drawings by Savadier and photographs and reproductions from The Jewish Museum, New York. A bibliography and an index conclude the book.

Schwartz, Howard. *The Day the Rabbi Disappeared: Jewish Holiday Tales of Magic*. Illustrated by Monique Passicot. New York: Penguin Putnam Books for Young Readers, 2000. 80p.
Grades: 4–8. Schwartz has retold twelve holiday tales filled with magic and adventure sure to entrance readers. Black-and-white illustrations capture the magic and the excitement. A glossary and a list of sources conclude the book.

The Jewish Holidays Video Guide. Bala Cynwyd, Penn.: Schlessinger Video Productions-Library Video Company, 1990. 75 min.
Grades: 7 and up. This award-winning video introduces students to the Cohen family as they participate in major Jewish holidays including: Passover, Hanukkah, Rosh Hashanah, Yom Kippur, Sukkot, Shavout, Purim, and Shabbat. Ed Asner, Theodore Bikel, Monty Hall, and Judge Wapner also share their favorite holiday memories. This video is from the Jewish Traditions series.

EXPLORATIONS

1. After reading *Jewish Holidays All Year Round: A Family Treasury* (Cooper, 2002), ask students why they think illustrations by Savadier and reproductions from The Jewish Museum, New York, were both included in the book. How did the illustrations and the reproductions help them comprehend the material? What would they have missed if only illustrations were included? What would they have missed if only reproductions were included?

2. After viewing *The Jewish Holidays Video Guide*, ask students what impact hearing celebrities' comments had on their understanding of the holiday. Did the comments add or detract from what they learned?

TEACHER RESOURCES

Books in this section contain detailed information about holidays around the world, Jewish celebrations, an encyclopedia of Christmas, and Chinese festivals. These books provide teachers with background information to support their classroom teaching and enable them to help students find answers to questions that arise as they study celebrations and holidays.

BOOK CHOICES

Burghardt, Linda. Jewish Holiday Traditions: *Joyful Celebrations from Rosh Hashana to Shavuot.* New York: Kensington Publishing, 2001. 294p.
The traditions, history, activities, and recipes are described for twelve Jewish holidays including: Rosh Hashanah, Yom Kippur, Sukkot, Simchat Torah, Hanukkah, Tu b'Shevat, Purim, Passover, Yo Ha'atzmaut, Lagb'Omer, Shavuot, and Sabbat. While the focus of the book is on ideas for celebrating these holidays at home, the book is a useful, well-organized resource for teachers and librarians. Blessings, a calendar, a glossary, recommendations for further reading, and an index all complement the text.

Gulevich, Tanya. *Encyclopedia of Christmas.* Illustrated by Mary Ann Stavros-Lanning. Detroit, Mich.: Omnigraphics, 2000. 734p.
Religious observances, history, legends, symbols and more surround Christmas. This comprehensive volume contains a well-researched collection of entries related to the celebration of this special day all around the world. Books for further research, a bibliography, Web sites, and an index are included.

Gulevich, Tanya. *Encyclopedia of Easter, Carnival and Lent.* Illustrated by Mary Ann Stavros-Lanning. Detroit, Mich.: Omnigraphics, 2001. 729p.
Folkore, history, legends, customs, and symbols associated with Easter and related holidays are described in this encyclopedia.

Entries explore Easter and Carnival celebrations around the world. A bibliography, Web sites, and an index are included.

Henderson, Helene, and Sue E. Thompson. *Holidays, Festivals, and Celebrations of the World Dictionary*, 3rd ed. Detroit, Mich.: Omnigraphics, 2002. 822p.
Over two thousand observances are described in short paragraphs that include contact information and Web sites. Local celebrations from all fifty states and from over one hundred nations are arranged alphabetically. This handy quick reference source includes a variety of indexes for quickly locating celebrations. Tourist information sources, a bibliography, and Web sites are included.

MacDonald, Margaret Read, editor. *The Folklore of World Holidays*. Detroit, Mich.: Gale Research, 1998. 841p.
Explore the legends and folklore of holidays from over one hundred fifty countries around the world. The detailed descriptions of the holidays are arranged chronologically. Bibliographic information and books for further reading are included for many of the entries.

Marling, Karol Ann. *Merry Christmas! Celebrating America's Greatest Holiday*. Cambridge, Mass.: Harvard University Press, 2000. 442p.
This view of Christmas through the media of popular culture discusses how the "things" of Christmas came to mean so much and to play such a prominent role in the holiday. Some of the chapters are about wrappings of Christmas, business, shopping, Christmas past, trees, and Santa Claus. This book can be of great use to teachers and librarians.

Santino, Jack. *All Around the Year: Holidays and Celebrations in American Life*. Urbana, Ill.: University of Illinois Press, 1994. 227p.
The author's personal recollections of holidays and the recollections of others provide personal glimpses into American holidays and celebrations, both traditional ones and not-so-traditional ones. The celebrations describe the common elements found in celebrations across America, but readers also learn how families have added traditions specific to their region or to their own family.

Scharfstein, Sol. *Understanding Jewish Holidays and Customs: Historical and Contemporary*. Hoboken, N.J.: KTAV Publishing House, 1999. 186p.

Scharfstein presents the historical basis for Jewish holidays and customs, explains how and why they have evolved, and describes the present-day holidays and customs. He also explains differences in the holidays and customs of Reform, Conservative, and Reconstructionist Judaism. The side margins of the pages are filled with captioned photographs and reproductions that help readers understand the text. An index concludes the book.

Stepanchuk, Carol, and Charles Wong. *Mooncakes and Ghosts: Festivals of China*. San Francisco: China Books and Periodicals, 1991. 143p.
Concise descriptions of Chinese festivals accompanied by stories and quotes explain the history, rituals, and traditions. Black-and-white photographs, illustrations, and maps along with some color plates are included. An appendix of information related to the holidays and a bibliography conclude the book.

Thompson, Sue Ellen, ed. *Halloween Program Sourcebook*. Detroit, Mich.: Omnigraphics, 1999. 694p.
The book begins with an introduction to Halloween. Stories, legends, strange happenings, poems, plays, activities, and recipes perfect for celebrating Halloween are all found in this resource book. Many of the selections easily lend themselves to dramatic presentations. An index concludes the book.

Thompson, Sue Ellen, ed. *Holiday Symbols*, 2nd ed. Detroit, Mich.: Omnigraphics, 2000. 694p.
Information on the origins and significance of over nine hundred holiday symbols can be found in this reference book. The entries include information on the type of holiday, when and where the holiday is celebrated, a list of associated symbols, a list of related holidays, brief essay on the origin of the holiday, and a list of further reading. A general index and an index of symbols are included.

Thompson, Sue Ellen, ed. *Thanksgiving Program* Sourcebook. Detroit, Mich.: Omnigraphics, 1999. 350p.
The introduction to Thanksgiving contains information on the origins, the evolution, and the significance of this harvest festival. Stories, poems, prayers, songs, plays, activities, and recipes for celebrating Thanksgiving are found within the pages of this book. Also included are a bibliography, Web sites, an author index, a title index, and an index to the first lines of the poetry in the book.

Tucker, Cathy C. *Christmas Worldwide: A Guide to Customs and Traditions*. Philadelphia, Penn.: Xlibris, 2000. 333p.
From Antigua to Wales the Christmas celebrations of sixty-eight countries taking place from Advent to the Epiphany are explored. The entries are brief, yet thorough. When making connections between the celebrations of different countries the index is a valuable resource. Entries such as "cleaning as tradition" and "fireworks" reveal that numerous countries share these traditions. A selected bibliography, addresses for obtaining additional information, and an index conclude the book.

REFERENCES

Vidrine, Beverly B. *A Mardi Gras Dictionary*. Lafayette, La.: Sunflower Press, 1994.

SPECIAL CELEBRATIONS 18

Religious and national celebrations and holidays occur throughout the year, making each month special. Other special occasions that are more local or personal in nature highlight the year, as well, such as bar mitzvahs, bat mitzvahs, birthdays, circuses, fairs, fiestas, jamborees, graduations, Native American celebrations, quinceañeras, snow days, Tooth Fairy visits, and weddings. As students study, the special celebrations below they discover experiences they have in common with other people around the world. Additionally, they develop an understanding and acceptance of people from other cultures, as they learn about their birthday, wedding, and Tooth Fairy customs. Although not on any calendar, completely unplanned, spontaneous celebrations can transform an ordinary day into something special; we just have to learn to recognize them. In the books annotated below, Byrd Baylor and Cynthia Rylant share ideas for turning ordinary and not-so-ordinary events into special celebrations.

BOOK AND MEDIA CHOICES

Rylant, Cynthia. *The Wonderful Happens*. Illustrated by Coco Dowley. New York: Simon & Schuster Books for Young Readers, 2000. Unp.
Grades: P–3. Rylant uses free verse to encourage readers to stop and appreciate the simple pleasures of life from fresh bread to spider webs, to birds, to flowers, to worms, to clocks. In the first part of the book, detailed borders surround the bright primary colored folk art illustrations. Towards the end of the book the exuberant illustrations break out of the constraints of borders and fill the double-page spreads edge-to-edge.

Baylor, Bryd. *I'm In Charge of Celebrations*. Illustrated by Peter Parnall. New York: Charles Scribner's Sons, 1986. Unp.
Grades: 1–5. In this joyful poem, a young woman revels in the wonders of the desert as she celebrates dust devils, rainbows, green clouds, coyotes, falling stars, and her own special New Year's Day. Celebrations, she tells readers, are for days when something out of the ordinary happens that causes the heart to pound. She records these special days in a notebook and celebrates them each year. The prose is written in narrow columns in stark white spaces accompanied by illustrations of abstract visualizations painted with intense colors. This book also is available on audiocassette.

BAR MITZVAHS AND BAT MITZVAHS

For Jewish people, a bar mitzvah is a coming of age ceremony for thirteen-year-old boys and a bat mitzvah is a coming of age ceremony for twelve-year-old girls. The ceremony signifies that they are ready to accept responsibility for their actions and for the religious obligations of a Jewish adult (Goldin, 1995). References to bar mitzvahs date back to the thirteenth century. Formal ceremonies for girls date back only as far as the mid-1900s and not all Jewish communities conduct bat mitzvahs (Goldin, 1995). Bar mitzvah and bat mitzvah ceremonies include reading in public worship from the Torah and the Prophets (Scharfstein, 1999). These ceremonies involve months of preparation as the young adults study the Torah, rehearse the ceremony, and prepare for the celebration.

BOOK AND MEDIA CHOICES

Goldin, Barbara Diamond. *Bat Mitzvah: A Jewish Girl's Coming of Age*. Illustrated by Erika Weihs. New York: Viking, 1995. 139p.
Grades: 5 and up. The first part of the book provides background information on the role of women throughout Jewish history. The second part of the book contains information on the preparation, the ceremony, the celebration, and what happens afterward. The author's personal experiences in preparing girls for the ceremony make this book an invaluable resource for those anticipating their own bat mitzvah. The book concludes with a glossary, source notes, and an index.

1. Bar mitzvahs commemorate boys coming of age and bat mitzvahs commemorate girls coming of age. However, as discussed in *Bat Mitzvah: A Jewish Girl's Coming of Age* (Goldin, 1995), bat mitzvahs have only recently been celebrated and not all Jewish groups celebrate them. Engage students in a discussion of why they think bat mitzvahs are not as universally accepted as bar mitzvahs are.

BIRTHDAYS

Birthday celebrations are as unique as the people who celebrate them. They might include parties at a skating rink, a bowling alley, a fast food restaurant, or at home. Cakes are commonly part of the birthday celebration, but the kinds of cakes vary according to individual preferences, and not every birthday includes a cake. Some people have traditional birthday cakes with "Happy Birthday" written on top and others select their favorite kind of cake such as, pineapple upside down cake. Long ago people believed that the smoke from candles on birthday cakes carried their prayers to the gods who lived in the sky, and making a wish while blowing out candles is a modern adaptation of this old custom (Erlbach, 1997). American birthday parties borrow from different cultures such as the popular Mexican piñata that has replaced Pin the Tail on the Donkey at some American birthday parties (Menard, 2000). As students read the books below they discover ideas for traditions to incorporate into their own birthday parties.

BOOK AND MEDIA CHOICES

Birthday Party Singalongs. CD. Redway, Calif.: Music for Little People, 2001.
Grades: P–2. Twelve birthday songs are included on this music CD, presented for everyone to sing along. Included on the CD are "Happy Birthday," "Hokey Pokey," "Piñata," and "Ring Around the Rosie."

Knight, Margy Burns. *Welcoming Babies*. Illustrated by Anne Sibley O'Brien. Gardiner, Maine: Tilbury House, 1994. Unp.

Grades: P–2. This is a multiethnic look at how new babies are welcomed into the world. Singing, kissing, naming, and blessing are a few of the ways that babies are welcomed. Colorful pastel illustrations fill the pages and present a warm, glowing portrait of the ways births are celebrated around the world. Notes at the end of the book provide additional information on the customs described and the culture of the people in the illustrations.

Selkowe, Valrie M. *Happy Birthday to Me!* Illustrated by John Sandford. New York: HarperCollins, 2001. Unp.
Grades: P–3. One morning rabbit finds a key that opens a gate. Beyond the gate, a path leads through a garden and into the pink house where wondrous things are happening. Dolls are dancing, the horse is rocking, and pigs are squealing about a cake with candles. When the piano starts playing, everyone sings "Happy Birthday" to rabbit. The text runs across the two-page spreads in curving white banners superimposed on the charming, detailed illustrations.

de Groat, Diane. *Happy Birthday to You, You Belong in a Zoo*. New York: Morrow Junior Books, 1999. Unp.
Grades: P–4. When Gilbert gets an invitation to Lewis's birthday party, he assumes Lewis will now be nice to him at school. However, Lewis continues to be mean and tells Gilbert the only reason he got an invitation is because his mother said he had to invite all the boys in the class. Gilbert picks out a frying pan for Lewis's birthday present. When Lewis opens the present Gilbert brought, Lewis and Gilbert are both pleasantly surprised.

Look, Lenore. Henry's *First-Moon Birthday*. Illustrated by Yumi Heo. 40 pages. New York: Simon & Schuster, 2001.
Grades: K–2. Jenny and her grandmother get up early to prepare for Henry's one-month birthday. Big sister Jenny tells the story as she helps with all of the preparations for this very special occasion. The book provides a glimpse into the Chinese culture through this Chinese American family's celebration. Pigs' feet, red eggs, ginger soup, and good luck messages are all prepared for this celebration shared with the extended family. Child-like illustrations help to convey the story as told by Jenny.

Hopkins, Lee Bennett, selector. *Happy Birthday*. Illustrated by Hilary Knight. New York: Simon & Schuster, 1991. 26p.
Grades: K–3. This small book of short birthday poems has delightful illustrations that capture the joy and happiness of these special days.

The collection, chosen by poet Lee Bennett Hopkins, includes poems by Myra Cohn Livingston, Dr. Seuss, and Aileen Fisher, among others. Children will enjoy both reading the poems and listening to them.

Yolen, Jane. *Mouse's Birthday*. Illustrated by Bruce Degen. New York: G.P. Putnam's Sons, 1993. 26p.
Grades: K–3. Mouse lives in a tiny little house with barely enough room for himself. But on his birthday cat, dog, cow, horse, and farmer come to bring gifts and all crowd into his house. What happens when mouse blows out the candle on his cake surprises everyone?

Lankford, Mary D. *Birthdays around the World*. Illustrated by Karen Dugan. New York: Harper Collins, 2002. 32p.
Grades: K–4. For thousands of years around the world, people have rejoiced at the birth of a new baby and each year birthdays are remembered and celebrated. This book examines the birthday customs from seven different countries: Finland, Malaysia, Mexico, the Netherlands, New Zealand, the Philippines, and Sweden. Readers can make connections between their birthday celebrations and the celebrations in other lands. They may also find new ways to celebrate their next birthday. The book also discusses birthday superstitions, an around the world birthday party, and contains a bibliography and an index.

Polacco, Patricia. *Some Birthday!* New York: Simon & Schuster Books for Young Readers, 1991. 24p.
Grades: 1–3. A little girl and her brother are spending the summer with their father, their grandmother, and their cousin Billy. She cannot understand why Daddy has not mentioned her birthday at all. When he comes home from work, he says they should all go down to the Clay Pits to look for and take a picture of the Monster of the Clay Pit Bottoms. Along the way, the readers find out why this was the best birthday ever.

Craven, Jerry. *Celebrations*. Vero Beach, Fla.: Rourke Publications, 1996. 32p.
Grades: 2–6. The birth of a child is a special occasion marked by different celebrations some indicating rites of passage throughout life. In China, a child's future is predicted on the first birthday and in Japan third, fifth, and seventh birthdays are special. Rites of passage include the Native American dream-quest for twelve-year-old boys and a dance for thirteen-year-old girls; for thirteen-year-old

Jewish boys it is the bar mitzvah and for twelve-year-old girls it is the bat mitzvah; Latino girls have a quinciñera on their fifteenth birthday; and in some countries the twenty-first birthday is marked by a "key party." Color photographs accompany the brief descriptions of birthday celebrations. A glossary and an index are included. This book is from the Customs, Costumes, and Cultures series.

Erlbach, Arlene. *Happy Birthday, Everywhere!* Illustrated by Sharon Lane Holm. Brookfield, Conn.: The Millbrook Press, 1997. 48p.
Grades: 4–6. The games, foods, and customs associated with birthday celebrations in nineteen different countries are described in colorful two page spreads. Each entry includes either directions for playing a game, instructions for creating crafts, or recipes for special foods. For example, a Russian birthday party might include the clothesline game where prizes are hung on a string and blindfolded guests select a prize to take home. The book includes a bibliography.

Hurwitz, Johanna, editor. *Birthday Surprises: Ten Great Stories to Unwrap.* New York: Beech Tree Books, 1995. 118p.
Grades: 5 and up. Johanna Hurwitz approached children's authors and asked them each to write a story based on the same plot. The plot involves a child who receives many birthday presents, but one of the presents is an empty box. The stories include historical fiction, a poem, a modern fairy tale, a collection of letters, and fantasy. The book includes stories by these authors: David A. Adler, Ellen Conford, Pam Conrad, James Howe, Johanna Hurwitz, Karla Kuskin, Ann M. Martin, Richard Peck, Barbara Ann Porter, and Jane Yolen.

EXPLORATIONS

1. Rather than introducing *Happy Birthday to Me!* (Selkowe, 2001) by reading the title to the students, conceal the title and tell the students that they are going to guess the ending to the story. Stop reading either just before the pigs and the birthday cake or just before the song is sung and ask the students to predict how the story will end.

2. *Celebrations* (Craven, 1996) includes information about coming of age celebrations for Native American and Jewish girls and boys. However, Mexican Americans only have a celebration for girls and not for boys. Engage students in a discussion of why they think this is so.

3. Ask students to make a list of games they have played at birthday parties. While reading *Happy Birthday, Everywhere!* (Erlbach, 1997) have students make connections between games they have played at birthday parties and the games played at birthday parties in other parts of the world.

4. Before talking about birthdays, have the students brainstorm a list of words describing birthday cakes. Then, have the students use the words to write descriptions of their perfect birthday cake.

5. Prior to reading *Birthday Surprises: Ten Great Stories to Unwrap* (Hurwitz, 1995), have the students discuss what they would think if they unwrapped a present and nothing was inside the box. Explain to the students that Hurwitz contacted different authors and had them write stories about an empty birthday present. After reading the stories, have students talk in small groups about their ideas for a story about receiving an empty box for their birthday. Then, have the students write a story about receiving an empty box for a birthday present.

CIRCUSES, FAIRS, FIESTAS, AND JAMBOREES

Circuses, fairs, fiestas, and jamborees are a conglomeration of sights, smells, and sounds that tickle the senses. Whirling rides, flashing lights, colorful booths, and brightly colored games of chance tantalize the eyes. The smells of cotton candy, funnel cakes, popcorn, candy apples, and corn dogs delight the nose. Screams from those on the carnival rides, the clanking, whooshing noises of the carnival rides, and shouts from winners of the games of chance fill the air. As night falls the lights become brighter and the evening takes on a magical air.

BOOK AND MEDIA CHOICES

Circus Magic. CD and Audiocassette. Huntington, Calif.: Youngheart Music, 1999.

Grades: P–2. Celebrate the circus with these lively tunes sung by Linda Arnold. Included are recordings of: "Circus Train," "Singing Ringmaster," and "Clover the Clown."

Crews, Donald. *Night at the Fair*. New York: Greenwillow Books, 1998. Unp.
Grades: P–2. At night, the lights of the fair glow and sparkle. The air fills with the smells of corndogs, popcorn, and sausage; the shouts of the winners of the games; and whirling, screeches of the carnival rides. It is a magical night that all to soon ends.

Duncan, Lois. *Song of the Circus*. Illustrated by Meg Cundiff. New York: Penguin Putnam Books for Young Readers, 2002. Unp.
Grades: P–2. Two circus children fend off a ferocious, hungry tiger that is looking for a tasty meal. This is a rollicking romp through the chain reaction at a circus as performers topple and fall. Young readers recognize the performers and their acts.

Greene, Rhonda Gowler. *Jamboree Day*. Illustrated by Jason Wolff. New York: Scholastic, 2001. Unp.
Grades: P–2. This lively, playful, rhyming text introduces a variety of jungle animals as they head for the jamboree. Coconut milk, banana splits, balloons, train rides, limbo, bands, and dancing are the order of the day. As the sun sinks in the sky, the animals leave for home. Full-page, colorful illustrations filled with whimsical smiling animals depict the gaiety and excitement of the jamboree.

Stoeke, Janet Morgan. *Minerva Louise at the Fair*. New York: Dutton Children's Books, 2000. Unp.
Grades: P–2. Minerva was sleeping in the wheelbarrow one night instead of the hen house when she heard fireworks and decided to investigate. She discovers the county fair and takes in all the sights. When she gets sleepy, she climbs into an empty nest. She awakens the next morning to discover she has won a blue ribbon.

Ancona, George. *Fiesta Fireworks*. New York: Lothrop, Lee & Shepard Books, 1998. Unp.
Grades: 1–4. The Mexican town of Tultepec is famous for the fireworks the townspeople produce. Each year they hold a fiesta to ask their patron saint, San Juan de Dios, to protect them in their dangerous work. While the book is about the Tultepec festival, similar festivals are held throughout Mexico as every town has a patron saint. Vibrant color photographs explode with the excitement of the

preparations and the celebration of this festival. An author's note, a map of Mexico, and a glossary conclude the book. A note on the title page reminds readers of the dangers of fireworks.

Lewin, Ted. *Fair*. New York: Lothrop, Lee & Shepard, 1997. Unp. Grades: 1–4. When it is time for the county fair, the deserted fairground is magically transformed with carnival rides, tents, pens for animals, cables, and lights. Lewin describes the sights, sounds, and thrills of a county fair in words and full-page color illustrations. Tasty foods, games of skill, a sideshow of strange creatures, animal judging, cooking contests, and an assortment of other activities fill the days. Then, the fair ends and the fairgrounds revert to their dormant, deserted state.

EXPLORATION

1. While reading *Night at the Fair* (Crews, 1998), focus the attention of students on the black background of the illustrations depicting night. Provide the students with an opportunity to paint pictures or have them create collages on black construction paper.

2. Prior to reading *Song of the Circus* (Duncan, 2002), have students talk about their memories of trips to the circus.

3. After reading *Jamboree Day* (Greene, 2001), write some of the rhyming words on the board and show students how the words have similar endings. Then, let the children think up rhyming words to share with each other.

4. Read both *Minerva Louise at the Fair* (Stoeke, 2000) and *Fair* (Lewin, 1997) to the students. Then, engage the students in a discussion of how the stories about the fair differ based on the perspective of the characters telling the stories.

GRADUATIONS

Graduation marks the end of one stage of schooling, and perhaps the beginning of another. Students may graduate from kindergarten, sixth grade, eighth grade, and high school. Each graduation is a time for remembering the past and thinking ahead to the future. Graduation ceremonies include speeches, music, caps, gowns, and diplomas. Parties often follow the ceremonies, where parents, relatives, and friends present the graduate with gifts. The graduations in the books below include the ordinary and the unusual, but they all signify a rite of passage.

BOOK AND MEDIA CHOICES

Dr. Seuss. *Oh, the Places You'll Go!* New York: Random House, 1990. Unp.
Grades: K–8. Graduates young and old appreciate the wit and wisdom of Dr. Seuss as he encourages them to venture out and experience what life has to offer. The journey is filled with ups and downs but Dr. Seuss is sure they will succeed. Bright, busy pages filled with rhyming text and imaginative pictures depict the adventuresome journey.

Park, Barbara. *Junie B. Jones is a Graduation Girl.* Illustrated by Denise Brunkus. New York: Random House, 2001. 69p.
Grades: 1–3. Junie B. and her classmates in Room Nine are graduating from kindergarten. Rumors abound. One student declares their "brains and feet are going to double in size." Another announces they are getting "cats and gowns." The children are sent home with their white caps and gowns, but Junie B.'s does not stay white for long. Just before the graduation ceremony her classmates rally around Junie B. and her spotted gown.

Park, Barbara. *The Graduation of Jake Moon.* New York: Atheneum Books for Young Readers, 2000. 115p.
Grades: 4–6. Graduation does not just mean moving from one grade to the next, sometimes graduation means moving from one stage of a relationship to another. Jake's grandfather, Skelly, has always supported Jake and his friends by providing them with the support and self-confidence they need to succeed. As Skelly sinks deeper and deeper into the oblivion of Alzheimer's disease, Jake finds it difficult to understand and accept his grandfather's bizarre behavior. He resents his grandfather and does not want his friends to know about his grandfather's illness and his behavior. During Jake's graduation ceremony, his grandfather wanders onto stage and Jake discovers within himself the courage to walk up and escort his grandfather off the stage. The book concludes with contact information for the Alzheimer's Association National Office and Web sites for obtaining more information about Alzheimer's disease.

Anderson, Janet S. *Going through the Gate*. New York: Dutton Children's Books, 1997. 134p.
Grades: 5–8. Miss Clough has been teaching in this one-room schoolhouse for a very long time. Before her students leave for middle school she gives them a private graduation ceremony that profoundly changes their lives. Other graduates in the town cannot talk about the ceremony and throughout the book the suspense builds as tantalizing clues about the ceremony are revealed.

EXPLORATIONS

1. At the end of *Junie B. Jones is a Graduation Girl* (Park, 2001), her friends all decorate their white caps and gowns to match Junie B.'s spotted cap and gown. Ask the students what would have happened if her friends had not decorated their caps and gowns to match Junie B's. Discuss with the students how Junie B.'s classmates prevented her from the embarrassment of having the only spotted gown on stage.

2. Skelly in *The Graduation of Jake Moon* (Park, 2000) was a very special grandfather. Ask the students to return to the text and record examples of the things Skelly did that made him so special.

3. Before reading *The Graduation of Jake Moon* (Park, 2000) have the students use the Web sites in the book to learn about Alzheimer's disease or have them write to the Alzheimer's Association National Office to obtain additional information about the disease.

NATIVE AMERICAN CELEBRATIONS

American Indian Day or Native Americans' Day was first celebrated on the second Saturday in May 1916 (Henderson and Thompson, 2002). In some states the fourth Friday in September is set aside to honor Native Americans. This holiday celebrates the unique contributions of Native Americans and focuses on improving their living conditions. When teaching about Native Americans it is important to avoid stereotypes and to present information about the different tribes and their unique cultures and contributions to American life

(Reese, 1996; Franklin, Roach, and Snyder, 1993). The book annotations below contain information on Native American celebrations that honor their unique heritage including the powwow, the Potlatch, and Buffalo Days. (See Itse Selu.)

BOOK AND MEDIA CHOICES

Pow Wow. Video. Bala Cynwyd, Penn.: Schlessinger Video Productions-Library Video Company, 1996. 25 min.
Grades: K–4. Native American dancers, musicians, songs, and stories introduce students to the Native American powwow. Information about different tribes and their beliefs help students understand the important contributions Native Americans have made to our culture. Curriculum correlation documents are available to assist teachers as they incorporate this video into their social studies curriculum. This video is part of the Holidays for Children series.

Kalman, Bobbie. *Celebrating the Powwow*. New York: Crabtree Publishing, 1997. 32p.
Grades: 2–4. The book provides a brief look at a Native American powwow. Readers learn about customs and symbols that are important to Native Americans. Preparations for the powwow include the making of drums and clothing. Dances and dance competitions are the highlights of this grand occasion as shown in the color photographs accompanying the text. A glossary and an index conclude the book.

Liptak, Karen. *North American Indian Ceremonies*. New York: Franklin Watts, 1992. 63p.
Grades: 2–5. Ceremonies are an important part of the lives of Native Americans, which celebrate major life events such as birth, puberty, and marriage. Other ceremonies are for giving thanks and for healing. Color photographs and illustrations accompany the text. The book includes a glossary, books for further reading, and an index.

Ancona, George. *Powwow*. San Diego: Harcourt Brace Jovanovich, 1993. Unp.
Grades: 2–6. Bright, colorful photographs show the traditional Crow Fair. This is a time for celebrating the Native American culture and heritage with dances, eating, and competitions. Well-researched descriptive text explains the traditions associated with this lively celebration.

Come Celebrate with Me: Native American Powwow. Video. Morris Plains, N.J.: Lucerne Media, 2001. 10 min.
Grades: 3–6. Viewers learn about the traditions and customs that are part of the Native American powwow. A teacher's guide is included.

Hoyt-Goldsmith, Diane. *Buffalo Days*. Photographs by Lawrence Migdale. New York: Holiday House, 1997. 32p.
Grades: 3–6. Clarence Three Irons, Jr. and his family are members of the Crow Indian tribe who are working to reestablish buffalo herds on the tribe's lands. Readers learn how the once plentiful buffalo herds were decimated leaving the Crow, the Cheyenne, and other Native American tribes without a livelihood. The buffalo herds have been reestablished and the Crow nation celebrates the importance of the buffalo during the third week of August with Buffalo Days. Tipis are set up, traditional clothing is worn, plus there are parades, rodeo competitions, horse races, and dancing as the Crow nation celebrates.

Hoyt-Goldsmith, Diane. *Potlatch: A Tsimshian Celebration*. Photographs by Lawrence Migdale. New York: Holiday House, 1997. 32p.
Grades: 3–6. David R. Boxley, a thirteen-year-old, tells readers about a potlatch held in Metlakatla, Alaska by the Tsimshian tribe. The potlatch was to honor David's great-grandfather. Before the time of written records potlatches served to establish rank, privileges, ownership, and inheritance. Legends, stories, songs, and dances transmit the history of the tribe. These social gatherings reunited clans from different villages and were marked by the giving away of elaborate, expensive gifts. Often families would give away all of their possessions, so for many years laws prohibited potlatches. Photographs, maps, and reproductions enhance the well-researched, detailed text. A glossary and an index are included.

Into the Circle: An Introduction to Native American Powwows. Video. Bala Cynwyd, Penn.: Schlessinger Video Productions-Library Video Company, 1992. 60 min.
Grades: 7 and up. Viewers meet Native Americans as they gather for a powwow in Oklahoma. Live action shots show the dances, ceremonies, and songs performed by the Native Americans. Interviews with the tribal elders and the performers provide viewers with a personal introduction to this ancient ceremony.

EXPLORATIONS

1. Prior to reading *Buffalo Days* (Hoyt-Goldsmith, 1997), show students the picture on page eleven, which shows a man standing on a mound of buffalo bones, and read the quote by Joe Medicine Crow on the last page of the book. Based on these stimuli, have students make predictions about what they will learn from the book.

2. Before reading *Potlatch: A Tsimshian Celebration* (Hoyt-Goldsmith, 1997), ask students to look closely at the drawing around the photograph on the cover of the book. They were created by David Boxley, who introduces readers to the Potlatch.

3. Students interested in learning more about potlatches can visit an online exhibit sponsored by Peabody Museum of Archaeology and Ethnology located at www.peabody.harvard.edu/potlatch.

4. Before showing *Into the Circle: An Introduction to Native American Powwows*, preview the video and create questions to focus student attention while they watch the video, and for the students to use as they discuss the video afterward.

QUINCEAÑERAS

When an Aztec girl reached the age of fifteen, she was considered ready to assume the role of an adult and this is perhaps the origin of the quinceañera ritual (King, 1998). In 1521, the Spanish conquered the Aztecs and introduced the Roman Catholic religion. Hence, the quinceañera is a blend of native Aztec initiation rites and of western Christian religion (Lankford, 1994). Family members and friends are invited to this rite of passage, which may be celebrated by a religious ceremony followed by a party or simply a party. These celebrations range from the simple to the elaborate. Some families have sponsors who pay for particular items associated with the ceremony such as the girl's dress or the band for the party (Menard, 2000). The books below provide details about the different traditions associated with quinceañeras.

Book and Media Choices

Hoyt-Goldsmith, Diane. *Celebrating a Quinceañera: A Latina's 15th Birthday Celebration*. Photographs by Lawrence Migdale. New York: Holiday House, 2002. 32p.
Grades: 3–6. While everyone's birthday is special to the celebrant and family, the fifteenth birthday is extra-special to Hispanic girls. This day marks the end of childhood and the beginning of the girl's life as an adult. Special foods are prepared, special friends are included, special clothes are worn, and certain religious teachings are observed. This in the story of Ariana and her cousin Cynthia as they prepare for this special birthday celebration. The book concludes with a glossary and an index.

Lankford, Mary D. *Quinceañera: A Latina's Journey to Womanhood*. Photographs by Jesse Herrera. Brookfield, Conn.: The Millbrook Press, 1994. 47p.
Grades: 4–8. Martha Jimenez was born in Mexico, but grew up in Texas. She and her parents spent over a year planning and preparing for her quinceañera. The preparations included a trip to Mexico to purchase her dress. Color photographs combined with brief paragraphs tell the story of Martha's special day. Books for further reading and an index are included.

King, Elizabeth. *Quinceañera: Celebrating Fifteen*. New York: Dutton Children's Books, 1998. 40p.
Grades: 6–9. Readers follow along as two young California girls prepare for their quinceañeras in honor of their fifteen birthdays. Elaborate dresses are bought, decorations are made, and special foods are ordered including an ornate cake, the pastel. Dance lessons are given to the young ladies and their honor courts. The book concludes with information on the origins of the celebration.

Explorations

1. *Quinceañera: Celebrating Fifteen* (King, 1998) is about two different girls celebrating their quinceañeras. Students can complete a Venn diagram detailing the similarities and differences between the two girls' celebrations.

2. Have students think about the quinceañera celebrations they read about or have attended. Ask them to imagine

they are at a quinceañera and record the sights, sounds, smells, and tastes that come to mind.

Senses Chart	
	Quinceañera
Sights	
Sounds	
Smells	
Tastes	

Figure 18-1. Completing the senses chart requires the students to use their imaginations and prior knowledge.

SNOW DAYS

When the snow continues to fall and blankets the earth and nothing is moving in the white wilderness, it is a snow day. The normal routine is suspended, schools and businesses close, families and friends celebrate, and everyone enjoys the unexpected holiday. The books describe the wonder and the excitement of an unexpected day off.

BOOK AND MEDIA CHOICES

Plourde, Lynn. *Snow Day*. Illustrated by Hideko Takahashi. New York: Simon & Schuster, 2001. Unp.
Grades: P–1. Readers join a cozy family of four as they experience all the pleasures of a gift from nature, a snow day. Steaming oatmeal, a crackling fireplace, games, munchies, snow angels, and hot chocolate all combine to make it a perfect day. The onomatopoeia and adjectives found in the text paint wonderful word pictures for readers that complement the warm acrylic illustrations.

Lakin, Patricia. *Snow Day!* Illustrated by Scott Nash. New York: Penguin Putnam Books for Young Readers, 2002. Unp.

Grades: P–2. Four friends awake to glorious fresh snow and decide to go sledding. Suddenly, it dawns on them it is a school day, so they head back inside. Reporting in as Principal Sam, Principal Pam, Principal Will, and Principal Jill, they call the local news station and cancel school. Then, it is off for a day of sledding.

George, Lindsay Barrett. *Who's Been Here?* New York: William Morrow, 1995. Unp.
Grades: P–3. As they trudge through the woods on the way to their sledding hill two children encounter a variety of animals in the winter wonderland. As the children walk they carefully examine nature's signs to determine which animal is nearby. The repeated question, "Who's been here?" gives students the chance to guess which animal is on the next page. Large realistic illustrations display the animals and make this a great book for reading aloud to groups of children.

Joosse, Barbara M. *Snow Day!* Illustrated by Jennifer Plecas. New York: Clarion Books, 1995. Unp.
Grades: P–3. Robby and his dog, Zippy, cannot wait to get outside and enjoy last night's snowfall. Soon the rest of the family joins them. Snowball fights, snow angels, warm cocoa, and a toasty fire make for a perfect snow day with the family. Colorful full-page illustrations capture the frozen, white day and the warm, family relationship.

EXPLORATIONS

1. Ask students what they like to do on snow days? After discussing what they do on snow days, have them write about their favorite snow day activity.

2. After reading *Snow Day* (Plourde, 2001) or *Snow Day!* (Joose, 1995), have students talk about the ways the characters in the story warmed up after spending time in the snow. Then, ask students to share their favorite ways of warming up after playing in the snow.

3. While reading *Who's Been Here?* (George, 1995), stop and have students carefully examine the clues in the illustrations before they guess what animal will be on the next page.

```
DIRECTIONS................................................
            Please leare me
$2.00 or$1.00 or more
       Sign your name with
  the pen
```

TOOTH FAIRY VISITS

Losing a tooth is a sign of growing up and for some students may be a distressing event. Traditions surrounding the losing of teeth vary from family to family, region to region, and country to country. Before discussing the Tooth Fairy, ask students to share their experiences with losing a tooth.

BOOK AND MEDIA CHOICES

Wilhelm, Hans. *I Lost My Tooth*. New York: Scholastic, 1999. Unp.
Grades: P–1. When Puppy's tooth falls out and he loses it, he decides to take a picture of the gap in his teeth and stick it under his pillow for the Tooth Fairy. Sure enough the next morning the picture is gone and treats are under his pillow. The easy-to-read text and the familiar story make this a favorite for young readers. This book is from the Hello Reader!—Level 1 series.

Bourgeois, Paulette. *Franklin and the Tooth Fairy*. Illustrated by Brenda Clark. New York: Scholastic, 1996. Unp.
Grades: P–2. Franklin's friends are losing their teeth, putting them under their pillows, and receiving presents in exchange from the Tooth Fairy. He learns that losing teeth is also a sign of growing up. Poor Franklin—turtles have no teeth, so he will not be getting any presents; and how will he know he is growing up? His parents help him understand that it is okay to be different and that they recognize he is growing up.

Olson, Mary W. *Nice Try Tooth Fairy*. Illustrated by Katherine Tillotson. New York: Simon & Schuster Books for Young Readers, 2000. Unp.
Grades: P–2. When Grandfather comes to visit, Emma wants to show him the tooth she lost. Since the Tooth Fairy has already collected the tooth, Emma writes a note requesting that the tooth be returned for just one day. Eager to oblige, each night the Tooth Fairy delivers a different tooth. However, they are not Emma's, so she is visited by an assortment of animals coming to reclaim their teeth. The story is told in the letters that Emma writes the Tooth Fairy each night as she attempts to retrieve her tooth. Colorful, cluttered illustrations depict a patient Emma's bedroom and a harried Tooth Fairy's office.

Grambling, Lois G. *This Whole Tooth Fairy Thing's Nothing But a Big Rip-Off!* Illustrated by Thomas Payne. Tarrytown, N.Y.: Marshall Cavendish, 2002. Unp.
Grades: P–3. When the rain awakens Little Hippo and he discovers that his tooth is still under his pillow, he announces in a loud voice, "This whole Tooth Fairy thing's nothing but a big rip-off!" Having overheard his declaration the sneezing, drenched Tooth Fairy flies into his bedroom and plops on his bed. She enlists his aid in making her last stop of the evening and takes a short nap in his bed while he completes her rounds. The rich oil paintings capture the characters' expressions and delight young readers.

Middleton, Charlotte. *Tabitha's Terrifically Tough Tooth*. New York: Phyllis Fogelman Books, 2001. Unp.
Grades: P–3. Tabitha has a wobbly tooth that just will not come out. She spends the day trying different methods for getting her tooth to pop out of her mouth. Just when she gives up, she sneezes and her tooth goes flying across the room. Youngsters who have encountered Tabitha's problem easily make connections between her dilemma and their own experiences.

Jay, Betsy. *Jane vs. the Tooth Fairy*. Illustrated by Lori Osiecki. Flagstaff, Ariz.: Rising Moon, 2000. Unp.
Grades: K–3. When she discovers her loose tooth, Jane decides she wants to keep it. She does not share the excitement of her parents, her neighbor, or her grandmother about this new development. Her best efforts to retain the tooth fail and the inevitable happens. Children wondering about losing teeth and unconvinced that new ones will grow, relate to this humorous story. The scratchboard illus-

trations were scanned into Photoshop and digitally painted. Appealing, small illustrations are scattered throughout the text and enhance readers' understanding.

O'Connor, Jane. *Dear Tooth Fairy*. Illustrated by Joy Allen. New York: Grosset & Dunlap, 2002. 48p.
Grades: 1–2. As class picture day looms, Robby is concerned because he is the only one in the class who has not lost any baby teeth. All of his classmates' smiles are filled with gaping holes. His mother suggests that he write to the Tooth Fairy about his concerns. What follows is a series of letters between the worried Robby and the reassuring Tooth Fairy. Young readers relate to Robby and discover that this is a book they can read on their own. This book is from the All Aboard Reading series.

Beeler, Selby B. *Throw Your Tooth on the Roof: Tooth Traditions from Around the World*. Illustrated by G. Brian Karas. New York: Houghton Mifflin, 1998. Unp.
Grades: 1–4. With the simple question "What do you do when you lose a tooth?" came the customs described in this book. Throwing a tooth on the roof, leaving it for the Tooth Fairy or tooth mouse, and turning it into jewelry are just a few of the traditions included in the book. A map of the world, information about teeth, and a glossary are included. An author's note concludes the book describing how she researched the book and telling readers that one country may have many different traditions and some countries share traditions.

EXPLORATIONS

1. In *Nice Try Tooth Fairy* (Olson, 2000) and *Dear Tooth Fairy* (O'Connor, 2002), the children write letters to the Tooth Fairy. Ask the students about letters they might have written to the Tooth Fairy. Students who have not written to the Tooth Fairy may have written to Santa Claus and they can share their experiences.

2. The letters written in *Nice Try Tooth Fairy* (Olson, 2000) and *Dear Tooth Fairy* (O'Connor, 2002) are examples of informal letters. Point out the structure of the letters to the students as a way to introduce letter writing.

3. Before reading *Tabitha's Terrifically Tough Tooth* (Middleton, 2001), tell students that Tabitha has a loose

tooth that does not want to come out. Ask them for ideas on how she can get her tooth to come out.

4. In *Jane vs. the Tooth Fairy* (Jay, 2000), Jane does not want to lose her tooth. Invite students to discuss their feeling about losing their first tooth. Alternatively, ask students why they think Jane does not want to lose her tooth.

5. Before reading *Throw Your Tooth on the Roof: Tooth Traditions from Around the World* (Beeler, 1998), ask students what happens when they lose a tooth. Write their responses on the board. As the book is being read, help students make connections between their tooth traditions and the ones listed in the book.

WEDDINGS

Weddings are very personal, very special occasions. The books annotated below reflect cultural variations, family variations, and the personal preferences of the wedding couple. Weddings take place in churches, in city halls, on beaches, in houses, in parks, and in other places that have special meanings for the bridal couple. Weddings range from simple family affairs to elaborate social celebrations. The books annotated below explain cultural traditions associated with weddings and some of them examine weddings from the perspective of children.

BOOK AND MEDIA CHOICES

Cox, Judy. *Now We Can Have a Wedding!* Illustrated by DyAnne DiSalvo-Ryan. New York: Holiday House, 1998. Unp.
Grades: P–3. When a couple in the apartment building falls in love and decides to marry, everyone in the building prepares food from

their country for the wedding. Readers follow along as the bride's younger sister, Sally, visits each apartment and helps each of the tenets prepare an ethnic dish for the wedding including tai shio-yaki, steamed cakes, and biscotti. As each dish is finished the cook declares, "Now we can have a wedding." A glossary of wedding delicacies concludes the book.

Furgang, Kathy. *Flower Girl*. Illustrated by Harley Jessup. New York: Viking Children's Books, 2003. Unp.
Grades: P–3. A trip to the attic to try on Grandma's wedding veil and examine Mama's wedding dress convinces Anna that just maybe being a flower girl in Aunt Julie's wedding will not be so bad after all. Ink and watercolor illustrations capture Anna's emotions and changing perception of what it will be like to participate in the wedding.

Gibbons, Faye. *Mountain Wedding*. Illustrated by Ted Rand. New York: Morrow Junior Books, 1996. Unp.
Grades: P–3. Ms. Searcy and Mr. Long are at the preacher's house ready to be married. They have the wagon loaded with their belongings, Mr. Long's seven children dressed in their hand-me-down best, and Ms. Searcy's five children in their mended city clothes. The children are not ready for this union and when a swarm of bees frightens the farm animals and the mules harnessed to the loaded wagon bedlam breaks loose. The mules careen down the road leaving a trail of belongings behind them and the families race off after them gathering household items as they run. By the time the mules come to a halt and the children have worked together to retrieve their belongings, they are ready to become a family. Clever, humorous illustrations show a large brood of active, mischievous, loving children.

Hines, Anna Grossnickle. *When We Married Gary*. New York: Greenwillow Books, 1996. Unp.
Grades: P–3. Based on her own experience, the author tells of her life as a single mother with two young girls. When she marries Gary, her daughter refers to their family as a puzzle. Some how the puzzle does not fit together with their father, but it does with Gary. This is a loving portrait of a special family.

Johnson, Angela. *The Wedding*. Illustrated by David Soman. New York: Orchard Books, 1999. Unp.
Grades: K–2. Collage and black crayon illustrations portray the nuances and emotions of a family wedding seen through the eyes of

a younger sister. The preparations, the wedding, and the lingering memories are all here to savor and share.

Zalben, Jane Breskin. *Beni's First Wedding*. New York: Henry Holt, 1998. Unp.
Grades: K–3. When Uncle Izzy decides to marry Sashi, Beni is asked to be the page boy and carry the wedding ring up the aisle on a pillow. As he walks up the aisle a gushing aunt remarks about how cute he looks. As he turns to see who is speaking, he tilts the pillow and the ring rolls away. Cousin Max reclaims the ring and joins the wedding party. This is a heartwarming look at a Jewish wedding celebration. The book concludes with a recipe for honey wedding cake, a glossary, and information on the religious wedding customs of Judaism, Christianity, Islam, Hinduism, Sikhism, and Buddhism.

Schick, Eleanor. *Navajo Wedding: A Diné Marriage Ceremony*. Tarrytown, N.Y.: Marshall Cavendish, 1999. 40p.
Grades: K–4. Readers join a Caucasian girl and her family in the home of a Navajo bride on her wedding day. Throughout the day, the Navajo family explains the customs and traditions of this special day. Soft, colored-pencil illustrations bring the wedding to life and capture the warmth and joy of this Navajo ceremony.

Willner-Pardo, Gina. *Spider Storch's Desperate Deal*. Illustrated by Nick Sharratt. New York: Albert Whitman, 1999. 60p.
Grades: 2–4. Spider does not want to be the ring bearer in a wedding, he does not want to walk down the aisle with Mary Grace Brennerman, the flower girl, and most of all he does not want his friends to find out about this. He makes a series of deals with Mary Grace to keep her from telling his friends, but in the end decides that being a ring bearer was not so bad after all.

Soto, Gary. *Snapshots from the Wedding*. Illustrated by Stephanie Garcia. New York: G.P. Putnam's Sons, 1997. Unp.
Grades: 2–5. Maya, the flower girl, takes readers on a delightful tour of a wedding seen through her sharp eyes. She points out an untied shoelace on the ring bearer, Tio Juan itching in his new suit, and reminds readers that pitted black olives are for wearing on fingertips before eating. Sculpy clay artwork and found objects arranged in shadow boxes were used to create the snapshots of this Latino-American wedding.

Compton, Anita. *Marriage Customs*. New York: Thomson Learning, 1993.
Grades: 3–6. Wedding traditions and rituals from a variety of religions are described in this book. The author makes comparisons between the different ceremonies. Readers discover that marriage is celebrated in different ways, but there are similarities. A glossary, books to read, and an index are included. This book is from the Comparing Religions series.

EXPLORATIONS

1. Prior to reading *The Wedding* (Johnson, 1999) or *Beni's First Wedding* (Zalben, 1998), use *Inspiration* software to create a concept map depicting what students know about weddings. After reading the book, return to the concept map and ask the students what they learned about weddings that can be added. Then, work with the students to organize the information into appropriate categories, such as ceremony, food, guests, and clothing.

2. Prior to reading *Flower Girl* (Furgang, 2003), help the students make connections between their life and Anna's life by asking them if they have ever changed their minds about something.

3. After reading *Mountain Wedding* (Gibbons, 1996), ask the students why the families were ready to marry after they chased down the horses. What brought about changes in how the family members felt about each other? What evidence can they find in the illustrations to support their answers?

4. After reading *Snapshots from the Wedding* (Soto, 1997), return to the illustrations and have children describe what they see in the pictures. Call their attention to the fact that in some illustrations the artist has only included parts of people, such as only the feet and socks of the children rather than the whole child. She is focusing readers' attention on the important parts. They can use this technique in their own artwork rather than drawing the whole person.

5. After reading *Spider Storch's Desperate Deal* (Willner-Pardo, 1999), provide students with questions to guide their discussion of the book. How does Spider initially feel about being in the wedding? How do his feelings change?

Why do his feelings change? Remind the students to return to the book to find support for their answers.

6. After reading *Marriage Customs* (Compton, 1993), ask students what they found were the common elements in the marriage ceremonies.

VISITING DAYS

Visiting days are special days that really have no specific date on the calendar. They are unfortunately something that affect many of today's children. When a parent is incarcerated, opportunities to visit with them may be infrequent. On visiting day, they try to share all the news, events, and special occasions that occurred since their last visit. For these children and their parents visiting day is a celebration. In the pages of books, children want to find children just like themselves with similar problems and concerns. For some children this book enables them to see themselves and their parents and grandparents.

BOOK AND MEDIA CHOICES

Woodson, Jacqueline. *Visiting Day*. Illustrated by James E. Ransome. New York: Scholastic Press, 2002. 30p.
Grades: 1–8. A young girl wakes up to her grandmother frying chicken in preparation for a long bus ride. She thinks about seeing her daddy later in the day. The bus takes them to a big stone and concrete building where her father is serving time in prison. Their visit is happy and joyful as they share recollections of their days since their last monthly visit. The colorful paintings inspire belief and warmth. The book concludes with an author's note and an illustrator's note.

EXPLORATIONS

1. Before reading *Visiting Day* (Woodson, 2002), ask the students about what they do when they go to visit someone. Read the book aloud and then let the students direct the discussion that follows. This book may also just be a book on your shelf that you know is there for when you realize a child can relate to the story.

2. After reading *Visiting Day* (Woodson, 2002), share the last two sentences on the dust jacket with the students: "Love knows no boundaries. Here is a strong family that understands the meaning of unconditional love." Write the words "unconditional love" on the board and ask the students what the words mean to them. Then, have them discuss the unconditional love exhibited by the characters in the book.

REFERENCES

Erlbach, Arlene. 1997. *Happy Birthday, Everywhere!* Brookfield, Conn.: The Millbrook Press.

Franklin, Mary R., Patricia B. Roach, and Juanita K. Snyder. 1993. "Beyond Feathers and Tomahawks: Lessons from Literature." *Social Studies and the Young Learner* 6, no.2 (November/December): 13–17.

Goldin, Barbara Diamond. 1995. *Bat Mitzvah: A Jewish Girl's Coming of Age*. New York: Viking.

Henderson, Helene, and Sue E. Thompson. 2002. *Holidays, Festivals, and Celebrations of the World Dictionary*, 3rd ed. Detroit, Mich.: Omnigraphics.

Inspiration Ver. 7.0. Inspiration Software, Inc., Portland, Ore.

King, Elizabeth. 1998. *Quinceañera: Celebrating Fifteen*. New York: Dutton Children's Books.

Lankford, Mary D. 1994. *Quinceañera: A Latina's Journey to Womanhood*. Brookfield, Conn.: The Millbrook Press.

Menard, Valerie. 2000. *The Latino Holiday Book: From Cinco de Mayo to Dia de los Muertos—The Celebrations and Traditions of Hispanic Americans*. New York: Marlowe.

Reese, Debbie. 1996. "Teaching Young Children about Native Americans." *ERIC Digest*, ED394744.

Scharfstein, Sol. 1999. *Understanding Jewish Holidays and Customs: Historical and Contemporary*. Hoboken, N.J.: KTAV Publishing House.

Author Index

Adler, David, 46, 178, 225, 406

Ahlberg, Allan, 53, 205

Ahlberg, Janet, 53, 205

Ahsan, M. M., 101, 107, 190, 191

Alden, Laura, 43, 336, 338

Alexander, Sue, 32, 189, 190

Aliki, 328, 331

Allen, Judy, ed., 295, 298

Amado, Elisa, 27, 100, 107, 148, 150

Ammon, Richard, 205

Ancona, George, 33, 35, 56, 64, 75, 78, 89, 252, 253, 273, 392, 408, 412

Andersen, Hans Christian, 42, 285, 289–291

Anderson, Douglas Eric, 346, 348

Anderson, Janet S., 10, 35, 72, 86, 411

Anderson, Laurie Halse, 10, 35, 164, 169, 196, 217

Andrade, Mary J., 147, 149, 150, 170

Anno, Mitsumasa, 289

Antle, Nancy, 82, 155, 157

Arnosky, Jim, 295, 298

Asch, Frank, 47, 293,

Ashworth, Leon, 80, 89, 152, 153

Auch, Mary Jane, 260, 264

Baker, Liza, 43, 310, 313

Barba, Roberta H., xvii, xx

Barkin, Carol, 93, 107, 137, 144, 150, 153, 161, 170, 212, 217, 219, 229, 231, 242, 248, 299, 302, 310, 319

Barner, Bob, 383, 387

Barrett, Anna Pearl, 344

Barrett, Judi, 138, 141, 344

Barta, James J., xviii, xix

Barth, Edna, 8, 10, 11, 14–16, 69, 70, 71, 82–85, 141, 166, 209, 240, 242, 263, 265, 273, 280

Bartoletti, Susan Campbell, 115,

Bateman, Teresa, 72, 87, 155, 170, 352, 354

Bauer, Marion Dane, 43, 120, 129, 310, 313, 329, 331

Baylor, Bryd, 401, 402

Beeler, Selby B., 36, 421, 422

Bennet, Kelly, 17, 48, 299

Berger, Gilda, 65, 76, 89, 394

Berlin, Irving, 15, 47, 259, 264, 350, 354

Bernhard, Emery, 376

Bial, Raymond, 82, 166

Bierhorst, John, 69, 202, 203

Birdseye, Tom, 25, 355

Blake, Sally S., 111, 129

Blue, Rose, 394

Blumberg, Rhoda, 369, 370

Bohannon, Lisa Frederiksen, 21, 370

Bourgeois, Paulette, 36, 419

Branch, Muriel Miller, 58, 343, 345

Bredeson, Carmen, 7, 46, 112

Brown, Marc, 287

Brown, Tricia, 184

Browne, Anthony, 289

Bruchac, Margaret, 10, 68, 166, 169, 170

Bryant, Barry, 291, 292

Buck, Pearl S., 208, 212

Bulla, Robert Clyde, 14, 48, 236, 239, 241, 242, 248, 299, 301

Bunting, Eve, 19, 31, 40, 51, 56, 66, 139, 142, 143, 162, 178, 181, 205, 211, 330–332, 337, 338

Burghardt, Linda, 95, 99, 107, 175, 191, 266, 273, 323, 324, 332, 324, 396

Burroway, Janet, 151

Calhoun, Mary, 201, 202

Capucilli, Alyssa Satin, 236

Carlson, Lori Marie, 28, 39, 51, 118, 120, 222, 223–225, 229

Carlson, Nancy L., 7, 51, 118, 120

Carr, Jan, 42, 236

Carrier, Roch, 53, 69, 221, 222

Carus, Louise, ed., 194

Catrow, David, 61, 351, 354

Cazet, Denys, 55, 140, 237
Chambers, Catherine, 70, 146, 253, 257
Chandler, Clare, 377
Chandler, Gary, 17, 71, 86, 296
Chandler, Joel Harris, 128
The Children's Museum, Boston, 63, 74, 77, 88, 105–107, 389, 390
Chinn, Karen, 52, 185, 187
Chorao, Kay, 201
Christina, Maria Urrutia, 58, 305, 307
Ciavonne, Jean, 28, 198, 199
Claro, Nicole, 128,
Cleary, Beverly, 312, 314
Clements, Andrew, 19, 43, 336, 338, 339
Coerr, Eleanor, 26, 64, 74, 78, 88, 364
Coffin, Tristram Potter, ed., 367, 372
Cohen, Barbara, 68, 165
Cohen, Hennig, ed., 367, 372
Cohn, Janice, 31, 66, 76, 79, 179, 181
Coil, Suzanne M., 252, 274
Cole, Babette, 237, 240
Collier, Christopher, 126
Collier, James Lincoln, 126
Collins, David R., 113, 115
Colvin, Carolyn, xvii, xx
Compestine, Ying Chang, 110, 177, 184, 185, 187, 191
Compton, Anita, 36, 426, 427
Cooper, Ilene, 65, 69, 76, 79, 84, 89, 95, 96, 107, 395
Corey, Shana, 21, 164, 368, 370
Corwin, Judith Hoffman, 377
Cotton, Jacqueline S., 9, 47, 154, 156
Cowley, Joy, 40, 161
Cox, Judy, 36, 423
Craven, Jerry, 405, 406
Creaser, Barbara, xv, xvii, xix
Crews, Donald, 408, 409
Cristina, Maria, 29, 58, 305, 307
Dalgliesh, Alice, 352
Dau, Elizabeth, xv, xvii, xix
Davies, Valentine, 209
de Atiles, Julia Reguero, xi, xiv
De Capua, Sarah, 124
de Groat, Diane, 14, 34, 162, 237, 404
de Paola, Tomie, 16, 27, 28, 45, 195, 196, 198, 199, 209, 217, 223, 278, 367, 385, 387
Demi, 23, 24, 50, 63, 110, 111, 186, 188, 291, 292
Denise, Christopher, 287, 288
Dever, Martha T., xviii, xix
Diamond, Barbara J., xiv, xv, xvii, xx
Dickens, Charles, 11, 83, 209
Dickinson, Terence, 355, 356, 361
Dimidjian, Victoria Jean, xv, xvi, xx
Dr. Seuss, 11, 35, 41, 204, 211, 405, 410

Donnelly, Judy, 164
Dorris, Michael, 166
Dorros, Arthur, 252
Dues, Greg, 145, 170
Duncan, Lois, 408, 409
Dunlop, Eileen, 85, 280, 283
Erlbach, Arlene, 31, 34, 66, 76, 179, 207, 211, 376, 377, 379–382, 403, 406,407, 428
Erlbach, Herb, 377
Erricker, Clive, 291, 302, 389
Erricker, Jane, 291, 302, 389
Farndon, John, 111
Farris, Christine King, 13, 59, 78, 226,
Feinberg, Barbara Silberdick, 363, 364, 372
Ferry, Joseph, 341, 342
Fishman, Cathy Goldberg, 30, 32, 50, 65, 97, 266, 267
Flanagan, Alice K., 8, 14, 161, 170, 179, 236, 238, 248
Foster, Genevieve, 85, 245, 247
Foster, Joanna, 85, 245, 247
Fox, Paula, 289
Fradin, Dennis Brindell, 11, 69, 207, 235, 243, 248
Franklin, Mary R., 412, 428
Freedman, Russell, 114, 244, 246
Freeman, Don, 231, 233,
Freeman, Dorothy Rhodes, 214, 279
French, Fiona, 18, 43, 54, 201, 256, 257, 310, 313
French, Vivian, 310
Friedrich, Otto, 261, 264
Friedrich, Priscilla, 261, 264
Fritz, Jean, 21, 124, 369
Furgang, Kathy, 45, 424, 426
Gaeddert, Louann, 86, 317, 319
Gaines, Ann Graham, 243, 245
Gallagher, Carole S., 8, 132
Gardeski, Christina Mia, 8, 22, 94, 95, 131–133, 144
Gardner, Robert, 17, 86, 296,
Gay, Kathlyn, 82, 155
Gay, Martin, 82, 155
Geisel, Theodor S., 11, 35, 41, 204, 211, 405, 410
Gelb, Steven A., 193, 218
Gellman, Ellie, 30, 100
George, Lindsay Barrett, 57, 418
Gerace, Frank E., 109, 129, 193, 218, 303, 319, 379
Ghazi, Suhaib Hamid, 22, 39, 50, 101, 103
Gibala–Broxholm, Scott, 40, 138, 141
Gibbons, Faye, 424, 426
Gibbons, Gail, 16, 42, 47, 51, 54, 58, 139, 256, 259, 261, 278, 293, 297
Giblin, James Cross, 20, 243, 246, 352
Gilchrist, Cherry, 67, 81, 376
Glassman, Peter, 55, 311, 314
Gliori, Debi, 328, 331

Gnojewski, Carol, 13, 29, 59, 65, 70, 75, 226, 305–307, 319

Goldin, Barbara Diamond, 30, 32–34, 80, 100, 266, 267, 271, 272, 324, 402, 403, 428

Gore, Willma Willis, 351

Goring, Ruth, 195, 218, 305, 319

Goss, Clay, 12, 69, 84, 215

Goss, Linda, 12, 69, 84, 215

Goudvis, Anne, 115, 129

Gourley, Catherine, 7, 67, 81, 113, 116

Grace, Catherine O'Neil, 10, 68, 166, 169, 170

Graham, Kevin, 17, 71, 86, 296

Grambling, Lois G., 420

Grant, R. G., 78, 88, 365, 366

Green, Carl R., 359, 361

Greene, Carol, 35, 44, 51, 138, 142, 408, 409

Greene, Rhonda Gowler, 35, 44, 408, 409

Greenfield, Eloise, 263, 264

Grier, Ella, 12, 45, 213, 216,

Griest, Lisa, 263, 265

Grimes, Nikki, 53, 204, 211

Gross, Clay, 69, 394

Gross, Judith, 69, 394

Gulevich, Tanya, 396

Guy, John, 152

Hague, Michael, comp., 15, 263, 263

Hall, Diane, 63, 74, 104, 107, 131, 144, 182, 191, 173, 274, 388, 389, 391

Hamanaka, Sheila, comp., 26, 365, 366

Hamilton, Martha, 287, 288

Hamilton, Virginia, 289

Harlin, 346, 348

Harness, Cheryl, 51, 162, 167, 208, 244, 246

Harris, Zoe, 64, 75, 78, 195, 218, 392

Harvey, Stephanie, 115, 129, 136, 144

Haskins, Jim, 71, 86, 317, 318

Haynes, Charles C., xvii, xx

Henderson, Helene, ed., 104, 107, 112, 123, 129, 134, 144, 194, 196, 218, 231, 248, 283, 284, 286, 291, 302, 310, 319, 324–326, 328, 333, 366, 372, 397, 411, 428

Henkes, Kevin, 42, 258,

Herman, John, 19, 340

Hest, Amy, 154, 156

Hildebrandt, Ziporah, 42, 268, 271

Hiller, Peter, 343, 348

Hines, Anna Grossnickle, 424

Hintz, Kate, 213, 214, 218

Hintz, Martin, 213, 214, 218

Hodges, Margaret, 202, 203

Hoffman, Ernest Theodor Amadeus, 206

Hoffman, Mary, 330

Hogrogian, Nonny, 200

Hopkins, Lee Bennett, selector, 56, 404

Hopkinson, Deborah, 148, 170, 212, 218, 330, 332

Hoyt-Goldsmith, Diane, 7, 22–24, 27, 28, 31, 32, 34, 35, 62–64, 66, 73, 74, 77–80, 88, 101–103, 107, 113, 115, 119, 121, 148, 180, 182–184, 187, 191, 199, 213, 215, 218, 221, 229, 253, 270, 272, 274, 327, 333, 413–415

Hubbell, Patricia, 38, 49, 384

Hurwitz, Johanna, 330, 332, 406, 407

Hutchins, Pat, 328, 331

Isler, Claudia, 125, 127

Jackson, Alison, 42, 237

Jackson, Garnet, 163

James, Elizabeth, 93, 107, 137, 144, 150, 153, 170, 212, 217, 219, 229, 231, 242, 248, 299, 302 310, 319

James, Helen Foster, 342, 348

Jay, Betsy, 36, 57, 420, 422

Johnson, Angela, 424, 426

Johnson, Mildred, 226

Johnston, Tony, 27, 147, 149, 170

Jones, Amy Robin, 69, 215

Jones, Diana Wynne, 140, 143

Jones, Lynda, 378

Joosse, Barbara M., 35, 57, 147, 150, 212, 218, 332, 333, 418

Kadodwala, Dilip, 22, 24, 54, 64, 74, 93, 94, 95, 107, 273

Kalman, Bobbie, 33, 62, 412

Kamma, Anne, 10, 68, 165, 169

Karenga, Maulana, 12, 84, 213, 215

Kellogg, Steven, 300, 301

Kelly, Sheila, 7, 39, 118, 120

Kerven, Rosalind, 23, 104, 105

Kessler, Christina, 119, 121

Kimball, Stanley B., 360

Kimmel, Eric A., 31, 50, 52, 95, 97, 99, 107, 177, 261

Kimmelman, Leslie, 30, 38, 51, 96, 98, 162, 167, 269, 394

Kindersley, Anabel, 196, 218, 256, 273, 274, 276, 284, 307, 319, 378

Kindersley, Barnabas, 378

King, Elizabeth, 35, 414, 415, 428

King, Martin Luther, Jr., 226, 228

Kitada, Shin, 25, 64, 355, 356

Klayman, Michael, 65, 76, 394

Klee, Sheila, 125, 127

Knight, Hal, 44, 360

Knight, Margy Burns, 34, 44, 403

Knowlton, Laurie, 53, 200

Koscielniak, Bruce, 14, 232, 233

Koss, Amy Goldman, 79, 180, 181

Koutsky, Jan Dale, 7, 51, 119, 121

Kramer, Barbara, 135, 136

Krasno, Rena, 63, 74, 77, 88, 276, 284, 309, 319, 389

Kreitler, Peter Gwilliam, 341, 343

Krensky, Stephen, 329
Krishnaswami, Uma, 24, 42, 273
Kroll, Steven, 25, 43, 232, 234, 260, 264, 304, 339, 342
Kroll, Virginia, 309
Krull, Kathleen, 148
Kuhn, Betsy, 18, 70, 86, 317, 318
Lakin, Patricia, 35, 44, 51, 163, 167, 417
Landau, Elaine, 8, 9, 10, 14, 16, 20, 60, 68, 71, 72, 132, 133, 154, 160, 164, 170, 239, 242, 252, 277, 279, 284, 292, 296, 302, 351
Lankford, Mary D., 34, 56, 378, 382, 405, 414, 415, 428
Lasky, Kathryn, 149, 150
Leebrick, Kristal, 125,
Leslie, Clare Walker, 109, 129, 193, 218, 303, 319, 335, 348, 379
Leuck, Laura, 18, 55, 311
Levin, Pamela, 73, 87, 369
Levine, Abby, 14, 232, 234
Lewin, Ted, 35, 56, 409
Lin, Grace, 23, 39, 110, 111, 129
Liptak, Karen, 412
Livingston, Myra Cohn, xiii, 76, 383, 405
Look, Lenore, 404
Lord, John Vernon, 151
Luenn, Nancy, 217, 218, 378, 382
Lyles, Lois, 386, 387
Maass, Robert, 17, 294
Maccarone, Grace, 41, 200
Macdonald, Fiona, 308
MacDonald, Margaret Read, ed., 397
MacGill–Callahan, Sheila, 45, 278, 281, 282
MacMillan, Dianne M., 15, 22–24, 27, 52, 55, 60, 64, 65, 68, 70, 75, 93, 94, 102, 107, 122, 129, 165, 182, 186, 214, 243, 253, 275, 276, 284, 307, 309, 319, 326, 327
Maguire, Gregory, 239, 242
Maitland, Barbara, 238, 241
Mak, Kam, 388, 390
Manuel, Lynn, 148, 171, 207, 212, 332, 333
Manushkin, Fran, 32, 54, 66, 268, 270, 304
Marchant, Kerena, 23, 104, 105, 107
Markham, Marion M., 279, 282, 283, 287, 288
Marling, Karol Ann, 397
Marrin, Albert, 245
Maruki, Toshi, 365,
Marx, David F., 13, 22, 30, 38, 39, 41, 96, 98, 101, 220
Matthews, Mary, 50, 102, 103
McCaughrean, Geraldine, 118, 120
McClester, Cedric, 84, 216,
McCoy, Karen Kawamoto, 25, 326
McKeown, Margaret G., xix, xx
McKissack, Frederick L., 72, 87, 344, 345
McKissack, Patricia C., 72, 87, 344, 345

McLeod, Elaine, 61, 294
McMullan, Kate, 14, 233
Medearis, Angela Shelf, 214
Meinbach, Anita Meyer, 156, 171
Melmed, Laura Krauss, 139, 142
Meltzer, Milton, 8, 132
Melvern, Linda, 135, 136
Menard, Valerie, 89, 131, 134, 144, 252, 274, 305, 319, 392, 403, 414, 428
Merrick, Patrick, 15, 20, 61, 262, 350
Middleton, Charlotte, 420, 421
Milich, Melissa, 262,
Minarik, Else Holmelund, 16, 286
Moehn, Heather, xii, 95, 99, 101, 107, 112, 123, 129, 137, 145, 152, 171, 175, 191, 193, 194, 196, 198, 199, 203, 218, 255, 267, 274, 283, 284, 286, 302, 304, 310, 320, 323, 327, 333, 335, 338, 339, 356, 361, 379
Moline, Steve, 290, 301
Moore, Clement, 11, 41, 204, 211
Moore, Margaret A., xiv, xv, xvii, xx
Moorman, Margaret, 384
Mora, Pat, 18, 55, 60, 112, 115, 312, 314
Mulvihill, Margaret, 146
Murphy, Patricia J., 9, 46, 157, 383
Musa, Diana, xvi, xx
Musleah, Rahel, 65, 76, 394
Myers, Walter Dean, 70, 86, 312, 314
Nerlove, Miriam, 266, 267
Newman, Lesléa, 177, 191, 346, 347
NgGheong–Lum, Roseline, 357, 358
Nolan, Janet, 71, 280, 283
O' Connor, Jane, 36, 57, 421
Olson, Mary W., 57, 240, 421
Orozco, José–Luis, 64, 75, 391, 393
Osborne, Mary Pope, 165, 169, 331, 332
Owens, Mary Beth, 384
Palacios, Argentina, 29, 79, 306, 307
Pandell, Karen, 291, 292
Pang, Valerie Ooka, xvii, xx
Park, Barbara, 35, 55, 57, 238, 241, 410, 411
Parker, Toni Tent, 42, 259, 264
Pascoe, Elaine, 9, 68, 157–159, 171
Patterson, Katherine, 207, 289, 312
Penner, Lucille Recht, 67, 81, 225, 229, 315, 320, 386
Pennington, Daniel, 33, 62, 127–129
Peterson, Melissa, 197, 198
Pettit, Jayne, 84, 227, 228
Plain, Nancy, 80, 89, 358
Plourde, Lynn, 7, 35, 44, 51, 119, 120, 331, 333, 417, 418
Podwal, Mark, 177, 181
Polacco, Patricia, 18, 261, 262, 264, 316, 318, 405
Porter, A. P., 57, 213
Poydar, Nancy, 8, 14, 40, 138, 141, 238, 240

Presilla, Maricel E., 78, 89, 392, 393
Prince–Clarke, Heather, xvi, xx
Pushker, Gloria Teles, 98, 178, 269
Rael, Elsa Okon, 163, 168, 169
Ransom, Candice F., 316
Rappaport, Doreen, 13, 46, 225, 227, 228
Rattigan, Jama Kim, 13, 220, 221
Rau, Dana Meachen, 13, 14, 50, 53, 55, 96, 97, 99, 107, 220, 222, 238
Ray, Deborah Kogan, 60, 316
Reese, Debbie, 161, 171, 412, 428
Rex, Michael, 40, 137, 141
Ribak-Rosenthal, Nina, xvii, xx
Riehecky, Janet, 25, 307, 308
Riley, Linnea Asplind, 11, 41, 204, 210
Ringgold, Faith, 226
Roach, Patricia B., 412, 428
Robbins, Ken, 151
Roberts-Davis, Tanya, 67, 81, 114, 116
Robinson, Barbara, 11, 208
Robinson, Fay, 8, 24, 140, 142, 186
Rockwell, Anne, 46, 60, 112, 115, 237
Rollins, Charlemae Hill, 69, 83, 209, 212
Roop, Connie, 128
Rosen, Michael J., 31, 40, 176, 179, 181, 212, 218
Roth, Carol, 42, 236
Rothenberg, Joan, 269
Rothlein, Liz, 156, 171
Rotner, Shelley, 7, 39, 118, 120
Ruelle, Karen Gray, 16, 286
Russell, Ching Yeung, 23, 106
Russell, Todd T., xvii, xx
Ryan, Pam Muñoz, 19, 114, 117, 340, 342
Rylant, Cynthia, 206, 211, 401
Sachar, Louis, 59, 124, 126
St. George, Judith, 15, 244, 246
St. Pierre, Stephanie, 341, 342
Salisbury, Cynthia, 73, 87, 370
Salley, Coleen, 286, 288
Sanderson, Ruth, 146
Sandler, Martin W., 15, 70, 85, 244, 246, 316
Sanford, William R., 359, 361
Santino, Jack, 283, 284, 397
Scharfstein, Sol, 96, 99, 107, 175, 189, 191, 266, 274, 323, 333, 397, 402, 228
Schecter, Ellen, 270
Schick, Eleanor, 36, 45, 415
Schmidt, Patricia R., xvi, xix, xx
Schoberle, Cecile, 236
Schomp, Virginia, 308
Schotter, Roni, 54, 269
Schwartz, Howard, 395
Scieszka, Jon, 165, 171, 331, 332
Selkowe, Valrie M., 44, 56, 404, 406
Sendak, Maurice, 289

Shannon, David, 206, 211
Shaw, Jean M., 111, 129
Shepard, Aaron, 194, 195
Shields, Carol Diggory, 39, 118
Sigerman, Harriet, 368, 372
Silverman, Erica, 52, 271, 274, 304
Silverman, Maida, 178
Simon, Charnan, 359, 360
Simon, Norma, 32, 66, 270
Simonds, Nina, 63, 74, 77, 88, 105–107, 389, 390
Singer, Alan, xv, xx
Singer, Judith Y., xv, xx
Sisulu, Elinor Batezat, 59, 60, 158, 159
Skrepcinski, Denice, 386, 387
Slate, Joseph, 28, 82, 155, 157, 223
Slovenz-Low, Madeline, 185
Smalls, Irene, 19, 43, 56, 336, 337, 339
Smalls-Hector, Irene, 311, 314
Snyder, Juanita K., 412, 428
Soto, Gary, 36, 425, 426
Spies, Karen, 67, 131, 144, 153, 161, 171, 184, 191, 242, 248, 292, 299, 302, 305, 315, 320, 385
Spinelli, Eileen, 295, 298, 336
Steele, Anitra T., xv, xx
Stein, R. Conrad, 134, 135, 144
Stepanchuk, Carol, 77, 88, 105, 107, 272, 274, 398
Steptoe, Javaka, 19, 72, 87, 338
Stevens, Kathryn, 357
Stevenson, James, 16, 239, 241, 262, 264, 286, 288
Stock, Melissa, 386, 387
Stoeke, Janet Morgan, 44, 408, 409
Stone, Tanya Lee, 40, 176
Streissguth, Tom, 357, 358
Sullivan, George, 244, 246
Summer, L. S., 70, 84, 227, 228
Swartz, Leslie, 63, 74, 77, 88, 105–107, 389, 390
Taylor, Barbara, xix, xx
Taylor, Charles, 72, 87, 345
Tazewell, Charles, 53, 201, 203
Thiesing, Lisa, 332, 333
Thompkins, Gail E., 254, 274
Thompson, Jan, 145, 171, 196, 199, 218, 255, 256, 274
Thompson, Lauren, 54, 257
Thompson, Sue Ellen, ed., 104, 107, 112, 123, 129, 134, 144, 194, 196, 218, 231, 248, 283, 284, 286, 291, 302, 310, 319, 324–326, 328, 333, 366, 372, 397, 398, 411, 428
Thornhill, Jan, 293
Tompert, Ann, 194, 279, 282, 283
Tran, MyLuong, xvii, xx
Tucker, Cathy C., 399
Tucker, Kathy, 58, 278
Tudor, Tasha, 385

Updike, John, 38, 49, 383, 387

Van Allsburg, Chris, 11, 53, 205, 294, 298

Vidrine, Beverly B., 254, 393, 399

Viesti, Joe, 63, 74, 104, 107, 131, 144, 182, 191, 173, 274, 388, 389, 391

Wade, Mary Dodson, 29, 45, 58, 305, 306

Wallace, Nancy Elizabeth, 17, 61, 294

Wallner, Alexandra, 340, 342

Walsh, Joseph J., 83, 210, 211

Walton, Rick, 329

Warrick, Karen Clemens, 17, 300–302

Waters, Kate, 185

Weatherford, Carole Boston, 344, 345

Weilerstein, Sadie Rose, 96, 98

Weiss, Mitch, 287, 288

Wells, Rosemary, 15, 259

Welsey, Valerie Wilson, 45, 58, 343, 345

Weninger, Brigitte, 262

West, Delno C., 352

West, Jean M., 352

West, Robin, 310, 320

Wiencirz, Gerlinde, 259

Wildsmith, Brian, 42, 256, 257, 367

Wilhelm, Hans, 419

Willhoite, Michael, 346, 347

Williams, Suzanne, 64, 75, 78, 195, 218, 392

Willner–Pardo, Gina, 425, 426

Winchester, Faith, 105, 107, 137, 144, 182, 191, 213, 218, 222, 224, 229, 272, 274, 291, 302, 385, 387, 388, 391

Winne, Joanne, 31, 40, 176

Wisniewski, David, 140

Withrow, Sarah, 346, 347

Wolkstein, Diane, 32, 266, 267

Wong, Charles, 272, 274, 398

Wong, Janet S., 20, 24, 41, 47, 184, 187, 350, 354

Wood, Douglas, 19, 56, 311, 314, 337, 338

Woodson, Jacqueline, 36, 427, 428

Yep, Laurence, 365

Yin, 206, 211

Yolen, Jane, 337, 376, 405

Yopp, Hallie Kay, 168, 171

Yopp, Ruth Helen, 168, 171

Young, Ed., 240

Zalben, Jane Breskin, 30, 32, 79, 96, 100, 137, 144, 180, 181, 189, 268, 286, 302, 336, 348, 386, 425, 426

Ziefert, Harriet, 13, 20, 40, 41, 55, 161, 176, 180, 220, 312, 314, 349, 353

Zolotow, Charlotte, 260

ILLUSTRATOR INDEX

Allen, Joy, 36, 57, 421

Andersen, Bethanne, 330

Anderson, Earl, 259

Andreasen, Dan, 339

Antram, David, 308

Apperley, Dawn, 40, 176

Arndt, Ursula, 8, 10, 11, 14, 15, 20, 69-71, 82-85, 141, 166, 209, 240, 263, 280, 352

Arnold, Tedd, 55, 311

August, Louise, 30, 100

Barragan M., Paula S., 18, 55, 312

Bassett, Jeri, 232,

Beier, Ellen, 316

Benioff, Carol, 207

Berelson, Howard, 29, 79, 306

Bernhard, Durga, 376

Binch, Caroline, 330

Bittinger, Ned, 32, 54, 268

Bloom, Lloyd, 178

Boddy, Joe, 96

Branch, Willis, 58, 343

Brett, Jan, 41, 204

Brewster, Patience, 304

Brimberg, Sisse, 10, 166

Brooker, Kyrsten, 177

Brown, Jane Clark, 207

Brown, Judith Gwyn, 208

Brown, Rick, 176

Brunkus, Denise, 35, 55, 57, 238, 410

Bryan, Ashley, 12, 69, 83, 84, 209, 215

Buchanan, Yvonne, 344

Buehner, Mark, 18, 55, 208, 311

Byard, Carole, 12, 69, 84, 215

Cann, Helen, 81, 376

Casilla, Robert, 46, 225

Catalanotto, Peter, 65, 76, 89, 394

Cepeda, Joe, 40, 161

Chau, Tungwai, 185

Chen, Ju-Hong, 25, 355

Chen, Yong, 262

Chodos-Irvine, Margaret, 47, 350

Choi, Yangsook, 41, 184

Clair, Donna, 28, 198

Clark, Brenda, 36, 419

Cocca-Leffler, Maryann, 164, 330

Cockroft, Jason, 7, 51, 119

Cole, Henry, 139

Collicott, Sharleen, 138

Collier, Bryan, 13, 46, 225

Colon, Raul, 60, 112, 201

Cooney, Barbara, 69, 202

Cooper, Floyd, 12, 69, 84, 215

Cooper, Martha, 185

Coulson, Cotton, 10, 166

Cote, Nancy, 14, 51, 162, 232

Craig, Helen, 260

Croll, Carolyn, 163

Cundiff, Meg, 408

Cushman, Doug, 19, 56, 311, 337

Cyrus, Kurt, 51, 139

Dacey, Bob, 32, 66, 270

Davalos, Felipe, 28, 223

de Groat, Diane, 40, 79, 162, 180

de Paola, Tomie, 124, 209

Degen, Bruce, 405

Diamond, Donna, 79, 180

Diaz, David, 205

Dieterichs, Shelley, 14, 238

Dillon, Diane, 12, 69, 84, 87, 215, 344

Dillon, Leo, 12, 69, 84, 87, 215, 344

DiSalvo-Ryan, DyAnne, 21, 36, 179, 369, 423

Dodson, Bert, 10, 165

Donohue, Dorothy, 42, 236

Dooling, Michael, 243

Doughty, Rebecca, 55, 312

Dowley, Coco, 401

Drudop, Walter Lyon, 119
Duffy, Danie Mark, 165
Dugan, Karen, 34, 56, 378, 405
Edelson, Wendy, 194
Eitan, Ora, 394
Elwell, Peter, 43, 310
Estrada, Pau, 287
Ewing, Carolyn S., 52, 178
Farnsworth, Bill, 31, 66, 76, 79, 179
Faulkner, Matt, 10, 164
Feldman, Lynne, 394
Ferrer, Ismael Espinosa, 78, 89, 392
Fisher, Leonard Everett, xiii, 383
Frazee, Marla, 304
Garcia, Stephanie, 36, 425
Garland, Michael, 194
Garns, Allen, 329
Gilchrist, Jan Spivey, 12, 69, 84, 215, 263
Goode, Diane, 206
Goodell, Jon, 31, 52, 177
Gore, Leonid, 32, 189
Graef, Renée, 206
Green, Jonathan, 12, 69, 84, 215
Hafner, Marylin, 269
Hahner, Chris, 286
Hairs, Joya, 27, 148
Hall, Melanie W., 30, 50, 65, 97, 266
Harris, Jennifer Beck, 42, 236
Hays, Michael, 43, 311, 336
Helquist, Brett, 164
Heo, 404
Herrera, Jesse, 415
Hierstein, Judith, 98, 178, 269
Hillenbrand, Will, 45, 278
Himmelman, John, 30, 38, 96, 269
Hines, Lewis, 114
Hohag, Linda, 43, 336
Holm, Sharon Lane, 17, 34, 86, 296, 376, 377, 406
Hsu-Flanders, Lillian, 13, 220
Hu, Ying-Hwa, 52, 185
Hyman, Trina Schart, 38, 49, 383
Iwai, Melissa, 31, 40, 176, 197, 336
James, John, 308
Jerome, Karen A., 279
Jessup, Harley, 45, 424
Karas, G. Brian, 36, 421
Kawasaki, Shauna Mooney, 30, 100
Kleven, Eliza, 64, 75, 391
Knight, Christopher, 56, 149
Knight, Hilary, 56, 404
Kovalski, Maryann, 163
Krenina, Katya, 261
Kubick, Dana, 18, 43, 310
Kubiak, Kasi, 200, 53
Kwas, Susan Estelle, 14, 239

Ladwig, Ted, 202
Lambert, Stephen, 118
LaRochelle, David, 238
Lewis, Earl B., 50, 102
Livney, Varda, 19, 43, 336
Lunelli, Giuliano, 259
Maione, Heather Harms, 330
Manson, Christopher, 352
Marcellino, Fred, 289
Martinez, Ed, 28, 223
Masiello, Raph, 19, 114, 340
McCue, Lisa, 15, 259
McGovern, Kevin, 19, 56, 337
McGrory, Anik, 33, 324
McLaren, Chesley, 21, 368
McPhail, David, 43, 310
Meddaugh, Susan, 19, 56, 337
Micich, Paul, 53, 201
Migdale, Lawrence, 7, 22–24, 27, 28, 31, 32, 34, 35, 62-64, 66, 73, 76-80, 88, 102, 113, 119, 148, 180, 183, 187, 199, 215, 253, 270, 413, 415
Miglio, Paige, 329
Miller, Edward, 262
Miller, Gustaf, 20, 47, 349
Minter, Daniel, 214
Mitani, Yukihiko, 25, 64, 355
Morgan, Mary, 369
Munsinger, Lynn, 47, 350
Murdocca, Sal, 165
Muth, Jon J., 50, 97
Nakata, Hiroe, 39, 118
Nash, Scott, 44, 417
Natti, Susanna, 329
Nelson, Kadir, 53, 204
Nidenoff, Michele, 378
Nonnast, Marie, 352
Noyce, Robert R., 360
O'Brien, Anne Sibley, 34, 44, 403
O'Brien, John, 87, 352
Ohlsson, Ib, 67, 81, 386
Ortiz, Fran, 184
Osborne, Mitchel, 252
Osiecki, Lori, 36, 57, 420
Parnall, Peter, 402
Passicot, Monique, 395
Patrick, Pamela, 205
Payne, Thomas, 420
Pelletier, Gilles, 53, 69, 221
Pinkney, Jerry, 12, 69, 84, 215, 289
Plecas, Jennifer, 35, 57, 418
Popp, K. Wendy, 31, 66, 178
Porter, Janice Lee, 57, 213
Potter, Giselle, 147
Raglin, Tim, 51, 138
Rand, Ted, 424

Ransome, James E., 36, 427
Rayyan, Omar, 22, 39, 50, 101
Rockwell, Lizzy, 46, 60, 112
Roop, Peter, 128
Roraback, Robin, 19, 42, 268, 340
Rotner, Shelley, 39, 118
Roundtree, Katherine, 25, 43, 309
Saaf, Donald, 261
Sanchez, Enrique O., 148
Sandford, John, 44, 56, 58, 278, 404
Savadier, Elivia, 65, 76, 79, 89, 395
Schindler, S.D., 13, 41, 220
Schoenherr, John, 337
Schories, Pat, 236
Schuett, Stacey, 48, 51, 163, 299
Schumacher, Claire, 40, 161
Selznick, Brian, 338
Sharratt, Nick, 425
Shine, Andrea, 263
Small, David, 15, 244
Smith, Lane, 331
Smith, Mavis, 14, 233
So, Meilo, 63, 74, 77, 88, 389
Soentpiet, Chris, 13, 59, 206, 226
Soman, David, 424
Soper, Patrick, 254
Souza, Diana, 346
Stahl, Ben F., 71, 280
Stasiak, Krystyna, 25, 306
Stavros-Lanning, Mary Ann, 396
Stevens, Janet, 260, 286
Stewart, Don, 33, 62, 127
Sugita, Toru, 63, 74, 77, 88, 389

Takahashi, Hideko, 35, 44, 417
Taylor, John B., 291
Tharlet, Eve, 262
Thompson, John, 376
Tiegreen, Alan, 312
Tillotson, Katherine, 57, 420
Tong, Zhan, 388
Tusa, Tricia, 42, 237,
Uyehara, Elizabeth, 54, 257
Van Wright, Cornelius, 52, 185
Viesti, Joe, 63, 74, 388, 389, 391
Waldman, Neil, 32, 80, 270, 271
Ward, John, 45, 213
Warnick, Elsa, 295
Watson, Wendy, 38, 49, 384
Weihs, Erika, 32–34, 66, 266, 270, 402
Weissman, Bari, 394
Wijngaard, Juan, 32, 266
Williams, Sam, 41, 200,
Wilson, Sharon, 45, 58-60, 158, 343
Winter, Jeanette, 27, 147
Wolff, Jason, 35, 44, 408
Woo, Yolanda Garfias, 64, 75, 78, 392
Wood, Colleen, 61, 294
Wummer, Amy, 59, 124
Xuan, Sheng Yong, 110
Yao, Carolina, 25, 326
Yayo, 386
Young, Ed, 26, 76, 364
Young, May O'Keefe, 65, 394
Zhang, Christopher Zhong-Yuan, 106
Zwerger, Lisbeth, 11, 83, 209

TITLE INDEX

Abe Lincoln Goes to Washington, 1837–1865, 244, 246

Abraham Lincoln, 244, 246

African–American Holidays, 144, 218, 385-387

All Around the Year: Holidays and Celebrations in American Life, 284, 397

All Saints, All Souls, and Halloween, 146

Amanda Dade's New Years Parade, 13, 41, 220

The Amazing Christmas Extravaganza, 206, 211

America! A Celebration of Freedom from Our Nation's Finest, 19, 340

The American Flag, 341, 342

American Prophet, 360

An Amish Christmas, 205

The Ancient Celtic Festivals and How We Celebrate Them Today, 129, 218, 319, 348, 379

Angel to Angel: A Mother's Gift of Love, 71, 86, 312, 314

Angels of Mercy: The Army Nurses of World War II, 18, 71, 86, 317, 318

Anthology for the Earth, 295, 298

Apple Pie 4th of July, 20, 47, 350, 354

April Fool!, 286

The April Fool's Day Mystery, 287, 288

April Fools!, 16, 286

Arbor Day, 17, 48, 61, 299, 300

Arthur's April Fool, 287

Asian Holidays, 107, 191, 274, 388

The Baker's Dozen: A St. Nicholas Tale, 194, 195

The Ballad of Valentine, 42, 237

Barrilete: A Kite for Day of the Dead, 27, 100, 107, 148, 150

Bat Mitzvah: A Jewish Girl's Coming of Age, 33, 34, 402, 403, 428

Be Blest: A Celebration of Season, 384

Before and After: A Book of Nature Timescapes, 293

Behold the Trees, 32, 189, 190

Beni's First Wedding, 425, 426

The Best Christmas Pageant Ever, 11, 208,

Bethlehem: With Words from the Authorized Version of the King James Bible, 201

Betsy Ross, 340, 342

The Big Bunny and the Easter Eggs, 260, 264

Big Pig Saves Valentine's Day, 236

The Birds' Gift: A Ukrainian Easter Story, 261

Birthday Party Singalongs, 34, 44, 56, 403

Birthday Surprises: Ten Great Stories to Unwrap, 406, 407

Birthdays around the World, 34, 56, 405

Biscuit's Valentine's Day, 236

Black, Blue & Gray: African Americans in the Civil War, 71, 86, 317, 318

Bloomers!, 369

Bluebird Summer, 148, 170, 212, 218, 330, 332

Bon Odori Dancer, 25, 326

The Bones of Fred McFee, 51, 139, 142, 143

The Bookstore Valentine, 238, 241

Box Girl, 347, 348

Brigham Young: Mormon and Pioneer, 359, 360

Brigham Young: Pioneer and Mormon Leader, 359, 361

Brooms Are For Flying!, 40, 137, 141

Buddha, 24, 291, 292

Buddhist Festivals, 389

Buffalo Days, 34, 62, 73, 413, 414

Bunnies on the Go: Getting from Place to Place, 329

The Bunny Who Found Easter, 260

By the Dawn's Early Light: The Story of the Star-Spangled Banner, 339, 342

Cakes and Miracles: A Purim Tale, 266, 267

A Calendar of Festivals, 67, 81, 376

Career Day, 46, 60, 112, 115

Carlos, Light the Farolito, 28, 198, 199

Carnaval, 253, 273

Carnival, 253

A Carp for Kimiko, 25, 43, 309

Catholic Customs and Traditions, 170

Celebrate 2, 384

Celebrate! In Central America, 144, 391

Celebrate! In South Asia, 63, 74, 107, 191, 274, 388

Celebrate! In Southeast Asia, 63, 74, 389

Celebrate! Stories of the Jewish Holidays, 65, 76, 89, 394

Celebrate: A Book of Jewish Holidays, 394

Celebrating a Quinceañera: A Latina's15th Birthday Celebration, 35, 415

Celebrating Chinese New Year, 24, 187, 191

Celebrating Earth Day: A Sourcebook of Activities and Experiments, 17, 86, 296

Celebrating Hanukkah, 31, 66, 76, 79, 180

Celebrating Kwanzaa, 215, 218

Celebrating Passover, 32, 66, 76, 80, 270, 272, 274

Celebrating Ramadan, 22, 63, 74, 77, 102, 103, 107, 221, 229

Celebrating the Green: The History of St. Patrick's Day, 16, 85, 280

Celebrating the Powwow, 33, 62, 412

Celebration: The Story of American Holidays, 67, 81, 320, 386

Celebrations, 218, 274, 284, 319, 383, 405, 406

Celebrations of Light: A Year of Holidays around the World, 217, 218, 378, 382

Chanukah at Home, 177

Chanukah Lights Everywhere, 31, 40, 176, 181

The Cherokee Indians, 128

Chicken Sunday, 262, 264

A Child Was Born: A First Nativity Book, 41, 200

A Child's Calendar, 38, 383, 387

A Child's Hanukkah, 31, 49, 52, 177

Children Just Like Me–Celebrations, 378

Chinese New Year, 24, 52, 184, 186, 187

Chinese New Year: A Time for Parades, Family, and Friends, 24, 186

Chinese Shadow Puppet Theater, 23, 106

Christian Festivals, 171, 218, 274

Christmas, 11, 69, 207

Christmas around the World, 376, 378, 379, 382

A Christmas Carol, 11, 83, 209

Christmas Day in the Morning, 208, 212

Christmas Gif': An Anthology of Christmas Poems, Songs, and Stories Written By and About African Americans, 69, 83, 209, 212

Christmas in the Country, 206, 211

The Christmas Menorahs: How a Town Fought Hate, 31, 66, 76, 79, 179, 181

The Christmas Story, 201

The Christmas Thingamajig, 148, 171, 207, 212, 332, 333

Christmas Unwrapped: The History of Christmas, 11, 83, 209, 211

Christmas Worldwide: A Guide to Customs and Traditions, 399

Christmas: Celebrating Life, Giving, and Kindness, 207, 211

Christopher Columbus and the Discovery of the New World, 132

Cinco de Mayo, 29, 45, 58, 65, 305-307

Cinco de Mayo: Celebrating Hispanic Pride, 29, 65, 75, 306, 319

Cinco de Mayo: Yesterday and Today, 29, 305, 307

Circus Magic, 35, 44, 407

Civil War, 316

Columbus and the World around Him, 8, 132

Columbus Day, 8, 132, 133, 144

Columbus Day: Celebrating a Famous Explorer, 8, 132, 133

Come Celebrate with Me: Native American Powwow, 33, 73, 413

Come Celebrate with Me: Obon – Japanese Festival of Spirits, 25, 326

The Constitution, 126,

Creating the Constitution, 1787, 126

Crossing the Tressle, 82, 155, 157

Crunch, Smash, Trash!: Monster Machines that Recycle, 17, 61, 294, 297

D is for Dreidel: A Hanukkah Alphabet Book, 40, 176

Daddy's Roommate, 346, 347

Dance, Sing, Remember: A Celebration of Jewish Holidays, 394

The Day Gogo Went to Vote, 59, 60, 158, 159

Day of the Dead, 27, 147, 149, 170

Day of the Dead: A Mexican American Celebration, 27, 148, 333

The Day the Rabbi Disappeared: Jewish Holiday Tales of Magic, 395

Days of the Dead, 149, 150

Days of Jubilee: The End of Slavery in the United States, 72, 87, 344, 345

Dear Santa, Please Come to the 19th Floor, 206, 211

Dear Tooth Fairy, 36, 57, 421

December, 205, 211

Divali, 22, 94, 95, 107

Diwali, 22, 94, 95

DJ's Choice: Easter Bunny's Favorite Songs, 15, 41, 54, 260

Dumpling Soup, 13, 220, 221

The Earth and I, 47, 293

Earth Day: Keeping Our Planet Clean, 71, 296

Easter, 42, 54, 70, 256, 257, 259, 261

Easter Bunnies, 15, 262

The Easter Bunny That Overslept, 261, 264

The Easter Egg Farm, 260, 264

Easter Parade, 15, 259, 263, 264

The Easter Story, 42, 256, 257

Easter: with Words from the King James Bible, 54, 256, 257

Election Day, 9, 46, 59, 60, 158, 159

Elizabeth Cady Stanton: Leader of the Fight for Women's Rights, 73, 87, 370

Elizabeth Cady Stanton: The Right is Ours, 372

Encyclopedia of Christmas, 396

Encyclopedia of Easter, Carnival and Lent, 396

The Environment, 296

Environmental Songs for Kids, 17, 61, 293

Epossumondas, 286, 288

Equality: A History of the Women's Movement in America, 21, 368

Esperanza Rising, 114, 117

Esther's Story, 32, 266, 267

Failure is Impossible: The Story of Susan B. Anthony, 21, 370

Fair, 56, 409

The Family Haggadah, 270

Farmworker's Friend: The Story of Cesar Chavez, 113, 115

Fat Chance Thanksgiving, 51, 163, 167

Father's Day, 43, 336, 337

Father's Day Blues: What Do You Do about Father's Day When All You Have are Mothers?, 19, 56, 337

Feliz Nochebuena, Feliz Navidad: Christmas Feasts of the Hispanic Caribbean, 78, 89, 392, 393

Festival of Lights: The Story of Hanukkah, 52, 178

Festivals, xiii

Field Trips: Bug Hunting, Animal Tracking, Bird-Watching, and Shore Walking with Jim Arnosky, 295, 298

Fiesta Fireworks, 35, 56, 408

The Fiestas, 64, 75, 78, 89, 392

Fiestas: A Year of Latin American Songs of Celebration, 64, 75, 391, 393

Fireworks, Picnics, and Flags: The Story of the Fourth of July Symbols, 20, 352

First Christmas Record for Children, 11, 41, 53, 204

The First Christmas, 200-203

The First Noel: A Child's Book of Christmas Carols to Play and Sing, 200

The First Thanksgiving, 163

The Flag We Love, 19, 340, 342

Flight, 111

Floating Lanterns and Golden Shrines: Celebrating Japanese Festivals, 63, 74, 77, 88, 284, 319, 389

Flower Girl, 45, 424, 426

Fluffy Meets the Groundhog, 14, 233, 235

The Folklore of American Holidays, 372

The Folklore of World Holidays, 397

The Fool of the World and the Flying Ship, 287

Four Stupid Cupids, 239, 242

Fourth of July Fireworks, 20, 350

The Fourth of July Story, 352

France, 274, 299, 357, 358, 361

Franklin and the Tooth Fairy, 36, 419

Freedom's Gifts: A Juneteenth Story, 45, 58, 343, 345

Friends and Enemies, 86, 317, 319

Fright Night Flight, 139, 142

Garbage, 17, 47, 86, 293, 294, 297, 298

Geoffrey Groundhog Predicts the Weather, 14, 232, 233

George Washington and the Founding of a Nation, 245

George Washington: A Picture Book Biography, 243, 246

George Washington: Our First President, 243, 245

George Washington's World, 85, 245, 247

Gershon's Monster: A Story for the Jewish New Year, 50, 97, 99

Ghost Wings, 147, 150, 212, 218, 332, 333

The Giant Jam Sandwich, 151

God Bless America, 47, 350, 354

Going through the Gate, 35, 72, 86, 411

Good Girl Work: Factories, Sweatshops, and How Women Changed Their Role in the American Workforce, 7, 67, 81, 113, 116

Good Yontif: A Picture Book of the Jewish Year, 394

The Graduation of Jake Moon, 410, 411

The Graph Club, 152, 170

Graph Master, 152, 170

Gracias, the Thanksgiving Turkey, 40, 161

The Great Big Especially Beautiful Easter Egg, 262, 264

The Great Gilly Hopkins, 312

Gregory's Shadow, 231, 233

Gretchen Groundhog, It's Your Day, 14, 232, 234

Groundhog Day, 232, 234

Guests, 166

Guy Fawkes, 80, 89, 152, 153

Halloween, 8, 139

Halloween Is. . ., 51, 139

Halloween Program Sourcebook, 398

Halloween Tales: Spooky Pack, 8, 141

Halloween: Costumes and Treats on All Hallow's Eve, 8, 140, 142

Halloweenies, 140

Hanna's Christmas, 197, 198

Hanukkah/Passover, 31, 52, 54, 66, 178, 270, 271

Hanukkah: Celebrating the Holiday of Lights, 31, 66, 76, 179

Happy Birthday, 44, 56, 404

Happy Birthday to Me!, 56, 404, 406

Happy Birthday to You, You Belong in a Zoo, 34, 404

Happy Birthday, Everywhere!, 34, 406, 407, 428

Happy Easter, Davy!, 262

Happy New Year!, 376

A Happy New Year's Day, 53, 69, 221, 222

Happy New Year!/Kung-his fa-ts'ai, 24, 186, 188

Happy New Year, Beni, 96

Happy New Year, Everywhere!, 376, 379, 380, 382

Happy Passover, Rosie, 268

Harvest Celebrations, 377

Harvest Festivals Around the World, 377

Hats Off for the Fourth of July!, 20, 47, 349, 353

The Haunted History of Halloween, 8, 141, 142

Hearts, Cupids, and Red Roses: The Story of the Valentine Symbols, 14, 70, 84, 240, 242

Heather Has Two Mommies, 346, 347

Henry's First-Moon Birthday, 404

Hiroshima, 365

Hiroshima and Nagasaki, 78, 88, 364, 365, 366, 372

Hiroshima No Pika, 365

Hispanic Holidays, 391

Hoang Anh: A Vietnamese-American Boy, 23, 64, 78, 88, 183, 191

Hoaxes and Deceptions, 288

Holi, 24, 42, 54, 64, 74, 273

The Holiday Handbook, 107, 144, 170, 217, 248, 319

Holiday Symbols, 398

Holidays and Celebrations, 218, 319

Holidays, Festivals, and Celebrations of the World Dictionary, 107, 129, 144, 218, 248, 284, 319, 333, 361, 372, 397,428

Holly, Reindeer, and Colored Lights: The Story of the Christmas Symbols, 11, 69, 83, 209

Home for the Holidays: The History of Thanksgiving, 10, 82, 167, 170

Hooray for Grandparents' Day, 7, 39, 51, 118, 120

Hooray! It's Passover, 269

How the Grinch Stole Christmas, 11, 41, 204, 211

How I Saved Hanukkah, 79, 180, 181

Hurray for Three Kings' Day, 28, 223, 224

HyperStudio, 121, 129

I Don't Want to Go to Camp, 330-332

I Have a Dream, 226, 228

I Lost My Tooth, 419

I Love You Because You're You, 43, 310, 313

I See What You Mean: Children at Work with Visual Information, 301

I'm In Charge of Celebrations, 402

Id-Ul-Fitr, 23, 104, 105, 107

If a Bus Could Talk: The Story of Rosa Parks, 226

If You Lived with the Cherokee, 128

If You Were At. . . the First Thanksgiving, 10, 68, 165, 169

In Daddy's Arms I Am Tall: African Americans Celebrating Fathers, 19, 72, 87, 338

Independence Day, 20, 61, 350, 351

Independence Day – Birthday of the United States, 20, 72, 351

Independence Day: As American as Apple Pie, 353

Independence Day: History of July 4th, 20, 353

Inspiration, 135, 144, 191, 218, 221, 229, 426, 428

Into the Circle: An Introduction to Native American Powwows, 33, 88, 413, 414

It's Ground Hog Day, 232, 234

It's Kwanzaa Time!, 12, 69, 84, 215

Itse Selu: Cherokee Harvest Festival, 33, 62, 127-129

Jamboree Day, 35, 44, 408, 409

Jane vs. the Tooth Fairy, 36, 57, 420, 422

The Janitor's Boy, 338, 339

Japan, 333

Japan in the Days of the Samurai, 308

Japanese Boys' Festival, 25, 307, 308

Japanese Children's Day and the Obon Festival, 24, 55, 276, 284, 309, 319, 326, 327

Jewish Holiday Traditions: Joyful Celebrations from Rosh Hashanah to Shavuot, 107, 191, 273, 332, 396

Jewish Holidays All Year Round: A Family Treasury, 65, 76, 79, 107, 395

The Jewish Holidays Video Guide, 89, 395, 396

John Chapman: The Legendary Johnny Appleseed, 17, 300-302

Johnny Appleseed, 300, 301

The Jolly Christmas Postman, 53, 205

Jonathan and His Mommy, 311, 314

Juneteenth Jamboree, 344, 345

Juneteenth: A Celebration of Freedom, 72, 87, 345

Juneteenth: Celebrating Freedom in Texas, 344

Juneteenth: Freedom Day, 58, 343, 345

Junie B. Jones and the Mushy Gushy Valentine, 55, 238, 241

Junie B. Jones is a Graduation Girl, 35, 57, 410, 411

Just a Dream, 294, 298

K'tonton's Yom Kippur Kitten, 96, 98

Kevin and His Daddy, 43, 336

Kids & the Environment, 17, 71, 295

Kids around the World Celebrate, 378

Kids at Work, 114

Kids on Strike, 115

Kite Flying, 39, 110, 129

Kites: Magic Wishes That Fly Up to the Sky, 23, 50, 63, 110

Kwanzaa, 12, 45, 57, 69, 213-215, 217

Kwanzaa for Young People (and Everyone Else!), 12, 57, 214

Kwanzaa: A Celebration of Family, Community, and Culture, 12, 84, 215

Kwanzaa: Everything You Always Wanted to Know But Didn't Know Where to Ask, 84, 216

Kwanzaa: Why We Celebrate It the Way We Do, 214, 218

Labor Day, 7, 46, 112

Labor Day: Celebrating the Work We Do, 7, 114, 117

The Lady of Guadalupe, 27, 195, 196, 217

Language Arts: Content and Teaching Strategies, 274

Las Posadas: A Hispanic Christmas Celebration, 28, 199

The Last Snake in Ireland: A Story about St. Patrick, 45, 278, 281, 282

The Latino Holiday Book: From Cinco de Mayo to Dia de los Muertos–the Celebrations and Traditions of Hispanic Americans, 89, 134, 144, 274, 319, 392, 428

Learning from the Dalai Lama: Secrets of the Wheel of Time, 291, 292

Legacies: Using Children's Literature in the Classroom, 171

The Legend of Old Befana, 28, 223

Legends of Ten Chinese Traditional Festivals, 388

Leo & Blossom's Sukkah, 30, 100

The Leprechaun in the Basement, 58, 278

Lessons from Mother Earth, 61, 294

Let's Get Ready for Hanukkah, 31, 40, 176

Light the Lights: A Story About Celebrating Hanukkah and Christmas, 384

Lilies, Rabbits, and Painted Eggs: The Story of the Easter Symbols, 15, 70, 85, 263, 265, 273

Lincoln: A Photobiography, 244, 246

Lion Dancer: Ernie Wan's Chinese New Year, 185

Lionel in the Summer, 329

Literature-Based Reading Activities, 171

The Little Match Girl, 289, 291

The Littlest Angel, 53, 201, 203

Lost at the White House: A 1909 Easter Story, 263, 265

Lost in the War, 82, 155, 157

Lots of Grandparents, 7, 39, 118, 120

Louis XVI, Marie-Antoinette and the French Revolution, 80, 89, 358

Love One Another: The Last Days of Jesus, 54, 257

Love to Moma: A Tribute to Mothers, 18, 55, 312, 314

Love You, Soldier, 154, 156

Lucky Pennies and Hot Chocolate, 39, 118

Madeleine Albright: First Woman Secretary of State, 135, 136

The Magic Menorah: A Modern Chanukah Tale, 79, 180, 181

Magid Fasts for Ramadan, 50, 102, 103

Make Me a Peanut Butter Sandwich (and a Glass of Milk), 151

The March on Washington, 70, 84, 227

Mardi Gras, 253

Mardi Gras!, 252, 274

A Mardi Gras Dictionary, 253, 393, 399

Mardi Gras in New Orleans, 253

Mardi Gras: A Cajun Country Celebration, 253

Mardi Gras: Parades, Costumes, and Parties, 252

Maria Molina and the Day of the Dead, 148

Marriage Customs, 36, 246, 427

Martin Luther King, Jr. Day, 13, 46, 59, 225

Martin Luther King, Jr., Day: Honoring a Man of Peace, 13, 59, 70, 226

Martin Luther King, Jr.: A Man with a Dream, 84, 227, 228

Martin Luther King, Jr.: The Man and the Dream, 13, 84, 227, 229

Martin's Big Words: the Life of Dr. Martin Luther King, Jr., 13, 46, 225

Marvin Redpost: Class President, 59, 124, 126

Marvin's Best Christmas Ever, 207

Mary, 367

Mary: The Mother of Jesus, 367

Mathematics for Young Children, 129

Matzah Ball Soup, 269, 271

The Matzah That Papa Brought Home, 32, 54, 268, 271

Max's Chocolate Chicken, 15, 259

Memorial Day/Veterans Day, 9, 18, 47, 60, 154, 156, 316, 318

The Menorah Story, 177, 181

Merry Christmas! Celebrating America's Greatest Holiday, 397

Merry Christmas! Everywhere, 377

Mexican Independence Day and Cinco de Mayo, 27, 65, 122, 129

Mexico's Day of the Dead, 27, 149, 150

Michael Hague's Family Easter Treasury, 15, 263

Microsoft PowerPoint, 121, 129

Migrant Worker: A Boy from the Rio Grande Valley, 7, 113, 115

Milly and the Macy's Parade, 164

Minerva Louise at the Fair, 44, 408, 409

Minnie and Moo Meet Frankenswine, 55, 140

Minnie and Moo Will You Be My Valentine?, 237, 238

Miracle on 34th Street, 209

Miriam's Cup: A Passover Story, 32, 66, 270

Miz Fannie Mae's Fine New Easter Hat, 262

Moon Festival, 23, 106

Moonbeams, Dumplings and Dragon Boats, 63, 74, 77, 88, 105-107, 389, 390

Mooncakes and Ghosts: Festivals of China, 107, 274, 398

The Mormons, 360

A Mountain of Blintzes, 33, 324

Mountain Wedding, 424, 426

Mouse's Birthday, 405

Mr. Bear's Vacation, 328, 331

Mud Flat April Fool, 16, 286, 288

Multicultural Literacy: Mirroring the Reality of the Classroom, xiv, xx

Multimedia Collections: United States Constitution, 125

Muslim Festivals, 107, 191

Molly's Pilgrim, 68, 165

My Brother Martin: A Sister Remembers Growing Up with the Rev. Dr. Martin Luther King, Jr., 13, 59, 226,

My Chinatown: One Year in Poems, 388, 390

My Daddy Was a Soldier: A World War II Story, 60, 316

My First Passover Board Book, 42, 268

My Grandfather's Clock, 118, 120

My Great-Grandmother's Gourd, 119, 121

My Little Valentine, 42, 236

My Monster Mama Loves Me So, 18, 55, 311

My Mother is Mine, 43, 310, 313

My Working Mom, 55, 311, 314

My Very On Mother's Day: A Book of Cooking and Crafts, 320

The Nativity: Mary Remembers, 53, 200

Navajo Wedding: A Diné Marriage Ceremony, 36, 45, 425

New Year's Day, 13, 41, 53, 220, 222

Nice Try Tooth Fairy, 57, 420, 421

Night at the Fair, 408, 409

The Night Before Christmas, 11, 41, 177, 204, 211

Night Lights: A Sukkot Story, 30, 100

The Night of Las Posadas, 28, 198, 199

Night Shift Daddy, 336

Nonfiction Matters: Reading, Writing, and Research in Grades 3–5, 144

Noodlehead Stories: World Tales Kids Can Read and Tell, 287, 288

North American Indian Ceremonies, 412

Not For Ourselves Alone: The Story of Elizabeth Cady Stanton and Susan B. Anthony, 369

Now We Can Have a Wedding!, 36, 423

Nutcracker, 206

O Jerusalem, 376

Oh, the Places You'll Go!, 35, 410

Old Glory, 19, 340, 342

On Purim, 32, 266, 267

On Rosh Hashanah and Yom Kippur, 30, 50, 65, 97

On the Campaign Trail, 82, 158

On the Morn of Mayfest, 271, 274, 304

On the Wings of Peace: In Memory of Hiroshima and Nagasaki, 26, 365, 366

One Candle, 31, 66, 178, 181

111 Days to Zion: The Day-by-Day Trek of the Mormon Pioneers, 360

One Woman, One Vote, 370, 371

One Yellow Daffodil: A Hanukkah Story, 178

Our Eight Nights of Hanukkah, 179, 181

Our National Anthem, 341, 342

Our National Holidays, 46, 67, 144, 170, 191, 248, 383, 386, 387

Owen's Marshmallow Chick, 42, 258

Owl Moon, 337

Painted Eggs and Chocolate Bunnies, 42, 259, 264

Papa's Christmas Gift, 208

Parade Day: Marching through the Calendar Year, 383, 387

The Passover Journey: A Seder Companion, 32, 80, 271, 272

Passover Magic, 54, 269

Patrick: Patron Saint of Ireland, 16, 45, 278

Pearl Plants a Tree, 32, 189

Pen Pals, 7, 51, 119, 121

A Perfect Father's Day, 19, 56, 337, 338

The Perfectly Horrible Halloween, 8, 40, 138, 141

A Picture Book of Martin Luther King, Jr., 46, 225

The Pilgrims and Me, 164

Piñatas & Smiling Skeletons: Celebrating Mexican Festivals, 64, 75, 78, 218, 392

Pink and Say, 18, 316, 318

The Pledge of Allegiance, 339, 341

The Polar Express, 11, 53, 205

Potlatch: A Tsimshian Celebration, 34, 62, 73, 413, 414

Pow Wow, 412

The Powhattan, 82, 166

Powwow, 33, 412

A Present for Mom, 18, 43, 310, 313

Presidents, 15, 70, 85, 244, 246

Presidents Day, 15, 47, 60, 242, 243, 245

The Promise Quilt, 316

Pueblo Storyteller, 119, 121

Purim, 266, 267

Queen of the May, 304

Quinceañera: A Latina's Journey to Womanhood, 78, 415, 428

Quinceañera: Celebrating Fifteen, 35, 78, 415, 428

Rabbit Moon, 38, 49, 384

Ramadan, 22, 39, 50, 63, 101, 102, 103

Ramadan and Id al-Fitr, 22, 102

Ramona and Her Mother, 312, 314

The Real St. Nicholas: Tales of Generosity and Hope from around the World, 194

Rechenka's Eggs, 261

Recycle Every Day!, 17, 61, 294

Recycle: A Handbook for Kids, 47, 293

Recycling, 17, 86, 296

Red Eggs & Dragon Boats: Celebrating Chinese Festivals, 77, 88, 390

Red, White, Blue and Uncle Who?: The Stories behind Some of America's Patriotic Symbols, 19, 72, 87, 155, 170, 340, 352, 354

Rhyme Time Valentine, 14, 238, 240

The Right to Free Speech, 125, 127

The Right to Vote, 9, 68, 158, 159, 171

Rivka's First Thanksgiving, 163, 168, 169

Roses Are Pink, Your Feet Really Stink, 14, 237

Rosh Hashanah and Yom Kippur, 30, 38, 50, 96-98, 107

Rosh Hashanah/Yom Kippur, 30, 38, 50, 65, 97, 99

Round the Turkey: A Grateful Thanksgiving, 51, 162, 167

Runaway Dreidel!, 177, 191

The Runaway Rice Cake, 177, 185, 187, 191

Sadako, 26, 74, 364

Sadako and the Thousand Paper Cranes, 26, 64, 78, 88, 364

St. Nicholas, 194

St. Patrick, 279, 283

St. Patrick's Day, 16, 58, 71, 278, 279, 284

The St. Patrick's Day Shamrock Mystery, 279, 282, 283

The St. Patrick's Day Shillelagh, 71, 280, 283

St. Patrick's Day: Parades, Shamrocks, and Leprechauns, 16, 71, 85, 280

Saints: Lives and Illuminations, 146

Sam and the Lucky Money, 52, 185, 187

A Samurai Castle, 308

Scary Fright, Are You All Right?, 40, 138, 141

Secret Father's Day Present: A Lift-the-Flap Story, 19, 43, 336, 338

The Secret Stars, 28, 223, 224

Serving on a Jury, 124,

Seven Days of Kwanzaa: A Holiday Step Book, 12, 45, 213, 214, 216

Seven Spools of Thread: A Kwanzaa Story, 214

Shamrocks, Harps, and Shillelaghs: The Story of St. Patrick's Day Symbols, 280

Sharing Blessings: Children's Stories for Exploring the Spirit of the Jewish Holidays, 65, 76, 394

A Shepherd's Gift, 201, 202

Shh! We're Writing the Constitution, 124,

Silent Night: the Song and It's Story, 202, 203

Silly Celebrations! Activities for the Strangest Holidays You've Never Heard Of, 386, 387

1621: A New Look at Thanksgiving, 10, 68, 166, 169, 170

Snapshots from the Wedding, 36, 425, 426

Snow Day, 35, 44, 417, 418

Snow Day!, 35, 44, 57, 417

So You Want to Be President?, 15, 244, 246

Some Birthday!, 405

Somebody Loves You, Mr. Hatch,

Song for the Whooping Crane, 295, 298

A Song of Stars, 25, 355

Song of the Circus, 408, 409

Sound the Shofar! A Story for Rosh Hashanah and Yom Kippur, 30, 38, 96, 98

Spider Storch's Desperate Deal, 425, 426

Spirit Child: A Story of the Nativity, 69, 202

Starring Grace, 330

Statue of Liberty, 72, 87, 353

The Steadfast Tin Soldier, 289, 290

The Story of Kites, 110

The Story of Passover, 32, 66, 270

The Story of Punxsutawney Phil: Fearless Forecaster, 14, 233

The Story of Tanabata, 25, 64, 355, 356

The Story of the Three Wise Kings, 28, 223

The Story of Valentine's Day, 14, 239, 241, 242, 248

Strategies that Work: Teaching Comprehension to Enhance Understanding, 129

Summer Reading is Killing Me, 165, 171, 331, 332

Summer Star Gazing, 356, 361

Summer with Elisa, 330, 332

Susan B. Anthony: Fighter for Women's Rights, 73, 87, 369

Sweet Hearts, 42, 236

Tabitha's Terrifically Tough Tooth, 420, 421

Tales of St. Patrick, 85, 280, 283

Tamar's Sukkah, 30, 100

A Teacher's Guide to Religion in the Public Schools, xx

Teddy's Easter Secret, 259

Tet: Vietnamese New Year, 23, 52, 64, 182

Thank You, Grandpa, 7, 51, 119, 120, 331, 333

Thank You, Sarah!!!: The Woman Who Saved Thanksgiving, 10, 164, 169, 217

Thanksgiving, 10, 51, 163, 170

Thanksgiving Day, 68, 165

Thanksgiving Day: A Time to be Thankful, 10, 164, 170

Thanksgiving on Thursday, 165, 169

Thanksgiving Program Sourcebook, 398

Thanksgiving Wish, 212, 218

The Hajj: One American's Pilgrimage to Mecca, 24, 190

The Nutcracker Music Game, 208

The 13 Days of Halloween, 51, 138, 142

31 Uses for a Mother, 55, 312, 314

This Is Our Seder, 42, 268, 271

This Next New Year, 24, 41, 184, 187

This Whole Tooth Fairy Thing's Nothing But a Big Rip-Off!, 420

Those Summers, 328, 331

Three Young Pilgrims, 51, 162, 167

Through the Eyes of the Soul, Day of the Dead in México, 149, 170

Throw Your Tooth on the Roof: Tooth Traditions from Around the World, 36, 421, 422

A Time to Keep, 385

TimeLiner, 159, 171

To Every Season: A Family Holiday Cookbook, 144, 348, 386

Toby Belfer and the High Holy Days, 98,

Toby Belfer Never Had a Christmas Tree, 178

Toby Belfer's Seder: A Passover Story Retold, 269, 270

Tomas and the Library Lady, 60, 112, 115

Tonight is Carnival, 252

The Treasury of Saints and Martyrs, 146

A Tree Is a Plant, 48, 299, 301

Truelove, 237, 240

Tudor and Stuart Life, 152

A Turkey for Thanksgiving, 40, 162

Turkeys, Pilgrims, and Indian Corn, 10, 82, 166

The 12 Days of Christmas, 11, 204, 210

The U.S. Constitution & the Bill of Rights, 126

Ugly Duckling, 289, 290

Uncle Sam and Old Glory: Symbols of America, 352

Under the Christmas Tree, 53, 204

Understanding Jewish Holidays and Customs: Historical and Contemporary, 107, 191, 274, 333, 397, 428

United Nations, 135, 136

The United Nations, 135, 144

United States Constitution, 46, 59, 124

The United States Constitution, 125

United We Stand: Flying the American Flag, 342, 343

Valentine's Day, 14, 55, 237, 238

Valentine's Day: Candy, Love, and Hearts, 14, 239, 242

Veterans Day, 9, 47, 154, 156

Veterans Day: Remembering Our War Heroes, 9, 60, 68, 154

Vietnam War, 82, 155

A Village Full of Valentines, 239, 241

The Viper, 332, 333

Visiting Day, 36, 427, 428

Viva Mexico! The Story of Benito Juarez and Cinco de Mayo, 29, 79, 306, 307

Voices of the Heart, 240

Volunteering for a Political Campaign, 68, 125, 127

Voting and Elections, 9, 46, 157

Washington's Birthday, 243

We Need to Go to School: Voices of the Rugmark Children, 67, 81, 114, 116

We the Kids: The Preamble to the Constitution of the United States, 351, 354

We're Going on a Picnic, 328, 331

The Wedding, 424, 426

Welcoming Babies, 34, 44, 403

Were They Wise Men or Three Kings?: Book of Christmas Questions, 83, 210, 211

What a Year, 385, 387

What Dads Can't Do, 19, 56, 337, 338

What is Hanukkah?, 176, 180

What is Thanksgiving?, 40, 161

What Moms Can't Do, 311, 314

When I Go Camping with Grandma, 129, 329, 331

When We Married Gary, 424

Which Witch is Which?, 138, 141

Who's Been Here?, 57, 418

Witch's Business, 140, 143

Witches, Pumpkins, and Grinning Ghosts: The Story of the Halloween Symbols, 8, 141

The Wonderful Happens, 401

You Forgot Your Skirt, Amelia Bloomer, 21, 368, 370

You Want Women to Vote, Lizzie Stanton?, 21, 369

World Holidays: A Watts Guide for Children, 107, 129, 144, 171, 191, 218, 274, 320, 333, 348, 361, 379

Zigazak! A Magical Hanukkah Night, 31, 52, 177

SUBJECT INDEX

Abenaki, 163
Adams, Abigail, 368
Adams, John, 368
Advent, 4, 193, 199, 399
Africa, 146, 208, 257
Albright, Madeleine, 135, 136
Allah, 101, 190
All Hallow's Even, 137
All Saints' Day, 4, 96, 104, 105, 137, 141, 145–147, 326
All Souls' Day, 4, 96, 104, 105, 145–147, 325, 326
Alzheimer's disease, 410, 411
Andersen, Hans Christian, 286, 289
Anthony, Susan B., 368–371
Appleseed, Johnny, 299–302
April Fools Day, 5, 6, 16, 285–289, 383
Arbor Day, xii, 5, 6, 17, 48, 61, 189, 285, 299–302
Armistice Day, See Veterans Day.
Ash Wednesday, 251, 254
Assumption Day, 5, 363, 355–367
atomic bomb, 364–366
Australia, 377, 379
autumn equinox, 109
Aztec, 148, 202, 203, 414
baker's dozen, 194
bar mitzvah, 5, 34, 401–403, 406
Bastille Day, 5, 80, 89, 349, 356–358
bat mitzvah, 5, 33, 401–403, 406
Battle of Puebla, 305, 306
Befana, 223,
Belgium, 376
Bethlehem, 193, 198-201
Bill of Rights, 158
birthday, xii, 5, 34, 44, 56, 383, 385, 401, 403–407
Bolivia, 377
Bon Festival, See Obon Festival.
Bon Odori, 325–327
bonfire, 152, 273, 376

Brazil, 252, 253, 254, 376, 378
Buddha, 291, 292, 388, 389
Buffalo Days, 34, 62, 73, 412–414
Calle Ocho, 252
Canada, 112, 131, 221, 253, 376, 377, 379
Career Day, 112, 115
carnaval, 251, 253, 273
carnival, 4, 251–255, 378, 391, 396
carp, 307–309
Carter, Jimmy, 117
categorizing, 217
cause-and-effect, 143, 263, 288, 295, 324, 325
celebrations of light, 93–95, 175–182, 184–188, 198–199, 212–217, 219–222, 378, 382
Celts, 137, 140, 303, 375, 379
Central America, 131
Cerelia, 160,
Chang E, 105, 106
Chanukah, See Hanukkah.
Chapman, Johnny, See Johnny Appleseed.
character analysis, 117, 156, 157, 307, 319
character sketch, 136, 348
character traits, 146
Chavez, César, 113, 115, 116, 225,
Cherokee, 127–129
Cheyenne, 413
Children's Day, See Kodomono–Hi.
Chile, 376
China, 105, 106, 109–112, 134, 184–186, 240, 324, 327, 328, 376, 378, 398, 404, 405
Chinese Lunar Calendar, 109
Chinese New Year, See Xin Nian.
Ch'ing Ming. See Qing Ming.
Chongyang Jie, 4, 39, 50, 63, 109–112, 388
choral reading, 366
Christmas, 4, 6, 11, 41, 53, 69, 83, 94, 95, 138, 193, 200–212, 261, 376, 378, 382–384, 397

Cinco de Mayo, 5, 29, 45, 58, 65, 75, 79, 303, 305–307, 392
circle map, 301
circus, 5, 35, 44, 56, 401, 407–409
Citizenship Day, 4, 109, 123–127
Civil War, 242, 244, 315, 316–318
cleaning traditions, 93, 127, 147, 182, 184, 267, 272, 325
Clear Brightness Festival, See Qing Ming.
Columbia, 376
Columbus, Christopher, 131–134
Columbus Day, 4, 6, 8, 131–134, 383, 391
coming of age ceremonies, 402,403, 405, 414–416
commemorating the dead, 96, 145, 146–150, 182, 183, 272, 325–327
comparisons, 100, 103, 120, 122, 123, 128,141, 142, 169, 188, 224, 255, 270, 272, 304, 327, 354, 355, 358, 379–382
concept map, 135, 197, 221, 360, 426
conflict resolution, 213, 217
Constitution Day, See Citizenship Day.
Constitutional Amendment, Fifteenth, 157
Constitutional Amendment, Nineteenth, 157, 364, 368–371
Constitutional Amendment, Twenty-sixth, 157
Constitutional Convention, 124, 125
Costa Rica, 139
costume, 138, 139, 146, 252, 253, 266, 267, 270
Crow, 413
Cuba, 135, 252, 392
Cuban Missile Crisis, 135
cumulative tale, 139, 268, 271, 304
Czech Republic, 257
Dalai Lama, 291, 292
Day of the Dead, See Dia de los Muertos.
Day of the Race, See El Dia de la Raza.
Days of Awe, 95
death, See commemorating the dead.
Declaration of Independence, 350
definitions, 181, 182
Deng Jie, 175, 185, 389
Denmark, 196
Dia de los Muertos, 4, 27, 96, 100, 104, 105, 145, 147–150, 326, 391, 392
diary, 113, 266, 267, 360
Disabled American Veterans, 153
Diwali (Divali), 4, 22, 93–95, 219, 384
Dodd, Sonora Louise Smart, 335, 336
Dolls Festival, See Hina Matsuri.
Double Nine Festival, See Chongyang Jie.
Dragon Boat Festival, See. Duanwu Jie.
Dragon Dance, 184, 185
dramatization, 106, 139, 143, 146, 151, 194, 198, 212, 267, 330, 345, 398
Duanwu Jie, 5, 323, 327, 328, 389, 390
Dust Bowl, 114

Earth Day, 5, 6, 17, 47, 61, 71, 86, 189, 285, 292–299
Easter, 4, 6, 15, 42, 54, 70, 85, 251, 255–265, 383, 396
egg hunt, 257, 259
egg rolling, 258, 263, 265
Egypt, 251, 255, 267, 268, 270
Eid-Al-Adha, 4, 24, 175, 190, 191
El Dia de la Raza, 131
El Dia de los Reyes, See Epiphany.
Election Day, 4, 6, 9, 46, 59, 60, 68, 82, 145, 157–160, 368
Emancipation Proclamation, 343–345
England, 134, 150, 152,153, 165, 243, 277, 279, 285, 350, 379
Epiphany, 4, 28, 219, 222–224, 391, 399
Electoral College, 158
Environmental Protection Agency, 292, 297
Esther, 251, 266, 267
Ethiopia, 376, 377, 379
Europe, 146, 254
fair, 5, 35, 44, 56, 401, 407–409
fairytale, 289
family, nontraditional, 336, 337, 346–348
Fassika, 256
fasting, 95–99,101–103, 251, 255
Fat Tuesday, See Mardi Gras.
Father's Day, 5, 6, 19, 43, 56, 72, 87, 335–338
Fawkes, Guy152, 153
Feast of the Harvets, See Shavuot.
Feast of Our Lady of the Harvest. See Assumption Day.
Feast of Tabernacles, See Sukkot.
feelings chart, 98, 167, 168
Festival of Color, See Holi.
Festival of the Dead, See Obon.
Festival of the Flowers, See Hana Matsuri.
Festival of the Milky Way, See Tanabata.
Festival of the Weeks, See Shavuot.
Festivals of Light, 93, 94
fiesta, 5, 35, 44, 56, 401, 407, 408
Finland, 196, 405
fireworks, xi, 184, 219, 220, 222, 258, 263, 349–353, 388, 399
Flag Day, 5, 6, 19, 335, 339–343
flow diagram, 290
Forest of the Martyrs, 189
Fourth of July, 5, 6, 20, 47, 61, 72, 87, 123, 261, 343, 349–355, 357, 358, 383
France, 252, 277, 285, 356–358, 377
Franklin, Benjamin, 124, 125
French Revolution, 356–358
Gandhi, Mohandas, 113, 115, 224, 225
garbage, 292–299
Germany, 231, 376, 379
Ghana, 376

Good Friday, 251, 255
graduation, 5, 35, 57, 72, 401, 409–411
grandfather, 100, 117–121, 148, 150, 207,
grandmother, 117–121, 147, 148, 150, 197, 207,
    212, 223, 262, 269, 294, 312, 329–332, 420
grandparent, 117–121, 206, 330, 331
Grandparents' Day, 4, 6, 7, 39, 51, 109, 117–121
graph, 152
Great Britain, See England.
Greece, 257, 377, 379
Green Corn Festival, See Itse Selu.
Grinch, 204, 211
Groundhog Day, 4, 14, 6, 231–235
Guatemala, 110, 148, 379
Gunpowder Plot, 152, 153
Guy Fawkes Day, 4, 80, 89, 145, 152, 153
Haiti, 376
Hajj, 190, 191
Hale, Sara Josephina, 161, 164, 169, 196
Halloween, 4, 6, 8, 40, 51, 131, 137–143, 146, 261,
    376, 383, 398
Haman, 266
Hana Matsuri, 5, 24, 285, 291, 292
Hanukkah, 4, 31, 40, 52, 66, 76, 79, 94, 95,
    175–182, 378, 384, 395, 396
Harambee, 137
harvest festival, 99, 100, 127–129, 137, 160–170,
    213, 251, 272–273, 324, 325, 377
Harvest Festival, See Sukkot.
Harvest Festival for Our Lady of the Flowers. See
    Assumption.
Harvest Moon, 127
Hayes, Dennis, 292
Hidalgo, Father Miguel, 122
Hina Matsuri, 5, 24, 275, 285, 307, 388, 389
Hindu, 93, 94, 273, 285
Hiroshima Day, 5, 26, 64, 74, 78, 88, 363–366
Holi, 4, 24, 42, 54, 64, 74, 251, 272–273, 285, 376,
    388
Holocaust, 178, 179, 181, 189
Holy Thursday, See Maundy Thursday.
Holy Trinity, 277
homeless, 185, 187, 205
Hong Kong, 328
Iceland, 377
Id al-Fitr, See Id-Ul-Fitr.
Id-Ul-Fitr, 4, 23, 93, 96, 101, 104–105, 145, 147,
    326, 378, 388
Iftar, 101
Independence Days, 109, 122, 123, 305, 335,
    343–346, 349–355, 356–358
India, 95, 110, 376, 377
International Children's Book Day, 5, 285, 289–291
Iran, 376
Ireland, 139, 257, 275, 277–283
Israel, 189, 376, 378

Israelites, 99, 267, 268, 270
Italy, 131, 208, 258, 263, 283, 379
Itse Selu, 4, 33, 63, 99, 106, 109, 127–129, 161,
    170
Jackson, Andrew, 352
Jamaica, 377
jamboree, 5, 35, 44, 56, 401, 407–409
Japan, 110, 237, 275, 276, 285, 291, 307–309,
    323, 325–327, 355, 356, 364–366, 376–378,
    405
Jarvis, Anna, 310
Jefferson, Thomas, 353
Jerusalem, 175, 255, 256, 376
Jesus, 175, 193, 198–203, 255, 256, 376
Jewish Arbor Day, See Tu Bi–Shevat.
Juarez, Benito, 122, 306
Juneteenth, 5, 45, 58, 72, 87, 335, 343–346
Junkanoo, 213
jury, 124
Kalachakra, 291
Kamishibai, 355
Karenga, Maulana, 213, 215
Key, Francis Scott, 339, 342
King, Martin Luther, Jr., 115, 224–229
Kitchen God, 184, 388
kite, 109–112, 148, 150, 307
Kodomono-Hi, 5, 25, 43, 55, 303, 307, 309, 310,
    388, 389
Korean War, 153, 155, 157
Kwanzaa, 4, 6, 12, 45, 57, 69, 84, 193, 212–217,
    376, 378
Labor Day, 4, 6, 7, 46, 60, 67, 81, 109, 112–117,
    225, 383
Lakshmi, 93, 94
Lantern Festival, See Deng Jie.
Las Posadas, 4, 28, 193, 198, 199, 391
Last Supper, 256
Latin America, 146–150, 198, 224, 258, 263
Lebanon, 377
legend, 194, 278–280, 300, 355, 356, 387, 392,
    396–398, 413
Lei Day, 303
Lent, 4, 101, 251–256, 396
Lincoln, Abraham, 161, 164, 167, 169, 231, 243,
    244, 246, 247, 318
Loch Ness Monster, 278
Lupercalia, 236, 239
magic, 269, 286, 287, 395
mandala, 292
Mardi Gras, 4, 251–255, 378, 379
Martin Luther King, Jr. Day, 4, 6, 13, 46, 59, 70, 84,
    115, 219, 224–229, 383, 384
matzah, 268–270
Maundy Thursday, 251, 255
May Day, 5, 303–305
Mayflower, 162, 232

McQuade, Marian, 117

Memorial Day, 5, 6, 18, 47, 60, 71, 86, 153, 303, 315–319, 383

Mennonite, 317

menorah, 175–181

Mexican Independence Day, 4, 27, 65, 75, 109, 122, 123, 305, 349, 357

Mexico, 110, 114, 122, 123, 139, 147–150, 193, 195, 196, 198, 208, 224, 258, 263, 305–307, 376–379, 405

Mid–Autumn Moon Festival, See Zhongqiu Jie.

migrant worker, 112–117

miracle, 194, 206, 236

moon cakes, 105

Montagu, John, 150

Mormon Pioneer Day, 5, 349, 359–361

Morton, Julius Sterling, 285, 299

Mother's Day, 5, 6, 18, 43, 55, 71, 86, 303, 310–315, 384

Mott, Lucretia, 370

moving, 148, 198

Muhammad, 101, 102

mural, 142, 247, 265, 307, 366

Muslim, 101–105, 190–191, 392

Nagasaki, 364–366

Nanticoke, 163

national anthem, 341, 342

National Arbor Day Foundation, 299, 300

National Cemetery in Arlington, Virginia, 153, 154, 316

National Sandwich Day, 4, 145, 150–152,

Native American, 62, 67, 81, 127–129, 132, 145, 161, 163, 165, 166, 169,170, 377, 401, 405, 406, 411–414, 425

Native American's Day, 411

Navajo, 425

Nelson, Gaylord, 292

Nepal, 114, 116

Netherlands, 405

New Year's Day, 4, 6, 13, 41, 53, 69, 94, 95, 219–222, 376, 378, 388

New Zealand, 405

new clothes traditions, 94, 182, 184, 186, 187, 262, 324

Nigeria, 376, 377, 378

Nixon, Richard, 117

Nobel Peace Prize, 255

noise making, 110, 184, 219, 220, 222, 266, 349, 376

noodlehead stories, 286–288

North America, 132

Norway, 196

note taking, 245, 246, 283, 295, 298, 393

Now Ruz, 275

Obon Festival, 5, 25, 145, 147, 276, 323, 325–327, 378, 384, 389

opinion chart, 234

Our Lady of Guadalupe Day, 4, 27, 193, 195,196

Pakistan, 95, 104

Palm Sunday, 251, 255, 256

pancake racing, 254

parade, xi, 123, 146, 161, 163, 164, 184–187, 219, 220, 251–253, 259, 263, 266, 277, 280, 344, 345, 349, 350, 353, 383, 413

Parks, Rosa, 226

Passover, 4, 32, 42, 54, 66, 76, 80, 96, 251, 255, 267–277, 323, 383, 395, 396

patterning, 111

pen pals, 119, 121

Pentecost, 324

Persian Gulf War, 155

persistence, 132, 164, 196

personal responses, 115, 116

perspective, 257, 424, 425

Peru, 252

Pesach, See Passover.

Philippines, 377, 379, 405

Pilgrims, 145, 161–170, 198

Plimoth Plantation, 163, 164, 166, 169, 170

Pledge of Allegiance, 339, 341

poetry, 139, 167, 204, 209, 263, 312, 338, 365, 376, 382–384, 386–388, 404

Powhatan, 166

Poland, 163, 164, 377

political campaign, 125, 127

pollution, 294

Portugal, 258, 263

potlatch, 34, 62, 73, 74, 413, 414

powwow, 33, 63, 73, 88, 412, 413

prediction, 139, 157, 234, 245, 331, 353, 406, 418

president, 124, 126, 242–247

Presidents' Day, 4, 6, 15, 47, 60, 70, 85, 231, 242–247, 383

problem solution structure, 281

Pueblo, 119–121

Puerto Rico, 112, 131, 224, 377, 392

Punxsutawney Phil, 231

puppet, 105, 106, 279, 306

Purim, 4, 32, 251, 266–267, 376, 395, 396

pysanky, 261, 262, 264

Qing Ming, xii, 4, 96, 104, 105, 145, 147, 251, 272, 326, 389

questioning, 105, 122, 211, 271, 309, 370, 386, 426

quinceañera, 5, 35, 78, 401, 406, 414–416,

Ramadan, 4, 22, 39, 50, 63, 74, 77, 93, 101–104, 378

ranking, 241

recycle, 292–299

resolutions, 95, 98, 213, 219

retelling, 181, 272

Revere, Paul, 350

Revolutionary War, 155, 344
Rosh Hashanah, 4, 30, 38, 50, 65, 94–99, 101, 219, 395, 396
Ross, Betsy, 340
Rugmark Foundation, 114,116
Russia, 165, 257, 261, 287, 406
St. Joseph's Day, 5, 275, 283
St. Nicholas, 207, 210
St. Nicholas Day, 5, 193, 194,195, 275
St. Patrick's Day, 4, 6, 16, 45, 58, 71, 85, 275, 277–283, 383
Samurai, 307, 308
sandwich, 150–152,
Santa Claus, 193, 194, 203–212, 222
Santa Lucia Day, 4, 193, 196–198
Saturnalia, 203
Scotland, 219, 285, 376
senses, 106, 222, 416
sensory words, 121, 298, 301
sequence of events, 142, 199, 210, 211, 353
Serbia, 377
Shavuot, 5, 33, 96, 323–325, 395, 396
shofar, 95, 96, 98
Siddhartha, 291
Simchat Torah, 4, 30, 93, 99–101
slave, 213, 268, 277, 279, 343–346
slavery, 114, 194, 246, 251, 267, 316, 335, 343–346
Smith, Joseph, 359, 360
snow day, 5, 35, 44, 57, 401, 417, 418
Soviet Union, 134
Social Studies Curriculum Themes
    Asian, 63, 64, 74, 77, 78, 88
    Central American and Hispanic, 64, 65, 75, 78, 79, 89
    citizenship, 59,60
    European, 80, 89
    families, 38–58
    Jewish, 65, 66, 76, 79, 80, 89
    Native American, 62, 73, 88
    patriotic, 60, 61
    traditional American holidays, 67–73, 81, 87
Spain, 131, 258, 263, 305, 392
spring equinox, 275
Stanton, Elizabeth Cady, 368–371
Star Festival, See Tanabata.
Statue of Liberty, 353
Stonewall Rebellion, 5, 335, 346–348
story map, 199, 241, 282, 283
storyteller, 286
storytelling, 288, 355, 356
South America, 131, 132
Sudan, 119, 121
Suhur, 101
sukkah, 99–101

Sukkot, 4, xii, 30, 93, 96, 99–101, 106, 160, 161, 170, 395, 396
summer excursions, 5, 120, 323, 328–332
summer solstice, 323, 335
Summer Triangle, 355, 356
Sweden, 196–198, 257, 258, 263, 379, 405
Tanabata, 5, 25, 64, 349, 355, 356, 376
Tango-no-sekku, 5, 25, 303, 307–309
tashlikh, 95, 96
TET Nguyen-Dan, 4, 23, 52, 64, 78, 94, 96, 104, 105, 145, 147, 175, 219, 326, 389
Thailand, 110
Thanksgiving Day, 4, 6, 10, 40, 51, 68, 82, 99, 106, 145, 149, 160–170, 378, 383, 398
thingamajig, 148, 208
Three Kings Day, See Epiphany.
time travel, 331
timeline, 159, 228, 342, 361
Tobago, 254, 376
Tomb of the Unknown, 153
Tooth Fairy, 5, 36, 57, 401, 419–422
Trail of Tears, 128
Trinidad, 254, 376
Truman, Harry, 339
Tsimshian, 413
Tu Bi-Shevat, 4, 32, 175, 189–191, 396
Twelfth Night, See Epiphany.
Ukraine, 261, 262
United Nations, 131, 134–136
United Nations Day, 4, 131, 134–136
United States Constitution, 109, 123–127, 344, 351, 368
vacation, See summer excursions.
Valentine's Day, 4, 6, 14, 42, 55, 70, 84, 231, 235–242, 383
Venezuela, 224
Venn diagram, 327, 415
vernal equinox, 275
Vesak, 291, 376, 388
Vespucci, Amerigo, 132
veteran, 153, 304
Veterans Day, 4, 6, 9, 47, 60, 68, 82, 145, 153–157, 315
Vietnam, 182–183, 376
Vietnam Veterans Memorial, 155, 157, 352
Vietnam War, 153, 155, 157
Vietnamese New Year, See TET Nguyen–Dan.
Virgin Islands, 112
Virgin Mary, Mother of Jesus, 195,196, 198–203, 303, 366–367
visiting day, 5, 36, 427, 428
vocabulary development, 103, 113, 121, 156, 159, 227, 246, 254, 280, 298, 370, 371, 393, 428
voting, 157–160, 368–371
Wampanoag, 161. 166
Washington, George, 161, 231, 242–247, 352

wedding, 5, 36, 45, 401, 423–427

West Indies, 131

White House, 263

Wilson, Woodrow, 339

winter solstice, 193, 196, 209, 379

Wise Men, 200, 211, 221–224

Women's Equality Day, 5, 6, 21, 73, 87, 157, 363, 368–371

World War I, 153

World War II, 153–157, 179, 263, 264, 316–318, 363–366

writing activities

general, 115, 117, 133, 142, 143, 150, 211, 241, 242, 246, 254, 264, 288, 297, 318, 338, 387, 407

glossary, 103

letters, 163, 164, 168, 169, 330, 407, 420, 421

lists, 111, 120, 126, 134, 187, 288, 297, 298, 314, 331, 338, 345, 354, 355, 361

poetry, 167, 233, 235, 314, 342

Xin Nian, xi, 4, 24, 41, 52, 94, 175, 184–188, 219, 378, 390

Yom Kippur, 4, 30, 38, 50, 65, 93, 95–100, 104, 105,145, 147, 326, 395, 396

Young, Brigham, 359–261

Zakat-ul-Fitr, 104

Zapotec, 306

Zhongqiu Jie, 4, 23, 93, 99, 105,106, 160, 161, 170

About the Authors

Kathryn I. Matthew was born in Oakland, California. She received graduate and undergraduate degrees from the University of New Orleans. She received an Ed.D. in Curriculum and Instruction with an emphasis on technology and reading from the University of Houston. She has taught in elementary schools in Texas and Louisiana as a classroom teacher, English as a Second Language Specialist, and Technology Specialist. At the university level she has taught children's literature, reading, language arts, technology, and research classes. Kathryn co-authored *Reading, Comprehension: Books and Strategies for the Elementary Curriculum*; *Technology, Reading, and Language Arts*; and the *Neal-Schuman Guide to Recommended Children's Books and Media for Use with Every Elementary Subject*. She and her husband, Chip, live in Sugar Land, Texas.

Joy L. Lowe was born in Minden, Louisiana. She received graduate and undergraduate degrees from Centenary College of Louisiana, Louisiana Tech University, and Louisiana State University. She received a Ph.D. in Library and Information Science from the University of North Texas. A former school and public librarian, she taught library science at Louisiana Tech University for 25 years. Joy co-authored the *Neal-Schuman Guide to Recommended Children's Books and Media for Use with Every Elementary Subject*. She currently lives in Ruston, Louisiana, with her husband, Perry.